Fostering Accountability

FOSTERING ACCOUNTABILITY

Using Evidence to Guide and Improve Child Welfare Policy

Edited by

Mark F. Testa
John Poertner

2010

OXFORD
UNIVERSITY PRESS

Oxford University Press, Inc., publishes works that further
Oxford University's objective of excellence
in research, scholarship, and education.

Oxford   New York
Auckland   Cape Town   Dar es Salaam   Hong Kong   Karachi
Kuala Lumpur   Madrid   Melbourne   Mexico City   Nairobi
New Delhi   Shanghai   Taipei   Toronto

With offices in
Argentina   Austria   Brazil   Chile   Czech Republic   France   Greece
Guatemala   Hungary   Italy   Japan   Poland   Portugal   Singapore
South Korea   Switzerland   Thailand   Turkey   Ukraine   Vietnam

Published by Oxford University Press, Inc.
198 Madison Avenue, New York, New York 10016

www.oup.com

Oxford is a registered trademark of Oxford University Press.

Library of Congress Cataloging-in-Publication Data
Fostering accountability : using evidence to guide and improve child
welfare policy/edited by Mark F. Testa and John Poertner.
p. cm.
Includes bibliographical references and index.
ISBN 978-0-19-532130-2
1. Child welfare—Government policy—United States.
2. Foster home care—United States.   3. Child welfare—United States.
4. Family services—United States.
I. Testa, Mark.   II. Poertner, John.
HV741.F674 2009
362.7—dc22
2009031030

1 3 5 7 9 8 6 4 2

Printed in the United States of America
on acid-free paper

ACKNOWLEDGMENTS

This work owes much to the experiences we gained as former directors of the Children and Family Research Center in the School of Social Work at the University of Illinois at Urbana—Champaign. We are especially grateful to Jill Doner Kagle, former Dean of the School of Social Work, Richard Herman, former Chancellor of the University of Illinois, Jess McDonald, former Director of the Illinois Department of Children and Family Services, and Susan Wells, former Center director, for their efforts in the creation of the Center. We are also thankful to Benjamin Wolf, Joseph Loftus, and Tina Tchen for their assistance in defining the Center's role under the *B.H.* Consent Decree. We appreciate the continued support given by Dean Wynne Korr of the School of Social Work and Bryan Samuels, former director, and Erwin McEwen, current director, of the Illinois Department of Children and Family Services.

Many of the contributors to this volume first came together under a discretionary grant, Mentoring Research Partnerships for State Child Welfare Programs (Award No: 90-CW-1103), that the U.S. Department of Health and Human Services awarded to the Illinois Department of Children and Family Services in support of the Office of the DCFS Research Director to provide consultation, technical assistance, and mentorship to the states of Oklahoma, Rhode Island, and Nevada. Key chapters of this edited volume are based on the papers from the final cumulative program report, *Building Analytical Capacity for Child Welfare Programs in State Systems*, submitted to the U.S. Department of Health and Human Services in June 2005. We also thank the Pew Charitable Trusts for its funding of *Fostering Results*, a public education campaign managed by the Children and Family Research Center to educate lawmakers and citizens about the need for federal financing reform and improved court oversight of child welfare cases. Chapter 9 is based on an unpublished draft report prepared for this project. We also wish to acknowledge the support and technical assistance of Casey Family Programs in the preparation of the report on which Chapter 11 is based.

Lastly, we are appreciative of the comments and the recommendations made by several anonymous reviewers of our draft manuscript. We would also like to acknowledge the assistance of John Rogers, Senior Statistician at Westat, in preparing the power calculations presented in Chapter 5 and to thank Joseph Doyle, the Alfred Henry and Jean Morrison Hayes Career Development Associate Professor of Economics in the MIT Sloan School of Management, for his review of Chapter 7.

CONTENTS

CONTRIBUTORS

Tom McDonald
Professor and Associate Dean
School of Social Welfare
University of Kansas
Lawrence, Kansas

Terry Moore
Research Associate
School of Social Welfare
University of Kansas
Lawrence, Kansas

John Poertner
Professor Emeritus
University of Illinois at Urbana-Champaign
Urbana, Illinois

Michael Shaver
Executive Vice President and Chief Operating Officer
Children's Home + Aid
Chicago, Illinois

Ken Taylor
Executive Director
Wisconsin Council on Children and Families
Madison, Wisconsin

Mark F. Testa
Sandra Reeves Spears and John B. Turner Distinguished Professor
School of Social Work
University of North Carolina at Chapel Hill
Chapel Hill, North Carolina

Joan Levy Zlotnik
Director
Social Work Policy Institute
National Association of Social Workers Foundation
Washington, District of Columbia

Fostering Accountability

1

INTRODUCTION

Mark F. Testa

Critical inquiry and the acceptance of the fallibility of authority have long animated the search for scientific knowledge and truth. What is modern is the legitimacy of asking for the empirical evidence for a particular policy choice and the refusal to accept unquestioningly those justifications based solely on hierarchy, tradition, or faith (Mayhew, 1997). Although it may seem that these interests have always been central concerns of the human services professions, it is only in recent decades that it has become both commonplace and expected to ask doctors for a second opinion, to subject professional wisdom to scientific validation, and to certify public management by evaluating actual results. The reasons for this heightened interest appear to have less to do with more enlightened opinion than with the increased brute-force capacity for data processing and information retrieval in the human services. Before computers, search-engines, and the World Wide Web, people's ready acceptance of the dependability of professional judgment and the reliability of product guarantees was both pervasive and necessary (Giddens, 1990). It was simply too costly to gather all the information and evidence necessary to verify the adequacy of a professional's opinion or to test the reliability of a product's performance in advance of making a decision. You had to accept on trust a physician's diagnosis that a recommended operation was necessary or a salesman's assurance that a certain brand of car would start reliably in the morning.

Trust in professional certificates, advanced educational degrees, brand names, and other symbolic tokens of professional probity and product reliability is still a pervasive background force in modern life. The major difference today compared to a generation ago is that many clients and stakeholders now can almost effortlessly and instantaneously retrieve massive quantities of data and information to support, supplement, or contradict the advice they once naively accepted because of a person's prestige, status, or position in a hierarchy. Increasingly this "show me" attitude is being institutionalized in our dealings with service professionals, public officials, and government bureaucrats. It is fast becoming the new standard by which we determine whether we are being adequately served by the contractual and fiduciary agents who are accountable to us individually as consumers and collectively as citizens for acting on our behalf in health, education, social work, and other human services.

Accountability and Agency Relationships

Results-oriented accountability (ROA) is about holding professionals and organizations answerable for the results (outcomes) of a chosen course of action rather than just for the fulfillment of assigned activities and duties (processes). ROA expands the authority to intervene in what broadly may be called "principal–agent relationships" (Jensen & Meckling, 1976; Kiser, 1999) beyond checks against violations of agent integrity, i.e., actions that deviate from standards of responsible behavior and best practice, to demands that agents show valid evidence of their success in bringing about improvements in the outcomes valued by their individual and public principals.

There are many agency relationships in child welfare.[1] The caseworker is accountable for monitoring the safety and well-being of the child in foster care. The foster parent is accountable for providing safe and stable care of the foster child. The child welfare administrator is accountable for the effective and efficient implementation of permanency plans and other child welfare policies. The juvenile court judge is accountable for balancing the best interests of the child against the rights of the parents.

Accountability in agency relationships is normally ensured in free enterprise and democratic systems by the principals themselves who ultimately can take legal action against agents for wrongful private or public acts. In the case of child-principals, however, they do not hold power of full citizenship to make enforceable agreements or to seek enforcement of their own interests (Bross, 1997). Instead they are dependent on parents or other legal guardians to enter into agency relationships on their behalf and to protect their interests. When it is the parent or legal guardian who is culpable or suspected of the wrongful action, then it becomes incumbent on the state as *parens patriae* (parent of the country) to intervene and, if necessary, to assume the role of guardian temporarily until the parent or private guardian is able to resume parental responsibilities or the state lawfully reassigns these responsibilities to another adult or organization. In the interim, the state takes responsibility for the child's welfare as her or his public agent, while simultaneously acting as a principal in holding other agents accountable for meeting the child's needs in a long chain of principal–agent relationships that extends from policymaker, judge, and public administrator to service provider, caseworker, and caregiver.

Although accountability and responsibility are intertwined, the two concepts are separable to some degree. Whereas parents are responsible for the safety, care, and future well-being of their children, they are not ordinarily accountable to anyone else for their parenting practices except in the narrow sense of not violating child abuse and neglect laws. Institutions of family privacy render most caregiving in the home opaque to external surveillance. Conversely state child welfare administrators are accountable under federal law for the rate of child reabuse in their states even though they are only partially responsible for creating the conditions and providing the resources necessary for safe and healthful parenting.

The incomplete overlap between accountability and responsibility creates obvious tensions that agents may attempt to resolve by gaining greater control over the conditions and resources that impact children's outcomes. For example, a physician may take protective custody of a prematurely born infant because she or he is not confident that the parents are capable of meeting the infant's complex medical needs on their own. A judge may terminate the rights of parents who repeatedly abandon the care of their child and reassign child care responsibilities to the state child welfare department. In each case, the responsibility of the hospital or the department is enlarged on the presumption that with fuller control corporate agents will be better able to ensure the outcomes of child health or family permanence for which they are held accountable.

Alternatively, the tensions can be mitigated by narrowing the scope of accountability to only those conditions and resources over which agents exercise direct control. For example, a group of national organizations issued a 2004 report on measuring the performance of juvenile courts in child abuse and neglect cases (The American Bar Association, The National Center for State Courts, & The National Council of Juvenile and Family Court Judges, 2004). Although the organizations agreed on measures of child safety and family permanence, they declined to include child well-being, stating that "it is premature at this time to have courts adopt measures of well-being when consensus does not exist on measures for which courts have direct responsibility, such as safety of children, appropriate removal of children from their homes, successful achievement of permanency, and length of time in foster care" (p. 19). A similar argument could be made for further narrowing the scope of judicial accountability to only those legal processes over which courts exercise direct control, such as receipt of written notice, appointment of legal counsel, and adjudication within specified timeframes.

A core contention of this book is that quantitative accountability systems based narrowly on process or output-oriented measures will tend to distort agency performance over time by providing incentives and opportunities for agents to defect from their contractual commitments and fiduciary obligations. Accountability systems based on a more diffuse and balanced set of outcomes are more likely to reduce "agency risks," such as goal displacement, opportunistic gaming, and fraud, and to encourage a more experimentalist approach toward effectively accomplishing the broader and longer-term aims of social policy.

Even though ROA depends ultimately on having an enforceable right to take responsibility for agency relationships, it should be stressed that neither expanding state control to full legal responsibility for a child nor narrowing the scope of accountability to only those processes under an authority's immediate control is responsive to what the public ordinarily expects when it holds public agents accountable for the safety, permanence, and well-being of children. ROA operates on the premise that public and other corporate agents will be accountable for outcomes and processes that are only incompletely their responsibilities. Therefore, to achieve the desired results, public agents have to become both knowledgeable about the efficacy and effectiveness of professional practices and public policies (scientific validity) and skillful in how best to persuade, motivate, reward, and, as a last resort, compel other agents and corporate partners to act on and refine this knowledge without encouraging defections from the best interests of their principals to whom they owe shared responsibilities (agency integrity).

Dimensions of Accountability

What makes individual and corporate agents more or less accountable in terms of the validity of their actions and the integrity of their agency relationships? In general, there is greater accountability when the scope of interest in the desired results is defined diffusely rather than narrowly (Heimer & Staffen, 1998). It is more difficult to substitute procedural compliance for the substantive attainment of end goals when child welfare outcomes are broadly construed in terms of child well-being rather than narrowly in terms of agency processes or a limited focus on physical safety. For example, even though the timeliness of child maltreatment investigations can be a useful indicator of system responsiveness, it is a poor substitute for more direct measures of children's safety and health. Likewise, although child safety is the paramount concern, removal of children from neglectful homes should never displace other goals of continuity, stability, and permanence, which are also crucial to the overall well-being of the child.

The literature on accountability is replete with examples of goal displacement, opportunistic gaming, and outright fraud when policymakers and administrators try to hold agents accountable for production quotas, response times, and output targets. Rothstein (2009) recounts the classic case of output targets set by Soviet industrial planners for the number of shoes to be produced. Some factories responded to the threat of penalties for production shortfalls by using their limited supply of leather to produce shoes that were much too small for most of the public to wear. Similarly the use of arrest quotas is alleged to encourage "juking the stats"[2] in law enforcement by rewarding arrests for minor infractions at the expense of more effective crime-prevention activities that are more time consuming and less easily quantified. Likewise in child welfare, the provision in the Adoption and Safe Families Act of 1997 that states initiate termination of parental rights (TPR) petitions in circumstances in which children have been in foster care for longer than 15 out of the most recent 22 months has been faulted for increasing the numerical output of "legal orphans" without actually improving their prospects for legal permanence (Barth, Wulczyn, & Crea, 2005).

Considering the above examples, it is understandable that some observers would tie the temptation to evade substantive responsibilities to the rise of quantitative accountability systems at the expense of qualitative ones (Rothstein, 2009). Instead of framing the problem as one of measurement scale, however, it might be more helpful to characterize the problem as one of *construct validity*. As explicated by Shadish, Cook, and Campbell (2002), construct validity refers to the goodness of match between a particular measure and the higher-order construct that the measure is supposed to represent. For example, most would agree that inferring the safety of children from how rapidly investigators respond to allegations of child maltreatment provides an incomplete match at best. The number of substantiated reports of maltreatment per 1000 children is closer to the mark, but the sizable variation in substantiation rates across communities and among investigators for similar cases (Doyle, 2007) raises questions about the accuracy of the measure. Simply counting all reports, regardless of substantiation finding, does not necessarily improve construct validity and may actually worsen it, for example, when abuse reports are filed to discredit an opposing party in child custody disputes. Even if such instances of misuse were eliminated and variations in substantiation rates were reduced, the problem of unreported child maltreatment would still remain, which federal estimates put somewhere from one-fourth to one-third of all recognized instances of child abuse and neglect (Sedlak & Broadhurst, 1996).

As advances are made in improving the construct validity of child safety indicators, it will become more difficult to justify the substitution of output-based measures for more results-oriented indicators. The same applies to other child welfare outcome constructs, such as continuity of care, placement stability, legal permanence, and child well-being. But improving the measurement of each child welfare outcome separately will not adequately address the problems of goal displacement and other agency risks. ROA in child welfare depends on the monitoring of a counterbalanced set of indicators, which reflects the interrelated nature of child welfare outcomes (Webster, Usher, Needell, & Wildfire, 2008). Focusing on speedier family reunifications, for example, without considering the consequences for rates of reentry into foster care may satisfy the letter of accountability but certainly violate its spirit.

The importance of assessing agency performance in light of changes in a counterbalanced set of indicators of child welfare outcomes touches on a second dimension of accountability: the more transparent the agency's accounting for its performance, the more accountable the agency is. Transparency makes visible to principals and other stakeholders the conditions that propelled a course of action and any important facts that may help explain observed accomplishments as well as shortfalls. For example, an annual decline in the rate of institutionalizing children under the age of 12 years old should not be touted as a system accomplishment if the change is attributable mainly to a large influx of infants into foster care. Likewise a drop-off in reunification rates should not be greeted with alarm if the change was preceded by a sharp decline in the pool of children who can be quickly reunified because of more successful family preservation efforts.

Transparency frequently entails drilling down into the data in order to distinguish genuine success from spurious associations. It also involves making the findings publicly available and the data accessible to others for verification and replication purposes. Opacity is the opposite situation in which findings are suppressed and access to data is restricted, especially if the findings might prove unflattering to the initiator of the action. "Spinning the results" so that any minor improvement is portrayed as a statistically valid change is also a form of opacity that obscures agency accountability.

Threats to what Shadish et al. (2002) call *statistical conclusion validity* are much less of a concern in child welfare now that computerized records keeping can generate samples of sufficient size (e.g., thousands of cases) so that sampling error is small enough to ignore. More often the problem is the opposite one in which any change, no matter how trivial, can be proclaimed statistically significant when large administrative databases are analyzed. Because any difference found after testing an entire population is, by definition, significant at the highest possible level, it is questionable whether statistical significance should be used at all as is currently done in federal reviews to benchmark improvements when administrative data are available for all children in foster care.

Despite the availability of large administrative databases, inadequate sample size still remains a major problem in child welfare. The need for valid clinical data, behavioral assessments, and client satisfaction reports, which are less reliably collected as part of routine administrative data systems, makes it necessary to draw smaller sized samples for intensive case review in order to render qualitative judgments about agency performance and child well-being. The time and effort required to conduct such reviews are so intensive that cost constraints typically hold down sample sizes to numbers that are much too small to reach statistically valid conclusions either about the need for improvement or the effectiveness of program improvement plans. A 2001 report by the U.S. Government Accountability Office (GAO) calculated that the sample size of 50 cases that the federal government used in the past for on-site reviews of state child welfare performance yielded sample estimates of attributes (such as child gender) whose margin of error was plus or minus 14 percentage points (U.S. GAO, 2004). If gender equity were a concern, such a level of variability would pose obvious limitations on assessing whether a problem even existed, let alone judging whether progress had been made toward reducing gender disparity.

Another aspect of transparency involves reporting information in sufficient detail to permit principals and other stakeholders to distinguish genuine improvements from spurious statistical associations. Much of the federal government's reporting on child welfare outcomes presents data on only gross differences or crude effect sizes without carefully considering how changes in population characteristics might affect the results. As noted, changes in the age distribution of children taken into foster care could easily mislead people into believing that genuine progress is being made in reducing child institutionalization rates when the only real change is the lower average age at foster care entry. Disentangling policy and programmatic influences on outcomes from demographic determinants is what the literature calls risk or case-mix adjustment (Iezzoni, 2003). The goal is to assess whether differences and effect sizes retain their practical importance and statistical significance after appropriate statistical adjustments have been made for demographic characteristics and other pre-existing conditions.

Discounting spurious change while owning up to the need for genuine improvement puts a premium on the evidence-supported use of discretion to attain the desired results. The more knowledgeable agents are about what works and how effective interventions are across different populations and contexts prior to settling on a particular course of action, the more accountable the system can become. Flexibility in the choice of alternative courses of action is necessary in order to tailor results to particular circumstances, but unbridled discretion is the antithesis of evidence-supported practice and may cause harm even if intentions are good. ROA expects that discretion will be constrained by the best scientifically credible evidence of a practice's efficacy, effectiveness, and efficiency in accomplishing the desired results.

A scientific assessment that withstands challenges to the credibility of its findings across variations in populations, interventions, and contexts is said to be *externally valid* (Shadish et al., 2002). Learning that an intervention, which is efficacious in preventing the births of substance-exposed infants in Chicago (Ryan, Choi, Hong, Hernandez, & Larrison, 2008), is also effective in preventing births in rural Illinois instills greater confidence in the generalizability of the results. The most valid evidence comes from a systematic research review (SSR) of a wide and unbiased selection of published and unpublished studies in which population units are randomly assigned to one or more interventions and to some comparison condition in which the intervention is withheld, such as a waiting list, services-as-usual, or no-treatment control group (Littell, 2008). Although increasing, the number of SRRs on which to base best practice standards in child welfare is pitifully small. The dearth of scientifically credible studies means that standards of practice must be based either on findings from related fields in which the external validity of the results for child welfare populations is uncertain or on less rigorous quasi-experimental research, observational studies, and the consensual wisdom of child welfare experts.

The weaker the scientific evidence is for a chosen course of action, the more important it is for agents to follow up with scientifically valid evaluations of their interventions. The stronger the empirical evidence is in support of the causal efficacy of the intervention, the more *internally valid* the inference is (Shadish et al., 2002). As with external validity, the strongest evidence for the internal validity of an intervention comes from randomized controlled experiments (Ollendick & King, 2004).

It is sometimes suggested that experimental evaluations are too costly or unwieldy to be of much practical use in child welfare. There are also ethical objections to the use of random assignment. But uncontrolled experimentation on vulnerable children and families by well-meaning child welfare agents is no more ethical than controlled experimentation that seeks to augment the evidence base of child welfare knowledge. Child welfare (IV-E waiver) demonstrations have shown how such practical and ethical concerns can be satisfactorily addressed (see Chapter 7, this volume). However with the loss of IV-E waiver authority in 2006 (see Chapter 9, this volume), the continued reticence of child welfare systems to engage in routine randomized controlled experimentation threatens future gains in holding public child welfare accountable for this important dimension of causality.

Testing the efficacy, effectiveness, and efficiency of a course of action is necessary but not sufficient for ensuring accountability for results. Outcomes must also be subjected to a second-loop, usually qualitative review by program principals and other stakeholders to ensure that the accomplishments are the intended ones and that the results are compatible with other important end values. This involves taking a second look at the construct validity of the intervention (logic) model and assessing the goodness of match between its underlying theory of action and the intervention's intended and unintended impact on outcomes. Because some end values will invariably be compromised and improvements are always possible, ROA encourages the continuous revision of existing practices in light of new knowledge about the impact of those practices. This reflexive adaptation to contingencies creates an aura of unsettledness that is characteristic of all evidence-supported knowledge in the policy sciences. Although the lack of certainty sometimes invites the return of practices based on hierarchy, tradition, and faith, scientifically credible evidence still remains the most dependable source of knowledge about the world to which modern democratic societies can aspire (Giddens, 1990).

Framework of Results-Oriented Accountability

The book is organized around a framework of ROA that seeks to strengthen the validity of child welfare knowledge and to improve the integrity of child welfare policy and practice by reducing agency risks to the best interests of children. The stages we describe—outcomes monitoring, data analysis, research review, evaluation, and quality improvement—line up with the five dimensions of accountability and four types of validity as illustrated in the following (see Fig. 1.1). This framework shares important commonalities with related approaches in the human services such as the sequential framework for enhancing evidence-based public health (Brownson, Baker, Leet, & Gillespie, 2003) and the cycle for evidence-based child welfare practice development (Child Welfare Services Stakeholders Group, 2003).

Each of these approaches cycles through a similar sequence that asks the following questions: (1) Are the desired results broadly defined and validly measured to ensure that children's best interests are served? (2) Is the gap between desired and actual results of practical importance and statistical significance to warrant taking corrective action? (3) What potential courses of corrective action are supported by empirical evidence and how strongly? (4) How efficacious, effective, and efficient are the implemented actions in accomplishing the desired results? and (5) Should the implemented actions be continued, improved, or discontinued or should the desired outcomes, logic model, and underlying theory of action be redefined? Each of these questions is addressed in some detail in subsequent chapters.

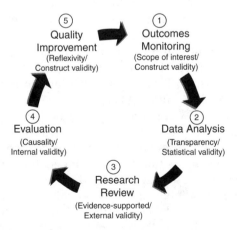

Figure 1.1 Cycle of results-oriented accountability.

The roots of ROA can be traced back to the pragmatic theory of experimental inquiry and reflexive regulation that John Dewey and others espoused during the first half of the twentieth century:

> Wherever purposes are employed deliberately and systematically for the sake of certain desired social results, there it is possible, within limits, to determine the connection between the human factor and the actual occurrence, and thus to get a complete social fact, namely, the actual external occurrence in its human relationships. (Dewey, 1931, p. 276)

Substitute the terms "intervention" and "outcome" for "human factor" and "occurrence" and we arrive at the key proposition that is at the core of ROA. The psychologist, Donald T. Campbell, and his colleagues helped to fill in the details of the "within limits" part of the above quotation with their now classic inventory of threats to valid scientific inferences in evaluation research (Campbell & Stanley, 1963; Cook & Campbell, 1979; Shadish et al., 2002). The framework that we advance in this volume, however, departs from Campbell's (1988) vision of an "experimenting society" by adopting the accountability perspective that he believed spawned more problems that it solved (Campbell, 1984).

Campbell ended up opposing the routine use of outcome indicators to improve public management. He believed that monitoring and evaluating agency units, e.g., schools, departments, and courts, invariably lead to the corruption of the indicators used to monitor results and to the degradation of the agency relationships that program evaluation is supposed to improve (Campbell, 1984). We acknowledge these agency risks as real threats and provide some examples of such performance distortions in subsequent chapters. But rather than eschew the use of quantitative outcomes for guiding and improving public management, our goal is to take cognizance of such threats in order to structure a framework of ROA that can help decrease these agency risks and increase the opportunities for responsible public management.

This book advocates holding judges, administrators, and service providers accountable for child welfare outcomes. But it differs from the minimum-standards setting and high-stakes monitoring that the federal government used in No Child Left Behind (NCLB) and the Children and Family Services Review (CFSR). Such approaches assume that the federal government (the principal) has sufficient foreknowledge to establish national outcome standards that adequately serve the best interests of children and that the imposition of financial penalties or other sanctions for shortfalls is sufficient to induce states (the agents) to improve performance. ROA takes a different tack. Under this framework, the federal government sets broad goals and metrics, and state administrators seek to advance these ends locally through outcomes monitoring, data analysis, evidence-supported intervention, rigorous evaluation, and continuous quality improvement. In exchange for federal support, states routinely report back on goals and metrics to public principals and other stakeholders who participate in regular peer reviews or "learning forums" (Moynihan, 2005) that discuss results from experimental evaluations or observational studies that compare performance with past history or to similar jurisdictions that match up on child demographics, intervention rates, and other relevant conditions. Shortfalls are not penalized by withholding federal funds, but instead dollars are reinvested back into additional analysis, research review, and evaluation. In this regard, the approach aligns with the hope Donald Campbell once expressed for program evaluation in which findings of trivial or even undesirable effects would result in funding boosts for the same administrative unit to continue working on the same problem with alternative and hopefully more promising approaches that take account of lessons learned (Campbell, 1984).

Organization of the Volume

This volume is organized using the ROA framework depicted in Figure 1.1. This constitutes an approach toward assessing the merits of alternative policies by using scientifically valid evidence of their impact on outcomes as opposed to establishing their consistency with canon, tradition, and faith. Chapter 2 introduces an analytical framework for classifying the different value tensions and agency risks that characterize historical shifts in policies and programs to bring safety, permanence, and well-being to the lives of abused, neglected, and other vulnerable children. Our aim is not to suggest that ROA can entirely resolve these value tensions or totally eliminate agency risks. In fact, we make the opposite argument that these tensions and risks are inherent features of U.S. child welfare policies, which have helped to drive periodic cycles of child welfare reform throughout the nation's history. Although the instrumental goal is to guide child welfare policy based on the best scientifically credible evidence, there is a reflexive aspect to this process that also measures progress in terms of narrowing the scope of ideological conflict, moderating the swings of the political pendulum, and acknowledging that any particular policy choice sacrifices, a bit a least, some other cherished value of civil society.

Chapter 3 explicates the framework of ROA. As described, ROA conceives of child welfare policy and management as cycling through five sequential stages: (1) outcomes monitoring, (2) data analysis, (3) research review, (4) evaluation, and (5) quality improvement. Chapters 4 through 8 present practical descriptions of each stage. Some of the material in these chapters can be quite demanding for readers with limited statistical training. We have tried to put the more challenging materials in appendices. We believe that it is important to include these technical appendices because public administrators and other agents are increasingly being called on to demonstrate or attest to the efficacy, effectiveness, and efficiency of child welfare polices by drawing on research findings that employ statistically rigorous methods of data analysis. The push toward statistical rigor is very much connected to the themes introduced in Chapter 2. As long as most of the voting public subscribed to a grand evolutionary narrative that larger, more centralized, and more bureaucratic government provided the best pathway to improved general welfare, demonstrating accountability was simply a matter of counting up recipients, calculating participation rates, and tracking other program outputs, such as the numbers of school lunches distributed, the timeliness of child protective investigations completed, and the fraction of eligible families receiving public assistance. But with the breakdown in consensus over the inevitability and desirability of a universal welfare state, accountability increasingly has turned toward demanding evidence of the success of planned interventions, tracing the pathways from cause to effect, attending to the unintended consequences, and evaluating the long-term impact on child safety, family permanence, and future well-being. Shoring up an evidence base for rendering such summary judgments requires increased familiarity with statistical methods that are sufficiently rigorous to support a confident conclusion about efficacy, effectiveness, and efficiency and to withstand skepticism of the results (Rossi, Lipsey, & Freeman, 2004).

Chapter 4 by Tom McDonald and Mark F. Testa provides an overview of the first stage of ROA—the routine monitoring of child welfare outcomes. It focuses on the federal Child and Family Services Reviews (CFSRs) and the proposed Chafee National Youth in Transition Database (NYTD). They call for strengthening these monitoring systems by adopting the methods of longitudinal data analysis and tracking entry cohorts to facilitate this type of analyses. They draw attention to the problems of selectivity, truncation, and censoring, which if not properly taken into account can misguide practitioners' and administrators' assessment of child welfare trends and system performance. They also consider what may be necessary to shore up the weakest area of the CFSR process, which is the monitoring of child well-being. The current reliance on small samples of case reviews is insufficient for drawing reliable or valid conclusions about agency performance in promoting child well-being. They conclude with a set of criteria for assessing both the validity and integrity of an outcomes-monitoring system.

Chapter 5 by Mark F. Testa builds on the previous chapter's discussion of the limitations of the existing CFSR outcomes indicators that rely heavily on cross-sectional samples of active cases and exit cohort samples of children discharged from foster care. It reviews some of the challenges of analyzing child welfare outcomes when program and policy changes are still in the process of implementation and discusses recent advances in longitudinal data analysis of time-to-outcome data. The chapter also provides an overview of the concept of statistical power and discusses the importance of distinguishing between statistical and practical significance when assessing agency performance. It concludes with an illustration of how greater transparency can be brought to the analysis of family reunification trends in Illinois through statistical risk adjustment for variations in child demographic characteristics, family needs, and other conditions of the populations served by the child welfare system.

Different professions have settled on different ways of defining various levels of evidence for rendering a summary judgment about the efficacy, effectiveness, and efficiency of evidence-supported interventions. Chapter 6 by John Poertner spotlights the efforts of different "technical communities" (MacRae, 1985) in synthesizing the results of randomized controlled trials of social interventions. He offers step-by-step guidelines for conducting research reviews and promoting the use of evidence-supported interventions through policy, training, and quality improvement, which sets the stage for the evaluation of promising and innovative practices.

Chapter 7 by Mark F. Testa makes a case for more routine use of randomized controlled experiments in child welfare than is currently the practice. Although it is the gold standard in many related fields such as medicine, education, mental health, and criminology, many child welfare administrators find randomized controlled experiments to be ethically suspect and of limited use because of the lengthy observational period before a summative judgment can be confidently rendered. The ethical objection usually concerns the appropriateness of constraining practitioner discretion by experimental protocols that allocate persons or other units to treatment and control conditions. The problem with this objection is that some practitioners advocate specific interventions as though they were certain of the benefits without adequate evidence of this fact. The randomized controlled experiment, which is the only scientifically proven method of testing causal relations from empirical data, constitutes a justifiable interference with agent discretion whenever the evidence for the efficacy or effectiveness of the intervention is weak. The chapter offers the example of the Illinois subsidized guardianship demonstration, which is one of the largest randomized controlled experiments in child welfare implemented under a federal IV-E waiver.

Although it is the gold standard of causal inference, there are situations in which controlled experimentation is inadvisable, unethical, or just impossible. Chapter 7 also discusses a variety of statistical methods that statisticians and econometricians have developed for estimating the genuine causal effect of an intervention on an outcome in observational studies in which nonrandom allocation or agent selection is involved. These methods also extend to randomized encouragement designs in which population units are encouraged to comply with an intended treatment but self-selection, agent selection, and subject attrition make the units that actually participate in the treatment a nonrandom subsample of the population originally assigned to the intervention group, e.g., the subset of families offered the option of subsidized guardianship by caseworkers.

The lengthy observational period required for many experimental and observational studies in child welfare has lead to greater interest in formative evaluations for guiding quality improvement (Rossi et al., 2004). Chapter 8 by Terry Moore offers practical advice for opening up the proverbial "black box" of evaluation research and developing data-tracking systems for continuous monitoring of service implementation, program outputs, and longer-term outcomes. He discusses the importance of fostering a results-oriented organizational culture that communicates the attitudes, behaviors, and values of ROA.

Chapters 9 to 11 examine three different institutional mechanisms for implementing ROA in service demonstrations, program budgeting, and university research and training partnerships. One of the more ambitious federal efforts to institutionalize the evaluation stage of ROA in child welfare was the Title IV-E waiver demonstration program that the U.S. Congress authorized in 1994. It permitted as many as 10 states per year to conduct demonstration projects by waiving certain requirements of titles IV-B and IV-E to encourage rigorous evaluations of new approaches to the delivery of child welfare services. Since 1996, 24 states have implemented 34 demonstrations components through 30 IV-E waiver agreements. The majority were evaluated using randomized controlled experiments. Chapter 9 by Mark Testa reviews the history of the IV-E waiver program and discusses some alternative proposals for promoting flexibility and innovation. In 2006, Congress did not renew the Health and Human Services' (HHS) authority to grant new child welfare waivers. This chapter offers a set of recommendations for improving the use of IV-E waivers if Congress were ever to revive this program to promote ROA in child welfare.

Chapter 10 by Ken Taylor and Michael Shaver discusses performance-based contracting (PBC) and budgeting in public child welfare, drawing on their experiences in implementing PBC in Chicago and Philadelphia. Their approach incorporated research design elements, such as rotational assignment and risk adjustment, to improve the monitoring of the performance of contractual service agents. They relied on market-pricing systems to motivate quality improvement and to achieve budgetary efficiencies.

Chapter 11 by Joan Levy Zlotnik reviews the history of university/agency partnerships in child welfare research and training. The establishment of closer research ties between universities and public agencies has frequently grown out of the desire to forge tighter linkages between universities and child welfare departments in the training of students and staff for public service careers. Many of the obstacles that have impeded educational collaborations in the past also can affect research partnerships, so this chapter's review of the past record of these relations can help to clarify the opportunities and challenges involved in translating evidence-based research and education from the academy to the field of public child welfare.

The volume concludes with Chapter 12 by Mark F. Testa and John Poertner, which considers the future of ROA and the use of empirical evidence to guide and improve child welfare policy. It assesses where current child welfare policy stands on each of five dimensions of ROA outlined in Chapter 1. It considers the alternative directions that ROA might take in child welfare with respect to the accountability mismatch between the enlarged scope of public interest and the limited technical capacity of states to meet rigorous standards of evidence. The chapter offers some thoughts about the future of waivers and the flexible funding of child welfare interventions, the continued viability of market-oriented solutions to the principal–agent problem, and the role of university–agency partnerships in fostering accountability in child welfare.

Research in the Service of Child Welfare Reform

Many of the practical lessons described in this book stem from the co-editors' respective experiences as former directors of the Children and Family Research Center (CFRC) in the School of Social Work of the University of Illinois at Urbana-Champaign. The CFRC was established in 1996 under a cooperative agreement between the University and the Illinois Department of Children and Family Services (DCFS) to fulfill the following four purposes:

- The CFRC will inform public policy decisions and practice by reporting on the results of DCFS efforts for children and families within the responsibility of the DCFS. This will extend to collecting administrative and survey data on critical policy, process, and need indicators that are linked to outcomes for children and families. Information generated from this effort will be publicly available to the Governor, the General Assembly, the courts, and other interested parties.
- The CFRC will initiate and carry out a research agenda in collaboration with a range of local, state, and national stakeholders, which helps advance public child welfare reforms and scientific knowledge about child safety, family permanence, and child and family well-being.
- The CFRC will operate a program of research that promotes the development of best practice by preparing systematic research reviews, engaging in experimental evaluations of innovative child welfare demonstrations, conducting intensive program audits of service performance, and providing the DCFS with technical assistance.

- The CFRC will recruit outstanding scholars, practitioners, managers, and students to positions of academic and professional leadership in child welfare research, administration, and education in Illinois, and attract funding for collaborative work with the DCFS and other research organizations. The CFRC will share findings with the research community and larger public through journal and book publications, public presentations, and talks at research and professional conferences.

The impetus for the creation of the CFRC was a federal consent decree, *B.H. vs. McDonald* (N0. 88 C 5599, N.D. Ill.), which the DCFS and the Illinois American Civil Liberties Union (ACLU) entered into in 1991. The decree obligated the DCFS to institute a range of reforms intended to improve the conditions of foster children under its care and custody. In 1995, the parties agreed to a supplemental order that retired the use of a court-appointed monitor and provided for the establishment of an independent research center to report on the results of DCFS' efforts to comply with the decree's provisions. The intention was to shift the monitoring functions from a compliance-oriented focus on organizational procedures to a results-oriented focus on improved outcomes for children and families within the responsibility of the DCFS.

The primary motivations for the change arose from the impatience of both the plaintiffs' attorneys and the new DCFS leadership with the slow pace of reform and their disenchantment with a "theory of action" that naively assumed that substantive improvements would automatically flow from procedural changes, such as reduced cases-to-worker ratios, tighter response times, and definite target dates for completing organizational reforms. Between the time the *B.H.* lawsuit was filed in 1988 and the consent decree was signed in 1991, the number of children under the care and custody of the DCFS rose from 16,900 to 23,800. On the eve of the filing of the 1995 supplemental order, the number of foster children in Illinois had ballooned to 48,200. This growth was fueled by a series of high profile abuse and neglect cases (Shapiro, 1999) and by a wide-open definition of child neglect that brought children into care when parents were absent, even when they were living safely with kin (Testa, 1997). By 1996, there were 17.1 foster children in Illinois for every 1000 children under 18 years old—the highest prevalence rate in the nation (Petit & Curtis, 1997).

Both the Governor's Office and the Illinois General Assembly lost confidence in DCFS leadership as a result of the cost overruns and annual DCFS supplemental appropriations that were running into the hundreds of millions of dollars. The decree's cases-to-worker formulas and procedural requirements automatically drove additional spending for the hiring of additional DCFS staff and the purchase of contractual services in order to keep pace with the caseload's rapid growth. It soon became obvious to all the parties that unless the DCFS began producing tangible results in terms of safer children left with or returned to birth families, more children discharged to permanent homes, and fewer children in long-term foster care, there was a strong possibility that the Governor's Office would pull out of the *B.H.* decree and that the General Assembly would proceed with proposed legislation to dismantle the DCFS.

The blueprint for the ROA framework for the new CFRC was drawn up by the DCFS Office of the Research Director (ORD) at the request of the then DCFS Director, Jess McDonald, under a planning grant from the Chicago Community Trust (Illinois Department of Children and Family Services, 1995a). The DCFS Director had earlier established the ORD under a memorandum of understanding he signed in 1994 with the School of Social Service Administration (SSA) at the University of Chicago. The responsibilities of the ORD were to coordinate all external research that was funded or approved by the DCFS and to initiate a program of internal research that would enhance the analytical capacity of the DCFS in the development of child welfare programs and policies. I was jointly appointed as DCFS Research Director in 1994 by the DCFS and SSA. I divided my time between directing the ORD and fulfilling my reduced teaching load and other academic responsibilities as an SSA faculty member.

The first major undertaking of the ORD was an outgrowth of research that I had earlier initiated as a consultant to the DCFS on its Home of Relative (HMR) foster care program. The HMR program recruited, approved, and licensed the relatives of foster children to serve as their foster parents under boarding arrangements similar to those traditionally used to support and supervise the care provided by nonrelated foster parents. Much of the growth in the Illinois foster care caseload since the mid-1980s had been accommodated by the placement of children with relative foster parents. This development was particularly pronounced among African-American children in the city of Chicago, the state's largest metropolitan area. The proportion of nonemergency placements of African-American children with relative foster parents jumped from 39% of the 2056 children placed in 1987 to 61% of the 3974 children placed in 1991 (Testa, 1997). Analysis of administrative data, audits of case files, surveys of HMR program participants, and focus groups with kinship caregivers suggested at the time that unless the DCFS initiated major reforms to its practice of taking children into child protective custody from safe and stable kinship care, the Illinois caseload could easily swell to twice its size (Testa, 1993).

The HMR Reform Plan that the ORD drafted to address these issues (Illinois Department of Children and Family Services, 1995b) was legislated by the General Assembly and implemented by DCFS in June of 1995. In anticipation of these policy changes, quarterly admissions to the HMR program dropped 15% from 4350 children in the third quarter of 1994 to

3700 in the second quarter of 1995 as children already in informal kinship care arrangements were afforded extended family support services and diverted from formal foster care. After the implementation of the HMR Reform Plan's changes in the structure of foster care subsidies paid to licensed and nonlicensed caregivers, admissions dropped another 23% to 2850 children in the fourth quarter of 1995.

The experiences of the ACLU and the DCFS leadership with the research-guided design of the HMR Reform Plan and its outcomes monitoring system that the ORD developed with the Chapin Hall Center for Children stimulated interest in applying this approach to performance monitoring under the *B.H.* decree. Because of the need to assure external stakeholders of the neutrality of the monitoring process, it was decided to locate the functions in an external research program at the School of Social Work (SSW) of the University of Illinois at Urbana-Champaign. In 2002, the ORD was consolidated into the CFRC in order to improve coordination between the internal and external research programs of the Department and the University.[3]

The research programs of both the ORD and CFRC have been widely credited with helping to turn around the public child welfare system in Illinois from one overwhelmed by child neglect cases, which President Clinton once referred disparagingly to as happening "not in Calcutta but in Chicago" (Shapiro, 1999), to what the Congressional Research Quarterly highlighted in 2005 as the "gold standard" of child care (Jost, 2005). The turnaround began with the HMR Reform Plan, which the Chicago Tribune lauded on the plan's one-year anniversary as helping to curtail the "relentless growth in the number of abused and neglected children washing into the system" (Dold, 1996). A few months later in September 1996, the ORD helped craft the IV-E federal waiver application to implement an innovative subsidized guardianship program to provide an alternative permanency option for children who had been backlogged in long-term kinship foster care (see Chapter 7, this volume). The next year, the ORD provided the analytical and staff support for the implementation of the performance-based contracting program that the DCFS Executive Deputy Director, Joseph Loftus, developed to leverage the resources necessary to sustain family stability and expedite the achievement of permanency outcomes for children in foster care (see Chapter 11, this volume).

The apparent successes of these interventions were first visible in the increased numbers of children discharged to permanent homes and in the reduced numbers remaining in long-term foster care. By March 1997, the number of children discharged to permanent homes exceeded for the first time in a decade the number of children admitted into foster care. The end-of-quarter caseload of open foster care cases peaked at 51,800 children and then declined steadily to 30,800 children in the second quarter of 2000. It was at this time that the number of children in publicly supported permanent homes with relatives, adoptive parents, and legal guardians surpassed the number of children in publicly subsidized foster care. At present, the number of children in permanent homes exceeds the foster care count by a margin of 37,000 to 16,000 children.

Subsequent chapters will consider the extent to which these results in Illinois can be attributed to the policy initiatives that the DCFS pursued in the late 1990s. Similar caseload turnarounds occurred in the states of New York (foster care caseloads peaked in 1991) and California (caseloads peaked in 1999). Nationally, aggregate foster care numbers show a gradual decline after 1999 as well. The point is not whether Illinois truly deserves its accolades as a gold standard (Jost, 2005), but rather to illustrate how the state's use of ROA and reliance on research evidence helped to develop, guide, evaluate, and alter the course of child welfare policies and their public management at critical junctures in the *B.H.* reform process.

The general consensus is that the shift from indeterminate foster care to kinship support and family permanence in Illinois helped to end the double digit percentage growth in foster care caseloads and deficit spending that had characterized the Illinois child welfare system for most of the late 1980s and early 1990s. But this apparent success could have turned into a pyrrhic victory if the long-term results were such that in terms of safety more children were put in jeopardy, breakdowns in adoptive and guardianship homes escalated, and the placement stability and emotional well-being deteriorated for the remaining children in long-term foster care.

The DCFS was aided in steering clear of these potential hazards by the ROA system that the ORD and CFRC helped to put in place to manage and evaluate the reform efforts. The implementation of a Child Endangerment and Risk Assessment Protocol (CERAP) in collaboration with the American Humane Association coupled with the evaluation reports that the CFRC prepared annually beginning in 1997 assuaged worries that lower rates of child removal were leaving more children at risk of reabuse and neglect. As annual admissions to foster care declined from a high of 15,000 in the mid-1990s to 5800 in the late 1990s, CERAP evaluations showed that Illinois' safety record was also improving: the recurrence rate among children previously investigated for abuse and neglect declined from 2.0% in 1996 to 1.2% in 2000 (Fluke, Edwards, & Johnson, 1997; Fuller & Wells, 1998).

The reflexive adaptation to unexpected contingencies that accompanied HMR Reform and subsequent permanency reforms also helped to identify the need for mid-course corrections. When the evidence showed that reunification rates with birth families were relatively unaffected by the state's permanency initiatives, the ORD initiated a series of focus groups and studies that identified parental drug abuse and low recovery rates as possible contributors to the underperformance (Marsh, D'Aunno, & Smith, 2000; Smith & Testa, 2002). In 1999, the DCFS applied for its second IV-E federal waiver application to improve reunification and other family permanency and safety outcomes by assisting birth parents to obtain needed alcohol and other drug abuse (AODA) treatment services and negotiate the expectations associated with drug recovery and concurrent permanency planning. The final CFRC evaluation report on the 5-year AODA demonstration showed that whereas the intervention significantly boosted reunification rates in the experimental group higher than in the comparison group, the levels of improvement were much lower than anticipated (Ryan, 2006). Further analyses led to the hypothesis that outreach services must also assist birth parents in achieving progress within the co-existing problem areas of domestic violence, mental health, and housing—in addition to substance abuse—if family reunification is to succeed (Marsh, Ryan, Choi, & Testa, 2006). In 2006, the U.S. Department of Health and Human Services approved the DCFS' application to extend its IV-E AODA waiver for another 5 years and to expand the scope of services provided to include screenings, assessments, and referrals to housing, mental health, and domestic violence services (U.S. Department of Health and Human Services, 2004).

Similarly, when the final CFRC evaluation report of the Illinois subsidized guardianship IV-E waiver demonstration indicated that fewer families of youth aged 14 to 18 years old had actually availed themselves of this option than what had originally been projected, the ORD initiated a series of focus groups and studies that pinpointed the loss of independent living and other transition services as a possible explanation for the low take-up rates (Testa, Cohen, & Smith, 2003). In 2004, the U.S. Department of Health and Human Services approved the DCFS' application to extend its IV-E subsidized guardianship waiver to offer federal independent living and other transition services, then available only to youth who aged out of the child welfare system, to youth who are adopted or enter subsidized guardianship at or after the age of 14 years old (U.S. Department of Health and Human Services, 2004).

Using Evidence to Guide and Improve Child Welfare Policy

As the preceding examples illustrate, ROA draws from a wider pool of scientific knowledge and methods—participant observation, focus groups, social surveys—than what is sometimes narrowly construed as empirically or evidence-supported interventions (Chambless & Hollon, 1998; Barth, 2008). The misperception that evidence comes only from quantitative studies, preferably randomized experiments, confuses methods with scientific goals, as educational researcher David Berliner (2002) points out:

> (E)thnographic research is crucial, as are case studies, survey research, time series, design experiments, action research, and other means to collect reliable evidence for engaging in unfettered argument about education issues. A single method is not what government should be promoting for educational researchers. It would do better by promoting argument, discourse, and discussion. (Berliner, 2002, p. 20)

The same argument applies to child welfare research. For this reason, the phrase "evidence-informed" is sometimes preferred over "evidence-based" in order to acknowledge the interplay between evidence and interpretation in advancing practice, policy, and scientific knowledge (Hargreaves, 1999). Similarly, the phrase "evidence-supported" is sometimes juxtaposed against "evidence-based" in order to differentiate the "stuff" of evidence-supported interventions (ESI) from the "process" of evidence-based practice (EBP) (Hughes & Potter, 2008).

ROA is our short-hand for discussing both the stuff of ESI and the process of EBP without trespassing too clumsily on distinctions that are continuing to be drawn and negotiated in the field. Client participation and the interpretative understanding of the intentions, motivations, and values of the principals and agents of public policy are components of ROA that are just as crucial as randomized controlled trials for shoring up scientific confidence in the validity of an ESI. The processes of ROA encompass client involvement in the definition of outcomes as indicators of success, the informed consent to participate in studies, the selection of research questions for research review, the search for alternative explanations when expectations are not fulfilled, and the feedback to administrators and policymakers even when operations appear to be working as intended. At the same time, our support for mixed methods does not mean that we believe that observational studies are just as valid as experimental ones in drawing causal inferences about the efficacy of an ESI. Nor does it mean that qualitative and quantitative inquiries occupy the same ranking on a hierarchical scale of scientific evidence. The qualitative feedback from direct service clients, participant observation, focus groups, and survey research must eventually be translated into "well-built scientific questions" (Richardson, Wilson, Nishikawa, & Hayward, 1995) and applied field experiments and service demonstrations in order to test and support the efficacy, effectiveness, and efficiency of program interventions. Conversely, the coordination of the quantitative results with the qualitative feedback from clients, practitioners, and researchers through peer review and learning forums constitutes an essential ingredient in the integration of ethical, evidentiary, and practical concerns that define the process and philosophy of EBP as envisioned by its originators (Sackett, Rosenberg, Gray, Haynes, & Richardson, 1996; Gambrill, 2006).

The penchant for choosing a particular scientific method to the exclusion of all others or omitting clients and critics from reflexive feedback loops is endemic to bureaucratic processes that reinforce what Argyris and Schön (1996) call "single-loop" learning in organizations. This refers to instrumental learning that seeks to improve the performance of organizational tasks but "in ways that leaves the values of a theory of action unchanged" (Argyris & Schön, 1996, 20). Single-loop learning tends to breed "legalism," that is, the disposition to adhere rigidly to the rules to the detriment of practical problem solving (Nonet & Selznick, 1978). A case in point is the federal provision cited above that instructs states to initiate TPR petitions in circumstances in which a child had been in foster care for longer than 15 out of the most recent 22 months. As Richard Barth and his colleagues (Barth et al., 2005) have observed:

> There seems to be negligible evidentiary support for ASFA's implicit assumption that TPRs would allow for improved child-specific recruitment and result in a vastly greater, national pool of adoptive families to provide permanency to older children. Instead, there is growing evidence that a substantial number of children will reside in foster care, or leave foster care to exits other than adoption, after their legal ties to their parents have been terminated. (Barth et al., 2005, p. 397)

Single-loop learning in this circumstance narrowly focuses agency performance on increasing the output of TPRs by automatically initiating petitions after the 15-of-22 month limit has been reached. It should be noted that ASFA does allow for some individualization of the law's impact by exempting children in kinship foster care, permitting agencies to demonstrate to a court that a TPR filing is contrary to the child's best interest, or postponing the filing date until efforts to reunify the family have been reasonably pursued [42 U.S.C. 675(5)]. But the law does not call for a systematic accounting of whether routine termination of parental rights or the exceptions to the rule actually improve the substantive results of safety, permanence, and well-being for children. ROA is meant to guard against these agency risks by ensuring a voice for clients and their affine agents as well as ethically obligating researchers and other fiduciary agents to provide a transparent account of the evidentiary status of their service interventions and the uncertainties associated with their policy choices. This affords an opportunity for what Argyris and Schön (1996) call "double-loop" learning that "results in a change in the values of theory-in-use, as well as in its strategies and assumptions (Argyris & Schön, 1996, p. 21). Double-loop learning entails not only a careful examination of the execution of organizational tasks but also a reflexive examination of the goals of the policy and whether they are worth pursuing. In the above example, questioning whether legal permanence is achievable by other pathways, such as legal guardianship that does not require TPR or considering whether the increased production of "legal orphans" may actually be a social harm rather than a collective good illustrates the reflexivity that characterizes ROA.

Conditions, Agency, and Outcomes

The double-loop learning fostered by ROA fits within a theory of action that recognizes that people exercise agency but not necessarily under conditions of their own choosing.[4] Agency in this context means "actions, activities, decisions and behaviors that represent some measure of meaningful choice" (Deacon & Mann, 1999, 413). Agency encompasses both the choices that people make in their own self-interest as well as on other people's behalf, i.e., agency relationships. It extends beyond the self-regarding motives of hierarchical and contractual agents (see the following section for definitions) to the other-regarding actions of affine or fiduciary agents on behalf of family, neighbors, clients, and fellow citizens. By acknowledging both the deterministic and voluntaristic components of social action, agency theory weaves together two explanatory perspectives that have historically been viewed as being opposed to one another.

On the one hand, there is the deterministic perspective that posits that people are products of their environment and that human behavior is best explained by the external conditions (threats and incentives) that constrain how they operate. On the other hand, there is the voluntaristic perspective that posits that people are autonomous agents who endeavor to alter the conditions of their actions rather than merely responding to external stimuli. Blending these two perspectives orients social research toward interpreting how the goal-oriented actions of interacting agents and principals combine to bring about system-level behavior and explaining how these actions in turn are shaped by the conditions that emanate from the system (Coleman, 1986).

An analysis of social outcomes as the product of both system conditions and agency relationships that are guided by self-interest and other-regarding values (LeGrand, 2003) assumes a more complex explanatory framework than the behavioral "black-box" model traditionally posited in evaluation research. In black-box evaluations, the focus is on estimating the effect of a change in conditions (inputs) on consequences (outputs) without attending to the intervening action orientations of the agents and principals. If intention or purpose is invoked, it is usually done in a post-hoc fashion to suggest a plausible interpretation of the various reasons why a casual result happened or did not happen as expected (Coleman, 1986). For example, black-box evaluations of the efficacy of intensive family preservation services (IFPS) in preventing children's removal from the home ask whether experimental families randomly assigned to IFPS (inputs) subsequently experienced lower rates of child removal (outputs) than control families from whom IFPS were withheld. Although additional measurements on the duration of treatment, intensity of worker contact, and number of services may be collected for supplementary "treatment-on-treated" (TOT) analyses (see Chapter 7, this volume), little more is needed than a reliable random assignment process and a valid measure of results to draw a reasonable causal inference about the impact of a controlled change in conditions on the outcome.

The limitations of the conditions-to-outcomes framework in social research have been pointed out repeatedly by critics who posit the importance of mediating and moderating processes that intervene between conditions and outcomes (Baron & Kenney, 1986). The sociologist Dennis Wrong (1961) warned of the pitfalls of an "oversocialized conception" of human behavior that emphasized conformity to normative constraints and ignored the propensities to defect from ethical obligations or cooperative relationships. There has been a similar tendency in child welfare to attribute parental deviance primarily to faulty learning or to environmental disadvantage. Building into child welfare research a wider conception of human agency, which allows for both self-interest and other-regarding motives, helps to steer clear of the reductionism associated with utilitarianism and market economics and the unwarranted assumptions about social beneficence associated with collectivism and the welfare state.

An enlarged "conditions-agency-outcome" framework is consistent with the conception of social workers as agents of change who are purposively oriented toward improving the conditions and outcomes of their client-principals. This "change-agent" model of ROA breaks free from the older "industrial model," which posits a deterministic relationship between resource inputs and client outputs (Friedman, 2005). By acknowledging the mediating and moderating effects of agent interests, motives, and intentions on client outcomes, ROA can be decoupled from the deterministic and behaviorist assumptions that are sometimes narrowly associated with EBP (Webb, 2001).

Types of Agency Relationships

The conditions-agency-outcomes framework of ROA can be built on four key agency relationships that correspond to the elementary relational models that anthropologist Alan Fiske (1992) identifies as structuring the ways in which purposive actions of individuals combine to produce social outcomes. This typology is elaborated on in Chapter 2, which discusses the various tensions and risks inherent in child welfare policy currently and historically.

The first relational model is "communal sharing," in which people who have a common heritage, group identity, or affinity with one another, such as a family, ethnicity, tribe, or other primordial solidarities, allocate goods and services without keeping track of who gets what. This relational model gives rise to a specific type of agency relationship that James Coleman (1990) calls *affine agency*, in which an agent, who closely identifies with the well-being of the principal, can be counted on to make choices in the best interests of the principal as if those interests were the agent's own interests.

Although affine relationships can be found in both primordial solidarities and bureaucratic organizations (French, 1995), the prototypical form is the bond between a mother and infant. As an agency relationship, the bond structures the reliable flow of nutrients, resources, and parental investments so that the infant-principal's self-interest in survival combines with the mother-agent's genetic interest in inclusive fitness to promote the health and safety of her offspring. Although evidence suggests that conditions of genetic relatedness and psychological attachment increase the likelihood of these desired social outcomes (Buss, 1999), it is the intervening choices of the parent to comply with or defect from the nurturing relationship that influences whether these desired outcomes will actually be achieved. In addition to defecting from responsible parenthood, there are other agency risks to a child's well-being that can arise from overinvestments in the affine relationship, such as feeding fetishes, excessive supervision, and certain forms of discipline. A social intervention that targets the conditions of child abuse and neglect without attending to the intervening orientations of the parent insufficiently safeguards the best interests of the child.

Another type of agency relationship that involves the restraint of self-interest in deference to contributing to the well-being of others can be termed *fiduciary agency* (Buchanan, 1988). It bears some similarity to communal sharing but more closely aligns with the relational model that Fiske labels "equality matching." Waiting your turn for a hospital procedure, reporting for jury duty, participating in a child-care cooperative, and casting your vote in a democratic election are some examples of equality matching systems. Fiduciary agents who are accountable for ensuring the dependability of such systems are entrusted with the responsibility of equitably allocating resources and ensuring that beneficiaries do not evade or jump the queue. The British National Health Service exemplifies the fiduciary agency relationship in the sense that staff reports that the desire to provide good quality service outweighs pecuniary gain as its primary motivation (Graham & Steele, 2001). Patients also absorb some of the costs of equality matching by waiting their turn for nonemergency medical care.

Cooperation in fiduciary agency relationships is reinforced by agents' internalization of values of ethical responsibility and professional probity and principals' placement of trust in the fairness and reliability of the equality matching system. Agent risks to principals' interests may again be of two sorts: defecting from norms of ethical responsibility, such as favoritism, shirking duties, and violating the public trust, or overinvesting in a fiduciary role that fosters paternalism, such as taking unilateral action for the "own good" of the recipient. Principal risks also involve the withholding of individual contributions to an equality matching system, such as "the free rider problem" that arises in generalized reciprocity systems, such as voluntary blood donation that Richard Titmuss described in his classic *The Gift Relationship* (1972). People voluntarily contribute blood with the diffuse expectation that their donations will be reciprocated at some future time should the need ever arise. Shirking your present obligation to donate blood undermines the generalized reciprocity system in the future by destroying contributors' trust in the norm of mutualism.

Many human services administrators and policymakers in the late twentieth century came to believe that the problems of self-interested defections from public service and paternalistic agency risk are best handled under the relational model that Fiske calls "market pricing" (LeGrand, 2003). An economic market for the exchange of private goods and services is the classic type of market pricing system in which individuals enter into *contractual agency* relationships in the context of competitive exchange to produce equilibrium prices and distribution of services. Similar ideas have been incorporated into the delivery of human services through the use of competitive "quasimarket" mechanisms, such as performance-based contracts, capitation funding, and service vouchers, to reward desired outputs and to sanction underperformance (see Chapter 11, this volume). These systems are "quasimarkets" because the state rather than the individual consumer provides the funding, and nonprofit and public agencies as well as for-profit groups can compete for business (LeGrand, 2003). Although market pricing systems are time-tested mechanisms for aligning individual self-interests with the efficient production of private goods and services, they are not without their own agency risks. In fact, agency theory originally emerged in economics as a way of dealing with contractual risks that arise from the divergence of agents' own interests from their principals' own interests and the better information they have about their own actions than the principals (Jensen & Meckling, 1976). Contractual agency theory focuses on the ways principals try to limit agency risk by screening prospective agents for trustworthiness, closely monitoring work efforts, and using various types of rewards and sanctions such as offering incentives for exemplary performance and canceling contracts for inadequate work (Kiser, 1999).

Rounding out the four types of agency relationships is what may be labeled *hierarchal agency*. This corresponds to the relational model that Fiske calls "authority ranking." Under this model, people are rank-ordered along some hierarchical dimension that accords persons higher in rank more resources, prerogatives, prestige, and deference than those lower in rank. Agency relations between the genders, across generational lines, and among kinfolk have traditionally been governed by this relational model. A prototypical agency relationship of this sort is filial piety. Throughout human history, the major agency risk in family relations has been defined from the point of view of the parents. It is the risk that children will fail to comply as adults with authority ranking norms of fealty, homage, and piety for the sake of the continuity, honor, and prosperity of the family lineage. Similar mechanisms of enforceable trust have evolved in many traditional cultures for resolving this parental investment dilemma.

Under ancient Chinese legal codes, for example, the patriarch had the authority to punish children, who by living apart from their family, failing to support parents in a decent manner, or marrying against parental wishes, defected from the norms of filial piety. Under Roman law, the patriarch even had the authority to take the life of an insubordinate son or wayward daughter and to dispose of an unhealthy newborn through exposure. Residues of hierarchal agency relationships can be found in the rights of parents to use corporal punishment, legal confinement of runaways, sanctions against juvenile uncontrollability and other status offenses as well as traditional customs of family duty, apprentices' obligations to their masters, and state enforcement of extended family liability laws. Under Elizabethan poor laws, for example, parents, grandparents, and even children of sufficient means were held legally liable for the support of dependent, disabled, and nonworking kin. These laws continued to be enforced in the United States as late as the 1970s under federal public assistance and child welfare programs. Now legal liability is limited to birth and adoptive parents, but residues of extended family liability persist today in the lower foster care subsidies that some jurisdictions pay to relatives than to nonrelatives in non-IV-E eligible, state-financed foster care programs.

Much of the modern history of child welfare as well as human services can be written from the perspective of egalitarian movements and political campaigns that have sought to detach agency relationships from hierarchal authority systems based on gender, kinship, and other ascribed statuses and to re-attach them to contractual agency relationships based on voluntary work and other commitments of limited liability (Janowitz, 1978). A related trend has been the break-up of affine systems of mutual care and protection from the primordial solidarities of extended kinship and local community and their restructuring around the conjugal nuclear family and the social welfare institutions of national citizenship (Marshall, 1964). One of the reasons that ROA is becoming a more prominent feature of contemporary child welfare and social policy in general is that that the evolutionary narrative that once guided public policy for much of the twentieth century is no longer sufficient for inspiring confidence in centralized bureaucratic capacity to meet the needs of children and families. It can no longer be taken for granted that the displacement of the welfare functions of primordial solidarities by centralized bureaucratic institutions is structurally inevitable, financially sustainable, or even socially desirable. The loss of public confidence has opened the way for alternative ideological visions to exert an influence on child welfare policy and practice (Sowell, 2002). These include neoconservatism that combines market pricing and authority ranking to justify limited government involvement in the economy and the revival of traditional family values; communalism that joins authority ranking with communal sharing to favor faith-based programs, block grants to local communities, and tribal sovereignty over child welfare matters; neoprogressivism that unites communal sharing and equality matching to advocate for greater public investments in the preservation of parent–child relationships no matter how fragile; and various market pricing and equality matching mechanisms that seek to bypass the intermediary agency of families and other primordial solidarities to equalize child developmental opportunities directly, such as universal preschool, adolescent reproductive health programs, and public trust funds that become available to children when they become adults.

In the next chapter, we present an analytical framework that charts these various ideological divisions and identifies the various value tensions and agency risks that have driven periodic cycles of child welfare reform in the past and may continue to influence policy in the future.

Notes

1. The phrases "principal–agent relationship" and "agency relationship" are used interchangeably in this book. Likewise the term "agency" is used in the general sense to refer to any number of principal–agent relationships in child welfare as well as in the narrower, more conventional sense to refer to the particular organization of a public or private child welfare agency.
2. This phrase comes from the HBO television series *The Wire*.
3. Until a full-time director could be hired, the SSW Dean, Jill Doner Kagle, asked me to serve as interim director of the CFRC. Dr. Susan Wells was later appointed the first CFRC director in August of 1996. Her responsibilities included administration of the Center, development of a collaborative agenda and program of research, fund-raising, and recruitment of child welfare scholars to advance the mission of the Center. The Associate Dean of SSW, Dr. John Poertner, was delegated to oversee the monitoring functions of the CFRC under the *B.H.* decree. After Dr. Wells left the Center in 2000 for the University of Minnesota, Dr. Poertner assumed the Center directorship until his retirement from the SSW in 2002. His retirement created an opening to resolve a longstanding confusion over the division of roles and responsibilities between the Department's internal research operations under the ORD and the external research program conducted by the CFRC. In 2002, I resigned my joint appointment as the DCFS Research Director to become director of the newly enlarged Center.
4. This is a deliberate paraphrasing of Marx's celebrated line: "Human beings make history but not under conditions of their own choosing" (Marx, 1969/ 1852).

References

Argyris, C., & Schön, D. A. (1996). *Organization learning II: Theory, method, and practice*. Reading, MA: Addison-Wesley.

Baron, R. M., & Kenney, D. A. (1986). The moderator-mediator variable distinction in social psychological research: Conceptual, strategic, and statistical considerations. *Journal of Personality and Social Psychology, 51*, 1173–1182.

Barth, R. P., Wulczyn, F., & Crea, T. (2005). From anticipation to evidence: Research on the Adoption and Safe Families Act. *The Virginia Journal of Social Policy and Law, 12*(3), 371–399.

Barth, R. P. (2008). The move to evidence-based practice: How well does it fit with child welfare services? *Journal of Public Child Welfare, 1*(2), 145–171.

Berliner, D. C. (2002) Educational research: The hardest science of all. *Educational Researcher, 31*(8), 18–20.

Bross, D. C. (1997). The legal context of child abuse and neglect: Balancing the rights of children and parents in a democratic society. In M. E. Helfer, R. S. Kempe, & R. D. Krugman (Eds.), *The battered child (3rd edition)*. Chicago: The University of Chicago Press.

Brownson, R. C., Baker, E. A., Leet, T. L., & Gillespie, K. N. (2003). *Evidence-based public health*. New York: Oxford University Press.

Buchanan, A. (1988). Principal/agent theory and decisionmaking in health care. *Bioethics, 2*(4), 317–331.

Buss, D. M. (1999). *Evolutionary psychology: The new science of the mind*. Boston: Allyn & Bacon.

Campbell, D. T. (1984). Can we be scientific in applied social science? In R. Conner, D. G. Altman, & C. Jackson (Eds.), *Evaluation studies review annual, 9*, 26–48.

Campbell, D. T. (1988). The experimenting society. In E. S. Overman (Ed.), *Methodology and epistemology for social science: Selected papers of Donald T. Campbell* (pp. 290–314). Chicago: The University of Chicago Press.

Campbell, D. T., & Stanley, J. C. (1963). Experimental and quasi-experimental designs for research in teaching. In N. L. Gage (Ed.), *Handbook of research on teaching* (pp. 171–246). Chicago: Rand McNally.

Chambless, D. L., & Hollon, S. D. (1998). Defining empirically supported therapies. *Journal of Consulting and Clinical Psychology, 66*(1), 7–18.

Child Welfare Services Stakeholders Group. (2003). *Child welfare redesign: The future of California's child welfare services, final report*. Sacramento, CA: CWS Stakeholders Group.

Coleman, J. S. (1986). Social theory, social research, and a theory of action. *American Journal of Sociology, 91*(6), 1309–1335.

Coleman, J. S. (1990). *Foundations of social theory*. Cambridge, MA: Belknap Press of Harvard University Press.

Cook, T. D., & Campbell, D. T. (1979). *Quasi-experimentation: Design and analysis for field settings*. Chicago: Rand McNally.

Deacon, A., & Mann, K. (1999). Agency, modernity and social policy. *Journal of Social Policy, 28*(3), 413–435.

Dewey, J. (1931). Social science and social control. *The New Republic, 62* (July 29), 276–277.

Dold, R. B. (1996). Family matters: DCFS push to let extended family members rear their relatives' kids on their own having a favorable impact. *Chicago Tribune*, July 26.

Doyle, J. J. (2007). Can't buy me love? Subsidizing the care of related children. *Journal of Public Economics, 91*, 281–304.

Fiske, A. (1992). The four elementary forms of sociality: Framework for a unified theory of social relations. *Psychological Review, 99*, 689–723.

Fluke, J., Edwards, M., & Johnson, W. (1997). *Outcome evaluation: CERAP safety assessment technical report*. Urbana, IL: Children and Family Research Center.

French, P. A. (1995). *Corporate ethics*. New York: Harcourt Brace College Publishers.

Friedman, M. (2005). *Trying hard is not good enough*. British Columbia, Canada: Trafford Publishing.

Fuller, T., & Wells, S. (1998). Illinois child endangerment risk assessment protocol (CERAP): *Technical report concerning the implementation and validation of the protocol*. Urbana, IL: Children and Family Research Center.

Gambrill, E. (2006). Evidence-based practice and policy: Choices ahead. *Research on Social Work Practice, 16*(3), 338–357.

Giddens, A. (1990). *The consequences of modernity*. Stanford, CA: Stanford University Press.

Graham, A., & Steele, J. (2001). *Optimising value: The motivation of doctors and managers in NHS*. London: Public Management Foundation.

Hargreaves, D. H. (1999). Revitalising educational research: Lessons from the past and proposals for the future. *Cambridge Journal of Education, 29*(2), 239–249.

Heimer, C. A., & Staffen, L. R. (1998). *For the sake of the children*. Chicago: The University of Chicago Press.

Hughes, R., & Potter, C. C. (2008). Guest editorial. *Journal of Public Child Welfare, 1*(2), 139–144.

Iezzoni, L. I. (2003). *Risk adjustment for measuring health care outcomes (3rd edition)*. Chicago: Health Administration Press.

Illinois Department of Children and Family Services. (1995a). *A proposal to the Chicago Community Trust to help establish a children and family research center*. Springfield, IL: Illinois Department of Children and Family Services.

Illinois Department of Children and Family Services. (1995b). *HMR Reform Plan*. Springfield, IL: Illinois Department of Children and Family Services.

Janowitz, M. (1978). *The last half-century: Societal change and politics in America*. Chicago: The University of Chicago Press.

Jensen, M. C., & Meckling, W. H. (1976). Theory of the firm: Managerial behavior, agency costs and ownership structure. *Journal of Financial Economics, 3*(4), 305–360.

Jost, K. (2005). Child welfare reform. *The CQ Researcher, 15*, 345–367.

Kiser, E. (1999). Comparing varieties of agency theory in economics, political science, and sociology: An illustration from state policy implementation. *Sociological Theory, 17*(2), 146–170.

Le Grand, J. (2003). *Motivation, agency, and public policy*. New York: Oxford University Press.

Littell, J. (2008). How do we know what works? The quality of published reviews of evidence-based practices. In D. Lindsey & A. Shlonsky (Eds.), *Child welfare research: Advances for practice and policy* (pp. 66–93). Oxford: Oxford University Press.

MacRae, D. Jr. (1985) *Policy indicators: Link between social sciences and public debate*. Chapel Hill: The University of North Carolina Press.

Marsh, J. C., D'Aunno, T. A., & Smith, B. D. (2000). Increasing access and providing social services to improve drug abuse treatment for women with children. *Addiction, 95*, 1237–1247.

Marsh, J. C., Ryan, J. P., Choi, S., & Testa, M. F. (2006). Integrated services for families with multiple problems: Obstacles to family unification. *Children and Youth Services Review, 28*(9), 1074–1087.

Marshall, T. H. (1964). *Class, citizenship, and social development*. Chicago: University of Chicago Press.

Marx, K. (1969/1852). *The eighteenth brumaire of Louis Bonaparte*. New York: International Publishers.

Mayhew, L. H. (1997). *The new public: Professional communication and the means of social influence*. Cambridge, UK: Cambridge University Press.

Moynihan, D. P. (2005). Goal-based learning and the future of performance management. *Public Administration Review, 65*(2), 203–216.

Nonet, P., & Selznick, P. (1978). *Law and society in transition: Toward responsive law*. New York: Harper Colophon Books.

Ollendick, T. H., & King, N. J. (2004). Empirically supported treatments for children and adolescents: Advances toward evidence-based practice. In P. M. Barrett & T. H. Ollendick (Eds.), *Handbook of interventions that work with children and adolescents: Prevention and treatment* (pp. 3–25). New York: John Wiley.

Petit, M. R., & Curtis, P. A. (1997). *Child abuse and neglect: A look at the states.* Washington, DC: CWLA Press.

Richardson, W. S., Wilson, M. C., Nishikawa, J., & Hayward, R. S. A. (1995). The well-built clinical question: A key to evidence-based decisions. *ACP Journal Club*, Nov/Dec. 123, A12.

Rossi, P. H., Lipsey, M. W., & Freeman, H. E. (2004). *Evaluation: A systematic approach (7th edition).* Thousand Oaks, CA: SAGE Publications.

Rothstein, R. (2009). *Lessons for child welfare accountability: What can we learn from accountability policy in public education and in other sectors?* Paper presented at the planning meeting on improving metrics of performance assessment in child welfare systems, National Research Council/Institute of Medicine Board on Children, Youth, and Families, Washington, DC, March 13, 2009.

Ryan, J. P. (2006). *Illinois alcohol and other drug abuse (AODA) waiver demonstration: Final evaluation report.* Urbana, IL: Children and Family Research Center.

Ryan, J. P, Choi, S., Hong, J. S., Hernandez, P., & Larrison, C. R. (2008). Recovery coaches and substance exposed births: An experiment in child welfare. *Child Abuse and Neglect, 32*(11), 1072–1079.

Sackett, D. L., Rosenberg, W. M. C., Gray, J. A. M., Haynes, R. B., & Richardson, W. S. (1996). Evidence-based medicine: What is it and what it isn't. *British Medical Journal, 312*, 71–72.

Sedlack A. J., & Broadhurst D. D. (1996). *Third national incidence study of child abuse and neglect* (contract no. 105–91–1800). Washington, DC: National Center on Child Abuse and Neglect.

Shadish, W. R., Cook, T. D., & Campbell, D. T. (2002). *Experimental and quasi-experimental designs for generalized causal inference.* Boston: Houghton Mifflin Company.

Shapiro, M. (1999). *Solomon's sword: Two families and the children the state took away.* New York: Times Books/Random House.

Smith, B. D., & Testa, M. F. (2002). The risk of subsequent maltreatment allegations in families with substance-exposed infants. *Child Abuse and Neglect, 26*, 97–114.

Sowell, T. (2002). *A conflict of visions: Ideological origins of political struggles.* New York: Basic Books.

Testa, M. (1993). *Home of relative (HMR) program: Interim report to the Illinois Department of Children and Family Services.* Chicago: School of Social Service Administration.

Testa, M. (1997). Kinship foster care in Illinois. In J. Duerr Berrick, R. Barth, & N. Gilbert (Eds.), *Child welfare research review, volume two* (pp. 101–129). New York: Columbia University Press.

Testa, M. F., Cohen, L., & Smith, G. (2003). *Illinois subsidized guardianship waiver demonstration: Final evaluation report.* Urbana, IL: Children and Family Research Center.

The American Bar Association, The National Center for State Courts, & The National Council of Juvenile and Family Court Judges. (2004). *Building a better court: Measuring and improving court performance and judicial workload in child abuse and neglect cases.* Washington, DC: Author.

Titmuss, R. M. (1972). *The gift relationship: From human blood to social policy.* New York: Vintage Books.

U. S. Department of Health and Human Services. (2004). Waiver authority terms and conditions, State of Illinois. Amended October 22, 2004 to extend the implementation date for the enhanced guardianship component from no later than September 30, 2004 to no later than June 30, 2005. Washington, DC: U.S. Department of Health and Human Services.

U. S. Government Accountability Office. (2004). Child and family services reviews: States and HHS face challenges in assessing and improving state performance. Testimony before the Subcommittee on Human Resources, Committee on Ways and Means, House of Representatives. Washington, DC: U.S. Government Accountability Office.

Webb, S. S. (2001). Some considerations on the validity of evidence-based practice in social work. *British Journal of Social Work, 31,* 57–79.

Webster, D., Usher, C. L., Needell, B., & Wildfire, J. (2008). Self-evaluation: Using data to guide policy and practice in public child welfare agencies. In D. Lindsey & A. Shlonsky (Eds.), *Child welfare research: Advances for practice and policy* (pp. 261–270). Oxford: Oxford University Press.

Wrong, D. H. (1961). The oversocialized conception of man in modern sociology. *American Sociological Review, 26*(2), 183–193.

2

CHILD WELFARE IN THE TWENTY-FIRST CENTURY

Outcomes, Value Tensions, and Agency Risks

Mark F. Testa and John Poertner

Child welfare is arguably the most complex, litigious, political, heartbreaking, frustrating, and rewarding human service endeavor. The scope and complexity of the problems facing children, families, and their communities are daunting. The number of state and federal laws and policies that govern public responses to these problems are demanding and confusing. The media attention that accompanies difficult and failed cases is heart wrenching and too frequently generates political intervention that may actually be counterproductive. This is only part of the context in which we propose a framework for results-oriented accountability (ROA). This framework helps child welfare agencies coordinate community and government responses to child and family problems while developing and implementing evidence-supported interventions (ESI) to enhance agency capacity for improving outcomes for children and families.

The purpose of this chapter is to provide a general overview of key public interests and organizational principles that shape and define the public role in child welfare. Public child welfare is concerned largely with three major issues: (1) the *safety* issue of what minimal standards of child protection should be enforced to reduce agency risks to the life and health of children; (2) the *permanency* issue of who should be delegated the discretion to act as agents of children's care and guardianship when protective standards are violated; and (3) the *well-being* issue of how the performance of parents, guardians, and other child-caring agents can be enhanced to promote children's optimal development. These three issues supply a general framework for defining the scope of public child welfare interest and for building a ROA system that can advance the safety, permanence, and well-being of abused and neglected children.

Safety, Permanence, and Well-Being

Public child welfare starts from the premise that most children will be safely and permanently looked after by at least one of their birth parents until they are of legal age to act as agents of their own interests and well-being. When this norm of "natural guardianship" cannot be fulfilled because of parental absence, incapacity, or failure to meet minimal protective standards, other social groups will usually intervene to support, supplement, or substitute for the protection and care of these children.

Child protective interventions are divided between those that are handled informally through the affine agency of family, friends, and concerned neighbors and those that are formally instigated through the fiduciary agency of mandated reporters and concerned citizens who contact child protective services (CPS). In 2004, an estimated 3.5 million referrals were made formally to CPS throughout the United States alleging that approximately 5.5 million children had been abused or neglected.[1] These referrals must then be screened, investigated, and when the safety of children is at risk an appropriate and safe response must be made.

Two out of three of CPS referrals in 2004 were determined to warrant further action and were forwarded for investigation or response by CPS workers. These referrals involved about 3.5 million children and set into motion a sequence of decisions that begin with the issue of *safety*: Is there sufficient grounds for finding that a child has been maltreated or is at substantial risk of maltreatment? In 2004, CPS workers found sufficient evidence of maltreatment or substantial risk of victimization for approximately 872,000 children referred for investigation or alternative response. Expressed as a fraction of the U.S. child population, this victimization rate is down from 134 per 10,000 children in 1990 to 119 per 10,000 children in 2004. The highest rate of victimization occurred in 1993, when the rate was 153 per 10,000 children. Findings of child victimization are assumed to represent only the "tip of the iceberg" of known or suspected incidents of child maltreatment. The federal government funds a National Incidence Study (NIS) that is designed to estimate the larger number of children that are believed by professionals to have been maltreated in addition to those formally referred to CPS. The fourth round of NIS was initiated in 2005. The last published figures from the third round in 1996 estimated that CPS investigated only 28% of the recognized children who had experienced harm from abuse or neglect (Sedlak & Broadhurst, 1996).

For the segment of children found by CPS to be victims of abuse or neglect, a decision must next be made about social *continuity*: Can victims safely be left or served in their own home, or, if they must they be removed, can they be placed with relatives or in other family settings that conserve their connections to siblings, classmates, friends, and neighbors? In approximately 4 out of 10 cases of child victimization, CPS will refrain from any follow-up involvement with the family. This can happen because CPS determines that the children are no longer at substantial risk of revictimization. For example, a nonparental perpetrator (such as a baby-sitter or ex-partner) may no longer be present in the home or involved in the child's care. Additionally, postinvestigation services may simply be unavailable, waiting lists too long, or caregivers too uncooperative; as a result, postinvestigation involvement with the family simply ends. For the remaining 60% or 518,000 child victims who are able to access postinvestigation services, CPS is expected to make "reasonable efforts" to prevent their removal and maintain them as an "intact family" case if it is desirable for the caregiver to stay involved in the care of the children and it is safe to do so.

At other times safety considerations will dictate that the children must be removed from their home and placed in state protective custody on an emergency or longer-term basis. CPS workers, police, and medical personnel made this removal decision for approximately 268,000 children in 2004. For children taken into protective custody on an emergency basis, CPS then has several days to make a legal case before a juvenile court judge that it is necessary to retain the children longer in foster care. In about 12% of removals, CPS allows protective custody to "lapse" without judicial review and the children are returned home. For the remaining 236,000 children taken into foster care, court proceedings are initiated to decide on temporary custody of the victim, the disposition of the dependency, neglect, or abuse petition, and if public guardianship of the foster child should be granted to the child welfare agency on a longer-term basis.

Disruption of regular parental care, even if the parenting is abusive or neglectful, can be extremely stressful for children. To minimize this trauma, federal law encourages community-based care with relatives or in foster family homes in close proximity to the children's home of origin. Since 1996, federal policy has favored children's placement in the homes of relatives that meet relevant state safety standards. An estimated 123,000 children were looked after by relative foster parents in 2004. Although national data are unavailable on the geographic proximity of kinship placements to parents' homes, state-specific data indicate that approximately 30–40% of children in kinship foster care in California and Illinois are placed within five miles of their parents' home (Children and Family Research Center, 2008a; Child Welfare Research Center, 2008). Seventy percent of children in sibling groups of two to three are placed together in the same kinship foster home in Illinois (Children and Family Research Center, 2008b).

Although generally beneficial, it is not always possible or in the best interest of children to be placed with relatives or near their home of origin. In these circumstances, the next best alternative is to create *stability* in foster children's lives by placing them in alternative substitute care settings: Can children be placed in the least-restrictive (family-like) setting that ensures stable care and treatment consistent with their needs? Substitute care placements can be arrayed along a restrictiveness scale from the most to the least family-like setting as follows: trial home visits, preadoptive homes, kinship foster homes, nonrelative foster family homes, supervised independent living, group homes, and institutions. At the end of September 2004, approximately 21,000 foster children were back in their parent's home on a trial basis. Because they were still in the legal custody of the state, these children are tallied as still in foster care. They accounted for 4% of all 517,000 children in U.S. foster care at that time. Another 21,000 children or 4% were placed in preadoptive home settings awaiting finalization of their adoptions. In addition to the 123,000 children or 28% looked after by relative foster parents, there were another 238,000 children or 46% placed in the foster family care of nonrelatives. Foster children in supervised independent living programs numbered approximately 6000 or 1% of the U.S. foster care population. Foster children in group homes accounted for 46,000 or 9% and children in child-care institutions another 52,000 or 10% of the foster care population. There were an additional 11,000 foster children or 2% whose location in September 2004 was unknown and they were classified as runaways.

Compared to September 1998, the number and percentage of U.S. foster children on runaway status have doubled. In addition, restrictiveness of foster care placements has also increased: 76% of children were in foster family care with either relatives or nonrelatives in 1998 compared to 70% in 2004, whereas 15% were in group homes or institutions in 1998 compared to 19% in 2004. During this period, the average number of placements per foster child also increased from 2.9 to 3.0, whereas the percentage with six or more placement rose from 11.1% to 12.2%. To some extent, these increases in runaways, restrictiveness of care, and placement instability correlate with the aging of the U.S. foster child population from a median of 9.6 years old in 1998 to 10.9 years old in 2004. This age shift reflects to a large extent the movement of younger children out of temporary foster care into permanent homes with adoptive parents and legal guardians rather than a change in the median age of children entering care, which dropped from 8.5 years old in 1998 to 8.1 years old in 2004.

After removal, child welfare agencies and the courts immediately begin deliberating the issue of *permanence*: Can the circumstances that led to removal be successfully ameliorated so that the child may be returned home, or if family reunification is not possible, can alternative permanent homes be found with relatives, adoptive parents, or legal guardians? In subsequent chapters, we make the argument that the longitudinal tracking of children who enter foster care (entry cohorts) from the date of case opening to the date of permanence or case closing at 18 or 21 years of age provides the best insight into permanency planning dynamics. Currently, however, the only national data available on permanency outcomes come from reports on foster children who have exited care (exit cohorts) during the year. In 2004, the United States as a whole answered the permanency question by reunifying approximately 54% of children who exited foster care, discharging another 16% to the custody of relatives or legal guardians (most of whom are also relatives), and finding adoptive homes for another 18% (most of whom are relatives or former foster parents). The remaining 12% either aged out of foster care at 18 years old or a few years later (8%), had their case closed after running away (2%), or were transferred to another public agency such as juvenile corrections or mental health (2%). The percentage of foster children exiting to these nonpermanent settings has declined slightly since 1998 while the percentage reunified with parents has dropped from 60% in 1998 and the percentages discharged to the custody of relatives, legal guardians, and adoptive parents has risen from 26% in 1998 to 34% in 2004.

For foster children under 18 years of age who are awaiting permanence, child welfare agencies as their public guardians have the obligation to oversee the promotion of their *well-being*: What measures can be taken to ensure that children's developmental opportunities for leading a rewarding and productive life are not unduly compromised by state intervention? The funneling down of 5.5 million annual child referrals for abuse and neglect to 300,000 annual child removals into foster care means that child welfare agencies and the courts are looking after the most vulnerable of the vulnerable. This child well-being challenge is further complicated by the fact that the residual groups of foster children who are unlikely quickly to attain family permanence constitute an increasingly older segment of public wards with special health, emotional, disability, and educational needs.

The best available information on the well-being of foster children comes from the National Survey of Child and Adolescent Well-Being (NSCAW). Initiated by the U.S. Department of Health and Human Services in 1999, the study includes a cohort of 5501 children from families that were investigated by state CPS for maltreatment. This core sample was supplemented by a sample of 727 foster children who had been in care for at least 1 year. Most of the data collected from caregivers, children (aged 9 and older), teachers, and caseworkers for active cases are longitudinal, providing up to four or five time points. The last wave of data collection for the CPS cohort was completed in November 2007. The length of follow-up ranged from 59 to 97 months after the close of the investigation depending on the child's age. The last wave of data collection for the supplemental sample of foster children occurred approximately 48 months after placement into foster care.

In 2009, the Children and Family Research Center released its second report on the well-being of foster children in Illinois (Hartnett, Bruhn, Helton, Fuller, & Steiner, 2009). The Illinois sample consisted of 655 children who were in foster care as of September 2003. The study used many of the same instruments developed for NSCAW to interview the caregivers, caseworkers, and children, aged 9 years and older. Because the instruments were the same for the Illinois and national study, comparisons could be drawn between the Illinois sample and the national supplemental sample of foster children.

Although the two samples differed with respect to data collection periods (2003 vs. 2001), child characteristics (e.g., length of time in foster care and placement type), and caregiver characteristics (e.g., ethnicity and family relationship), the two samples of children profiled remarkably similar on most standardized assessments of physical health, mental health, educational status, and community connections. For example, 8% of the national foster care sample had a serious injury, accident, or poisoning that required the attention of a physician or nurse compared to 7% of the Illinois sample; 27% of the national sample had gone to the emergency room or urgent care three or more times compared to the same percentage for Illinois foster children; and 20% of the national sample had not seen a dentist for a check-up in the last year compared to 19% of the Illinois sample.

The national and Illinois samples were also comparable on the proportions that scored in the borderline or clinical range for behavior problems (48% vs. 51%) according to caregiver reports, psychiatric hospitalization rates (9% vs. 11%), and self-reported symptoms of depression by children (6% vs. 4%). Although the national and Illinois foster child samples are statistically indistinguishable on most standardized physical and mental health measures, the overall levels of physical and mental well-being of foster children are substantially below the norms for the general population of children in the United States. For the sake of comparison, the proportion of children in the general population who score in the borderline or clinical range for behavior problems (17%) is one-third the proportion of the foster child population (48% to 51%) in Illinois and the nation as a whole. Substantial disparities also exist with regard to enrollment in special education classes: 39% of foster children versus 15% of students in Illinois (Hartnett et al., 2009) and rates of juvenile delinquency: 43.3 per 1000 victims of child maltreatment versus 27.8 per 1000 child population in Cook County, Illinois (Ryan & Testa, 2005). Although the Illinois DCFS cannot be held solely accountable for narrowing such disparities in health, education, and law abidance between foster children and the general population of children, the Department and the juvenile courts certainly bear major responsibility for safeguarding the well-being of abused and neglected children at each decision stage of child protective intervention.

Shared Accountability and Continuous Quality Improvement

The shared accountability for child welfare outcomes is acknowledged by Mark Hardin, Director of the National Child Welfare Resource Center on Legal and Judicial Issues, as follows: "Although the courts ultimately decide whether a child will be removed from the home, placed in foster care, or freed for adoption and determine the nature and extent of services provided to children, youth and their families, the input of child welfare workers affects all of these decisions" (Hardin, p. 705). This perspective places accountability for child welfare outcomes within the jurisdiction of the courts. Although not everyone would agree that the roles of CPS and child welfare agencies are secondary, there is little doubt that public child welfare operates in a complex and contentious legal environment of legislative standards setting, judicial oversight, federal audits, case reviews, class-action law suits, judicial consent decrees, and citizens review boards. Results-oriented quality improvement is intended to decrease the need for these overlapping levels of public accountability and judicial oversight. It refers to those administrative mechanisms of performance monitoring, policy analysis and planning, systematic research review, program evaluation, and continuous quality improvement that make "reflexive" use of information about the results of an activity as a means of reordering and redefining what that activity is. It is a subset of what the sociologist Anthony Giddens (1994) calls the "reflexive monitoring of social action" (Giddens, 1994). This concept applies not only to formal organizational activities but also to individual monitoring activities that rely on empirical results rather than on tradition, faith, or hierarchy to decide whether to conform to a particular pattern of behavior or to undertake an alternative course of action that promises more satisfactory results. When the process of evaluating the validity of a general course of action adheres to scientific methods of observation, prediction, control, and falsifiability, we may say that the process is evidence supported.

Although child welfare interventions are becoming more results oriented and evidence supported, both the courts and child welfare agencies largely exist to implement policies derived from state and federal child welfare laws that to some extent stem from tradition, faith, and hierarchy. The major difference from the past is that many of these new laws contain provisions for reflexively self-correcting some of the assumptions and factual premises on which they are based. Of all the child welfare laws, the most influential for ROA is the Adoption and Safe Families Act (ASFA) that the U.S. Congress passed in 1997. Under the authority of this Act and other federal child welfare policies, the U.S. Department of Health and Human Services (DHHS) designed a system of ROA and quality improvement (QI) that all states must adopt or else they risk losing federal funds. Much of DHHS' authority to design and implement such a system comes from Sec. 479a of ASFA. This section calls for an annual report to Congress on the performance of each state on a set of outcome measures that this Act requires the DHHS to develop. Implementation of this section by DHHS has been controversial,[2] but there is no doubt that the data collected and the procedures developed for performance assessment carry enormous potential for influencing the operations of state and local child welfare agencies and the courts.

The major vehicle for implementing the federal accountability and quality improvement system is the Child and Family Services Review (CFSR). According to DHHS:

> The Child and Family Services Reviews are designed to enable the Children's Bureau to ensure that State child welfare agency practice is in conformity with Federal child welfare requirements, to determine what is actually happening to children and families as they are engaged in State child welfare services, and to assist States to enhance their capacity to help children and families achieve positive outcomes. www.acf.hhs.gov/programs/cb/cwmonitoring/index.htm#cfsr.

During a CFSR, the review team assesses the state's substantial conformity to statistical benchmarks and standards in the domains of safety, continuity, stability, permanence, and well-being. The 23 items assessed during CFSR can be reordered according to the five stages of child protective intervention identified (see Table 2.1).

The CFSR process has two stages: system-level review and on-site case audits and interviews. The system-level review involves the completion of a "Statewide Assessment," which consists of a 20-page questionnaire (including instructions). This assessment instrument has five sections that include general information about each state agency, state child welfare agency characteristics with narrative responses on systemic factors, data profiles for the safety and permanency outcomes, a narrative assessment of the outcome areas and a self-assessment of the state's strengths and needs, and issues and locations for further examination through the onsite review. The case audit stage of the CFSR process includes case record reviews of a sample of children in foster care and those receiving in-home services. Data collection from these records is augmented with in-person interviews with children, parents, foster parents, caseworkers, and other professionals involved with the children.

When the CFSR indicates that a state's achievement level falls below the threshold for "substantial conformity," the state must develop a program improvement plan (PIP). Because no state was judged to be in "substantial conformity" in the first round of reviews, every jurisdiction was required to develop a program improvement plan.

The accountability and quality improvement provisions of the ASFA as implemented by DHHS have the potential to transform the operations of public child welfare agencies. It is impossible for states to escape public reporting of the DHHS outcome indicators, case reviews, or PIPs. Most states incorporate the DHHS outcome indicators in their reporting

TABLE 2.1   CFSR Items Ordered by Stage of Child Protective Intervention

Safety	**Children are, first and foremost, protected from abuse and neglect.**
	Item 1: Timeliness of initiating investigations of reports of child maltreatment
	Item 2: Repeat maltreatment
Continuity	**Children are safely maintained in their homes whenever possible and appropriate, or the continuity of family relationships and connections is preserved for children.**
	Item 3: Services to family to protect child(ren) in home and prevent removal or reentry into foster care
	Item 4: Risk assessment and safety management
	Item 11: Proximity of foster care placement
	Item 12: Placement with siblings
	Item 13: Visiting with parents and siblings in foster care
	Item 14: Preserving connections
	Item 15: Relative placement
	Item 16: Relationship of child in care with parents
Stability	**Children have stability in their living situations.**
	Item 6: Stability of foster care placement
Permanence	**Children have permanence in their living situations.**
	Item 7: Permanency goal for child
	Item 8: Reunification, guardianship, or permanent placement with relatives
	Item 9: Adoption
	Item 10: Other planned permanent living arrangement
	Item 5: Foster care reentries.
Well-Being	**Families have enhanced capacity to provide for their children's needs and children receive appropriate services to meet their educational needs and adequate services to meet their physical and mental health needs.**
	Item 17: Needs and services of child, parents, and foster parents
	Item 18: Child and family involvement in case planning
	Item 19: Caseworker visits with child
	Item 20: Caseworker visits with parent(s)
	Item 21: Educational needs of the child
	Item 22: Physical health of the child
	Item 23: Mental/behavioral health of the child

Adapted from http://www.acf.hhs.gov/programs/cb/cwmonitoring/tools_guide/procedures/appendixb.htm; last accessed September 1, 2009.

systems, conduct practice case reviews using DHHS instruments, and regularly review their PIPs.

Complying with these requirements and more importantly improving the outcomes for children and families require each state to operate within this results-oriented system. We believe that there is much that can be done to maximize the benefits for children and families by building on the DHHS framework with the model presented in the next chapter. However, before presenting the model and developing its components in subsequent chapters, it is important to recognize the value-laden features of public child welfare that influence agency behavior, public opinion, and policy. A society's values become behavioral norms that guide the behavior of its members including legislators and agency staff.

Scope of Public Interest

There is widespread agreement in both policy and practice circles that safety, continuity, stability, permanence, and well-being are the desired results of child protective intervention. Within this general consensus, however, there are conflicting points of view about the appropriate scope of public interest in ensuring these results and alternative perspectives on the optimal form of social organization for achieving these aims.[3]

The different points of view on the appropriate scope of public interest can be conceived as falling along a continuum from the narrow to the diffuse (Wolfe, 1978). Under a *narrow* scope of public interest, state intervention into private family life is justified only if the life or health of the child is jeopardized, e.g., when there is bodily injury, physical neglect, or outright abandonment. "State" here refers to government broadly defined, including legislative, judicial, and executive branches. Responsibility for other child welfare outcomes, such as continuity of relationships, stability of care, emotional attachments, and educational attainment, is believed best left to the discretion of birth parents, extended kin, and other communal associations. Only if these traditional affine agents of child welfare violate the wider standards of minimally adequate protection and care by abandoning, neglecting, or abusing their "natural responsibilities" may the state intervene as a last resort and reassign child-caring duties to bureaucratic agents, such as foster families, group homes, and institutions.

Alternatively, under a *diffuse* scope of public interest, state engagement with the family is encouraged whenever it promotes the well-being of children. This assumes that the state should take responsibility for all children whose interests are best served by universally guaranteeing them equal opportunities for development into productive workers and responsible citizens. Although the primary locus of discretion may still reside with birth families, state fiduciary agents are entrusted with the major responsibility for overseeing and safeguarding the well-being of all children.

Generally speaking, the scope of public interest in child welfare in the United States can be viewed as having widened from a narrow *safety* focus on the protection of children from parental cruelty and exploitation in the workforce in the late nineteenth century to a broader *permanency* concern with family continuity, placement stability, and legal permanence in the twentieth century. Now at the beginning of the twenty-first century, there is an enlarged public interest in equalizing child *well-being* opportunities, as reflected in the 1999 John H. Chafee Foster Care Independence Program (CFCIP) and 2001 No Child Left Behind Act (P.L. 107-110). Although the widening scope of public interest tends generally to reduce the responsibility and autonomy of parents, extended kin, and other communal associations in the protection, care, and development of children, there are occasionally exceptions to this trend, such as home schooling, informal kinship care, and the withholding of medical treatment in favor of spiritual healing. Political disputes over the appropriate scope of public interest in child welfare can also produce periodic reversals, such as the scaling back in the United States of social welfare spending in the 1980s and the ending of the open-ended federal entitlement of Aid to Families with Dependent Children (AFDC) in 1996 in favor of time-limited financial assistance and mandatory workforce participation of needy parents. Similar reactions against the entitlements and outcomes of the bureaucratic welfare state can be observed for other liberal democratic societies such as Denmark, Great Britain, and New Zealand (Korpi & Palme, 2003). Just how far a polity is prepared to shift the loci of discretion and responsibility from families to the state or back to families depends, to some extent, on the degree of confidence it places in two alternative principles of social organization: the primordial and the bureaucratic (Testa, 2001).

Primordial Solidarities and Bureaucratic Institutions

For most of human history, child protective interventions have been rooted in what sociologists call the "primordial solidarities" of kinship, community, and tribe (Shils, 1957; Coleman, 1990). Over the past several centuries, religious, voluntary, and other communal associations have assumed a greater role in the protection and care of vulnerable children. Most recently, the bureaucratic welfare state has emerged as a major guarantor of public child welfare both directly through its administration of CPS, family support programs, and substitute care interventions and indirectly through its licensing and subvention of the temporary and permanent placement of children with relatives, foster families, adoptive parents, and legal guardians.

The differentiation of child welfare functions out of primordial solidarities and their restructuring as specialized programs of the bureaucratic welfare state are manifestations of a broader transformation in the economic and social organization of modern societies. This process can be characterized as one in which human resources are lifted out of the primordial ecologies of extended family and local community and reinvested across vast spans of space and time into bureaucratic structures of economic exchange and social cooperation (Giddens, 1990; Lin, 2001). The splitting off of the nuclear family from the extended kin household, the spatial separation of residence and workplace, and more recently the worldwide reach of the Internet and other modes of telecommunications have made possible impressive gains in economic growth and social productivity. In the language of social capital theory, bridging social capital displaces bonding social capital as the key input for economic investment and social exchange (Putnam, 2000). At the same time, the decreased face-to-face presence and decreased proximity of trusted family, friends, and neighbors place unprecedented strains on traditional modes of child protection and care. To bridge this gap, modern bureaucratic institutions in the forms of CPS, health clinics, welfare offices, foster care agencies, juvenile courts, school boards, police departments, youth employment bureaus, and media censors have emerged to assume greater responsibility for overseeing, contributing to, and sometimes substituting for familial and communal investments in the protection, care, and development of children.

Child welfare workers once viewed this historical development largely in evolutionary terms. They joined social reformers at the turn of the twentieth century in redefining the appropriate unit of public responsibility from the smallest territorial unit to the largest national aggregation, substituting taxpayer obligation for kinship duty as the fairest allocation of social burden, promoting bureaucratic regularity over moral judgment as the proper aim of social administration, and discarding the traditional Poor Law principle of "less eligibility" in favor of income adequacy as the relevant standard of family assistance. The guiding policy assumption was that national market structures of economic achievement and federal programs of social equality would steadily dislodge individuals from their particularistic roles (Parsons, 1951) in kinship and local community networks and reattach them to their universalistic roles of life-long work and national citizenship (Marshall, 1964). Innovations in family law helped to advance this process by narrowing the scope of patriarchal authority over adult children and women and limiting family support liabilities to the conjugal nuclear family, consisting of a single breadwinner, his housewife, and their children.

For children who were deprived of nuclear family support or permanence of family care because of parental death, absence, disability, or failure to uphold minimal protective standards, state and federal governments partnered to support, supplement, or substitute for the children's protection and care. From the 1930s to the 1970s, the U.S federal and state programs of AFDC, subsidized foster care, child abuse protection and treatment, and adoption assistance steadily enlarged the public role in the protection, care, and development of dependent, neglected, and abused children. After the U.S. federal courts invalidated "substitute father" and "unsuitable parent" restrictions in the 1960s that had cut-off AFDC to dependent children in the homes of unmarried adults, AFDC support for the in-home and out-of-home care of dependent, neglected, and abused children greatly expanded. As a result, the national count of poor children plummeted and the preservation of homes with at least one birth parent rose to unprecedented levels. By the usual yardsticks of program participation, poverty reduction, and family continuity as indicators of child and family well-being, the widening net of federal social security programs in the 1960s was a major success. But as family organization diverged from the conjugal family ideal and public spending on dependent, neglected, and abused children continued to rise, the federal government cut back on program expansion in the 1980s and reversed policy direction in the 1990s. By the turn of the twenty-first century, there was a wide scale backlash against family income entitlements and the child welfare outcomes of the bureaucratic welfare state.

What processes should a liberal democratic society follow in the twenty-first century in deciding whether to narrow or broaden the scope of public responsibility for ensuring child welfare outcomes? Do the demands of a global economy call for further diminution of local authority and familial autonomy in the protection, care, and education of children? Are inherited customs, cultural traditions, and religious beliefs sufficient justification for different methods of child rearing? When should empirical evidence be demanded as proof of the efficacy of traditional practices in accomplishing desired child welfare outcomes? What is the proper balance between value-based discourse and evidence-supported knowledge in adjudicating among competing claims about child safety, family permanence, and adolescent well-being? These are some of the questions that policymakers, practitioners, clients, and citizens must learn to address as the "reflexive modernization" of family life increasingly calls into doubt traditional beliefs about marriage, family organization, and the status of children (Giddens, 1994; Beck, Bonss, & Lau, 2003).

The critical challenge we now face in child welfare is to how best to go about developing an ROA system that is responsive to the desires, impulses, and values of children and families while remaining true to scientifically validated processes of questioning traditional practices and evaluating social innovations in light of information about their effectiveness in accomplishing desired social ends. No longer can child welfare policymakers and practitioners simply take for granted that the unidirectional displacement of social welfare functions by centralized bureaucratic institutions is structurally inevitable, financially sustainable, or even socially desirable. The current process appears to be less one of total replacement than one in which primordial solidarities retain a delimited but significant role (Litwak, 1965; Janowitz and Suttles, 1979). The emerging pattern in public child welfare is one in which modern bureaucratic institutions must now learn to coexist with older primordial structures by creating reciprocal avenues of influence so that the macrofunctions of ensuring child safety, family permanence, and adolescent well-being can become better coordinated with the microprocesses of parental authority,

kin altruism, and communal solidarity that make possible the accomplishment of these broader collective aims.

In this next chapter, a model of results-oriented accountability is proposed for child welfare that responds to the need for better coordination
between primordial solidarities and bureaucratic institutions, incorporates and develops evidence-supported policies, and integrates these
efforts into improving the quality of public engagement and the efficacy
of child welfare interventions. We do not suggest that this model is easy to
develop or to manage in bureaucratic settings. We do believe that it is
possible and necessary to improve organizational learning capacity to
protect children, ensure that they have safe and permanent homes, and
promote their well-being, while at the same time respond to increased
public demands for fiscal efficiency and public accountability. Managing
such a model requires acknowledging the legal requirements in which
child welfare operates as well as the public expectations that frequently
reflect hotly contested and competing values. The next section presents an
analytical framework for categorizing the variety of safety, permanency,
and well-being issues that challenge the design, direction, and funding of
public child welfare policy and practice in the United States and other
liberal democratic societies.

Value Tensions and Agency Risks

The cross-classification of the two dimensions of scope of public interest
by form of social organization provides an analytical framework for
examining the history of public child welfare and charting the various
ideological divisions that drive periodic cycles of policy reform (see
Fig. 2.1). At the narrowest scope of public interest is the minimalist concern for child safety that guarantees those conditions only necessary for
children's physical survival and *health*. With a more diffuse scope of public
interest, a broader concern with child well-being arises that encompasses
those additional developmental processes of social attachment, encultura-
tion, and *education* that prepare children for productive work and responsible citizenship as adults. Permanence of caregiving relationships plays
a mediating role and makes available to dependent children the requisite
human, social, cultural, and financial capital necessary for their physical
survival and future social development (Webb, Dowd, Harden,
Landsverk, & Testa, 2010).

When family permanence is lacking because of parental absence, incapacity, or failure to uphold minimal protective standards, the state
will intervene with supportive and rehabilitative services in order to
maintain family *continuity* and conserve children's social connections to
siblings, relatives, neighbors, and friends (bonding social capital). If
family preservation and conservation of community connections prove

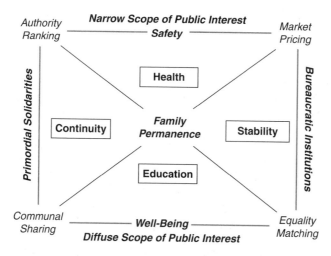

Figure 2.1 Analytical framework.

infeasible, the state will attempt to reconstruct some semblance of *stability* in children's lives by placing them in licensed foster homes or in more restrictive (less family-like settings) of group homes, child-care institutions, residential treatment centers, or secure detention facilities depending on their needs (bridging social capital).

Conservation of bonding social capital to maintain continuity as opposed to investment in bridging social capital to achieve stability each draws on different organizational principles for reducing what economists and lawyers call "agency risk" (Buchanan, 1988). As detailed in Chapter 1, agency in this context refers to more than just formal organizations. It also encompasses the choices and decisions made by both primordial and bureaucratic agents to whom are delegated the discretion to act on behalf of the interests of child-principals. Agency relationships in child welfare include, for example, the primordial relationships of biological child and birth parent, grandchild and grandparent, and American Indian child and tribal judge. They also include the bureaucratic relationships of foster child and foster parent, client and social worker, adopted child and adoptive parent, and ward and guardian. Agency risk refers to the problem of primordial and bureaucratic agents' imperfectly fulfilling the best interests of child-principals, for example, parental abuse and neglect, child sexual exploitation, foster care drift, professional malfeasance, and adoption disruption.

At each corner in Figure 2.1, we list one of the four relational models (Fiske, 1992) that were introduced in Chapter 1. The figure is a further elaboration of an analytical framework that was previously constructed to categorize periodic cycles of reform in child welfare (Testa, 2008). Each of the four relational models corresponds to a modal type of agency relationship at the corners of the intersecting poles of scope of public interest and form of social organization. Although the other types of agency relationships also operate in each of these four corners, it is the modal relationship that gives a particular combination of scope of interest and social organization its distinctive form. The social science literature offers many analogous concepts for drawing similar distinctions, such as Max Weber's classic typology of traditional, affectual, value-rational, and instrumental-rational action and Alejandro Portes and Julia Sensenbrenner's (1993) sources of social capital as enforceable trust, bounded solidarity, value introjection, and reciprocity exchange. We have chosen to rely on Alan Fiske's four relational models of authority ranking, communal sharing, equality matching, and market pricing because they combine in useful ways to describe different modes of reducing agency risk and enhancing agency performance in the protection, care, and education of abused and neglected children.

The *primordial* principle for reducing agency risk and improving agency performance draws largely from the relational models of communal sharing and authority ranking. The former holds that biological kinship, and its close approximations based on ethnicity, nationality, and religion, should take precedence when delegating rights and responsibilities to act as agents of children's well-being. Birth certification, paternity establishment, laws of relatedness, same-race matching, and federally recognized tribal membership are examples of administrative and judicial procedures for authenticating primordial agency. The assumption is that kin and other primordial agents naturally feel affinity for and closely identify with their children's well-being so they can be trusted to make caregiving choices that promote the best interests of the children as if they were their own interests.

The primordial model of authority ranking relies on the linear ordering of agency relationships along the hierarchical dimensions of gender, age, degree of relatedness, and other ascribed statuses, to enforce traditional norms of care, commitment, and trust among family, friends, and neighbors. These norms include, for example, filial piety that obligates children's reciprocation of parental investments by supporting their parents in old age (Hamilton, 1990), the enforcement of extended family liability under Elizabethan Poor Laws (Crowther, 1982), and the subordination of women's roles to unpaid domestic labor and caregiving tasks under patriarchal authority structures.

In contrast, the *bureaucratic* principle for reducing agency risk and enhancing agency performance draws largely from the relational models of market pricing and equality matching. The former holds that child-caring rights and responsibilities should not be automatically ascribed but instead achieved based on a comparative assessment of different child-caring agents' qualifications, abilities, and demonstrated performance in parenting irrespective of gender, kinship, race, or other ascribed characteristics. Attachment studies, psychological parent assessments, foster home licensing, termination of parental rights (TPR), and race-neutral selection of adoptive homes are examples of bureaucratic processes for reassigning parental rights and responsibilities. The assumption is that bureaucratic agents are best held accountable by financial incentives, performance contracts, and monitoring systems (e.g., supervision, home visits, and performance reviews) that discourage self-interested defections from norms of responsible child caring.

Whereas it is taken for granted that the interests of primordial agents and principals are likely to converge and divergences are rare, the assumption is that the interests of bureaucratic agents and principals are potentially in conflict. The bureaucratic model of equality matching relies on ethical codes, licensing tests, accreditation standards, educational degrees, and other symbolic tokens that signal agency integrity and guard against the risks that agents will defect from their fiduciary responsibilities and equitable decision making on behalf of children's best interests and well-being.

The coexistence of primordial and bureaucratic principles and practice remains a chronic source of organizational strain in child welfare policy. The intensity of the strain varies depending on whether agents are operating within a large centralized bureaucracy or within small localized offices. Whatever the scale of operations, child welfare agencies usually respond to agency risk by becoming rule-bound. Nonetheless, the unpredictable situations confronting families and the workers charged to help them must create some space for creativity and sensitivity in taking into account the different cultural traditions, folk beliefs, and informal rules on which primordial solidarities rely to promote communal cooperation and enforce mutual trust. Responding creatively to particular family problems while abiding by universalistic policy rules and at the same time using evidence-based policies and practices is a delicate balance that is difficult to manage.

Advances in medical technology, for example, have greatly increased the potential for the discretion of physicians to come into conflict with the preferences of parents in the treatment and care of children with complex medical needs, such as prematurity, respiratory disorders, and heart problems. Some faith-based groups, such as Christian Scientists and Jehovah's Witnesses, reject on religious grounds certain medical interventions even in life-threatening situations. Even though the parents believe they are acting in the "spiritual" best interests of their children, such beliefs come into conflict with child protection laws, such as the so-called "Baby-Doe Amendment" that Congress attached in 1984 to the federal Child Abuse Prevention and Treatment Act (CAPTA). The law requires states to have in place procedures for reporting allegations of the withholding of medically indicated treatment from disabled infants as medical neglect. In life-threatening emergencies, state child protective procedures allow attending physicians to take temporary custody of infants and to administer medical treatments in spite of parental opposition (Heimer & Staffen, 1998). Despite objections from medical associations, many states have laws that exempt from the definition of neglect parental reliance on prayer for the treatment of disease or refusal of medical treatment on religious grounds (Stanfield, 2000).

Similar tensions also characterize issues of family permanence. The primordial principle finds one of its fullest expressions in the 1978 Indian Child Welfare Act (ICWA) that upholds the sovereign authority of tribal nations to control the processes by which Native American children are removed from tribal homes and to ensure their placement with extended family members, other tribal foster homes, or other Indian families (Madrigal, 2001). The primordial principle also figures in the preference for kinship foster care that many American states added to their child welfare laws during the 1980s (Gleeson & Craig, 1994) and that Congress attached to the 1996 Personal Responsibility and Work Opportunity Reconciliation Act (PRWORA). The provision encourages states to place children with kin when such relatives meet relevant child protection standards. Efforts to extend primordial prerogatives beyond kinship and Native American culture to other ethnic and racial groups, however, came to a halt with the passage of the 1994 Multiethnic Placement Act (MEPA) and 1996 Interethnic Placement Act (IEPA). Both laws subordinate the primordial principle to bureaucratic procedures by outlawing the denial or delay of the placement or adoption of any child on the basis of race, color, or national origin. In 2006, the U.S. Congress further curbed kinship prerogatives by eliminating federal reimbursement for casework and child placement services to foster children in long-term extended family care that does not meet the same licensing standards and other bureaucratic certifications required for unrelated foster homes.

Looking at the same set of child welfare policies either through a primordial or bureaucratic lens can often yield opposite conclusions. For example, the 1994 MEPA and 1996 IEPA, which outlawed the use of race, color, or national origin in the selection of temporary or permanent homes for foster children in the United States, reinforce suspicions among minority groups about the country's commitment to the preservation of minority communities and cultures that are different from the ethnic identities of the majority of the population (Roberts, 2002). The overrepresentation of minority children in foster care in proportion to their numbers in the child population and at each prior and subsequent stage of child protective intervention raises doubts about the validity of bureaucratic claims to fairness, impartiality, and equal treatment (Derezotes, Poertner, & Testa, 2005). Similarly, ASFA's retention of federal adoption assistance entitlements after PRWORA ended welfare entitlements to needy families appears to tilt the scales away from birth families in favor of substitute homes. Most recently, the withdrawal of federal reimbursements under the Deficit Reduction Act of 2005 for the administrative costs of child placement, permanency planning, and other services to foster children in the homes of relatives that do not meet foster home licensing standards strikes many as another unwarranted attack against primordial principles.

Viewing these same policies through a bureaucratic lens invites a different interpretation. According to MEPA and IEPA proponents, these laws ended the outmoded practice of treating children as if they were the "property" of primordial groups (Bartholet, 1999). They contend that the surplus of minority children in foster care can best be eliminated by removing the intragroup placement preferences that needlessly deny or delay adoption for minority children who otherwise tend to languish in long-term foster care. There is suspicion that reasonable efforts requirements keep children in unsafe homes too long and too often return them to inadequate families. It is argued that kinship placement preferences routinely result in the placement of children in the homes of blood relatives who have only a passing acquaintance with the children or perpetuate the same family problems and intergenerational dysfunctions that caused the abuse or neglect in the first place. Furthermore exempting relatives from fulfilling the same foster home licensing requirements expected of non-relatives destroys the rational basis for paying foster parents a higher stipend than welfare recipients and allows them to bypass certification procedures that help filter out unsafe and unsuitable homes.

In the absence of coordinating mechanisms for reconciling these divergent interpretations, the unmediated clash of primordial and bureaucratic principles risks alienating parents, families, and local communities from broader public purposes and pushes child protective services and juvenile courts toward an overreliance on coercive measures to accomplish organizational goals. Because child abuse and neglect are shocking departures from norms of parental altruism and family mutualism, it is understandable that child protective agents would want to look beyond ascribed signs of commitment and trust and demand instead concrete demonstrations of agent reliability and commitment, such as compliance with service plans, completion of parenting classes, regular visitation with children, and licensing of prospective foster parents, before reassigning caregiving responsibilities back to birth parents or delegating them to relatives. Similarly, because the rules, tokens, and contracts used by bureaucratic institutions to reduce agency risk are alien to the traditional assurances of enforceable trust and bounded solidarity based on kinship, common ethnicity, neighborhood residence, and religious membership, it is understandable that public actions that ignore or transverse these boundaries would sometimes be viewed with skepticism and suspicion by parents, relatives, and other primordial agents. Both reactions are antithetical to the mutual trust necessary for cooperative child protection and care in modern societies.

The lack of consensus on how best to resolve these primordial and bureaucratic tensions contributes to the fragmentation of public child welfare policy at both central and local levels. Some groups favor narrowing the scope of public interest and restricting public support for dependent children in the custody of single parents in the hopes of reinvigorating paternalism and traditional family values. Others argue for the leveling of child developmental opportunities at the expense of family autonomy by accelerating TPRs and increasing financial subsidies for the adoption of abused and neglected children by state-approved families. Still others argue for delegating discretion back to local communities and primordial solidarities at the expense of bureaucratic principles through social service block-grants, government sponsored faith-based initiatives, or greater tribal sovereignty in child welfare matters. Which of these different directions future policy and practice should take is one of the most challenging and unsettling issues confronting public child welfare at the start of the second decade of the twenty-first century.

Cycles of Child Welfare Reform

U.S. child welfare shares an interesting and complex history with Great Britain and its former colonies, which dates back to the sixteenth century (McGowen, 2005). For analytical purposes, however, it is useful to start in the nineteenth century when free-market ideologists fused together the values of *laissez-faire* capitalism (market pricing) with paternalism (authority ranking) to justify narrowing the scope of public interest in child welfare to the minimal conditions necessary for protecting child safety. As described by the sociologist, Alan Wolfe (1978):

> The paternalistic theory of the child is intimately linked to the economic theory of laissez-faire. Just as in the (nineteenth) century it was held proper for the state to keep its hand off the private firm, it followed that the state should not intervene into the private family. Just as the remaining functions of the state were protective—tariffs and the creation of an economic infrastructure—so state intervention into family life could only occur if it also were protective of established values. In short, the world of nineteenth century capitalism was based at least in theory on a twin assertion of privatism: first for the firm and then for the family. (Wolfe, 1978, p. 427)

This dual assertion of (nuclear) family autonomy and individual achievement within the context of a capitalist economy freed human resources from the restraints of traditional authority structures and propelled exchange relations far beyond the local boundaries of kinship and community. The accompanying diminution of communal control over private family choices and the comparative anonymity of urban life multiplied the opportunities for calculative self-interest to impinge on traditional authority and primordial relationships of communal sharing among families, friends, and neighbors. Unencumbered by traditional norms and emancipated from the bounded solidarity of extended kinship and reciprocity exchange, adults were free to pursue a wider range of interests and to give fuller expression to their individuality and creativity.

With these greater economic and social freedoms, however, came greater risks of child dependency, neglect, and exploitation as economic downturns, industrial accidents, and other misfortunes left immigrant and working-class families on their own and isolated from traditional support networks to absorb the full brunt of their breadwinners' losses and failures in the marketplace. Many impoverished families sought to make up for these deficits by exchanging the labor of their minor children for wages in the marketplace. At the time, the patriarchal family was regarded as the principal and the children were viewed as agents of their parents' interests. As Eekelaar (2002) observes:

> From the earliest times, the basis for legal intervention in family matters was the protection of the interests of parents or other adults in the value which children represented for them. Thus, in medieval law (and up to at least 1660), "Wardship procedures were not designed with the purpose of facilitating judicial intervention into the lives of vulnerable infants" but to benefit the guardian from the ward's land and prospective marriage (Seymour, 1994) . . . . Common law did nothing about the child's interest in its relationship with its parents, either in ensuring that the father properly discharged his responsibilities under it, or in providing the child with remedies against third parties should they injure that interest. (Eekelaar, 2002, p. 383)

Even though the prevailing norms of paternalism and laissez-faire capitalism tolerated public indifference to other children's well-being and condoned the use of children as contractual agents in the marketplace, the increased visibility of child beggars and street orphans and the growing exploitation of child laborers in factories and sweat-shops stood in stark contrast to the basic democratic commitment to social equality. According to the political scientist James Fishkin (1983), the evolution of social policies in the United States can be characterized in terms of which two of three basic American values a particular policy upholds: achievement, equality, or family autonomy.

These three values correspond, respectively, to the concepts of market pricing, equality matching, and family permanence as displayed in Figure 2.1. The value of *achievement* embraces the market pricing principle that the allocation of social roles and economic rewards should be based solely on competitive economic performance or comparative bureaucratic assessment without regard to gender, race, national origin, or other ascribed characteristics. The value of *equality* embodies the equality matching principle that children should be universally guaranteed the minimally necessary developmental conditions to provide them with a realistic opportunity of leading economically productive and rewarding lives as adults. The third value of family *autonomy* recognizes the permanent rights of parents to guide the development of their children in accordance with their own cultural traditions, religious beliefs, and nepotistic interests. The social welfare policies of most liberal democratic societies embody to varying degrees all three of these values. Fishkin's argument, however, is that any social policy can at best maximize only two of these three basic values and by doing so logically rules out the third. His deduction identifies a powerful cultural and political dynamic that provides a compelling interpretation of recurrent cycles of public child welfare reform in the United States and in other liberal democratic societies.

The ideology of paternalism and laissez-faire capitalism that restrained public child protective intervention into autonomous family life unraveled in the late nineteenth century as the fragmentation of families and the impoverishment of dependent children exposed the limitations of family privatism and the unfettered pursuit of economic profit in a market economy. Confronted with a choice between sacrificing privatism in the economy or privatism in the family to accommodate the growing need for charitable aid and child protection, lawmakers chose to sacrifice the autonomy of poor families by making public assistance conditional on needy parents' relinquishment of their rights of child custody to renounce, in the words of T. H. Marshall (1964), "any claim to trespass on the territory of wages" (p. 88). The expanded scope of public interest in child safety and health initiated a new cycle of child welfare reform that emphasized the criminal prosecution of nonsupportive and neglectful parents and the construction of a child protective infrastructure that was built almost exclusively around the removal of dependent and abused children from parents and their placement in almshouses, orphanages, and, if available, "free" foster boarding homes.

The new ideology of "child rescue" established a basic floor of support for dependent, neglected, and abused children removed from parental custody but at a subsistence level that did not threaten the achievement principle of "less eligibility." As the historian Walter Trattner (1979) explains the concept:

> The doctrine of "less eligibility" [is] the notion that the status of those dependent on public assistance "shall not be made really or apparently so eligible [satisfactory] as the situation of the independent laborer of the lowest class." In other words, the condition of all welfare recipients, regardless of need or cause, should be worse off than that of the lowest paid self-supporting laborer. While relief should not be denied the poor, life should be made so miserable for them that they would rather work than accept public aid. (Trattner, 1979, p. 46)

The expanded public commitment to minimal developmental opportunity at the expense of family autonomy in order to uphold the value of competitive economic achievement is best exemplified in the operations of Societies for the Prevention of Cruelty to Children (SPCC). The movement originated in 1874 in New York and by 1910 had spawned more than 200 private anticruelty societies and humane associations across the United States (Costin, 1992). Its objective was to supply abused and neglected, immigrant and working-class children with minimal care and protection by separating them permanently from their families and placing them in institutions and foster homes that promised to instill the traits of thrift, hard work, and delayed gratification that were believed lacking in their own homes (Costin, 1992).

During this period, another wing of the child rescue movement dedicated itself to raising the bar of minimal child developmental opportunity, also at the expense of family autonomy, by promoting compulsory school education and reining in on the family's use of children as contractual agents in the marketplace. This change signaled a major cultural and legal shift in principal–agent relations away from the exploitation of children as agents of family interests toward the acknowledgment of the child as the principal and the recasting of the parental role as agent of the child's well-being. This redefinition of principal–agent relationships had been already accomplished among urban middle-class families by the mid-nineteenth century without government intervention (Zelizer, 1985). Child rescuers sought to extend these new principal–agent relations in the family by expanding legal restrictions on the market pricing of children's worth among immigrant and working-class families and cultivating middle-class norms of communal sharing within the narrowed context of the conjugal nuclear family. Legislation redefined the legal status of children from subjects of patriarchal domination (authority ranking) to partial citizens of the state (equality matching). Educators, preachers, and social workers encouraged immigrant and working-class families to stop viewing their children as economically useful assets (market pricing) and to cherish them, in the words of sociologist Viviana Zelizer (1985), as economically "worthless" but emotionally "priceless" objects of parental affection and altruism (communal sharing).

These legal and cultural shifts in family and child relationships helped to broaden the scope of public interest in child welfare as reflected in increased public investments in universal public education, restrictions on parental exploitation of children in the labor force, the forbiddance of the exchange of children for money in the foster care and adoption markets, and a national public health campaign to reduce infant and child mortality (Zelizer, 1985). The growing acceptance of governmental interventions to protect child life and health paralleled a growing public willingness to encroach on free-market pricing principles and to demand greater government regulation of the economy. As Trattner (1979) explains, these changes helped set the stage for another cycle of child welfare reform as the child rescue perspective that attributed family poverty and its causes to the moral failings of parents gradually gave way to a family preservation perspective that linked the problems of child dependency and neglect to broader social and economic conditions.

This change in outlook received its first official endorsement at the 1909 White House Conference on the Care of Dependent Children that proclaimed:

> Home life is the highest and finest product of civilization. It is the great molding force of mind and of character. Children should not be deprived of it except for urgent and compelling reasons. Children of parents of worthy character, suffering from temporary misfortune and children of reasonably efficient and deserving mothers who are without the support of the normal breadwinner, should, as a rule, be kept with their parents, such aid being given as may be necessary to maintain suitable homes for the rearing of the children.[4]

The premium placed on family continuity over child removal reflected another shift in value trade-offs. This time the principle of equality matching was joined together with the value of family permanence at the expense of market pricing in order to enrich child-caring environments in children's own homes. The new Progressive politics of the early twentieth century led to the invention of the juvenile court and probation services that favored in-home supervision over out-of-home care. This was followed by the passage of mother's pension programs, which started out in Illinois and Missouri (confined first to Kansas City) in 1911, and soon spread to another 37 states by 1919 (Leff, 1993). The laws authorized the use of county and state funds for the in-home care of dependent children by widows, disabled mothers, and, in some states, women deserted by husbands. These initiatives paved the way for the federalization of mother's pensions programs under federal Aid to Dependent Children of the 1935 Social Security Act.

Although family preservation was the preferred outcome, the first White House Conference also accepted the need for additional public investments on behalf of children who could not be cared for in their own homes. To support the recruitment, licensing, and subvention of additional foster boarding capacity, state and local governments appropriated funds to replace the dwindling supply of so-called "free" or "work" foster homes that prevailed at the turn of the twentieth century. Efforts were also undertaken in partnership with voluntary child welfare agencies to convert large congregate care facilities into intensive residential treatment centers or smaller (more family-like) cottage settings and group homes. As state and federal dollars began supporting a larger share of faith-based and voluntary foster care capacity through grants-in-aid and purchase-of-service agreements, the competence of contractual and fiduciary agents in safeguarding the interests and well-being of abused and neglected children came under increased public scrutiny.

The beginnings of an ROA movement in child welfare can be marked with Maas and Engler's (1959) ground-breaking study, *Children in Need of*

Parents. Their findings exposed the agency risks of multiple moves, uncertain identity, and psychological disturbance that accompanied the "drift" of foster children in indefinite foster care. A "permanency planning movement" arose in the 1970s that argued for reembedding foster children, who could not return home, in permanent substitute family relationships with adoptive parents, relatives, and legal guardians. The preference still was to retain abused and neglected children in their own home rather than remove them to more restrictive settings of foster family care, residential treatment, and independent living. But when this was not possible, the goal became finding the permanency option that best approximated those relational qualities of primordial solidarities that ensured safe and reliable care. These include the intention that the relationship will last permanently, a commitment to the continuity of family ties, a sense of belonging rooted in cultural norms and sanctioned by law, and a respected family identity that is relatively free of social stigma (Pike, Down, Emlen, Downs, & Care, 1977). These were qualities that were difficult to reproduce in bureaucratized care settings because of frequent staff turnover, the affective neutrality of professionals, and the narrow technical specialization of service providers.

Although permanency planning quickly became the new catchphrase in practice circles, public policy at the federal level, as is frequently the case, lagged behind research and local interests. It was not until the Adoption Assistance and Child Welfare Act of 1980 (P.L. 96-272) that prevention of placement by serving children in their own homes and decreasing the time children spent in foster care through permanency planning became federal policy. The larger federal child welfare role as evidenced in P.L. 96-272 and other laws such as the Child Abuse Prevention and Treatment Act (CAPTA), however, did not fully restore public confidence in child welfare. During this time, another shift in political momentum was underway that reawakened doubts about the premium placed on family continuity. The seeds of concern were planted during the 1960s with the so-called "rediscovery of child abuse" (Nelson, 1984). Discussion of child abuse as a public problem had been muted during the first part of the twentieth century as child welfare professionals distanced themselves from the child removal practices of the nineteenth century and emphasized instead the values of family autonomy and equal child developmental opportunity (Costin, 1992). This inattention abruptly ended in the 1960s when C. Henry Kempe and his colleagues published their seminal article, "The Battered Child Syndrome." Reviewing hospital records, radiological evidence, and clinical and psychiatric data, the authors concluded that the physical abuse of young children by parents or foster parents was a significant cause of permanent injury and death that demanded greater public attention (Kempe, Silverman, Steele, Droegemueller, & Silver, 1962). Their recommendation that child safety take priority over family continuity prefigured a major shift in orientation away from family preservation toward increased removal of abused and neglected children from their homes:

> All too often, despite the apparent cooperativeness of the parents and their apparent desire to have the child with them, the child returns to his home only to be assaulted again and suffer permanent brain damage or death. Therefore, the bias should be in favor of the child's safety; everything should be done to prevent repeated trauma, and the physician should not be satisfied to return the child to an environment where even a moderate risk of repetition exists. (Kempe et al., 1962, p. 24)

As had been the case with mothers' pension legislation, most states moved quickly to enact child abuse reporting laws. Patterned after model legislation disseminated by the U.S. Children's Bureau, reporting laws were first enacted in 10 states in 1963. By 1967, every state and the District of Columbia had passed some form of child abuse reporting law (Nelson, 1984). The laws at first embraced a narrow view of the problem of child safety in order to blunt opposition from groups fearful of government restrictions on parental discretion to discipline children physically (Nelson, 1984). Both the 1963 California and the 1965 Illinois laws included similar phrasing that mandated medical practitioners to report any children coming before them for examination, care, or treatment who may have suffered physical injury or disability by other than accidental means.[5] But soon afterward state legislatures expanded the number of mandated reporters and enlarged the scope of child maltreatment to include malnutrition, sexual abuse, emotional maltreatment, lack of supervision, and eventually excessive corporal punishment, substantial risk of harm, and intrauterine substance exposure. It was also during this time that misgivings began to be expressed about the living arrangements of the growing number of children in single-parent homes. Soon the federal centerpiece for maintaining family continuity—AFDC, renamed from the Aid to Dependent Children (ADC) in 1962—came under sharp attack.

Prior to ADC's creation in 1935, families with dependent children had little recourse but to turn to extended kin, local charities, and, if available, state mother's pension programs when their support systems failed them. Congress also created at this time federal old-age retirement (OAI) and assistance (OAA) programs as separate parts of the Social Security Act to assist retired persons and the dependent elderly. Between 1940 and 1965, the per-capita rate of ADC receipt by children more than doubled from 20 to 45 per 1000 children under age 18 years. During the same period, the per-capita rate of OAI/A receipt more than tripled from 223 to 817 per 1000 persons aged 65 years and older. From 1965 to 1975, OAI/A programs expanded at a more gradual pace as coverage of the elderly population neared a ceiling of 950 per 1000 aged 65 years and older. Meanwhile, AFDC coverage of dependent children increased at a much brisker pace from 45 per 1000 to 118 per 1000 in 1975 as the federal government curtailed "substitute father" and "unsuitable parent" restrictions that denied AFDC to dependent children in homes in which the adults were unmarried and cohabitating.

With nearly total coverage of the elderly population, the U.S. Congress "indexed" social security benefits to cost-of-living changes in 1972 and federalized supplementary security income (SSI) in 1974 for the remaining dependent elderly. This equalized payments across the nation and protected the erosion of old age benefits by inflation. These changes helped to halve the poverty rate among the elderly from 352 per 1000 in 1959 to 153 per 1000 in 1975. Unlike federal assistance to the elderly, monthly AFDC assistance in 1972 for a family of four varied by state from a low of $60 in Mississippi to a high of $375 in Alaska (U.S. Department of Health, Education, and Welfare, 1973). Although AFDC benefits were not indexed to inflation like old age benefits, child poverty rates also fell from 273 per 1000 in 1959 to 171 per 1000 in 1975. During this period, the percentage of elderly persons who were able to live apart from their adult children and other relatives rose from 80% in 1955 to 95% in 1975. The percentage of children without at least one parent in the home dropped from 4.3% in 1950 to 2.9% in 1970.

In terms of social equity and family autonomy, the widening net of social security programs between 1959 and 1975 scored major victories for both the young and old. Yet reactions to the news of these respective success stories were decidedly different. The phrase "welfare crisis" began to be applied to this period in U.S. history when the number of poor kids plummeted from 17.5 million children to 11.1 million children and AFDC coverage expanded from 23% to 79% of all poor children. Whether the news was delivered by Gil Steiner (1971), Charles Murray (1984), or Nathan Glazer (1988), the laments were nearly identical:

> By the early 1960s something that was increasingly being called a "crisis in welfare" was being analyzed. The number of mothers and children on welfare was increasing, not declining, as the social insurance system matured. And there was a second reason for the crisis: the composition of those on welfare was changing. The minor's widow was less and less in evidence. The women on welfare were those who had been divorced or deserted by living spouses, or, increasingly, had never been married at all and were the mothers of one or more illegitimate children. (Glazer, 1988, p. 23)

U.S. census data tell the basic story. After holding stable at around 10% between 1880 and 1960, the percentage of children less than 18 years old who resided in single-parent homes suddenly spiked to 20% in 1980 and then to 25% in 1990. Comparing the per-capita ratio of children living with widowed mothers to the ratio of children with never married mothers, the balance flipped from six widows for every never-married mother in 1960 to one widow for every six never-married mothers in 1991. Again there are many economic and social factors that contributed to the change in the proportion of children living in never-married, single-mother homes. From a values perspective, the charge that stuck was that AFDC enabled too many parents to shirk their family responsibilities and forgo the work ethic in favor of relying on public assistance for the support of their children. In terms of Fiskin's value trade-offs, the rhetorical claim created an opening wedge for the reassertion of the values of individual achievement and the protection of child developmental opportunity at the expense of family autonomy.

Sixty years after the creation of ADC, the U.S. Congress eliminated the AFDC program in 1996. The welfare entitlement for the in-home care of children was replaced by a block grant, Temporary Assistance for Needy Families (TANF). It permitted states to spend federal funds flexibly to serve families with children. The restrictions were that financial assistance to legally responsible parents could last no longer than 5 years and at least 50% of the single parents receiving assistance under TANF had to be engaged in some kind of work-related activity for at least 30 hours a week. The following year, Congress passed the Adoption and Safe Families Act (ASFA), which reasserted the paramountcy of child safety over family continuity, watered down reasonable efforts requirements to preserve and reunify birth families, mandated TPR for children in foster care longer than 15 out of 22 months, and awarded bonuses to states that increased the number of adoptions out of foster care.

Values and Evidence

In certain respects, it looks like ASFA returned child welfare policy full circle to the outcome preferences of the late nineteenth century with Congress's reassertion of the twin values of market achievement and child developmental opportunity at the expense of family autonomy. A major difference, however, is that ASFA also mandated the development of an ROA and QI system that states must adopt or risk losing federal funding. This provides an opportunity for the development of an alternative deliberative process to the sharp ideological swings in value trade-offs that have often driven public child welfare reform in the past. A more coordinated approach based on evidence to resolving Fishkin's value trade-off promises to legitimate state intervention in the private sphere of the family in order to uphold minimal child well-being, but in a way that does not convert children into clients of an all-pervasive welfare state or undermine the role and responsibility of family, kin, and community (Parton, 1999). Neither the revival of primordial principles of traditional authority and communal sharing nor the substitution of bureaucratic principles of market pricing and equality matching alone will be sufficient to meet the critical child welfare challenges of the twenty-first century. Further political polarization of the tensions between primordial solidarities and bureaucratic institutions not only strains the legitimacy of existing child welfare interventions but undercuts the mutual trust necessary for cooperative child welfare action.

To rebuild mutual trust, it will be important to create new opportunities for the impulses, desires, and values of families, kinship networks, ethnic groups, and faith-based communities to enter into the reflexive self-steering of bureaucratic institutions (Testa, 2008). This can be accomplished by refashioning out of existing accountability procedures in child welfare new coordinating mechanisms that enable children, parents, extended family members, foster parents, and concerned citizens to get straightforward explanations and accounts of the policies and decisions made on their behalf by public agents. A logical place to start is with the CFSR. In addition to supplying a framework for assessing the efficacy and effectiveness of the rules, tokens, and operations of state bureaucratic systems, it contains the mechanisms for acquiring a better understanding of the particularistic commitments and desires of children and families from on-site reviews and in-person interviews. Both sources of information are important: quantitative studies that ask how well empirical evidence stacks up in support of hypotheses such that intervention i increases outcome o better than counterfactual c and qualitative studies that inquire about the different cultural and political meanings that people bring to their private and public deliberations on how best to attain socially desirable results for children and families.

Many of the rancorous conflicts in child welfare arise over the failures of bureaucratic agents to cultivate an understanding of the traditional customs and subjective perspectives of the children and families that are the objects of social policy and to develop alternative means, if appropriate, for achieving the desired outcomes of safety, continuity, stability, permanence, and well-being. This was initially the situation with kinship foster care in the United States, which many perceived as posing an insurmountable barrier to legal permanence (Thornton, 1991; Burnette, 1997). After subsidized guardianship was introduced as an alternative permanency option under controlled experimental conditions, it was discovered that foster placements with kin yielded outcomes the same or superior to placements with nonkin (Testa, 2005). When kinship commitments no longer had to be forced into the nuclear family mold by TPR and adoption, relative foster parents were just as willing as nonrelatives to accept permanent legal responsibility for the children under their care (see Chapter 7, this volume).

Of course there will always be some traditional practices, such as child marriage, severe corporal punishment, and female genital mutilation, that are impossible to reconcile with universal child welfare values. And there will be value clashes that are more taxing to resolve as discussed in previous sections. The problem of reconciling the three basic values of family autonomy, achievement, and equality has been a recurrent challenge throughout American history. Compulsory education laws and child labor prohibitions in the nineteenth century and domestic law protections of women and children in the privacy of their homes in the twentieth century were initially resisted as unwarranted intrusions on contractual liberty and family autonomy. At the beginning of the twenty-first century, policy attention in child welfare turned to the question of whether after safety, it is always best to emphasize family continuity and community-based care over other well-being factors such as school quality, job opportunities, and other inputs to social mobility that might create additional discontinuity in children's lives (Bartholet, 1999; Barth, 1999). Should kinship care, community connections, and cultural heritage be upheld as intrinsic values in their own right, or should they be judged satisfactory only insofar as they adequately prepare neglected and abused children for the transition to self-sufficient and productive adulthood in a posttraditional, global economy?

Addressing these issues demands of policymakers, practitioners, judges, and administrators a willingness to grapple with the differences between judgments of fact or evidence and judgments of value. For example, it is a fact that children are poorer as a group than the elderly. But whether child poverty should be reduced by extending to families the same federal SSI benefits available to the elderly, ameliorated by removing children from their parents' custody, or simply tolerated as a child's lot in life is a judgment call that cannot be derived from statistical facts alone.

Frequently evidence leads to value judgments. For example, if it were established that poor children's average life expectancy could be extended by 5 years by giving their families benefits equivalent in value to SSI, would it be unethical to deny these families such an entitlement? This is still a judgment call but one that is based on evidence. With facts and values so intertwined, the difference between conclusions based on evidence and value judgments is easily obscured in policy discussions.

Public policy is society's expression of its most highly cherished values. Consider the following policy statements that underlie key child welfare outcomes:

- *Safety*: Children's safety is the primary concern of all child welfare services, particularly the safety of children who have been identified as victims of maltreatment.[6]
- *Continuity:* Children should be placed in a safe setting that is the least restrictive (most family like) and in close proximity to the parents' home.[7]
- *Stability*: Children are entitled to a stable and lasting family life and should not be deprived of it except for urgent and compelling reasons.[8]

- *Permanence:* Every child is entitled to a guardian of the person, either a natural guardian by birth or adoption or a legal guardian appointed by the court.[9]
- *Well-Being:* Children should receive adequate services to meet their educational, physical, and mental health needs.[10]

Each of these official policy pronouncements are expressions of public values. Most people would agree with each of them, but what about the following:

- *Safety:* Children should be deemed at substantial risk of revictimization if the alleged perpetrator is biologically unrelated to the children.
- *Continuity:* Foster children should be placed with relatives whenever family members make themselves known to the child welfare agency.
- *Stability:* Children should be removed from the foster home of a gay or lesbian couple who take up residence together.
- *Permanence:* Children who have been adopted should not be granted visitation rights with their biological siblings.
- *Well-Being:* Children should not be returned to the custody of parents if their reading and math achievement is likely to suffer.

Public child welfare involves, in part, the pursuit of society's values regarding identifiable groups of children that are the focus of public concern. Discussions of values are necessary to determine public policy. These discussions are not always agreeable, but they are a critical part of the democratic process. Consider again the ASFA example highlighted in the Introduction. To paraphrase, Section 102 of the ASFA says that states shall initiate a petition to terminate parental rights of foster children who have been in care longer than 15 out of the most recent 22 months. Where did the numbers "15" and "22" come from? Many child welfare professionals would argue that this rule does not give many parents enough time to kick harmful habits and to develop the capacity to provide their children with a safe and permanent home. Clearly "the 15 out of 22" is a value judgment. We as a society do not want children to spend long periods of their childhood in indefinite foster care.

But let us say that there was solid evidence that children in foster care longer than 15 months face only a slim possibility of ever returning home. How then should the policy be judged if the outcome turns out to be more "legal orphans" than children discharged to permanent legal homes? This example emphasizes the importance of monitoring systems and learning forums for holding public officials and bureaucratic agents accountable. Monitoring systems test the validity of particular policy choices and can challenge the substantive irrationality of an otherwise functionally efficient process, such as increasing TPRs.

In the endeavor to provide children who are victims of abuse and neglect with safe and permanent homes it is important to be able to distinguish value statements from evidence statements. This is in part because disputes over the validity of factual claims are settled differently from disputes over the priority of value claims. The empirical validation of factual assertions may be used to argue for a value claim, but it is the capacity of agents to argue persuasively on behalf of the interests of principals though reasoned discourse that settles a dispute regarding whether a value becomes a behavioral norm. Persuasion exercised in this fashion, that is, employing statements based on evidence and organized around credible appeals to the common interests of primordial and voluntary solidarities, provides systematic alternatives to coercive authority structures and unfettered market systems as a means of ordering child and family affairs (Mayhew, 1997).

Frequently, value disputes in public child welfare center on the relative importance of competing values. Not all values are equally important to different social groups. AFSA provides a clear example of a conflict over the comparative weight given to two highly held values: child safety and family permanence. The first section of this law seeks to clarify the reasonable efforts criteria of P.L. 96-272 to prevent removal or to reunify the child and family. This section includes the word "shall" six times. These are authoritative directives to states wishing to receive federal funds. They are also the voice of the electorate through Congressional action stating that child safety is a more important value when this appears to conflict with preserving the family or reunifying the child with his or her parents. Other things being equal, safety is more important than family preservation. Of course, in individual cases things are never exactly equal.

The apparent conflict in values between child safety and family reunification is common in child welfare, but it is perhaps better to frame the dispute as a difference in judgment over the choice of investing in parental capacity versus bureaucratic systems for managing agency risks to child safety. Certainly there can be no dispute that the protection of a child's life takes priority over parental interests in family permanence. A healthy child in the custody of strangers is clearly superior to the death of a child from neglect while in parental custody. What lies at the root of the apparent conflict between child safety and family permanence is the Fishkin trade-off between sacrificing market achievement in order to provide public resources to equalize opportunities for family permanence in single-parent households and violating family autonomy to fund alternative paid care that less directly infringes on patriarchal norms and market pricing principles. It is not too difficult to discern the Poor Law principle of "less eligibility" lurking in the following passage from journalist Heather MacDonald's (1994) polemic against family preservation in *The Public Interest*, which includes a quote from Patrick Murphy, who was the Cook County Public Guardian at the time:

> Finally, there are numerous possible ethical objections to family preservation. Patrick Murphy rejects the logic of showering benefits on the worst parents while the hard-working family next door is barely scraping by. "In most cases," he says, "giving money and services to parents who have abused their children does nothing but reward irresponsible and even criminal behavior." (MacDonald, 1994, p. 56)

It is useful to recognize when different value principles are conflicting rather than claims about evidence. Certainly it was not MacDonald's reading of the family preservation experiments of the 1990s, showing intensive family services were no more effective than ordinary in-home services in ensuring safe and stable homes, which led her to pen the following conclusion:

> Family preservation claims to stand for family autonomy against unwarranted state intrusion. Yet its nonjudgmental approach to family formation leads to just the opposite result: a growing number of "families" who can survive only with constant state support.... There is no evidence that social services can compensate for the lack of personal responsibility that is fueling America's epidemic of illegitimacy.... The child welfare system is not working because it is the wrong answer to the problems of illegitimacy and social dysfunction. (MacDonald, 1994, pp. 59–60)

Factual disputes are settled in a different manner. In child welfare, some are settled in court. The basics of this model can be used in a variety of ways including discussions within child welfare agencies. The elements of this process are rules regarding what facts are, a method of accumulating evidence on each side of a dispute, a way to "weigh" the evidence, and agreement that the side with the greater weight of evidence prevails. For example, when the facts of a particular child's safety are in dispute and this is submitted to a court for resolution, there are rules of evidence that help determine when a piece of information can be used to argue for a fact. There is also an adversarial procedure that permits someone to challenge evidence and facts in a variety of ways and present information to support their position. The judge is supposed to be the dispassionate examiner of the evidence and its support of the facts on each side of the argument and decides which side has the "weight of the evidence." Although this court process is very formal, it is a dominant model for resolving disputes about facts.

The scientific method is another model for resolving disputes about facts. As the philosopher Karl Popper (1994) observed, the scientific tradition is a tradition of criticism that contributes to knowledge by eliminating errors. In this tradition, factual statements are more properly regarded as hypotheses that survive scientific tests of their validity but remain in principle open to falsification at some future date. Whereas a fact is something that has been demonstrated (perhaps in court) to be true, a hypothesis is a claim that needs to be scientifically validated before we can be reasonably confident that it is probably true. The distinction is an important one but is often difficult to draw because facts from the scientific perspective are still only hypotheses that may yet be disproved. This is a lesson that the legal system painfully learned after DNA testing invalidated the "facts" of hundreds of judicial convictions of persons sentenced to death or imprisonment in the United States.

The debate over the value of preventing children from remaining in foster care for extended periods of time provides a useful example of the difference between facts and hypotheses. Congress expresses the value preference for permanence in ASFA by directing states to begin the process of TPR for children who have been in care 15 of the most recent 22 months. Those advocating that this time frame is too short often cite the example of parents struggling with substance abuse. The argument is that this is insufficient time for a parent to enter and successfully complete the initial phase of treatment let alone stabilize his or her life as a recovering person. Is this a fact or a hypothesis?

There are many child welfare workers who have many years of experience with parents' repeated relapses that have delayed reunification with their children. Many of them would claim it is a fact that the time limit of 15 of 22 months is too short. These experiences produce practice wisdom that is frequently expressed as "rules-of-thumb." For example, it is often stated that a parent with a substance abuse problem needs at least 1 year of recovering after successful treatment before he or she is capable of taking on the stressful task of caring for a child. Another "rule" is that substance abusers have frequent relapses before they are able to abstain from use for an extended period of time. These relapses are seen as normal and even welcomed occurrences because they signal that the person is closer to beginning the recovery process. Substance abuse treatment with frequent relapses followed by 1 year of recovery usually involves a period of time longer than 22 months. This practice wisdom has been built up over years of experience and is therefore accepted as sufficient evidence to establish this as a "fact."

Practice wisdom is real and useful and arises from the day-to-day experiences of workers. This experience is also limited to a set of experiences and established ways of doing the work. Workers who have different experiences may derive different rules. In other words, a rule derived from practice wisdom is evidence in the sense of being demonstrated to be true (by a person in a certain context). Yet, in another context, this rule may no longer be true. Practice wisdom needs to be submitted to more rigorous testing to be considered evidence beyond the experience of a select group of people.

Continuing with the substance abuse example, Joseph Ryan (2006) reported findings from the Illinois Alcohol and Other Drug Abuse (AODA) Waiver Demonstration showing that 8% of parents randomly assigned to an outreach program staffed by "recovery coaches" were able to be reunified with their children within 15 months of child removal compared to 4% in the control group. By the fifth year of the waiver demonstration, the reunification rate had edged up to 16% in the experimental group and 12% in the control group. This evidence shows that 50% of the 16% reunified in the experimental group occurred between the fifteenth month and the fifth year and 75% of the 12% reunified in the control group occurred during this period. On the one hand, a substantial portion of reunifications that do occur happen after 15 months. On the other hand, the experimental group achieved only marginally higher reunification rates. The small improvement in overall reunification rates raises questions about how much additional time beyond 15 months is truly necessary to achieve the desired results.

In another analysis of these data, the investigators found that 92% of parents had a co-occurring mental health, housing, or domestic violence problem in addition to substance abuse that significantly lowered their chances of getting their children back (Marsh, Ryan, Choi, & Testa, 2006). At the end of the first 5 years of the Illinois AODA waiver demonstration, two-thirds of the children were still in foster care. Despite the 15-out-of-22 month rule, 75% of the foster children were still carrying a return-home goal in their case plans (Ryan, 2006).

The AODA waiver demonstration shows the importance of subjecting practice "rules of thumb" and other hypotheses to rigorous testing to determine how well the predictions stand up to research "rules of evidence." A full discussion of these "rules" is beyond the scope of this chapter or book (see Shadish, Cook, & Campbell, 2002 for an excellent overview), but one useful idea borrows from the levels of evidence developed for judging evidence-supported interventions. These levels of evidence rank research in terms of the strength of the research. Perhaps the most important child welfare research questions are those about causality. For example, does a particular method of substance abuse, e.g., "recovery coaches," result in more children being reunified with their families? In other words, do recovery coaches cause an increase in reunification compared to situations in which these outreach services are withheld?

The research community considers research findings that are derived from randomized controlled experiments, such as the Illinois AODA Waiver demonstration, to be the strongest evidence of a cause-and-effect relationship (see Chapter 7, this volume). Randomized controlled experiments involve a large group of people assigned by some chance process (e.g., coin-toss, dice-roll, or table of random numbers) to two groups with each group receiving something different. One of the groups (intervention) receives the innovation, i.e., recovery coaches, and the other group (comparison) receives regular services or possibly nothing at all. The two groups are then closely monitored to determine the relative effects of the different treatments. There is greater transparency because random assignment eliminates most of the differences in average characteristics, such as age, severity of problem, or relapse history, between groups prior to the intervention. Any differences in average outcomes observed after the intervention can be confidently attributed to the treatment itself rather than to any preexisting group differences.

Some policymakers, administrators, and practitioners have reacted to the call for randomized controlled experiments in child welfare as too expensive, too complicated, and too time consuming, and perhaps unethical to be of routine benefit for day-to-day child welfare work. Such complaints appear to be one set of reasons that Congress neglected to reauthorize the IV-E child welfare waiver program in 2006, which had hitherto been the largest source of federal funding for randomized controlled experiments in child welfare (see Chapter 9, this volume). Fortunately, existing IV-E waiver demonstrations are able to continue and there is a lot of state and privately funded research that is going on across the country that meets these high standards of research evidence as well as other quasi-experimental and observational research that also can enrich the child welfare knowledge base. Compiling findings from this pool of research studies in a way that is useful to child welfare policymakers and practitioners is an important component of any system of quality improvement. This includes rating the research in terms of the level of evidence so that workers can compare claims for different treatment approaches.

The next chapter describes a system of results-oriented accountability in public child welfare that aims to be responsive to the impulses and values of primordial solidarities and political constituencies while adhering to scientifically validated processes of technical communities in assessing the efficacy and effectiveness of traditional and innovative solutions in accomplishing desired social ends. Even though this system privileges scientific evidence over other validity claims based on hierarchy, faith, and tradition, the technical community is not committed to a particular source of values except those of skepticism, disinterestedness, universalism, and knowledge sharing, which are integral to the scientific process itself (Merton, 1968).

Notes

1. All statistics, unless otherwise noted, come from the U.S. Children Bureau website at http://www.acf.hhs.gov/programs/cb/stats_research/index.htm#can. We chose 2004 as the reporting period because it was the latest year that data were consistently available for all programs and outcome measures presented in this section.
2. Discussion of the measurement of outcomes and the controversy surrounding the decisions made by DHHS are presented in Chapter 4.
3. This and subsequent sections build on concepts originally presented in Testa (2008).

4. http://www.libertynet.org/edcivic/whoukids.html; last accessed September 1, 2009.
5. California language cited in Nelson (1984) and Illinois language cited in Hugi (1983).
6. U. S. Department of Health and Human Services. (2004). *Child welfare outcomes 2001: Annual report. Safety, permanency, well-being.* Washington, DC: U. S. Government Printing Office.
7. U. S. Social Security Act, Sec. 475. [42 U. S.C. 675].
8. First White House Conference on the Care of Dependent Children, January 25, 1909.
9. U. S. Children's Bureau (1961) *Legislative guides for the termination of parental rights and responsibilities and the adoption of children,* No. 394, Washington, DC: U. S. Department of Health, Education, and Welfare.
10. U. S. Department of Health and Human Services. (2003). *Child and Family Services Reviews onsite review instrument and instructions.*

References

Barth, R. (1999). After safety, what is the goal of child welfare services: Permanency, family continuity, or social benefit? *International Journal of Social Welfare, 8*(4), 244–252.

Bartholet, E. (1999). *Nobody's children: Abuse and neglect, foster drift, and the adoption alternative.* Boston: Beacon Press.

Beck, U., Bonss, W., & Lau, C. (2003). The theory of reflexive modernization: Problematic, hypotheses and research programme. *Theory, Culture, and Society, 20*(2), 1–33.

Buchanan, A. (1988). Principal/agent theory and decisionmaking in health care. *Bioethics, 2*(4), 317–331.

Burnette, D. (1997). Grandparents raising grandchildren in the inner city. *Families in Society: The Journal of Contemporary Human Services, 78,* 489–501.

Child Welfare Research Center. (2008). *Child Welfare Services Reports for California.* Last accessed March 15, 2008 at http://cssr.berkeley.edu/CWSCMSreports/.

Children and Family Research Center. (2008a). Continuity of social ties: Of all children entering substitute care, what percentage is placed within five miles of their home of origin? Last accessed March 15, 2008 at http://xinia.social.uiuc.edu/outcomedata/factbook/indicator12.html.

Children and Family Research Center. (2008b). Continuity of social ties: Of all children placed into foster care at the end of the year, what percentage is placed with all their siblings? Last accessed March 15, 2008 at http://xinia.social.uiuc.edu/outcomedata/factbook/indicator13.html.

Coleman, J. S. (1990). *Foundations of social theory.* Cambridge, MA: The Belknap Press of Harvard University Press.

Costin, L. B. (1992). Cruelty to children: A dormant issue and its rediscovery, 1920–1960. *Social Service Review, 66*(2), 177–198.

Crowther, M. A. (1982). Family responsibility and state responsibility in Britain before the welfare state. *The Historical Journal, 25,* 131–145.

Derezotes, D. M., Poertner, J., & Testa, M. F. (Eds.) (2005). *Race matters in child welfare: The overrepresentation of African-American children in the system.* Washington, DC: CWLA Press.

Eekelaar, J. (2002). Child endangerment and child protection in England and Wales. In M. K. Rosenheim, F. E. Zimring, D. S. Tanenhaus, & B. Dohrn (Eds.),

A century of juvenile justice (pp. 381–412). Chicago: The University of Chicago Press.

Fishkin, J. S. (1983). *Justice, equal opportunity, and the family.* New Haven: Yale University Press.

Fiske, A. (1992). The four elementary forms of sociality: Framework for a unified theory of social relations. *Psychological Review, 99*(4), 689–723.

Glazer, N. (1988). *The limits of social policy.* Cambridge, MA: Harvard University Press.

Giddens, A. (1990). *The consequences of modernity.* Stanford, CA: Stanford University Press.

Giddens, A. (1994). *Beyond left and right: The future of radical politics.* Stanford, CA: Stanford University Press.

Gleeson, J. P., & Craig, L. C. (1994). Kinship care in child welfare: An analysis of states' policies. *Children and Youth Services Review, 16*(1/2), 7–31.

Hamilton, G. G. (1990). Patriarch, patrimonialism, and filial piety: A comparison of China and Western Europe. *The British Journal of Sociology, 41*(1), 77–104.

Hardin, M. (2005). The role of the legal and judicial system for children, youth and families in foster care. In G. P. Mallon & P. M. Hess (Eds.). *Child welfare for the twenty-first century: A handbook of practices, policies, and programs* (pp. 687–706). New York: Columbia University Press.

Hartnett, M., Bruhn, C., Helton, J., Fuller, T., & Steiner, L. (2009). *Illinois child well-being study: Year two final report.* Urbana, IL: Children and Family Research Center.

Hugi, R. (1983). *Children and the state: Responsibilities and expenditures.* Chicago: The Children's Policy Research Project.

Heimer, C. A., & Staffen, L. R. (1998). *For the sake of the children.* Chicago: The University of Chicago Press.

Janowitz, M., & Suttles, G. D. (1979). The social ecology of citizenship. In R. C. Sarri & Y. Hasenfeld (Eds.), *The management of human services* (pp. 80–104). New York: Columbia University Press.

Kempe, C. H, Silverman, F. N., Steele, B. F., Droegemueller, W., & Silver, H. K. (1962). The battered-child syndrome. *Journal of the American Medical Association, 181*, 17–24.

Korpi, W., & Palme, J. (2003). New politics and class politics in the context of austerity and globalization: Welfare state regress in 18 countries, 1975–95. *American Political Science Review, 97*(3), 425–446.

Leff, M. H. (1993). Consensus for reform: The mothers'-pension movement in the progressive era. *Social Service Review, 47*(3), 397–417.

Lin, N. (2001). *Social capital: A theory of social structure and action.* Cambridge, UK: Cambridge University Press.

Litwak, E. (1965). Extended kin relations in an industrial democratic society. In E. Shanas & G. F. Streib (Eds.), *Social structure and the family: Generational relations* (pp. 290–323). Englewood Cliffs, NJ: Prentice Hall.

Maas, H., & Engler, R. (1959). *Children in need of parents.* New York: Columbia University Press.

MacDonald, H. (1994). The ideology of "family preservation." *The Public Interest, 115* (Spring), 45–60.

Madrigal, L. (2001). Indian child welfare act: Partnership for preservation. *American Behavioral Scientist, 44*(9), 1505–1511.

Marsh, J., Ryan, J., Choi, S., & Testa, M. (2006). Integrated services for families with multiple problems: Obstacles to family reunification. *Children and Youth Services Review, 28,* 1074–1087.

Marshall, T. H. (1964). *Class, citizenship, and social development.* Chicago: The University of Chicago Press.

Mayhew, L. H. (1997). *The new public: Professional communication and the means of social influence.* Cambridge, UK: Cambridge University Press.

McGowen B. G. (2005). Historical evolution of child welfare services. In G. R. Mallon & P. McCartt Hess (Eds.), *Child welfare in the 21st century.* New York: Columbia University Press.

Merton, R. K. (1968). *Social theory and social structure.* New York: The Free Press

Murray, C. (1984). *Losing ground: American social policy 1950–1980.* New York: Basic Books.

Nelson, B. J. (1984). *Making an issue of child abuse: Political agenda setting for social problems.* Chicago: The University of Chicago Press.

Parton, N. (1999). Reconfiguring child welfare practices: Risk, advanced liberalism, and the government of freedom. In A. S. Chambon, A. Irving, & L. Epstein (Eds.), *Reading Foucault for social work* (pp. 101–130). New York: Columbia University Press.

Parson, T. (1951). *The social system.* New York: The Free Press.

Pike, V., Down, S., Emlen, A., Downs, G., & Care, D. (1977). *Permanent planning for children in foster care: A handbook for social workers.* (DHEW Pub. No. OHDS 77–30124) Washington, DC: U. S. Department of Health and Human Services.

Popper, K. R. (1994). *The myth of the framework: In defense of science and rationality.* (Edited by N.A. Notturno). New York: Routledge.

Portes, A., & Sensenbrenner, J. (1993). Embeddedness and immigration: Notes on the social determinants of economic action. *The American Journal of Sociology, 98* (6), 1320–1350.

Putnam, R. D. (2000). *Bowling alone: The collapse and revival of American community.* New York: Simon & Schuster.

Roberts, D. (2002). *Shattered bonds: The color of child welfare.* New York: Basic Books.

Ryan, J. P. (2006). *Illinois alcohol and other drug abuse (AODA) waiver demonstration: Final evaluation report.* Urbana, IL: Children and Family Research Center.

Ryan, J. P., & Testa, M. F. (2005). Child maltreatment and juvenile delinquency: Investigating the role of placement and placement instability. *Children and Youth Services Review, 27,* 227–249.

Sedlak, A. J., & Broadhurst, D.D. (1996). Executive summary of the third national incidence study of child abuse and neglect. Washington, DC: U.S. Department of Health and Human Services (www.childwelfare.gov/pubs/statsinfo/nis3.cfm#official, accessed September 1, 2009).

Seymour, J. (1994). *Parens patriae* and wardship powers: Their nature and origins. *Oxford Journal of Legal Studies, 14*(2), 159–188.

Shadish, W. R, Cook, T. D., & Campbell, D. T. (2002). *Experimental and quasi-experimental designs for generalized causal inference.* Boston: Houghton Mifflin Company.

Shils, E. (1957). Primordial, personal, sacred and civil ties: Some particular observations on the relationships of sociological research and theory. *The British Journal of Sociology, 8*(2), 130–145.

Stanfield, J. (2000). Faith healing and religious treatment exemptions to child endangerment laws: Should parents be allowed to refuse necessary medical treatment for their children based on religious beliefs? *Hamline Journal of Public Law and Policy, 22*(1), 45–86.

Steiner, G. Y. (1971). *The state of welfare*. Washington, DC: The Brookings Institution.

Testa, M. F. (2001). Kinship care and permanency. *Journal of Social Service Research, 28*(1), 25–43.

Testa, M. F. (2005). The quality of permanence—Lasting or binding?" *Virginia Journal of Social Policy and Law, 12*(3), 499–534.

Testa, M. F. (2008). New permanency strategies for children in foster care. In D. Lindsey & A. Shlonsky (Eds.), *Child welfare research* (pp. 108–124). Oxford: Oxford University Press.

Thornton, J. L. (1991). Permanency planning for children in kinship foster homes. *Child Welfare, 70*(5), 593–601.

Trattner, W. I. (1979). *From poor law to welfare state: A history of social welfare in American (4th edition)*. New York: The Free Press.

Webb, M. B., Dowd, K. L., Harden, B. J., Landsverk, J., & Testa, M. (Eds.) (2010). *Child welfare and child well-being: New perspectives from the national survey of child and adolescent well-being*. Oxford: Oxford University Press.

Wolfe, A. (1978). The child and the state: A second glance. *Contemporary Crises, 2*, 407–435.

Zelizer, V. A. (1985). *Pricing the priceless child: The changing social value of children*. New York: Basic Books.

3

LOGIC OF RESULTS-ORIENTED ACCOUNTABILITY

Populations, Interventions, Comparisons, and Outcomes

Mark F. Testa

Results-oriented accountability in public child welfare is pursued within a legal and administrative framework that expects that public fiduciary and contractual service agents, when called on, will be able to demonstrate the efficacy and effectiveness of their professional practices and policy interventions in achieving the desired outcomes of safety, continuity, stability, permanence, and well-being (substantive accountability). This supplements the longstanding concern that service delivery occurs in a legally acceptable manner (procedural accountability) as exemplified in fair hearings, IV-E eligibility audits, and administrative case reviews. Holding agents accountable for substantive results is a more recent development in child welfare and is best exemplified in judicial consent decrees, Children and Family Services Review (CFSR), and child welfare service demonstrations (IV-E waivers).

The demonstration of substantive accountability in child welfare increasingly involves principles of scientific reasoning. This includes the systematic employment of data and information systems, the appropriate use of social scientific theory and logic models, and the implementation of valid research designs and evaluation methods (Brownson, Baker, Leet, & Gillespie, 2003). Federal and state governments have encouraged the incorporation of such methods and procedures into the day-to-day operations of public child welfare systems by emphasizing evidence-supported interventions (ESI), demanding rigor in program evaluation designs, and importing social scientific data collection methods and analytical techniques into program review and quality improvement processes.

To facilitate the transfer of this knowledge, both governmental and nongovernmental organizations fund or sponsor resource centers, research consortia, and university–agency partnerships. These include, among others: the National Resource Centers funded by the U.S. Children's Bureau to provide onsite training and technical assistance to states, tribes, and public child welfare agencies in the preparation and implementation of the CFSR; the U.S. DHHS Child Welfare Information Gateway that provides access to print and electronic publications, Web sites, and online databases covering a wide range of child welfare topics; the nonprofit Campbell Collaboration (C2) composed of social scientists internationally, which produces and disseminates systematic reviews of research evidence on the efficacy and effectiveness of child welfare and other social interventions; the California Evidence-Based Clearinghouse for Child Welfare funded by the California Department of Social Services for the identification and dissemination of information regarding ESI relevant to child welfare; the National Working Group (NWG) sponsored by the Child Welfare League of America (CWLA) to improve the validity and reliability of federal child welfare data; and a variety of university–agency research and training partnerships, such as the Barton Child Law and Policy Clinic at Emory University, the Chapin Hall Center for Children at the University of Chicago, the Child Welfare Research Center at the University of California at Berkeley, the Children and Family Research Center at the University of Illinois at Urbana-Champaign, and the public–private Partners for Our Children at the University of Washington.

The goal of these university–agency partnerships is to create and sustain what Duncan MacRae (1985) has called a "technical community," which includes researchers and consultants working in collaboration with administrators and practitioners to deal with policy problems, oversee related research, and monitor the quality of the partnership's work on these activities. Although a technical community draws a substantial portion of its membership from professional and academic ranks, its audience is not just professional and academic peers but also consumers, policymakers, advocates, and the wider public. Reaching these target audiences requires the construction of bridging structures that can help reconcile the scientific rigor and significance demanded by technical communities with the value orientations and policy relevance expected by political and lay audiences.

University–agency partnerships can play a useful role in helping to bridge these technical and public interests. In child welfare, a common desire is enhancing the analytical capacity of public systems and building generalizable knowledge that can promote the attainment of child and family outcomes. This extends to identifying the gaps between actual and desired results, understanding the whys behind the deviations, acting on this information by generating promising solutions and conducting research reviews of the existing evidence, designing rigorous evaluations to test the impact of selected interventions, and maintaining continuous quality improvement systems to enhance the performance of child welfare agents. Chapter 11 by Joan Zlotnik in this volume discusses some of the opportunities and challenges involved in creating and sustaining university–agency partnerships. These endeavors share interests in evolving public child welfare into an evidence-informed system of expert knowledge, service delivery, and results-oriented accountability, which can be continuously reexamined and reflexively reformed in light of incoming information on child and family outcomes.

Cycle of Results-Oriented Accountability

The framework of results-oriented accountability outlined in Chapter 1 builds on a common foundation of clinical practice and policy management, which conceives of child welfare interventions as cycling through five successive stages as follows:

1. *Outcomes Monitoring*: Are the desired results broadly defined and validly measured to ensure that children's best interests are served?
2. *Data Analysis*: Is the gap between the desired and actual results of practical importance and statistical significance to warrant taking corrective action?
3. *Research Review*: What potential courses of corrective action are supported by empirical evidence and how strongly?
4. *Evaluation*: How efficacious, effective, and efficient are the implemented actions in accomplishing the desired results?
5. *Quality Improvement*: Should the implemented actions be continued, improved, or discontinued or should the desired outcomes, logic model, and underlying theory of action be redefined?

These five stages can be conceived in flow chart fashion as follows: (1) begin monitoring agency performance through routine tracking of statistical indicators of child and family outcomes; (2) identify important shortfalls and gather additional evidence on the underlying population conditions that may be contributing to the results; (3) if corrective action is warranted, formulate a well-built research question based on the gathered evidence and conduct a research review of previously tested interventions for achieving the desired results; (4) implement the most promising intervention and evaluate its causal efficacy and general effectiveness in reference to comparison groups using a research design that is commensurate with the strength of the existing evidence; and (5) if the results indicate progress, engage in continuous quality improvement activities to ensure that interventions are implemented in a reliable and improved manner (single-loop learning), or else after one or more unsuccessful trials, curtail current operations or develop an alternative theory of action for attaining the desired outcomes (double-loop learning). These five stages of results-oriented accountability are discussed briefly in the following sections and elaborated on more fully in subsequent chapters.

Outcomes Monitoring

Results-oriented accountability begins with the definition of a set of intended outcomes that individual and public principals want to see achieved. Outcomes monitoring involves making a preliminary descriptive assessment of whether public fiduciary or contractual service agents are making adequate progress toward achieving these intended results. In public child welfare, outcomes are defined in federal and state statutes, judicial consent decrees, international covenants, and other goal-setting processes. There is considerable agreement in policy, law, professional literature, and historical documents that the principal aims of child welfare intervention are safety, continuity, stability, permanence, and well-being (see Chapter 2, this volume).

To achieve these aims justly, it is important not only that service efficacy and effectiveness be validated but also that service provision be certified as consistent with general end values. Although not exhaustive, the following value declarations offer a set of prescriptive statements for monitoring service delivery and reconciling specific outcomes with more general end values[1]:

- *Equity:* Children have a right to fair and equal protection and care without regard to gender, race, culture, sexual orientation, language, national origin, ethnicity, and religion.
- *Voice:* Children who are capable of forming their own views shall be assured the right to express those views openly in regard to their preferences and well-being with due consideration given to those views in accordance with their age and maturity.
- *Efficiency:* Children are entitled to receive care and services that are efficiently and economically supported from private and public funding sources.
- *Solidarity:* Children are entitled to secure attachment relationships that connect them to enduring social networks of care, cooperation, and trust.

Outcomes monitoring in reference to these general end values typically involves a double-loop review of results after the single-loop review of system performance in accomplishing the particular outcomes of safety, continuity, stability, permanence, and well-being. For example, an increase in the stability of substitute care that results from placing a greater proportion of foster children in residential treatment facilities may be judged less desirable than maintaining children in less restrictive settings when the end values of efficiency and voice are also taken into account. An educational program that boosts scholastic scores among Native American children while neglecting the skills needed for maintaining social relationships within tribal communities might be deemed inadequate when the end value of solidarity is also considered important. Similarly a numerical boost in permanence from increased adoptions may be judged deficient on equity grounds if minority children are disproportionately impacted by the intervention.

Both particular outcomes and general end values should be jointly monitored to assess properly the overall performance of child protection and child welfare systems. The initial list of federal quantitative measures that was published in the February 2, 1999 issue of the *Federal Register* (Volume 64, Number 21) addressed particular outcomes such as reduced recurrence of child abuse or neglect once a child had come to the attention of the child protective system as well as general end values such as the reduction of racial and ethnic disparities in the median length of time in foster care, and system efficiencies such as the mean length of time between receipt of a child maltreatment report and the initiation of an investigation.

The final list of quantitative measures published in August of that year (*Federal Register*, Volume 21, Number 64) narrowed the list of indicators to a reduced set of safety, stability, and permanency measures. Six of these indicators were used in the first round of the CFSR that the federal government conducted to assess whether state child welfare systems were in substantial conformity with national standards. Some general end values, such as children's voice and the preservation of their attachment relationships, are also examined as part of the CFSR on-site case audits and interviews. Other end values such as cost–benefit efficiency and racial equity may be addressed at the quality improvement stage when a Program Improvement Plan (PIP) is developed.

The six national standards are described and reviewed in Chapter 4 by Tom McDonald and Mark Testa. Professor McDonald was a member of the original technical team that Health and Human Services (HHS) convened to advise it on the development of outcome measures to assess the performance of states in operating child protection and child welfare programs. The first round of CFSR was completed in April 2004. The process scored 26 of the 52 jurisdictions including the District of Columbia and Puerto Rico as falling below the reentry standard, 33 below the reunification standard, 35 below the maltreatment standard, 37 below the adoption standard, and 38 below the stability standard. When all 14 outcomes and systemic factors were considered, not one of the 52 jurisdictions was judged to be in substantial conformity with national standards. This shortfall prompted the next stage in the cycle of results-oriented accountability, which involves conducting statistical analyses and gathering other data to develop program plans that specify action steps for improving agency performance in each of the outcome areas for which the jurisdiction is judged not to be in substantial conformity with the national standards.

Data Analysis

When progress is being made toward attaining specified targets or effect sizes of suitable magnitude, the outcomes monitoring process continues for another round of review. Otherwise the detection of a worrisome gap between a valued result and an observed outcome signals the potential need for some corrective action or at least a reasonable accounting for the shortfall. When the gap is of both practical importance and statistical significance, a data analysis process should be initiated to distinguish the need for genuine improvement from population changes and other risk factors that may be contributing to the result.

The first step in judging whether a gap is worrisome enough to warrant corrective action is to decide a priori on a difference in rates or an effect size (odds ratio or relative risk) that corresponds to the smallest performance gap that would be deemed important enough to narrow. This is best done in conjunction with practitioners and administrators who are able to draw comparisons with history, other parts of the organization, a different geographic area, an established standard, or some other designated target. For example, if administrators peg the desired permanency rate for an entering cohort of foster children at 50% over a 2-year period (corresponding to a 2-year median length of stay) and past performance was at 45%, then the gap is 5 percentage points. If we settle on this gap as the minimum amount for taking corrective action and quality improvement then we would need to conduct a statistical analysis that is sufficiently "powered" to detect a difference or an effect size of this magnitude with a reasonable amount of confidence (see Chapter 5, this volume). The smaller the gap, the larger the sample must be to detect a statistically significant difference or effect size.

It should be stressed that initiating a corrective action program in response to an observed performance gap is merely a way of economizing and prioritizing the multitude of corrective actions that could be taken. The aphorism, "if it ain't broke, don't fix it," does not necessarily imply all is well. Needs assessment based on simple comparative assessments of change is still descriptive and must always be regarded as tentative. Additional statistical analysis, which identifies statistical associations with population conditions and other risk factors (conditional associational analysis), can help to reveal the extent to which the planned results are amenable to system improvement or are merely by-products of external (exogenous) changes that can both exaggerate the need for corrective action, e.g., a cocaine epidemic leading to slower reunification rates with addicted parents, as well as mask a deterioration in system performance, e.g., economic growth leading to fewer recurrences of neglect despite slower response times to reports of child maltreatment.

As interest shifts from outcomes monitoring to program planning, the simple descriptive assessment of difference or change no longer suffices as a valid guide for action. The problem is that the gap between observed progress and the desired outcome embodies both the net influence that is directly attributable to system performance as well as all the other observed and unobserved systematic and random influences on that outcome. Statisticians say that the effect of the child welfare intervention is *confounded* (mixed up) with the effects of all other influences on the outcome (Freedman, 2005).

Chapter 5 illustrates some of the data analysis methods that statisticians and econometricians have developed for disentangling confounding influences from the need for genuine system improvement. This helps to set the stage for the next phase of results-oriented accountability, which involves conducting a research review of the external validity of current and past studies of promising interventions to effectuate system improvements.

Research Review

A research review (RR) involves the explicit search and selection of relevant studies, assessment of their validity, and critical synthesis of their findings to reach an overall (tentative) conclusion about program efficacy (i.e., is the program impact genuine?) and program effectiveness (i.e., does the impact generalize across different populations of persons, places, and times?). Research reviews begin with the formulation of a well-built question that can be parsed into four components as follows:

P—The target population about which you wish to draw inferences, such as foster children aged 12 years or younger, abused and neglected children in intact families, or children in long-term foster care;

I—The intervention, whose efficacy and effectiveness you are interested in evaluating, such as intensive family preservation, subsidized guardianship, or family group conferences;

C—The alternative course of action with which you want to draw a comparison, such as no intervention, regular services, or a different intervention; and

O—The intended outcome you want to see achieved, such as child safety, family continuity, placement stability, adolescent well-being, or legal permanence.

These four components of a well-built question are grouped together under the acronym of PICO (Richardson, Wilson, Nishikawa, & Hayward,

1995). They can be arranged in any order to improve readability as long as all four components are referenced. Each of the following examples of well-built questions is reworded from existing protocols registered with the Campbell Collaboration (C2):

- Does Functional Family Therapy (*I*) compared to usual services, alternative services, placebo, or no treatment (*C*) improve prosocial behavior, positive parenting behavior, and family functioning (*O*) in families of youth aged 11 to 18 years old with behavioral problems (*P*)? (Littell, Bjørndal, Hamerstrøm, & Winvold, 2007).
- Are children under the age of 18 years who are removed from the home because of abuse or neglect (*P*) and formally placed out of the home with licensed or unlicensed kin caregivers (*I*) at lower risk of impermanence, reabuse, and reentry (*O*) than children placed with licensed, nonrelated foster parents (*C*)? (Winokur, Holtan, & Valentine, 2009).
- Is the out-of-home placement rate (*O*) for children and young persons under 18 years old (*P*) reduced when family group conferences are conducted (*I*) compared to decision-making processes that do not feature the generation of a plan by family members (*C*)? (Shlonsky et al., 2009).

When policy planning is done comprehensively with a view towards overall system reform, well-built questions can be consolidated into a research agenda for guiding choices in a program of research. There are several published examples of comprehensive research agendas that have been developed for public child welfare (National Association of Public Child Welfare Administrators, 2001; Johnson, Wells, Testa, & McDonald, 2003). Once one or more well-built research questions have been assembled, the next step in the policy planning cycle is to track down through computerized searches of bibliographic databases the best available evidence with which to answer the questions. This involves a systematic search of all potentially relevant studies and critical appraisal of the strength of the empirical evidence. It is important that research questions be framed in advance of the computerized search and that the search topic remain consistent even if it is later discovered that there is not much written about a particular topic. We ought to be as interested in identifying little investigated topics as we are in amply studied ones. A record of the keyword searches and how they are phrased should be maintained.

Most research reviews synthesize the existing literature using narrative descriptions and statistical summaries. To the extent that they attempt to quantify effect sizes over a large number of studies, they converge with *meta-analyses* (Shadish, Cook, & Campbell, 2002) and are usually referred to as systematic research reviews (SRR). In Chapter 6, John Poertner discusses various classificatory schemes for rank ordering the evidentiary strength of different studies for drawing causal inferences about intervention effects. Other areas of interest include the construct validity of outcome indicators, the fidelity of program implementation, and unintended sources of within-program variation (e.g., incomplete implementation, participant attrition, and treatment interactions).

Evaluation

Outcomes monitoring, data analysis, and RR constitute the preimplementation stages of results-oriented accountability. After implementation, attention turns to assessing the extent to which the implemented intervention or program is actually producing the intended results. As indicated, it is helpful to draw a distinction between program efficacy and program effectiveness. Each involves a different type of validity. Efficacy evaluations are concerned with internal validity and test whether the statistical association between the intervention and the outcome is spurious or results from a genuine causal relationship. Effectiveness evaluations are concerned with external validity and test whether a particular causal relationship generalizes over temporal and geographic variations in persons, interventions, comparisons, and outcomes.

Efficacy is necessary to but not sufficient for establishing effectiveness (Flay, 1986). Intervention effects that are identified under controlled experimental conditions may turn out differently when the intervention is implemented in the field or extended to other samples of persons and settings. Effectiveness studies can be conducted by replicating controlled randomized experiments in these other settings or by conducting a variety of conditional associational analyses of observational data.

When an intervention is untried or when the existing evidentiary level for a mature intervention is still weak, it is best whenever possible to mount a randomized controlled experiment in order to strengthen the internal validity of the study's inference about intervention effects. By leaving the selection of group participants to a chance process, such as flipping a coin, drawing a lottery ball, or consulting a table of random numbers, the laws of probability help to ensure that the intervention and comparison groups are, on average, statistically equivalent within the bounds of chance error on a wide range of measured and unmeasured conditions prior to the intervention. Establishing statistical equivalence between the intervention and comparison groups beforehand through random assignment allows for a straightforward assessment of the internal validity of the experimental intervention. Because random assignment minimizes selection bias by eliminating coordinating relationships between baseline conditions and the intervention group, the only substantive difference between the intervention and comparison groups is exposure to the intervention. Thus, any significant differences in outcomes may confidently be attributed to the intervention. To improve transparency in the reporting of randomized controlled experiments, an international group of statisticians, epidemiologists, researchers, and journal editors has developed the Consolidated Standards of Reporting Trials (CONSORT) (Moher, Schultz, & Altman, 2001). The CONSORT statement comprises a checklist and flow diagram for use in writing, reviewing, and evaluating reports of randomized controlled trials (RCT). The CONSORT statement is not currently in wide use in child welfare, but there are calls for its greater utilization by child welfare researchers (Littell, 2005; Gambrill, 2006).

If an intervention has already been deemed efficacious and effective from prior research reviews by a recognized entity such as the Campbell Collaboration, it may make sense to forgo randomization in favor of quasi-experimental methods for assessing external validity. Econometricians and statisticians have developed a variety of methods of controlling for confounding influences in observational studies to approximate the results that are obtainable under optimal experimental conditions. The problem is often characterized as one of *selection bias* because of the different ways that principals learn about programs and agents recruit and screen potential participants. As Bloom, Michalopoulos, Hill, and Lei (2002) describe the challenge:

> In practice, program and comparison groups may differ with respect to many factors that are related to their outcomes. These differences come about in ways that depend on how program and comparison group members are selected. Hence, they might reflect how (1) individuals learn about, apply for, and decide whether to participate in a program (self-selection), (2) program staff recruits and screens potential participants (staff selection), (3) families and individuals, who become part of a program or comparison group because of where they live or work, choose a residence or job (geographic selection), or (4) researchers choose a comparison group (researcher selection). For these reasons, estimating a program impact by a simple difference in mean outcomes may confound the true impact of the program with the effects of other factors. (Bloom et al., 2002, pp. 1–4)

Because of the great variety of selection factors associated with different types of population conditions and agency relationships in child welfare, we are never quite sure if the program effect being estimated is the genuine intervention effect or a biased (gross) estimate that mixes up (in reference to the *PICO* components) the direct causal effect of I on O with an indirect "spurious" relationship via unobserved population characteristics and agent choices, P. The greater the departure from the assumption of statistical independence (i.e., the observed and unobserved P are statistically equivalent on average for both I and C) and the stronger the effects of these P on the outcome, the larger will be the biased component of the observed intervention effect of I on O.

Econometricians and statisticians have developed a variety of statistical methods for handling selection biases in order to uncover the genuine causal effect of an intervention on an outcome. Linear regression analysis, propensity score and other matching methods, and instrumental variable analysis are common approaches for adjusting for selection biases in the absence of randomized controlled experimentation. But even when randomization is employed, these same methods are sometimes necessary, for example, when self-selection, agent selection, and subject attrition make the subsample that actually participates in the intervention a nonrandom subsample of the population originally assigned to the intervention group. These issues are explored more fully in Chapter 7.

Quality Improvement

The quality improvement stage of results-oriented accountability opens up the proverbial "black-box" of program evaluation. Knowing that a population has been randomly or pseudorandomly assigned to an intervention or comparison group seldom allows for full causal explanation of the effect and does not offer much interpretative insight into why expected outcomes are or are not being achieved. Improving the quality of practice and policy requires a deeper understanding of the intervening processes by which program inputs are disbursed within a service system and transformed into program outputs.

Issues of quality improvement often arise early in the implementation process when preliminary results first become available. Initially, quality improvement takes the form of repeating a single-loop learning cycle of planning, review, and evaluation several times as needed in an effort to steer agency performance toward the direction of outcome improvement. Sometimes the implemented actions correlate immediately with improved results, and the process can return to the initial stage of monitoring future progress. Other times the results will fall short of the desired targets or show no improvement, or else run contrary to other general end values, such as cost inefficiencies or inequitable impacts on selected subpopulations. In these circumstances, quality improvement entails a search for the "whys" behind inadequately performing interventions so that lessons can be learned and double-loop adjustments can be made if necessary. It is at this time that public agents are usually called on to provide a public accounting for their performance.

Accountability for results presumes a theory of action about the way improvements are expected to happen and an interpretive framework for organizing information and drawing inferences about the mediating and moderating effects of the intervening processes on outputs and outcomes. It is helpful to make these expected effects, theoretical assumptions, and interpretive framework explicit by constructing a logic model (Julian 1997; Schalock & Bonhamd, 2003) that fills in the intervening activities, outputs, and intermediate outcomes that are omitted in black-box evaluations.

There are a variety of designs for constructing logic models. One approach elaborates on the *PICO* framework presented above. These "path diagrams" bear some resemblance to the social indicator models that were once popular in the 1970s and 1980s (Land & Spilerman, 1975; Testa, 1988). Subsequent work on social indicator models has branched off into two related but distinctive directions: one that stresses a methodical approach to the analysis and measurement of social change and the other that emphasizes an evaluative approach to the planning and management of social policy (MacRae, 1985). Logic models are outshoots of the later. They aim to fill in the intervening activities that link interventions and population conditions to the short-term outputs produced by the activities and the longer-term outcomes these activities are expected to achieve (Julian, 1997). Logic models visually depict how a policy or program is supposed to work along with its underlying theoretical assumptions and associated interpretative framework (W. K. Kellogg Foundation, 2004).

Figure 3.1 overlays on top of the *PICO* framework the hypothesized intervening causal actions that link interventions and populations to services, procedures, and outputs that impact outcomes. The abbreviated descriptive items that appear in most logic models can be expanded into a series of declarative statements and expectations about desired changes, e.g., train workers in methods and procedures of delivering services to clients, decrease the length of time between the start of a legal process and a subsequent milestone, and reinforce children's sense of belonging and solidarity within a family setting.

Immediately below the causal model are spaces for the enumeration of the historical and external conditions that are not under the direct control of agents but that influence their activities and capacity to achieve the desired goals. Next are the assumptions of the theory of action and

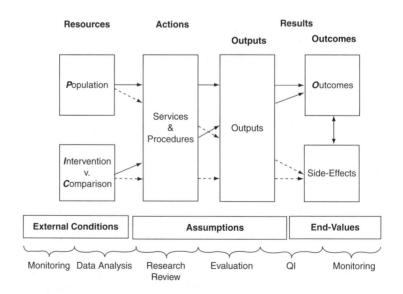

Figure 3.1 Components of a logic model.

agency relationships that are posited to effectuate the desired change. Finally there are the general end values for reconciling diverse outcomes and for evaluating the ultimate worth of the resulting change. Some general end values may be included in the causal portion of a logic model as an ultimate outcome, such as economic efficiency or subjective well-being. Others, such as equity, solidarity, and voice, function better as part of the underlying interpretative framework rather than as an intended result of a causal process because there is much debate about conditions under which they are desirable (Sowell, 2002). The technical appendix to this chapter describes these various components of the logic model in more detail. The following section illustrates the application of the logic model to the policies of Home of Relative (HMR) Reform in the state of Illinois.

The Logic of Home of Relative Reform in Illinois

On March 26, 1993, the *Chicago Tribune* carried a headline and story about the explosive growth in the HMR program in Illinois from 5500 children in June 1988 to 15,600 children as of September 1992 (Karwath, 1993). The story laid out ideas and hypotheses that had been advanced in an interim report that I had submitted a few months earlier to the Illinois DCFS (Testa, 1993). The report explained that the placement of abused and neglected children with grandparents, aunts, and uncles had been a longstanding practice in Illinois. What was unprecedented was the unrelenting rise in the number of new entries into the HMR program and the failure of reunifications, adoptions, and other exits to keep up with the growth. The result was a mounting backlog of children in long-term foster care (see Fig. 3.2).The sizable gap between the rapidly escalating placements and costs and the general public preference for keeping foster care caseloads and expenditures low created the political pressure that motivated the state to take a closer look at the reasons for the deviation from the desired state of affairs.

During the time that the *Tribune* story ran, I was conducting a series of focus groups with relative caregivers in Chicago to obtain better insight into their motivations, perceptions of children's needs, and their own long-term goals for the children under their care. The following excerpt from the transcripts of these focus groups offers some hypothesis-generating evidence about the different conditions and kinds of agency relationships that were contributing to the growth[2]:

> *Margaret:* "My daughter had dropped the children off. The first year was okay, but then it got sort of a hassle for me to have them, you know and pay my rent. I called. After I explained what the Aid was giving the children, a caseworker in the court said "Well that's not near enough to take care of those children. But if you prefer switching to DCFS, we would give you much more than what the Aid is giving you."

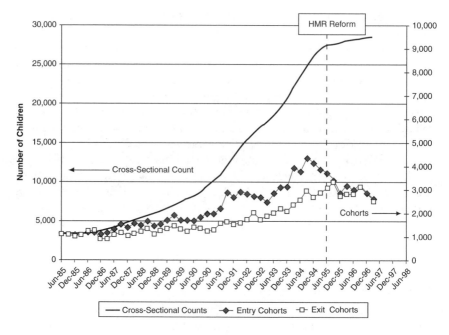

Figure 3.2 Kinship foster care caseflow dynamics in Illinois.

The HMR Interim Report (Testa, 1993) included a chart that showed the payment disparities to which the caseworker was referring. The differences in financial support that relatives could receive in foster care benefits ranged from three to five times as much money, depending on family size, than what they were entitled to receive under the old Aid to Families with Dependent Children (AFDC) program. These higher premiums were available to all relative caregivers who looked after children under the formal care and supervision of the state regardless of whether their homes were licensed as foster homes. This liberal payment policy expanded the 1979 ruling by the U.S. Supreme Court in *Miller vs. Youakim*, which prohibited Illinois and other states from denying relatives the same federal foster care benefits that foster parents received as long as the relatives met the same contractual and certification standards for foster home licensure.

Although there was a readiness among Illinois budget and legislative staff to view the payment disparities as providing an incentive for families to misrepresent children's needs for protective services, it was clear from discussions with workers in social agencies and the courts that they saw little difference between the circumstances of those affine (kinship) agents who had intervened informally on their own to remove children from conditions of abject poverty and parental drug addiction and the contractual (foster family) agents who had agreed to provide this care after formal investigation and the court-sanctioned removal of the children from the parent's home. Media focus on the failures of IDCFS to prevent the deaths of children under their supervision spurred the Department and the courts to take more children into legal custody even though they were safely looked after informally by extended family members. This blurring of the boundaries between the informal kinship care of dependent children and the formal kinship care of abused and neglected children opened the door to the incorporation of preexisting kinship arrangements into the formal foster care system (Testa, 1992). Previously, these arrangements would have been supported with much lower AFDC "child-only" grants.

In addition to the steady flow of new cases into the HMR program, Figure 3.2 shows that the lag in exits from the system also contributed to the build-up of children in long-term foster care. Statistical analyses revealed that rates of reunification and adoption from kinship homes were much lower than the rates for comparable children from foster family homes (Testa, 1997). The following excerpts from the focus group transcripts offer additional hypothesis-generating evidence about the reasons for the difference:

> *Margaret:* "My husband doesn't want to adopt because he said their mother was a good mother until she got into a little trouble and sent to prison. So, I felt not to adopt them because she's always been a good parent, and I thought she would settle herself down and she could get them back."
> *Judith:* "I understand that's what my daughter would have to do: give up her parental rights. But in doing so, she's denied any contact with this child. That's wrong. That is wrong."
> *Sandra:* "I told you earlier that I will adopt my two grandchildren, if it's necessary. I don't want to adopt those children. I want my daughter to have them, okay. But I will do all I can for them because I love them, and I will not let no one else adopt them."

As these passages indicate, the reluctance of some families to become parties to the termination of the parental rights of their daughters, sons, sisters, and brothers contributed to children's remaining in long-term kinship foster care. Although legal guardianship was a recognized alternative to adoption under the Social Security Act, caseworkers were reluctant to push this alternative permanency plan because it did not come with the same level of financial assistance as foster care and adoption did. Its underutilization was unfortunate because guardianship addresses many of the concerns that relatives express about adopting their own kin.

Under a transfer of guardianship, relatives are able to maintain their extended family identities as grandparents, aunts, and uncles instead of becoming mom and dad as adoption defines the relationship. The court awards legal custody of the children to the guardian, and the agency and court close their cases. Because rights are not terminated, birth parents retain rights of visitation and consent to adoption and may remain involved in their children's upbringing. If circumstances change in the future, parents can petition the courts to reopen the case and restore custody of the children back to them. Many older children also find consenting to guardianship less traumatic than consenting to adoption, which clears away another roadblock to permanence.

Intrigued with the prospect of a federally reimbursable permanency alternative to adoption when reunification was unlikely, the Illinois DCFS crafted a new foster placement status that mimicked some of the advantages of guardianship but without the transfer of legal custody that would have jeopardized the receipt of federal foster care funds. They dubbed the new status "delegated relative authority." It gave relatives the discretion to travel out of state, sign consents for medical and school-related matters, and release confidential information without first having to obtain clearance from DCFS (Testa, Shook, Cohen, & Woods, 1996). The Department commissioned me to oversee a needs-assessment survey of the extent to which caseworkers and kinship caregivers might find such a new arrangement both practical and appealing.

The Relative Caregiver Social Assessment Survey (RCSA) was completed by caseworkers from 11 private agencies on a sample of 1116 children who were not under their own agency's supervision (Testa et al., 1996). Roughly 35% of the children were reported by caregivers as already living with them at the time that the IDCFS took legal custody of the children. Most of these so-called "nonremoval" cases were brought into custody on an indicated finding of lack of supervision by the parents, some of whom had not been involved in their child's care for years.

Of the entire sample of children, assessment workers nominated 23% for delegated relative authority (DRA) status, 19% for adoption, and 5% for reunification.[3] Adoption recommendations were substantially higher than the 4% slated for adoption prior to reassessment, and reunification recommendations were much lower than the 20% that previously carried the goal of reunification. Although DRA promised to carve into the 68% of children who previously held the goal of long-term kinship foster care, workers still deemed this goal appropriate for 47% of the children after reassessment.

As the size of the HMR program increased from 17,500 in March 1993 to 25,900 in December 1994, both the Governor's Office and the General Assembly demanded swift action to stop the double-digit percentage increases in caseload growth. To deal with the backlog of children in long-term kinship foster care, the IDCFS moved forward with making DRA a state permanency planning option effective January 1995. A few months later, it announced its HMR Reform Plan to slow the intake of children into the foster care system.

The HMR Reform Plan was an interagency agreement between the IDCFS and the Illinois Department of Public Aid (IDPA). It proposed to reduce the removal rate by changing the way the state dealt with relative caregivers in two important ways: First, the Illinois legislature amended the definition of child neglect to exclude children in preexisting kinship care arrangements in which no immediate protective need existed. IDCFS stopped taking these children into state protective custody and instead began to offer their families Extended Family Support (EFS) Services to address the financial and legal authority problems that threatened the stability of these living arrangements. Second, the IDCFS implemented a single foster home licensing system in which relatives could participate if they applied and met those standards. The Department continued to place children in nonlicensed kinship care if the home passed basic safety and criminal-background checks. Although some legislative staff wanted to reduce the support of nonlicensed homes to the much lower "child only" grant to eliminate the payment disparity entirely with AFDC, both the Department and the *B.H.* plaintiffs' attorneys resisted imposing such a drastic cut. Instead foster children in nonlicensed kinship care would be supported at an intermediate level with a combination of payments from DPA and DCFS that equaled 100% of the AFDC child only Standard of Need (SON).[4] This was the minimal income that the state determined a family needed to maintain "a livelihood compatible with health and well being." In addition to DRA, the state extended its adoption assistance program to nonlicensed kin who wished to adopt children who could not be reunified and whom the courts deemed safe and suitable caregivers.

Figure 3.3 sketches out a logic model that adapts and expands the monitoring plan that I developed to monitor the implementation of the HMR Reform Plan (Illinois Department of Children and Family Services, 1995). The causal components of the logic model (top half) identify the key changes implemented under the HMR Reform Plan and their anticipated directional impacts, i.e., increase (+), decrease (−), or no effect (0), on the identified program outputs and child welfare outcomes. The interpretive components (bottom half) summarize the key historical and external conditions that defined the status of the service system prior to the reform and identify the major theoretical assumptions and agency relationships that were posited to effectuate the intended changes.

Budgetary efficiency, family autonomy, and kinship solidarity are the central end values that HMR Reform sought to reinforce. As indicated, adverse media attention to child deaths, concentrated poverty in urban neighborhoods, and an epidemic of cocaine addiction stimulated an avalanche of child abuse and neglect filings with the state. It was generally perceived that payment disparities between the amounts that relatives could receive in AFDC child-only grants and the much larger amounts they could obtain in foster care benefits encouraged the incorporation of preexisting informal kinship arrangements into the formal foster care system.

A reduction in the supply of formal kinship care providers (−) was anticipated to result from declining admissions due to the HMR Reform Plan's redefinition of child neglect and expansion of extended family support services. The average 30% reduction in state compensation to nonlicensed kinship caregivers was also expected to moderate program expansion on the assumption the financial disparity with AFDC public assistance encouraged the substitution of formal for informal kinship care.

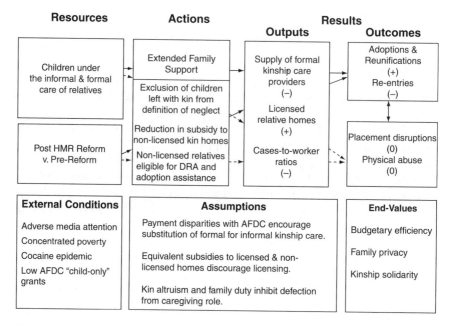

Figure 3.3 HMR reform logic model.

It was also anticipated that the reduction in payments in nonlicensed homes would provide an incentive for relatives to seek certification as licensed foster parents (+) by tying the higher reimbursement rate to foster home licensure. State payments for nonlicensed kinship care are ineligible for federal foster care reimbursement.

Cases-to-worker ratios (−) were expected eventually to fall as a result of the reduced workload expectations for children in DRA arrangements. The smaller financial losses incurred by nonlicensed kin were expected to stimulate more timely reunifications (+) while their eligibility for higher adoption assistance payments was expected to encourage adoptions (+). Assisting kinship caregivers in making a legally permanent commitment was also anticipated to reduce the rate of reentry (−) into the foster care system. The underlying assumption was that feelings of kin altruism and the sense of family duty would inhibit widespread defection from the caregiving role. Both placement disruptions and physical abuse were expected to remain unchanged (0) despite the reduction in the amount paid to nonlicensed kinship caregivers.

The attractiveness of a well-built logic model of intended policy change is that it allows for mid-course corrections by keeping stakeholders continuously apprised of progress toward or deviation from short-term outputs without holding off judgment until a summative evaluation of the impact on long-term outcomes can be completed (Shadish et al., 2002). The major drawback with the logic model for HMR Reform, however, was its heavy reliance on historical comparisons for drawing inferences about policy and program impacts. Valid assessments of system improvement are difficult to make because the postreform period may differ from the prereform period in other important ways than just the implemented changes. This interferes with the ability to draw valid inferences about causal impacts on outputs and outcomes. Another complication in the case of HMR Reform is that it was a bundle of reforms that could potentially exert contradictory influences on outputs and outcomes. For example, the redefinition of child neglect to exclude children already in the informal custody of kin might increase placement disruptions apart from the effects of payment changes by removing these very stable living arrangements from the pool of foster placements. In Chapter 7, I report on the results of a major longitudinal study of the impact of HMR Reform in Illinois (Doyle, 2007), which deals with these analytical complications by employing some recent developments in the statistical analysis of program and policy impacts.

Despite the limitations of relying on historical comparisons, the data charted in Figure 3.2 helped to sensitize policymakers to where HMR Reform appeared to be working as intended and where it seemed to be falling short of expectations. The trend line for entries shows that new kinship care cases began to drop several quarters before the HMR Reform Plan was officially put into effect (see Fig. 3.2). This anticipatory response is quite common in social policy as the details of a proposed change spread throughout the organization in advance of their official start date. The trend line for exits had been rising prior to HMR reform. It was anticipated that entry and exit lines would eventually cross by the end of 1995, but something unexpected happened instead: exits began to track the decline in entries (see Fig. 3.2). Rather than showing a drop in the active numbers of HMR cases as forecasted, the size of the program stabilized at approximately 28,000 cases. In addition, case tracking showed that the availability of DRA did not make much of a dent in the numbers of children that remained in long-term kinship foster care.

To understand the reasons behind the shortfalls, focus groups were convened with DCFS and private agency workers. It was learned that workers were hesitant about recommending DRA because they believed they would still be held liable if anything went wrong as legal custody still remained with the state. Also they perceived that their workloads would increase because they would be held accountable for a larger number of DRA cases than if the children remained in long-term kinship foster care. What was needed from their point of view was a new subsidized permanency option that transferred full legal responsibility from the state to the family and closed the administrative case. In effect they were asking for subsidized legal guardianship, which finally became available to Illinois in 1997 under a IV-E waiver granted by the federal government. This part of the story is picked up in Chapter 7.

Another related explanation for the stabilization of the HMR program stemmed from the recognition that the bottom lines of private agencies, which handled 80% of the HMR cases, would be adversely impacted by

the large-scale movement of children to permanent legal guardianship
and to adoptive homes with kin. Although it is difficult to acknowledge
that contractual agency interests can sometimes trump fiduciary agency
responsibilities, research shows that agency performance can be strongly
affected by financial incentives (Meezan & McBeath, 2008). In the case of
the HMR program, all of the financial incentives were stacked in favor of
retaining children in long-term foster care because funding to agencies
stopped after children were reunified or discharged to permanent homes.
Chapter 9 of this volume picks up this part of the story in its discussion of
Illinois' performance contracting program.

The next five chapters offer fuller accounts of the conceptual foundations of each of the stages of result-oriented accountability outlined in this
chapter and provide additional practical applications. It is my hope that
the example of HMR Reform presented in this chapter helps to convey the
cyclical nature of the process that moves from hypothesis-generating
qualitative evidence to more rigorous quantitative and experimental evidence and then loops back again to fine-tune performance or in a double-
loop to strengthen the construct validity of the underlying theory of
action. In this way, results-oriented accountability is both practice
informed and evidence supported in its efforts to improve the quality
and validity of services to families and children.

Technical Appendix 3A: Logic Models

Child welfare outcomes can be conceived of as the results of a service
system that operates on inputs of populations and interventions. A logic
model is a conceptual representation of the hypothesized intervening causal
actions that link populations and interventions to the services, procedures,
and outputs that impact the outcomes by valued principals and other
stakeholders. It rests on an interpretive framework that describes the key
historical and external conditions that define the state of the service system
prior to intervention and identify the major theoretical assumptions and
agency relationships that are posited to effectuate the desired change. The
framework includes an enumeration of general end values for reconciling
intended (outcomes) and unintended (side-effects) results and for evaluating the ultimate worth of the resulting change.

The causal and interpretive components of the logic model illustrated
in Figure 3.1 are defined as follows.

Causal Model

- *Resources*

    ○ *Intervention—Inputs that are alterable by agents and go into a service or
    program plan.* These can involve manipulations of the conditions

under which persons or organizations exercise agency, such as instrumental incentives. They can also include activities that are intended to improve agency performance, such as expressive support, counseling, and training. Inputs may encompass a wide range of financial, organizational, political, and community resources, such as funding levels, eligibility criteria, staff trainings, court orders, and altruistic appeals. These resources represent the nature and degree of the investment needed by the program to perform its expected activities and to obtain the desired outputs and outcomes (Taylor-Powell, Jones, & Henert, 2002).

○ *Population—Conditions of the service population that are preset prior to the intervention and not alterable by agents.* These can include factors such as age, race, maltreatment type, and diagnosis. Conditions usually refer to exogenous factors that confound the relationship between interventions and outcomes, which must be controlled to draw causal inferences (internal validity). They can also refer to moderating factors that amplify or attenuate the impact of an intervention, program, or service on outputs and outcomes for different subgroups of the population (external validity).

- *Actions*

   ○ *Services—Activities conducted or products created that are delivered to the service population.* Examples are financial subsidies, case planning activities, worker contacts, and team meetings.

   ○ *Procedures—Socially approved standards of service delivery that define the manner in which a population expects to receive services.* These can be measured in terms such as timeliness of investigation, restrictiveness of care, standards of evidence, equitable treatment, and due process of law.

   ○ *Outputs—Quantity of services delivered or products created.* These include frequency of worker contacts, numbers reached by a public education campaign, and amount of counseling hours. Outputs also include measures of the extent to which service delivery is consistent with procedural standards, such as child maltreatment investigations initiated within 24 hours of referral, legal representation of parents, and time to permanent placement. Outputs are tangible evidence that services were delivered in a socially sanctioned manner.

- *Results*

   ○ *Outcome—Intended changes in the conditions of the population that result from the program outputs.* Outcomes answer the counterfactual question: What will be different after the population has received the program's outputs compared to if they never received the outputs? Outcomes are not what a program does, but what happens for those being served because of what a program does.

- ○ *Side effects—Unintended consequences (positive and negative) of a specific intervention beyond its targeted impact.* Examples are cost overruns, substitution effects, or unanticipated positive results. Frequently included as a category in social indicator models (Land, 1975), side effects are commonly omitted from logic models. Because the double-loop learning that occurs during the quality improvement stage is often stimulated by information or protests about unintended consequences, it seems more appropriate to make this possibility explicit in the logic model.

Interpretive Framework

- • *External Conditions*
  Exogenous historical, political, economic, cultural, and social factors that are beyond an agent's control but influence the activities and capacity of the agent to achieve the desired outcomes. External conditions include macroeconomic trends, changes in political majorities, and cultural innovations that may necessitate a revision of activities, outcomes, and assumptions.

- • *Assumptions*
  Underlying beliefs and postulates about human nature, motivation, and purposive action that bring about change and help interpret why a specific intervention is expected to result in the desired outcome. Much of the attention to assumptions has arisen in reaction to the theory of action and agency relations underlying microeconomics, which posits that people are motivated to maximize their individual self-interest. Criticisms of this assumption as too sparse and unrealistic (Perrow, 1986) have led to a broadening of agency theory beyond contractual relations to include the altruism bestowed on principals by affine agents who share a social bond (Coleman, 1990); the general beneficence displayed by fiduciary agents who are motivated by an internalized sense of probity or service ethic (Buchanan, 1988); and the obedience to a law, command, or threat by agents who are in a subordinate hierarchical relationship with an authority figure or principal (Addams, 1996). Chapter 1 discussed the four relational models (authority-ranking, communal sharing, market pricing, and

equality matching) that underlie different types of agency relations. Although the self-interested motivation of contractual agents is commonly assumed in logic models that involve economic and financial incentives, the increased use of logic models in the planning, evaluation, and management of judicial interventions, family and community-based services, as well as usual professional services makes it important to be explicit about these other motivational and relational assumptions underlying the logic model.

- *End values*

  Outcomes that are intrinsically valued for their own sake. End values help define specific outcomes and can serve as more inclusive categories for reconciling tensions between different outcomes. The connections that are drawn between assumptions and relational models can also be done for the end values that people generally regard as desired outcomes in their own right. These include the end value of economic efficiency that links to the relational model of market pricing. When the resources, activities, and results in a logic model can all be expressed in comparable money terms, a benefit–cost analysis can be undertaken to approximate the decisions that might have been made in a private market (Haveman & Weisbrod, 1975). In this sense, net economic benefit is equivalent to market efficiency and can be used as a criterion for choosing among competing alternatives (MacRae, 1985).

  Voice is another end value, which drawing from Hirschman (1970) can be defined as the right of a subordinate in an authority-ranking relationship to express dissatisfaction, grievances, or proposals for a change in conditions. When voice is calibrated in terms of subjective well-being, it also provides a potential basis for trade-offs and reconciliation among competing alternatives (MacRae, 1985).

  Solidarity, which is associated with the relational model of communal sharing, is an end value about which there is far less consensus concerning its general desirability. Although forming secure attachment relationships in childhood is regarded as an essential condition for maintaining lasting commitments and cooperative relationships in adulthood (Bowlby, 1969) there is ambivalence about bounded solidarity or loyalty to a group as a value in its own sake. Modern relationships are increasingly characterized by commitments of "limited liability" (Janowitz, 1978), such that when the relationship stops satisfying an individual's wants and interests, the individual is free to exit the relationship (Giddens, 1990). For this reason, solidarity in logic models may also operate as an intermediate outcome or contributing condition to another end value in addition to being treated as an intrinsic value in its own right. Similarly, although there is a general acceptance of the end value of equity as a desired outcome, this consensus breaks down in a "conflict of visions" (Sowell, 2002) over whether equity should be defined in terms of equality matching (equality of outcomes) or market pricing (equality of process). Equity in the former sense of equalized probabilities of achieving given results is what Sowell calls the "unconstrained vision" of equality, whereas equity in the later sense of fair and equal treatment defines the "constrained vision" of equality. The constrained vision holds that rewards should be commensurate with individual competitive achievement in fair enterprise, whereas the unconstrained vision aims for the equalization of conditions so that all groups are uniformly well off regardless of individual achievement. Chapter 2 discussed this basic tension and presented Fishkin's argument that the two values of equality and achievement can be reconciled only at the expense of the third value of family autonomy (which affirms parental voice in matters of family solidarity). A logic model of this argument would allow for nonlinear relationships and periodic double-loop adjustments of specific outcomes as maximization of any two end values eventually leads to inconsistency with the third.

At the bottom of Figure 3.1 are the five stages of results-oriented accountability that are most closely related to each component of the logic model. The linkage of components to the different stages shows how a logic model can help tie together the cycle of results-oriented accountability in child welfare practice and policy.

Notes

1. This list parallels the general end values of equity, subjective well-being, economic benefit, and social integration, which Duncan MacRae includes in a more general system of policy indicators (MacRae, 1985).
2. Names of focus-group participants have been changed to preserve anonymity.
3. These distributions are based on a slightly larger sample size of 1297 children than the 1119 children in the published article by Testa et al. (1996).
4. The SON subsidy for one child was 30% lower than the licensed foster care subsidy and 150% higher than the AFDC "child only" grant that DPA paid nonlegally liable relatives to care for dependent children. The magnitude of the disparity increased for larger sibling groups because "child only" grants incorporated an "economy of scale" discount factor whereas the foster care amounts increased additively with each additional child in the home.

References

Addams, J. (1996). Principals and agents, colonialists and company men: The decay of colonial control in the Dutch East Indies. *American Sociological Review, 61*(1), 12–28.

Bloom, H. S., Michalopoulos, C., Hill, C. J., & Lei, Y. (2002). *Can nonexperimental comparison group methods match the findings from a random assignment evaluation of mandatory welfare-to-work programs?* New York: MDRC.

Bowlby, J. (1969). *Attachment and loss: Vol. 1. Attachment.* New York: Basic Books.

Brownson, R. C., Baker, E. A., Leet, T. L., & Gillespie, K. N. (2003). *Evidence-based public health.* New York: Oxford University Press.

Buchanan, A. (1988). Principal/agent theory and decision making in healthcare. *Bioethics, 2*(4), 317–333.

Coleman, J. S. (1990). *Foundations of social theory.* Cambridge, MA: Belknap Press of Harvard University Press.

Doyle, J. J. (2007). Can't buy me love? Subsidizing the care of related children. *Journal of Public Economics, 91,* 281–304.

Flay, B. A. (1986). Efficacy and effectiveness trials (and other phases of research) in the development of health promotion programs. *Preventive Medicine, 15,* 451–474.

Freedman, D. A. (2005). *Statistical models: Theory and practice.* Cambridge, UK: Cambridge University Press.

Gambrill, E. (2006). Evidence-based practice and policy: Choices ahead. *Research on Social Work Practice, 16*(3), 338–357.

Giddens, A. (1990). *The consequences of modernity.* Stanford, CA: Stanford University Press.

Haveman, R. H., & Weisbrod, B. A. (1975). Defining benefits of public programs: Some guidance for policy analysts. *Policy Analysis, 1*(1), 169–196.

Hirschman, A. O. (1970). *Exit, voice, and loyalty: Responses to decline in firms, organizations, and states.* Cambridge, MA: Harvard University Press.

Illinois Department of Children and Family Services. (1995). *HMR Reform Plan.* Springfield, IL: Department of Children and Family Services.

Janowitz, M. (1978). *The last half-century: Societal change and politics in America.* Chicago: The University of Chicago Press.

Johnson, M., Wells, S., Testa, M., & McDonald, J. (2003). Illinois child welfare research agenda: An approach to building consensus for practice-based research. *Child Welfare, 82*(1), 53–76.

Julian, D. A. (1997). The utilization of the logic model as a system level planning and evaluation device. *Evaluation and Program Planning, 20*(3), 251–257.

Karwath, R. (1993). Relatives' care for DCFS wards carries big price tag. *Chicago Tribune,* March 26, 1993, p. 1.

Land, K. C. (1975). Social indicators models: An overview. In K. C. Land & S. Spilerman (Eds.), *Social indicator models* (pp. 5–36). New York: Russell Sage Foundation.

Land, K. C., & Spilerman, S. (1975). *Social indicator models.* New York: Russell Sage Foundation.

Littell, J. H. (2005). Lessons from a systematic review of effects of multisystemic therapy. *Children and Youth Services Review, 27,* 445– 463.

Littell, J. H., Bjørndal, A., Hamerstrøm, K. T., & Winvold, A. (2007). Functional family therapy for families of youth (age 11–18) with behavior problems. *Title Proposal.* The Campbell Collaboration Library of Systematic Reviews. Last accessed September 1, 2009 at http://www.campbellcollaboration.org/library.php.

MacRae, D. Jr. (1985). *Policy indicators: Link between social sciences and public debate.* Chapel Hill: The University of North Carolina Press.

Meezan, W., & McBeath, B. (2008). Market-based disparities in foster care outcomes. *Children and Youth Services Review, 30*(4), 388–406.

Moher, D., Schultz, K. F., & Altman, D. G. (2001). The CONSORT statement: Revised recommendations for improving the quality of reports of parallel group randomized trials. *BMC Medical Research Methodology, 1*(2).

National Association of Public Child Welfare Administrators and The National Resource Center on Child Maltreatment. (2001). *A research agenda for public child welfare*. Washington, DC: NAPCWA, last accessed March 1, 2008 at http:// www.nrccps.org/PDF/Research-Agenda.pdf.

Perrow, C. (1986). Economic theories of organization. *Theory and Society, Special Double Issue: Structures of Capital, 15*(112), 11–45.

Richardson, W. S., Wilson, M. C., Nishikawa, J., & Hayward, R. S. A. (1995). The well-built clinical question: A key to evidence-based decisions. *ACP Journal Club,* Nov/Dec, 123:A12.

Schalock, R. L., & Bonhamd, G. S. (2003). Measuring outcomes and managing for results. *Evaluation and Program Planning, 26,* 229–235.

Shadish, W. R., Cook, T. D., & Campbell, D. T. (2002). *Experimental and quasi-experimental designs for generalized causal inference.* Boston: Houghton Mifflin Company.

Shlonsky, A., Backe-Hansen, E., Schumaker, K., Cook, C., Crampton, D., Saini, M., & Kowalski, K. (2009). Family group conferences for children at risk of abuse and neglect. *Title Proposal.* The Campbell Collaboration Library of Systematic Reviews. Last accessed September 1, 2009 at http://www.campbellcollaboration.org/library.php.

Sowell, T. (2002). *A conflict of visions: Ideological origins of political struggles.* New York: Basic Books.

Taylor-Powell, E., Jones, L., & Henert, E. (2002). Enhancing program performance with logic models. Last accessed March 30, 2007 at http://www.uwex.edu/ces/lmcourse/.

Testa, M. (1988). Data necessary to support national policy functions in foster care and adoption. *Technical appendix to the report of the advisory committee on adoption and foster care information.* Washington, DC: Administration for Children, Youth and Families, USDHHS.

Testa, M. (1992). Conditions of risk for substitute care. *Children and Youth Services Review, 14*(1/2), 27–36.

Testa, M. (1993). *Home of relative (HMR) program: Interim report to the Illinois Department of Children and Family Services.* Chicago: School of Social Service Administration.

Testa, M. (1997) Kinship foster care in Illinois. In J. Duerr Berrick, R. Barth, & N. Gilbert (Eds.), *Child welfare research review, volume two* (pp. 101–129). New York: Columbia University Press.

Testa, M., Shook, K., Cohen, L., & Woods, M. (1996). Permanency planning options for children in formal kinship care. In D. Wilson & S. Chipungu (Eds.), *Child Welfare. Special Issue: Kinship Care, 75*(5), 451–470.

Winokur, M., Holtan, A., & Valentine, D. (2009). Kinship care for the safety, permanency, and well-being of children removed from the home for maltreatment. *Title Proposal.* The Campbell Collaboration Library of Systematic Reviews. Last accessed September 1, 2009 at http://www.campbellcollaboration.org/library.php.

W. K. Kellogg Foundation. (2004). *Logic model development guide: Using logic models to bring together planning, evaluation, and action.* Battle Creek, MI: W. K. Kellogg Foundation.

4

OUTCOMES MONITORING
IN CHILD WELFARE

Tom McDonald and Mark F. Testa

The cycle of result-oriented accountability starts with an assessment of agency performance through regular tracking of statistical indicators of child and family outcomes, system processes, and compliance with procedural standards. For this monitoring of results to be effective there needs to be consensually agreed on child and family outcomes that are measured validly and reliably. Although this may seem obvious, the history of child welfare indicates that a consensus on child and family outcomes has been difficult to achieve and valid and reliable measurement continues to be a struggle.

Unfortunately, child welfare managers cannot suspend operations until these problems are solved. Children suffer abuse or neglect, reside in foster care, and "age out" of the child welfare system on a daily basis. As this chapter demonstrates, the best set of indicators of child and family outcomes has not yet been created. In fact, current public policy supports some less than ideal measures. Through an understanding of the strengths and weaknesses of outcome indicators, managers can make informed judgments about measures and use those that most accurately report on agency performance. This chapter will describe current policy followed by a discussion of its strengths and weaknesses.

Child Welfare Goals

As discussed in Chapter 2, child welfare as a social service, particularly the institution of foster care, began in the mid-1800s in the United States with a narrow focus on affording dependent and neglected children the minimum necessities of life. In exchange for their labor, children received food, shelter, and training to promote moral behavior and a strong work ethic. This narrow orientation gradually broadened over the next century "from rescuing the children of poor families and providing them a minimal level of sustenance, moral guidance, and work training . . . to providing the supports necessary to enable parents to care adequately for children in their own homes, arranging substitute care only on the basis of individualized assessment of case need" (McGowan, 2005, pp. 25–26). These different points of view on the appropriate scope of public interest in child welfare and the optimal form of social organization for accomplishing these purposes frequently clashed, causing the focus of child welfare policy and services to swing like a pendulum between upholding the rights of parents and preserving families to child saving with greater emphasis on alternative permanent placement options outside the family of origin.

Concerning American child welfare, clearly the dominating force in current practice remains the Adoption and Safe Families Act of 1997 (P.L. 105-89; ASFA), even though the Fostering Connections to Success and Improving Adoptions Act of 2008 (P.L. 110-351, FCSIAA) pulls back slightly in the direction of preserving extended family, sibling, and community connections (see Chapter 11, this volume). As the title of the AFSA suggests, the Act emphasized child safety and the severance of parental rights over family continuity and maintenance of the child in the home of origin. ASFA specifies key principles that form the basis of the law and make explicit the goals of child welfare.

- The safety of children is the paramount concern that must guide all child welfare services.
- Foster care is a temporary setting and not a place for children to grow up.
- Permanency planning efforts for children should begin as soon as a child enters foster care and should be expedited by the provision of services to families.
- The child welfare system must focus on results and accountability.
- Innovative approaches are needed to achieve the goals of safety, permanence, and well-being (P.L. 105–89).

The shift from the ready acceptance of foster care as a long-term solution for abused and neglected children to the view that it should serve as only a temporary setting while more permanent placement options are explored was not new to ASFA, but its passage certainly solidified this perspective. Long-term foster care has ceased to be an acceptable goal for children. What ASFA did not address, but later legislation attempted to rectify somewhat, is the reality that some children, despite the best efforts to reunite their families or find new families, end up growing up in foster care and do not exit to more permanent homes but simply age out of the system and are "emancipated" at age 18 years old to make it more or less on their own. Research has shown that rather than making a successful transition to living on their own, a significant percentage of these youth experience homelessness, unemployment, victimization, and dependence on various types of public assistance (Courtney & Dworsky, 2006; Georgiades, 2005; Collins, 2004; Lemon, Hines, & Merdinger, 2005; Freundlich & Avery, 2005; Reilly, 2003; Collins, 2001). This reality led to the passage of legislation that has major implications for defining and measuring outcomes in child welfare.

Federal funding for independent living services to youth in foster care between the ages of 16 and 21 years first became available with the passage of the Title IV-E Independent Living Initiative (P.L. 99-272) in 1986. Funding for services was expanded in 1999 with the passage of the Foster Care Independence Act (P.L. 106-169), which established the John H. Chafee Foster Care Independence Program (CFCIP) and removed minimum age requirements for the receipt of independent living services. The recently passed FCSIAA will also allow states to claim federal funds to continue foster care payments for older youth in care (and, in certain cases, guardianship or adoption assistance payments) up to the age of 21 when those youth are engaged in work, school, or a program designed to eliminate barriers to or promote employment or cannot engage in these activities due to a documented medical condition.

Included in the Foster Care Independence Act was a requirement for the Administration of Children and Families (ACF) to develop a data collection system that would track the independent living services that states provide to youth and to develop outcome measures that may be used to assess state performance in operating their independent living programs. This data system, which is called the Chafee National Youth in Transition Database (NYTD), is scheduled for full implementation in October 2010. As a result, in addition to the goals of safety and permanence provided by ASFA for all children entering the public child welfare system, the system will be held accountable for these additional child well-being outcomes for all youth who turn 17 years while in foster care:

- Increase in financial self-sufficiency
- Improve educational (academic or vocational) attainment
- Increase young people's positive connections with adults
- Reduce homelessness among young people
- Reduce high-risk behavior among young people
- Improve young people's access to health insurance

The focus of this chapter is on the definition and measurement of outcomes for child welfare under ASFA and CFCIP. ASFA is much further along in its implementation, so it provides more concrete material and experience for review. However, the proposed Chafee NYTD will have a major impact on state child welfare systems and offers some interesting contrasts in its planned implementation in comparison to that of ASFA.

Outcome Monitoring Under ASFA

Under performance provisions of ASFA, the Secretary of Health and Human Services (HHS) is directed to:

a. Use the Adoption and Foster Care Analysis and Reporting System to develop outcome measures to assess the performance of the states in operating their child protection and child welfare programs;
b. Develop a system of rating the states' performance relative to those outcome measures;
c. Require that the states provide the necessary information so that HHS can rate them. This requirement is tied to a state's receiving funding for its child welfare system;
d. Make an annual report to Congress regarding the performance of each state relative to the outcome measures. The report must assess the reasons for good and poor performance and make recommendations for improvement of performance (42 USC 679b).

These requirements have been operationalized through the Child and Family Services Reviews (CFSRs), which are described in the following section.

The Federal Child and Family Services Reviews

Phase One. The impetus for the CFSRs grew out of the general dissatisfaction among the states and federal government with prior federal reviews culminating in a mandate in the Social Security Amendments of 1994 (see section 1123A of the Social Security Act) for the Department of Health and Human Services to promulgate regulations for reviews of state child and family services programs under Titles IV-B and IV-E of the Social Security Act. In response to this legislation the ACF, in consultation with experts in the field of child welfare, developed the CFSRs to be a results-oriented, comprehensive monitoring system. The major goals as described in the final regulations implementing the CFSRs were to (1) focus on achieving the goals of safety, permanence, and well-being in state child welfare systems and (2) move child welfare systems toward achieving positive child and family outcomes while maintaining accountability (65 FR 4021). The CFSR procedures were designed to be a change to a results- and outcome-based review process as opposed to the prior emphasis on compliance with procedural requirements.

The first round of actual reviews was not begun until 2000 and was not completed (in every state, the District of Columbia, and Puerto Rico) until 2004. Information for each CFSR came from the following sources: (1) The Statewide Assessment, (2) case-level reviews conducted by a team of federal and state reviewers, (3) interviews with key stakeholders, and (4) state data from the Foster Care File of the Adoption and Foster Care Analysis and Reporting System (AFCARS) and the Child File of the National Child Abuse and Neglect Data System (NCANDS), or an alternative data source approved by the Children's Bureau. The CFSRs attempt to examine child welfare practices at the "ground level, capturing the interactions among caseworkers, children and families, and service providers, and determining the effects of those interactions on the children and families involved" (Milner, Mitchell, & Hornsby, 2005).

Using this information, the first round of the CFSR assessed state performances on seven outcomes and seven systemic factors. The systemic factors include (1) statewide information systems, (2) case review systems, (3) quality assurance systems, (4) staff and provider training, (5) service array, (6) agency responsiveness to the community, and (7) foster and adoptive parent licensing, recruitment, and retention. Each of the systemic factors subject to review is based on specific state plan requirements.

The seven outcomes shown in Figure 4.1 are most relevant to the focus on results-oriented accountability. For the most part, performance on the seven outcomes was determined through the results of the case reviews.

Safety	Permanence	Well-Being
• Children are first and foremost, protected from abuse and neglect • Children are safely maintained in their homes whenever possible and appropriate	• Children have permanence and stability in their living situations • The continuity of family relationships and connections is preserved for children	• Families have enhanced capacity to provide for their children's needs • Children receive appropriate services to meet their educational needs • Children receive adequate services to meet their physical and mental health needs

Figure 4.1 ASFA goals and CFSR outcomes.

However, in the first round of the CFSR, the assessment for two outcomes also included a state's performance on six national data measures that ACF adapted from measures developed in response to the requirements of section 479A of the Social Security Act.

Originally ACF's invitation to comment on child welfare outcomes and measures, which appeared in the *Federal Register* in February 1999, endorsed comparisons with "historical controls," i.e., the outcomes in previous years, as the best way to assess progress. This viewpoint was echoed in the first Annual Report to Congress on Child Welfare Outcomes issued in 1999:

> The outcome measures should be used to assess the continuous improvement of each State over time, rather than compare the performance of States with one another. Comparison across States on their performance on the outcome measures is difficult due to variations in State population demographics, programs, and policies and must be undertaken with great care. State performance is better assessed by tracking a State's own continuous improvement over time (pp. 2–3).

ACF later modified its position and moved forward with national quantitative standards in response to requests for more tangible, objective measures to assess conformity with the six quantitative indicators targeted by the CFSR. ACF established national standards for each of the six data measures, all of which were calculated from data reported by states to NCANDS and AFCARS. ACF described these six data measures and the national standards in the preamble to the final CFSR regulation, published in the *Federal Register* (65 FR 4024–4025). This same regulation provides information on how ACF calculated the national standards associated with each of the six data measures. The Department of Health and Human Services (DHHS) based national standards for data indicators on the 75th percentile of all states' performance for that indicator.

Subsequently, ACF issued information memoranda on the specific national standards that would be used in the initial CFSR implementation (see ACYF–CB–IM–00–11 and ACYF–CB–IM–01–07). The following performance measures and national standards were used during the first round of the CFSR as part of the assessment of a state's substantial conformity with CFSR Safety Outcome 1:

- Children are, first and foremost, protected from abuse and neglect:
  - Repeat maltreatment—Of all children who were victims of substantiated or indicated child abuse and/or neglect during the first 6 months of the reporting period, 6.1% or less had

another substantiated or indicated report within a 6-month period.

○ Maltreatment of children in foster care—Of all children who were in foster care during the reporting period, 0.57% or less were the subject of substantiated or indicated maltreatment by a foster parent or facility staff member.

The following performance measures and national standards were used as part of the assessment of a state's substantial conformity with CFSR Permanency Outcome 1:

• Children will have permanence and stability in their living situations:

  ○ Timeliness of reunification—Of all children who were reunified with their parents or caretakers at the time of discharge from foster care, 76.2% or more were reunified in less than 12 months from the time of the latest removal from home.
  ○ Reentry into foster care—Of all children who entered foster care during the reporting period, 8.6% or less were reentering foster care within 12 months of a prior foster care episode.
  ○ Timeliness to adoption—Of all children who exited foster care to a finalized adoption, 32% or more exited foster care in less than 24 months from the time of the latest removal from home.
  ○ Placement stability—Of all children who have been in foster care for less than 12 months from the time of the latest removal from home, 86.7% or more have had no more than two placement settings. *Federal Register*/Vol. 70, No. 214/Monday, November 7, 2005/Notices

These six performance measures are included in a State Data Profile that ACF prepares and transmits, using AFCARS and NCANDS data submitted by the state. It is important to note that these indicators (and the related national standards) that use the AFCARS and NCANDS data address only one of two safety outcomes and one of two permanency outcomes. No uniform national data indicators collected through AFCARS or NCANDS can be reviewed for well-being outcomes. The data sources for evaluating performance with respect to the child and family well-being outcomes came primarily from the on-site case reviews of a sample of 50 cases.

Results from the first completed wave of CFSRs were not encouraging. To receive a rating of "substantial conformity" for any outcome, at least 90% of the applicable cases reviewed must have been rated as having "substantially achieved" that outcome. In addition, for a state to be considered in substantial conformity with Safety Outcome 1 and Permanency Outcome 1, it was necessary for the state to meet the national standards for specified outcome measures. Only a small percentage of states achieved substantial conformity with any of the seven outcomes, and no state achieved substantial conformity with Permanency Outcome 1 (Children have permanence and stability in their living situations) or Well-Being Outcome 1 (Families have enhanced capacity to provide for their children's needs).

Phase Two. In November 2005, ACF announced its plan to replace the six national data measures used for the CFSR with six data composites addressing the child welfare domains of maltreatment recurrence, maltreatment in foster care, timeliness of adoptions, timeliness of reunifications, placement stability, and permanence for children. The proposed changes were based on a review of the first round of CFSRs in FY 2004 by a contracted consultant who convened a CFSR workgroup of state child welfare agency administrators and child welfare researchers and, based on input from this workgroup, produced a set of recommendations for ACF. The focus of this review was on safety and permanency outcome measures that could be constructed with the AFCARS and NCANDS data. Child and family well-being outcomes were not addressed. The reasons provided for the changes were that

- Expanding the scope of data pertaining to a particular child welfare domain will provide a more effective assessment of state performance.
- Data composites will provide a more holistic view of state performance in a particular domain than a single data measure can achieve.
- Data composites will ensure that the data component of a state's performance with regard to a particular domain will not depend on one measure.
- Data composites will allow the development of national standards that account for variation in state practices and policies.
- Data composites are being successfully used by the federal government to assess other programs. (*Federal Register*/Vol. 70, No. 214/Monday, November 7, 2005, pp. 67479–67489)

Final notice of the data measures, data composites, and national standards to be used in the Child and Family Services Reviews were published in the *Federal Register* in June 2006 and are reproduced here in Figure 4.2.

Outcome Monitoring Under Chafee NYTD

The final rule for NYTD was published February 26, 2008 and was effective as of April 28, 2008. Full implementation of NYTD will be October 1, 2010, with the first report with data due to ACF no later than May 15, 2011. As noted, the states will be expected to report on services delivered as well as outcomes achieved. The focus here is on the requirement for tracking youth

Composites and performance measures	Range	Median	National standard
Performance Measures Associated with Performance on CFSR Safety Outcome 1—Children Are, First and Foremost, Protected from Abuse and Neglect			
Of all children who were victims of a substantiated or indicated maltreatment allegation during the first 6 months of FY 2004, what percent were not victims of another substantiated or indicated maltreatment allegation during a 6-month period?	86.0–98.0	93.5	95.2 or higher.
Maltreatment of children in foster care: Of all children in foster care in FY 2004, what percent were not victims of a substantiated or indicated maltreatment by a foster parent or facility staff member?	99.07–100	99.68	99.67 or higher.
Composites, Components, and Performance Measures Associated with Performance on CFSR Permanency Outcome 1—Children Have Permanency and Stability in Their Living Situations			
Permanency Composite 1: Timeliness and Permanency of Reunification			
Scaled Scores for the Timeliness and Permanency of Reunification Composite incorporating two components and four measures.	50–150	96.1	106.7 or higher.
Component A. Timeliness of reunification:			
Of all children discharged from foster care to reunification in FY 2004 who had been in foster care for 8 days or longer, what percent were reunified in less than 12 months from the time of the latest removal from home? (This includes the Trial Home Visit adjustment.).	44.2–88.8	69.5	No Standard.
Of all children discharged from foster care to reunification in FY 2004 who had been in foster care for 8 days or longer, what was the median length of stay from the time of the most recent entry into foster care until discharge to reunification (in months)? (This includes the Trial Home Visit adjustment.)	2.0–13.7	6.5	No Standard.
Of all children entering foster care in the first 6 months of FY 2004 who remained in foster care for 8 days or longer, what percent were discharged from foster care to reunification in less than 12 months of the time of entry into foster care? (This includes the Trial Home Visit adjustment.)	15.7–65.4	35.3	No Standard
Component B. Permanency of reunification:			
Of all children discharged from foster care to reunification in FY 2003, what percent re-entered foster care in less than 12 months?	1.6–29.5	14.8	No Standard.
Composites, commponents, and performance measures	Range	Median	National standard
Permanency Composite 2: Timeliness of Adoptions			
Scaled scores for the Timeliness of Adoptions Composite incorporating three components and five measures.	50–150	96.5	102.1 or higher
Component A: Timeliness of adoptions of children discharged from foster care			
Of all children who were discharged from foster care to a finalized adoption in FY 2004, what percent was discharged in less than 24 months from the time of the latest removal from the home?	6.4–74.9	27.1	No Standard.
Of all children who were discharged from foster care to a finalized adoption in FY 2004, what was the median length of stay in foster care (in months) from the time of removal from the home to the time of discharge from foster care?	16.2–55.7	32.0	No Standard.
Component B: Progress Toward Adoption for Children Who Meet ASFA Time-in-Care Requirements			
Of all children in foster care on the first day of FY 2004 who were in foster care for 17 continuous months or longer, what percent were adopted before the end of the fiscal year?	8.0–25.1	18.0	No Standard.
Of all children in foster care on the first day of FY 2004 who were in foster care for 17 continuous months or longer, what percent became legally free for adoption (i.e., a TPR was granted for each living parent) within 6 months of the beginning of the fiscal year?	0.2–17.2	9.0	No Standard
Component C: Progress Toward Adoption of Children Who Are Legally Free for Adoption			
Of all children who became legally free for adoption during FY 2004, what percent were discharged from foster care to a finalized adoption in less than 12 months?	18.9–85.2	43.7	No Standard.
Permanency Composite 3: Achieving Permanency for Children in Foster Care			
Scaled scores for the Achieving Permanency Composite incorporating two components and three measures.	50–150	98.6	105.2 or higher.

Figure 4.2 Measures and composites to be used in the second round of the Child and Family Services Review (*Federal Register* 71:109, p. 32980).

Composites, commponents, and performance measures	Range	Median	National standard
Component A: Achieving Permanency for Children in Foster Care for Extended Periods of Time			
Of all children who were discharged from foster care and were legally free for adoption (i.e., there was a TPR for each living parent), what percent exited to a permanent home defined as adoption, guardianship, or reunification prior to their 18th birthday?	84.6–100.0	96.8	No Standard.
Of all children in foster care for 24 months or longer at the start of the fiscal year, what percent were discharged to permanency in less than 12 months and prior to their 18th birthday?	8.0–35.2	24.6	No Standard.
Component B: Children Emancipated Who Were in Foster Care for Extended Periods of Time			
Of all children who exited foster care with a discharge reason of emancipation or who reached their 18th birthday while in foster care, what percent were in foster care for 3 years or longer?	17.5–80.4	50.6	No Standard.
Composites, components and measures	Range	Median	National standard
Permanency Composite 4: Placement stability			
Scaled scores for the Placement Stability Composite incorporating three measures	50–150	102.0	108.2 or higher.
Of all children in foster care for 8 days or longer and less than 12 months, what percent had two or fewer placement settings?	64.7–97.1	82.4	No Standard.
Of all children in foster care for at least 12 months but less than 24 months, what percent had two or fewer placement settings?	37.0–82.3	59.5	No Standard.
Of all children in foster care for at least 24 months, what percent had two or fewer placement settings?	14.1–53.8	33.4	No Standard.

Figure 4.2 *(Continued).*

and measuring outcomes. The final rule identifies six outcomes that are shown in Figure 4.3 with a general description of the relevant data elements that will be used to operationalize their measurement. Appendix A of the final rule provides more specific identification of 58 data elements that will comprise the NYTD service component and Appendix B provides the 22 specific questions to be asked in the outcome survey.

Outcomes	Relevant Data Elements
Outcome 1: Increase young people's financial self-sufficiency	Current full-time employment, Current part-time employment, Employment-related skills, Social Security, Educational aid, Public financial assistance, Public food assistance, Public housing assistance, Other financial support
Outcome 2: Improve young people's educational (academic or vocational) attainment.	Highest educational certification received, Current enrollment/attendance.
Outcome 3: Improve young people's positive connections with adults.	Connection to adult.
Outcome 4: Reduce homelessness among young people.	Homelessness
Outcome 5: Reduce high-risk behavior among young people.	Substance abuse referral, Incarceration, Children, Marriage at child's birth.
Outcome 6: Improve young people's access to health insurance.	Medicaid, Other health insurance coverage, Health insurance type.

Figure 4.3 Chafee NYTD outcomes and relevant data elements (*Federal Register*, 73:38, February 26, 2008, pp. 10350–10355).

The proposed methodology requires that states survey a sample of youth for outcomes information regardless of whether they receive independent living services. Data are to be collected at three points in time: on or about the youth's seventeenth birthday while the youth is in foster care, 2 years later on or about the youth's nineteenth birthday, and again on or about the youth's twenty-first birthday regardless of whether they remain in foster care or are receiving independent services. States are required to collect outcome data on a new cohort of youth (17-year-old youths in foster care) every 3 years.

States will be provided with the option to select a random sample of youth for the survey or another accepted sampling methodology that ACF approves. The required sample size will be determined by standard formulas that generate a sufficient number of cases for valid estimates of population scores within a 10% margin of error. States with an estimated population of less than 5000 17-year-old youth in foster care will be able to use the Finite Population Correction because the sample size will constitute a large proportion of the population. This would appear to apply to all states except California. After applying an adjustment for an anticipated 30% attrition it is estimated that the sample sizes across all states will range from 79 to 341 youth.

It is believed that the population of youth ages 19 to 21 years is now mostly excluded from AFCARS and that the NYTD data collection and processing will be largely independent and not duplicative. Common IDs would permit merging of data sets.

Performance standards are not being proposed for the NYTD but could be developed after sufficient data are accumulated. Penalties are proposed for failure to comply with the data collection and reporting requirements that are enacted.

Strengths and Weaknesses of the Current Monitoring Systems

Adequacy of the Methodology

The child and family services review is a two-stage process. The first stage, referred to as the Statewide Assessment, relies primarily on AFCARS and NCANDS data. The second stage involves an on-site review of child and family service outcomes and systemic factors to further explore and corroborate the findings of the statewide assessment (National Resource Center for Child Welfare Data and Technology, 2006 State Data Profile Toolkit Section 1: Chapter 1).

The on-site portion of the review includes the following: (1) case record reviews, (2) interviews with children and families engaged in services, and (3) interviews with community stakeholders, such as the courts and community agencies, foster families, and caseworkers and service providers. The initial protocol for the case reviews called for a total sample of

50 cases divided between children in foster care and children remaining in their homes. The actual average number of case reviews conducted in the first round was 21 in-home cases and 28 foster care cases (Children's Bureau, 2006). In round two of the CFSRs the case review protocol calls for a sample of 75 in each state ranging across all program areas and drawn from at least three sites from across the state (National Resource Center for Child Welfare Data and Technology, 2006 State Data Profile Toolkit Section 1: Chapter 1).

The case reviews, which are the primary source of data on the well-being outcomes, also collect data on permanence and safety outcomes. No well-being outcome measures are constructed from the AFCARS or NCANDS data. To receive a rating of "substantial conformity" for the well-being outcomes, at least 90% of the applicable cases reviewed must have been rated as having "substantially achieved" that outcome. Median scores on the three well-being measures in the first round of CFSRs ranged from 63 to 80%. The new and larger proposed sample size of 75 cases divided at least in half for in-home and out-of-home cases would yield 30 to 40 cases to calculate an individual state's substantial conformity rate. The statistical power of a sample of this size would be sufficient to detect departures from near perfect proficiency at the 0.05 significance level (see Chapter 5, this volume). But it would be clearly inadequate for distinguishing with any precision the best from the worst states with regard to their ratings on the well-being measures. The proposed sample size of 75 cases would yield sample estimates of 75% substantial achievement in the population on well-being outcomes with a margin of error of approximately plus or minus 10 percentage points.

The on-site reviews can be viewed as an adequate methodology for identifying deviations from near perfect performance on well-being outcomes and for supplementing the findings from the analyses of AFCARS and NCANDS data with respect to the safety and permanency outcomes. The AFCARS is a federally mandated system for collecting data on children in foster care and children who have been adopted under the auspices of the state child welfare agency. AFCARS data are submitted semiannually on a federal fiscal year basis. NCANDS is a collaborative, voluntary information collection system that gathers and analyzes annual state statistics on all reports of abused and neglected children. NCANDS data are collected annually on a calendar year basis.

Because all children in foster care or reported for child maltreatment are included in these data sets, sampling size and statistical power to reliably measure outcomes are not an issue. A major criticism that has been made regarding the safety and permanency outcome measures used in the first round of CFSRs has been the use of exit cohort measures instead of entry cohorts (Martin Bishop, Grazian, McDonald, Testa, & Gatowski, 2002; Courtney, Needell, & Wulczyn, 2003; Zeller & Gamble, nd). The problem with exit cohort measures, which are based on discharge data, is that they do not provide a valid or reliable picture of the flow of children through the foster care system because they exclude cases that have not yet exited for the reporting period. This problem was in part a consequence of a provision of ASFA that the outcome measures should be developed, to the extent possible, from AFCARS. This mandatory data collection system was implemented in the mid-1990s to replace the voluntary reporting programs on which HHS had relied prior to 1974 and during the 1980s. In 1986, federal legislation authorized the HHS secretary to convene an advisory committee to study "the various methods of establishing, administering, and financing a system for the collection of data with respect to adoption and foster care in the United States" (Administration for Children, Youth, and Families, 1987: 49). The committee recommended the implementation of a mandatory reporting system that collected individual child-level, case information from the states.

Consultants to the committee recommended a longitudinal data analysis system that followed children's progress from the point of entry into foster care to the point of exit from public custody (Fanshel, Finch, & Grundy, 1987; Testa, 1987). Computerized information systems that collected longitudinal data on child cases were just becoming operational at the time in some of the larger child welfare jurisdictions. Many of the smaller state and county-operated systems, however, still lacked this capacity. As a result, the advisory committee settled on a more familiar cross-sectional design that was patterned after point-in-time counts of foster children in institutional facilities, public custody, or as part of the decennial enumeration of the U.S. population. The committee justified its decision stating that child-level data were to be used for "conducting program and policy analyses and generating reports, and not be used for tracking individual children" (Advisory Committee on Adoption and Foster Care Information, 1987: 46).

The federal AFCARS regulations that HHS published in 1993 patterned the reporting and analysis system after the point-in-time collection procedures more commonly in use by child welfare jurisdictions at the time. To maintain client confidentiality, states were given the option of either assigning sequential numbers to case data or encrypting case identifiers to protect confidentiality. Little consideration was given at the time to the implications of hampering the ability to link case-level data across reporting periods, which some federal officials perceived as violating the prohibition on tracking.[1] As long as AFCARS was able to generate point-in-time case counts and report retrospectively the number of foster care entries and exits for simulating yearly case flow dynamics, federal officials saw little need for retaining the capacity to track case progress longitudinally across reporting periods from the date of entry to the date of exit.

The importance of tracking AFCARS data longitudinally eventually came to light after Congress mandated the development of a set of outcome measures in 1997 to assess and rank state performance. Saddled with a data collection system that allowed only point-in-time description and retrospective reporting of outcomes, HHS did its best to make do with the available data. The department promulgated a list of indicators that was based mostly on cases that had either exited the foster care system or else remained active at the end of the reporting period. The major problem with most of these measures is that they selectively throw away cases and truncate the measurement of outcomes, which can misguide practitioners' and administrators' assessment of child welfare trends and system performance.

Selectivity and Censoring

The problems with the point-in-time and retrospective reporting structure of AFCARS can be illustrated with the three types of foster care samples that are generated by the stock and flow of cases in and out of foster care: (1) *cross-sectional counts* of active foster care cases (stocks), (2) *exit cohorts* of children discharged from foster care (outflow), and (3) *entry cohorts* of children coming into foster care (inflow). Figure 4.4 charts the annual changes in foster care case flow for the state of Illinois for federal fiscal years 1981–2006. The cross-sectional count of children in foster care is the sum of the number of children in care at the start of the reporting period (federal fiscal year) plus the cohort of children who enter care minus the cohort of children who exit care during the period. As illustrated in Figure 4.4, the cross-sectional count of foster children rises when the number of entries exceeds the number of exits from the system (point A) and declines when the number of exits exceeds the number of entries (point B).

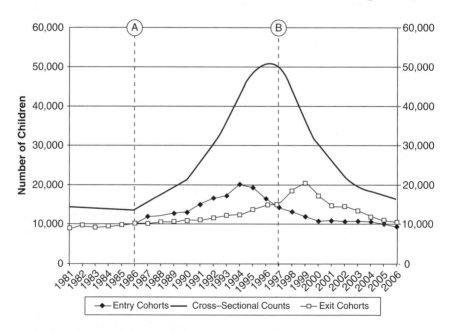

Figure 4.4 Illinois caseflow dynamics.

Considered all together, the three types of samples provide a complete statistical description of all children who have ever been served by the foster care system during a reporting period. The difficulty arises when outcome indicators are calculated for each type of sample separately. The problem is best understood as one of incomplete statistical description. Outcome indicators based on cross-sectional samples of active foster cases, for example, provide information only on still active child welfare cases, which as of a certain date have not attained the desired permanency outcomes of reunification, adoption, or guardianship. All that is known about the length of stay for these so-called *censored observations*—outcomes unseen by the observer—is that they are greater than the cumulative time the children thus far have spent in foster care. This is depicted in Figure 4.5, in which the open circles indicate observations that are censored at the end dates of each 6-month AFCARS reporting period. Because cross-sectional samples tend to omit cases that experience short durations of care, e.g., child 2, cross-sectional statistics tend to be slanted toward the experiences of children with the least statisfactory permanency outcomes.

Exit cohort samples suffer from the opposite kind of selection bias. The end points marked with an X indicate discharges from care. The four discharged cases between reporting periods 1B and 2B (children 1, 2, 5, and 7) constitute the exit cohort for this annual reporting period. Even though their lengths of stay are known exactly, i.e., *uncensored*, the times to discharge are observed only for the subset of ever-served children who experience a permanency outcome or exit for other reasons. Censored

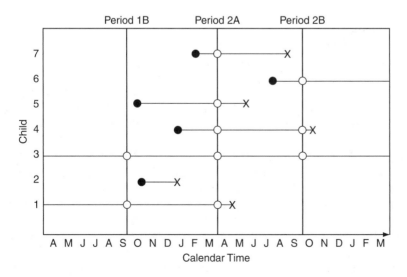

Figure 4.5 Selectivity and censoring in a hypothetical sample of seven subjects.

data for children just beginning a lengthy episode (child 6) or with an episode that spans several reporting periods (child 3) are overlooked.

Only entry cohort samples capture the experience of both uncensored and censored observations. Even though episodes of care that began prior to the start of the reporting period (children 1 and 3) are ignored, the outcomes for all children in an entry cohort are eventually observed in the long run. Cases with long durations of care must be tracked prospectively sometimes for years in order to observe the outcomes completely. Fortunately, methods of survival, failure-time, and event-history analysis can readily be applied to entry cohorts to model time-to-outcome data even in the absence of complete information (Shlonsky, Festinger, & Brookhart, 2006).

Time-to-Outcome Data

Statistics calculated from the three types of samples are sensitive both to the truncation of measurement and to the sample selectivity that arises from different cases being included or excluded as a result of case flow dynamics. This can be illustrated by comparing the median lengths of stay calculated for cross-sectional, exit cohort, and entry cohort samples. Although the measures sound similar, they measure different durations of time in care and can frequently yield very different assessments of performance trends.

Figure 4.6 shows the trend lines for three measures of median length of stay based on the different samples of cases. The median based on cross-sectional counts measures the cumulative amount of time that 50% of the children have spent in foster care at the end of the reporting period. This calculation yields on average the lengthiest of the three measures of median length of stay. This is because timely exits to permanence tend to be excluded from point-in-time calculations. Children with extended foster care episodes are likely to be counted in cross-sectional samples and children with shorter times in care are likely to be omitted.

Looking only at the exit cohort sample of children who leave care solves the censoring problem but at the expense of selecting a potentially biased subsample of foster children. The median length of stay for exit cohorts measures the cumulative amount of time that 50% of the children have spent in care at the point of discharge. These statistics point to sharply rising lengths of stay in Illinois between federal fiscal year 1994 and 1999 (points A and B). But this impression is largely an artifact of the reforms that the state implemented in the mid-1990s to expedite the discharge of foster children from long-term kinship foster care to adoption and guardianship (Testa, 2002). Counting only exits during this period gives the misleading impression that the median time that children were spending in care was rising.

The preferred solution is to track the time that all children spend in care. This is best done on an entry cohort of children placed into foster care.

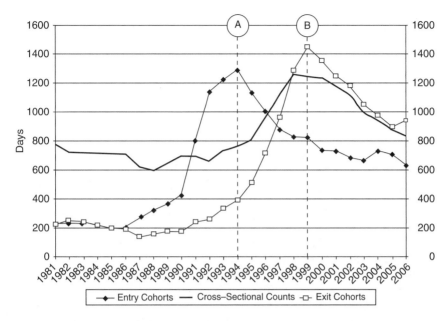

Figure 4.6 Three measures of median length of stay.

Calculations of length of stay for entry cohorts eventually capture the experiences of all children ever-served and in the interim provide valid estimates of the time that different fractions of children are expected to remain in care. As depicted in Figure 4.6, clocking the cumulative length of time that 50% of the children spend in care before discharge shows that the median length of stay was consistently declining during the period that both the exit cohort and cross-sectional estimates suggested the opposite was occurring. Prior to 2003, the federal *Child Welfare Outcomes* annual report calculated median lengths of stay only for the cross-sectional and exit cohort samples because of the barriers to linking case records across reporting periods. But as shown in Figure 4.6, ignoring the median time that entry cohorts spend in care can give erroneous signals about the performance of a child welfare system.[2] These distortions also extend to other outcome indicators that are based solely on cross-sectional or exit cohort samples.

Sensitivity Analysis of Censored Outcome Indicators

Many of the current federal indicators of child outcomes are affected by sample selectivity, truncated measurement, or other biases due to incomplete data. The national standard for family reunification, for example, still relies in part on the exit cohort sample of children reunified within the preceding annual reporting period. It looks backward at how long cases had been in foster care prior to reunification. Timeliness of adoptions also retains a retrospective measure in the construction of the composite score. Comparing these retrospective indicators based on exit cohorts to alternative prospective indicators based on entry cohorts can give very different readings on system performance.

The principal reason for the difference is that the federal retrospective measures again selectively include only reunified or adopted children in the year-to-year comparisons, whereas the alternative prospective measures track the experiences of all children entering foster care. Selectively discarding cases can give misleading signals to practitioners and administrators. Consider, for example, the cases depicted in Figure 4.5. During the annual reporting period between Period 1B and Period 2B, there were seven children ever served in foster care. We will assume that all four of the children who exited from care were reunified with their birth parents. Thus of the seven children ever served, just four would be included in the federal calculation of whether a state meets the national standard. Because three of the four reunifications occurred within 12 months of removal, the overall performance is 75%, which just falls short of the national reunification standard. But under what circumstances is it appropriate to exclude the three censored observations from the assessment? Beyond the statistical issues, ignoring censored observations might increase agency risks by rewarding bad practice (inadvertent or intentional). For example, curtailing reunification efforts for a child who has been in foster care for longer than 12 months drops child 1 from the exit cohort sample and pushes the retrospective measure of reunification above the national standard to 100%. States that defected in this fashion from fiduciary norms of permanency planning would always look better than states that appropriately reunified children after a year in foster care (Martin Bishop et al., 2002).

Table 4.1 illustrates the sensitivity of the federal reunification exit measure to different assumptions made about the three censored cases

TABLE 4.1 Sensitivity Analysis of Federal Reunification Measure Under Different Censoring Assumptions

		Reunified in Less Than 12 Months From Removal			
	Number of Children	Observed	Estimate A (Best Case)	Estimate B (Worst Case)	Estimate C
In care at end of reporting period	3	? + 0	2	0	1.5
Exited care during reporting period	4	3	3	3	3
Total N (%)	7	? + 0 + 3	5 (71.4%)	6 (42.9%)	4.5 (64.3%)

still in foster care. This illustration draws from a technical note by Shih (2002) on the problems of dealing with missing data and censoring in clinical trials. The missing data problem reflects the fact that the overall reunification rate within 12 months of removal for all seven ever-served children is unknown because the times to reunification are censored for two of the observations and (left) truncated for one (child 1). In this later case even though the actual time to reunification is unknown because of a missing entry date, it is obvious from the cumulative time spent in care that reunification for this child did not occur within 12 months from removal. The next three columns present a kind of sensitivity analysis of the possible impact of different assumptions about the remaining two censored observations.

Estimate A assumes that the two observations experience reunification immediately after the censoring date. Under the best of circumstances, the estimated percentage of children reunified within 12 months is 71.4%. Estimate B (42.9%) is the worst case scenario. It assumes that neither child is reunified within 12 months. Estimate C (64.3%) is in between these two extremes. It assumes that the proportion of children among the censored observations that would have been reunified within a year is the same as the proportion observed for the exit cohort sample (75%). This sensitivity analysis illustrates that even under the best of circumstances the proportion of children reunified in fewer than 12 months is less than the 75% obtained when only exits are counted and censored cases are ignored.

Other CFSR measures are similarly affected by the practice of treating truncated data as if they were *uncensored*, that is, as if the time to an event of interest were known exactly. *Truncation* is a form of censoring in which the occurrence of an event of interest is inexactly observed. All that is known about the times to the event is that it is less than (left truncated) or greater than (right truncated) a specific date or in between two dates (interval truncated data). The current CFSR of measures of placement stability, for example, treat truncated data on placement moves as if they were uncensored. The placement stability composite score is based on three measures that look at the number of placement settings for children in care: (1) more than 8 days but less than 12 months, (2) at least 12 months but less than 24 months, and (3) more than 24 months.

Treating censored data for children entering care near the end of the reporting period as though they were in stable care introduces obvious biases into the federal measurement of placement stability. Because the federal measure does not track all children for a full time period, the observation window for the first interval can vary from just 1 day (for children placed at the end of the federal fiscal year) to almost 12 months (for children placed at the start of the federal fiscal year). Similarly, including censored observations for children who exited care from their first or second placement introduces additional complications. Again the preferred solution to the problem of truncated measurement is to track placement changes prospectively for entry cohorts of children for a full year or more after their removal from the home. Event-history methods can handle right truncated data for children removed near the end of the reporting period, left truncated data for children in their fourth or higher-order placement setting, and interval truncated data, in which the timing of the third placement can be fixed only inexactly between upper and lower dates (Koh & Testa, 2008).

A different but related missing data problem is the incompleteness of information due to gaps in the outcome history. An example is the federal indicator of the institutionalization of children under the age of 12 years old that USDHHS reports to Congress (United States Department of Health and Human Services, nd). Even though the measure tracks the event of institutional care for an entry cohort sample, it is nonetheless incomplete because AFCARS data are available for only the last placement at the end of the 6-month reporting period. Children who were institutionalized immediately on entry would be missed if they were later transferred to a less restrictive setting prior to the end of the reporting period. As a consequence, children who enter foster care toward the end of the federal fiscal year would have a greater chance of being observed in a restrictive setting than children who enter care earlier in the year because first placements are more likely to involve shelter care. For example, only 50% of U.S. children under the age of 12 years who entered foster care at the start of federal fiscal year 2003 were still in their first placement setting at the close of the reporting period compared to 80% who entered foster care near the end of the fiscal year. The observed rates of institutionalization for the earlier and later cohorts were 90 per 1000 and 130 per 1000, respectively. Thus a state with decreasing numbers of children entering foster care could exhibit lower institutionalization rates than a state with rising numbers entering care even though the underlying incidence of the institutionalization of young children was the same in both states.

While policymakers have seemingly acknowledged the problem with exit cohort measures in the modifications to the second round of CFSRs, they have seen fit to add entry cohort measures while retaining measures based on discharge data. The problems with this approach are addressed more fully in a later section that looks at the outcome measures as a set. It should also be noted that the entry cohort measures that have been added in constructing the CFSR composite scores are extremely constrained by the limitations of the annual AFCARS data files, which do not directly allow for tracking beyond a 12-month period.

The proposed methodology for generating the NYTD is much stronger than that used in either the AFCARS or NCANDS analyses or case reviews under the CFSRs. Although the use of common identifiers will permit linking cases from NYTD with AFCARS, the NYTD is an independently generated data set. The 17 year olds in foster care are to be selected by random sampling or another accepted sampling methodology, and the same youths will be tracked for two observation periods at ages 19 and 21 years. Accepted statistical protocols are followed to calculate minimum sample sizes. States with 1000 17 year olds in foster care, for example, would draw a minimum random sample of 214 youth, which is sufficient to estimate the proportion of 17 year olds in foster care that are males within a 90% margin of error of plus/minus 5.6 percentage points.

Adequacy of the Individual Outcome Measures

Measures based on sample sizes much below the minimums set for the NYTD are too small to yield relatively precise scores. Sample sizes of 50 to 75 cases as are used for the on-site CFSR reviews cannot be adequate. Similarly, measures that utilize data from AFCARS or NCANDS may also be inadequate if the source data are not valid and reliable. Administrative data bases such as AFCARS and NCCANDS are known to have difficulty in achieving common definitions across states and ensuring data quality (General Accounting Office, 2003a,b). The latter are natural and inevitable difficulties, but with increased use of the data for monitoring outcomes it can be hoped that the quality and uniformity of the data will steadily improve.

Perhaps a greater concern for the CFSR system is the need to more clearly define and differentiate outcome and process measures. At the broadest conceptual level the three identified goals of child welfare—safety, permanence, and well-being—appear to be focusing on legitimate outcomes for these children and families. However, the seven slightly more operational definitions of these outcomes immediately begin to slip toward more process measures. This is particularly true for the three child and family well-being outcomes, which focus on services received rather than the outcomes of those services.

The indicators for Safety Outcome 1—Children are, first and foremost, protected from abuse and neglect—focus clearly on the outcome measures of recurrence of maltreatment and maltreatment while in foster care. The second safety outcome—Children are safely maintained in their homes whenever possible and appropriate—relies on the on-site case reviews.

For permanency outcome 1—Children have permanence and stability in their living situations—the major focus is appropriately on permanency outcomes of reunification and adoption. However, a fourth composite measure under this outcome looks at placement stability, which, arguably, is more of a process or output construct than an outcome of the child welfare system. The second permanency outcome—the continuity of family relationships and connections is preserved for children—relies on the on-site case reviews that, as previously discussed, are hampered by too small sample sizes for creating a reliable measure.

The six outcomes shown in Figure 4.3 for the NYTD resulted after ACF engaged in an information-gathering process with stakeholders. Three criteria were used in selecting and rejecting outcomes generated in this process: (1) the overall importance, (2) the relevance to assessing accountability of the state's CFCIP agency, and (3) the ease with which they could be measured. It is interesting to note the proposed outcomes that were rejected: a youth's access to essential documents; ethnic, cultural, and personal identity; social isolation; healthcare utilization (including mental health); leadership qualities; and general well-being, such as hopefulness, optimism, and resiliency. Some of these measures would be considered process measures (e.g., access to documents, healthcare utilization) whereas others refer to outcomes of a more expressive nature (e.g., identity, hopefulness, optimism). The adopted measures refer to outcomes of a more instrumental nature, particularly financial self-sufficiency, educational attainment, and homelessness. Arguably, positive connections to adults, reduced high-risk behavior, and access to health insurance are means to achieving healthy adulthood.

The Validity and Integrity of Outcomes Monitoring Systems

In their article "Managing for Outcomes: The Selection of Sets of Outcome Measures," Poertner, Moore, and McDonald (2008) point to the need to consider both the validity and integrity of a results-oriented accountability system. Validity refers to the efficacy and effectiveness of the system in attaining the outcomes valued by its principals. Integrity refers to the success of the system in discouraging defections from these broader public purposes by its agents. As discussed, results-oriented accountability begins with the definition of a counterbalanced set of outcomes as a whole because of the potential interactions that may occur between them. This is particularly important in the field of child welfare in which, as was argued in Chapter 2, different perspectives on serving the best interests of children are historically in tension with one another.

Poertner et al. (2008) propose seven criteria for evaluating the validity and integrity of a set of outcome measures:

1. The set of outcome measures should be understandable.
2. The set should contain as few measures as possible.
3. The costs and benefits of data collection should be considered.
4. The set of indicators should count all outcomes that occur as children move through the system.
5. Perverse incentives and other agency risks should be avoided.

6. A set of measures needs to be able to capture genuine change and avoid being susceptible to agent manipulation (e.g., goal displacement, opportunistic gaming, and outright fraud).
7. The set should include indicators that counterbalance each other.

Understandable Measures

Poertner et al. (2008) maintain that in addition to making sense to agency staff, administrators, and professionals in the child welfare field, outcome measures in child welfare should be transparent to and interpretable by individual principals and the general public. They offer the following litmus test for judging a set of outcome measures on this criterion: "Does your mother, father, aunt, or uncle understand?" They argue that outcome measures should be easy to understand not only by professionals and other agents but by parents, caregivers, citizens, and other principals.

This standard may not be totally realistic, necessary, or relevant. Whereas roughly 50% of all households in the United States invest in the stock market, most would have a hard time understanding an annual report from any of the companies in which they had investments. Bottom lines tend to suffice even when the public has a direct "investment" and risk. Public trust in child welfare tends to oscillate with anecdotal and sensational stories. A child dies in an abusive home, and the public demands that the system should be more safety oriented. Children are "wrongly" removed, and the system is denounced as insufficiently oriented toward family preservation. Public accountability in child welfare frequently asks agents to be answerable for both positive outcomes simultaneously—goals that are difficult to maximize at the same time in every case.

Nevertheless, the public has a right to expect that someone is minding the store. Accountability must include some "counting" and the numbers should at least make sense to an outside observer with moderate interest, competence, and background. At their more abstract levels, the three identified goals of safety, permanence, and well-being, and the seven outcomes under these goals (see Fig. 4.1), as well as the six Chafee outcomes seem quite understandable. In the first round of the CFSRs, the measures used to operationalize these outcomes were expressed as percentages. For example, one of the indicators of permanence was the timeliness of reunification, measured as the percentage of children reunified with their parents or caretakers that was reunified in less than 12 months. Although this measure is subject to selectivity and other measurement problems discussed earlier in this chapter, it would appear to be fairly understandable to most interested persons. The same could be said of the majority of other indicators in the first round of CFSRs, particularly those constructed from the AFCARS and NCCANDS data bases. Reporting of these percentages with some measure that provides a basis for comparison (e.g., threshold, range of scores, ranking) is fairly user friendly. However, the federal review process also imposed standards in interpreting these percentages that made the process of judging performance more explicit but less understandable to others. In the case of the example used here for "timely reunification" the threshold standard is that 76.2% of the cases had to be reunified in less than 12 months from the date of removal. Although this makes it easier to say that a state is either successful or not, the rationale for the choice of this threshold of success is much less understandable.[3]

The new composite measures that are being used in the second round of CFSRs are extremely difficult for nearly anyone to understand. The composite scores are obtained by summing weighted scores on multiple related individual measures. The initial measures are expressed most often as percentages or days. They are first converted to Z-scores so they no longer have any metric. The combined composite score then also has no metric and principals and agents do not readily know which individual items contributed most to the composite score. The final number of the composite score then has no real meaning other than in comparison to an equally obscure national standard that is different for every composite. Significant effort has been invested by some groups to make these technical matters more transparent by visually portraying the composites in graphic form, but the rationale behind weighting items differently still remains opaque to most workers and administrators.

No reports have yet been generated for the NYTD so the exact format is uncertain. However, it appears that at least for the initial phases of this outcome monitoring process interpretation would be straightforward and that most elements used to measure the six outcomes would be simply reported as the percentage answering "yes" or "no" to specific questions. Inclusion of some basis for an individual state's comparison (e.g., mean, median, percentile, or ranking) would readily enhance the interpretability of these data.

The Set Should Contain as Few Measures as Possible

Certainly one advantage of the composites used in the second round of CFSRs is that they potentially reduce the number of measures. Combining individual measures into a scale or composite score can reduce the utility of the data if the items being combined do not hang together conceptually and statistically. This would not appear to be a weakness of the composite scores. The composites include items that at least have face validity (i.e., the items in the Timeliness and Permanence of Reunification composite all relate to reunification and reentry). In addition, the composites were formed on the basis of a statistical analysis (principal components analysis or PCA) of actual data so the individual measures are known to be correlated with one another.

However, it should be remembered that the six data indicators generated from the AFCARS and NCCANDS data only measure two of the seven outcomes (safety outcome #1 and permanency outcome #1). A more complete representation of both the outcome and systemic indicators reported from the CFSRs is to be found in the State Data Profile, which is provided to the state prior to development of the Statewide Assessment. These profiles include the composites that are used to assess a state's conformity with timeliness and permanence of reunification, timeliness of adoption, achieving permanence for children in foster care, and placement stability. The data profiles also include statewide aggregate data indicators for which the Children's Bureau has established national standards used to determine substantial conformity as well as information that was provided in the first round of the CFSR.

An individual state's data profile is 16 pages long. The profile contains well over 100 rows of data with each row containing scores for 3 years. Some indicators in the data profile include counts and percentages for "unique" as well as "duplicated" cases. In its current form, the State Data Profile does not appear to be a functional report for focusing agency administrators and staff on what is important in assessing their performance.

Only 16 data elements (plus two more for youth out of foster care) are currently included in the proposed outcome survey for the NYTD. This would appear quite manageable and the elements are readily linked to the six outcomes. The danger is that as this process moves toward implementation additional elements and outcomes might be added.

The Costs and Benefits of Data Collection Should Be Considered

The challenge of constructing the best measures at the least cost takes considerable effort and thought. The CFSR measures and process cannot be faulted for lack of planning and discussion. As noted earlier in this chapter, although the CFSRs did not begin until 2000, the mandate from Congress to develop regulations for reviewing state CFSR programs came in 1994. The measures and process for constructing them came after years of consultation with experts in the child welfare field and after the instrument was field tested in 14 states before official implementation in 2000. The plan to develop data composites is a response to a recommendation made by an ACF consultant hired to study the CFSR process with input from a workgroup convened by the consultant at the end of the first round of CFSRs to assist in identifying areas needing improvement.

The considerable costs of data collection may be a useful argument for not implementing a new measure (Poertner et al., 2008). In part, CFSRs utilize existing data collection systems (NCAANDS and AFCARS) for which there have already been huge expenditures of federal and state dollars. This would appear to be a wise and efficient decision. However, sometimes existing data systems are inadequate for constructing meaningful outcome measures. As previously discussed, a major weakness of the outcome measures constructed from the AFCARS data in the first round of CFSRs was its use of exit cohorts rather than measures constructed from entry cohorts. Analyses based on entry cohorts require longitudinal data and the NCCANDS and AFCARS data bases are not routinely constructed this way. However, researchers in the field have successfully constructed the necessary longitudinal data bases from AFCARS and NCAANDS data files and most state data bases can be manipulated to construct longitudinal files for cohort analyses (Zeller & Gamble, nd; Testa, Koh, & Poertner, 2008). The notice of proposed rulemaking (NPRM) that ACF released in 2008 would modify the AFCARS reporting requirements along the lines required for longitudinal data analysis.

Although the second round of the CFSRs incorporates some entry cohort measures they tend to employ limited follow-up periods because of constraints of the federal data systems or are combined in composite scores with other measures. As an example, the "Timeliness and Permanence of Reunification" composite includes a cohort measure of reentry in which the entry cohort is restricted to the last 6 months of the previous year and a discharge measure of the percentage of reunified cases that were reunified in less than 12 months.

The on-site portion of the review includes the following: (1) case record reviews, (2) interviews with children and families engaged in services, and (3) interviews with community stakeholders, such as the courts and community agencies, foster families, and caseworkers and service providers. This effort represents a huge investment of dollars and staff time and produces imprecise information regarding state performance because of the small samples drawn for the case reviews. The costs simply outweigh the benefits. The current process should be viewed only as a supplemental qualitative study that identifies areas of weakness and could lend insight into agency performance if done in conjunction with a rigorous quantitative analysis based on data from the entire system or with a more statistically valid sample.

Estimates of exact costs of implementing the NYTD are not known. The Unfunded Mandates Reform Act (P.L. 104-4) requires agencies to prepare an assessment of anticipated costs and benefits before proposing any rule that may result in an annual expenditure by state, local, and tribal governments, in the aggregate, or by the private sector, of $100 million or more (adjusted annually for inflation). The view of ACF is that the proposed rule does not impose any mandates on state, local, or tribal governments, or the private sector that will result in an annual expenditure of $100 million or more. Many of the data processing costs that states incur as a result of NYTD may be eligible for federal financial participation at the 50% rate depending on whether the costs to develop and implement the NYTD are allowable costs under a state's approved planning document for SACWIS. States may also use their allotment of federal Chafee funds to implement NYTD. Additional costs to the federal government to develop and implement a system to collect NYTD data are expected to be minimal (*Federal Register*, 71:135)

The greater challenge to states in complying with the requirements of the NYTD is that it involves very different data collection methods than states are accustomed to carrying out in generating AFCARS and NCANDS data. State agencies are generally not experienced in conducting surveys and tracking clients after they exit programs. Contracting for these activities may be the most viable option for many states.

The Set of Indicators Should Count All Outcomes that Occur as Children Move through the System

The measures used in the first round of CFSRs were heavily focused on what happens early in a child's foster placement and did not capture general permanency information for children in foster care for a relatively long period of time. Nationally, about 50% of the children in foster care on any given day have been in foster care for about 2 years or longer. In 2004 over 22,000 children aged out of foster care nationally (Children Welfare League of America, 2006).

In response to this concern, ACF developed a new permanency composite measure: achieving permanence for children in foster care for long periods of time. The new composite measure consists of two components and three individual measures that attempt to focus on reducing the time in foster care and achieving permanence through a discharge to adoption, guardianship, or reunification rather than emancipation. These changes represent an improvement in the set of measures used for the CFSRs in the second round with regard to this criterion, but the measures themselves suffer from some of the previously discussed shortcomings (use of exit cohorts and limited use of entry cohorts).

The NYTD would further supplement missing information on older youth in foster care and would provide previously unavailable data on their outcomes after leaving foster care. These data are vital to recognizing that all children entering foster care will not achieve permanence through reunification or placement with another family.

The existing and proposed measures still suffer from a lack of attention to the front end of the child welfare system. None of the data indicators constructed from the AFCARS or NCCANDS data addresses entry rates into foster care. The Child Safety Profile contained in the State Data Profile does include substantiation or indicated rates and placement rates as a percentage of cases substantiated or indicated, but no national standards are provided and it is not clear how these are used in judging "substantial conformity."

Perverse Incentives Should Be Avoided

Perverse incentives are unintended consequences that are seldom seen before they occur. Avoidance requires careful planning before implementing a set of outcome measures and judicious monitoring after implementation. Major perverse incentive existed in the first round of CFSR outcome measures as a result of counting children in care during some time periods and not others. For example, reunifications were counted for the first 12 months and adoptions for the first 24 months in care. As noted, reunifications or adoptions occurring after these time periods could actually end up hurting the state's outcome performance score. Similarly, the CFSR's heavy reliance on cut-offs and other performance thresholds also can create incentives for caseworkers and administrators to concentrate their attention on children just above the thresholds. For example, with respect to the Round I reunification measure there was an incentive for administrators to focus agency efforts on speeding up the reunification process for children discharged during their thirteenth and fourteenth month in care and to ignore reunifications significantly below or above the threshold. The addition of measures for children in foster care for long periods of time, described in the previous section, somewhat reduces this potential for perverse incentives.

There also is a bias toward measures that emphasize nuclear family-based definitions of permanence. In the first round of CFSRs, legal guardianship and other planned permanent living arrangements with the extended family were not counted as permanency outcomes. Although not recognized as a separate indicator in the second round of CFSRs, legal guardianship is now included as a permanency outcome in constructing a permanency measure for children in foster care for an extended period of time.

On the other hand, neither version of the CFSRs includes indicators that are sensitive to the state's performance in keeping children out of foster care. This creates an agency risk for "creaming" by bringing children into foster care who could otherwise have been maintained in their own homes perhaps with some in-home services. Because such children are likely to be reunified quickly, widening the foster care net will show up as improved agency performance on the reunification measure unless it is counterbalanced by a measure that tracks the rate of child removals.

The proposed NYTD appears to have anticipated possible perverse incentives and other agency risks that could arise if the survey were limited to youth receiving independent services while in foster care. The final rule calls for surveying all (or a random sample of all) 17 year olds in foster care regardless of independent living services they are receiving or received. If only those receiving services were surveyed it might create an incentive to limit eligibility for services.

A Set of Measures Needs to be Able to Capture Genuine Changes and Avoid Being Susceptible to Administrative Manipulation

Perverse incentives, although unintended at the outset, can be subject to administrative manipulation if not corrected once they are recognized. The consequences of failing to monitor the front door of the child welfare system is probably well recognized now and has not been adequately addressed in the new measures.

Measures that are based on cut-offs and thresholds are more susceptible to manipulation. As an example, Poertner et al. (2008) point to the difficulty of defining a "placement setting" in constructing a measure of placement stability. The measure creates an additional risk for opportunistic gaming. Because the three individual measures of placement stability all define stability as "two or fewer placement settings," agents might focus on retaining children in undesirable second placements but pay little attention to foster home changes after a third move.

How the outcome indicators are used to motivate performance can also heighten or mitigate agency risks. Poertner et al. (2008) suggest that

> Another way to discourage administrative manipulation is to develop a culture that rewards openness and positive performance. . . . This requires a context that includes a tolerance for admitting errors, judgments based on substance, egalitarianism and a commitment to learning. Sets of outcome indicators used in this context will encourage learning and not manipulation (Poerter *et al.*, 2008, p. 14).

The CFSR review process results in a Final Report that is prepared within 30 days of the on-site review or resolution of any discrepancies in information collected during the Statewide Assessment and on-site review. The Final Report includes the written determination of substantial conformity for each of the outcomes and systemic factors reviewed. At the end of the on-site review, states determined not to have achieved substantial conformity in one or more of the areas assessed are required to develop and implement Program Improvement Plans addressing the area(s) of nonconformity. The CFSRs take a hierarchical approach to regulating agency relationships and "emphasize accountability through potential for financial penalties" (National Resource Center for Child Welfare Data and Technology, 2006 State Data Profile Toolkit Section 1, Pages 1–4). With regard to the national data measures, ACF has not required that a state meet the national standard in order to avoid financial penalties, only that the state demonstrates an agreed-on amount of progress in moving toward the standard. Nevertheless, this would not appear to be an optimal environment for discouraging gaming and manipulation of the assessment process and outcome scores.

Because the proposed NYTD does not include standards, states could not be penalized for failure to meet standards initially. However, the language in the proposed rules suggests that standards will be developed once data become available and there is considerable discussion of penalties for states failing to comply with data collection and reporting requirements. In general, the tone of the proposal seems consistent with the more punitive stance taken in the CFSRs.

The Set Should Include Indicators that Counterbalance Each Other

Chapter 2 outlined the challenges of a results-oriented accountability system in child welfare: the oscillations between a narrow focus on child safety and a diffuse public interest in child well-being, the ambivalence over agency relationships based on rule and procedure and those rooted in kinship, faith, and community, and the trade-offs between short-term reunification gains and long-term reentry risks. These tensions are well known and very difficult to balance in practice. Most administrators, supervisors, and caseworkers tend to focus on one goal or at best on several goals sequentially. One recent exception to this tendency is the advent of concurrent planning practices that expects workers to consider family continuity and alternative permanency outcomes simultaneously. Research has similarly tended to focus on predicting or impacting single outcomes. Exceptions are rare and analytic techniques are relatively new and complex (see, for example, Testa, 2002; McDonald, Poertner, & Jennings, 2009; McDonald, Bryson, & Poertner, 2006).

With the notable exception of the lack of attention to the removal of children discussed in previous sections, the CFSRs appear fairly balanced in the inclusion of counterbalancing outcome measures. The main problem is the difficulty in focusing attention simultaneously on these multiple outcomes. This problem begins with the construction of standards that are based on maximizing each individual outcome rather than any understanding of what optimum, balanced outcomes would look like. When one focuses on maximizing one outcome, say reunification, another, in this case reentry, is likely to suffer.

The application of some of the previously described criteria can be helpful in addressing this problem. Fewer measures that are readily understandable are easier to process simultaneously. Insights into the optimization of multiple outcomes will need further research.

Summary and Conclusions

The primary focus of outcomes monitoring in public child welfare is on the three goals identified in ASFA as safety, permanence, and well-being. At the abstract level of construct validity, these three goals form a reasonable and fairly comprehensive set of accountability criteria. However, in operationalizing particular measures to match these goals and in implementing protocols for monitoring agency performance, the current system has numerous limitations with respect to both the validity of individual measures and the consequences for goal displacement, opportunistic gaming, and other agency risks.

The CFSRs are the mechanism by which the federal government assesses performance in the areas of safety, permanence, and child and family well-being. The strongest component of the CFSRs is in the area of monitoring safety and permanency outcomes for children who come into foster care. This strength derives from the use of administrative data bases (NCANDS and AFCARS) that are well established, provide some degree of reliability and validity, and provide data on all children who enter foster care. These measures could be further strengthened if they fully embraced the logic behind the use of entry cohorts and constructed more complete longitudinal data files from the NCANDS and AFCARS files to support this type of analyses.

The child welfare system in the United States has always lacked an emphasis on prevention. The safety and permanency measures and protocols of the CFSRs reflect this failure in that they do not provide monitoring of initial incidents of abuse, neglect, or initial out-of-home placements. This shortcoming creates a potential bias in favor of removing children from their homes and placing them in foster care. Because placement rates per 1000 children are not monitored in the CFSRs, there is no disincentive to removing children at higher rates. In fact, states with a high placement rate are rewarded with high scores on reunification and reentry measures as many of these children could have been maintained in their own homes without placement and less likely to reenter foster care.

The weakest area of the CFSR process is in the monitoring of child well-being, which is totally reliant on the case reviews. We judge the methodology of the case reviews to be hampered by sample sizes that may be adequate for detecting departures from flawless performance but are much too small to draw reliable or meaningful inferences about quality improvement (see Chapter 5 for a further discussion).

The change in social values reflecting risk aversion to long-term foster care resulted in a type of myopia that ignored the reality that some children would continue to age-out of foster care despite all attempts to reunify them with their birth families or find other permanent homes. This is reflected in the first round of CFSR measures, which contained no information on these children and also created perverse incentives for discontinuing permanency planning efforts on behalf of older youth. If children did not reach reunification or adoption by the target dates of 1 year for reunification and 2 years for adoption, continued permanency planning could hurt the state's performance measures only if the children reached these permanency goals later on. This problem has been addressed in the second round of the CFSRs; however, the focus remains on measuring permanence and little attention is paid to youth who are aging out of foster care.

The creation of the Chafee NYTD provides a much stronger emphasis on accountability for youth who are aging out of foster care. Agencies are to be held accountable not only for the delivery of services to these youth but for the progress they make toward self-sufficiency and living healthy and productive lives as young adults.

The perspective brought by this initiative is absolutely critical to the development of a fully accountable child welfare system. The specified outcomes, operational measures, and methodology for data collection are excellent and could provide a model for similar efforts.

The CFSRs are conducted every 4 years in individual states. This cycle is insufficient for ensuring agency accountability. This fact coupled with the unwieldy reporting format of the CFSRs, concerns about data quality, and the lack of substate level information has prompted many states to design parallel or complementary data monitoring systems. Although this activity at the state level has been stimulated by activities at the federal level, the self-reflexive and pragmatic nature of state endeavors may hold greater promise for promoting a culture of accountability as an alternative to the penalty-driven systems that invite goal displacement, opportunistic gaming, and other agency risks.

Notes

1. The perceived prohibition against tracking gradually changed over time. The HHS official who staffed the 1986 Advisory Committee later extolled the merits of encryption "since it facilitates the analysis of data, as an encrypted number can be used to follow a particular case over time across a sequence of AFCARS 6-month reporting periods" (Collins, 1999). He correctly noted that encryption allows for longitudinal analysis while protecting the child's identity. But he admitted that it was not certain to what extent failing to require a unique encrypted identifier would restrict the longitudinal analysis of AFCARS data.
2. Discharge times at the 25th or 75th percentile can also be calculated, and the proportion discharged from care at 1, 2, or 3 years after entry can serve as useful benchmarks for gauging performance. Some defenders of the exit measures have portrayed the necessity of tracking entry cohorts as a limitation. But just because an entry cohort must be followed for 2 years to determine the proportion discharged within 24 months does not mean that the information on children entering 2 years earlier is any less timely than the information on children discharged within the last year. Both are equally as current as of the date of last reporting. The difference is that an entry cohort constitutes a well-defined sample with known time referents, whereas the exit cohort is a hodgepodge of selected cases originating in different periods.
3. DHHS based national standards for data indicators on the 75th percentile of all states' performance for that indicator. It is not clear why or how all states could be expected to perform better than average.

References

Administration for Children, Youth, and Families. (1987). *Report of the Advisory Committee on Adoption and Foster Care Information.* Washington, DC: Author.

Children's Bureau (2006). Findings from the Initial Child and Family Service Reviews, 2001–2004, http://www.acf.hhs.gov/programs/cb/cwmonitoring/results/sld001.htm.

Child Welfare League of America. (2006). Special tabulation of the Adoption and Foster Care Analysis Reporting System. Washington, DC: Author. Available at http://ndas.cwla.org/data_stats/access/predefined/Report.asp?PageMode=1&ReportID=324&GUID={76D12616-FB88-45E1-9660-C16A9FBA03F2}#Table.

Collins, R. (1999). The adoption and foster care analysis and reporting system: Implications for foster care policy. In P. A. Curtis, G. Dale Jr., & J. C. Kendall (Eds.). *The foster care crisis: Translating research into policy and practice* (pp. 45–59). Lincoln, NE: University of Nebraska Press.

Collins, M. E. (2001). Transition to adulthood for vulnerable youths: A review of research and implications for policy. *Social Service Review, 75*(2), 271–291.

Collins, M. E. (2004). Enhancing services to youths leaving foster care: Analysis of recent legislation and its potential impact. *Children and Youth Services Review, 26*(11), 1051–1065.

Courtney, M. E., & Dworsky, A. (2006). Early outcomes for young adults transitioning out-of-home care in the U.S. *Child and Family Social Work, 11*(3), 209–219.

Courtney, M., Needell, B., & Wulczyn, F. (2003). *National standards in the child and family series reviews: Time to improve on a good idea.* Paper prepared for the Joint Center for Poverty Research Child Welfare Services Research and Its Policy Implications.

Fanshel, D., Finch, S. J., & Grundy, J. F. (1987). Collection of data relating to adoption and foster care. *Technical appendix to the report of the advisory committee on adoption and foster care information.* Washington, DC: Administration for Children, Youth and Families, USDHHS.

Freundlich, M., & Avery R. J. (2005). Planning for permanency for youth in congregate care. *Children and Youth Services Review, 27*(2), 115–134.

General Accounting Office. (2003a). *Child Welfare: Most States Are Developing Statewide Information Systems, but the Reliability of Child Welfare Data Could Be Improved.* GAO-03-809. Washington, DC: July 31, 2003.

General Accounting Office. (2003b). *Child Welfare: States Face Challenges in Developing Information Systems and Reporting Reliable Child Welfare Data.* GAO-04-267T. Washington, DC: November 19, 2003.

Georgiades, S. (2005). A multi-outcome evaluation of an independent living program. *Child and Adolescent Social Work Journal, 22*(5–6), 417–439.

Koh, E., & Testa, M. F. (2008). Propensity score matching of children in kinship and non-kinship foster care: Do permanency outcomes still differ? *Social Work Research, 32,* 105–116.

Lemon, K., Hines, A. M., & Merdinger, J. (2005). From foster care to young adulthood: The role of independent living programs in supporting successful transitions. *Children and Youth Services Review, 27*(3), 251–270.

Martin Bishop, P., Grazian, L., McDonald, J., Testa, M., & Gatowski, S. (2002). The need for uniformity in national statistics and improvements in outcome indicators for child and family services reviews: Lessons learned from child welfare reform in Illinois." *Whittier Journal of Child & Family Advocacy, 1*(1), 1–36.

McDonald, T., Bryson, S., & Poertner, J. (2006). Balancing reunification and reentry goals. *Children and Youth Services Review, 28,* 47–58.

McDonald, T., Poertner, J., & Jennings, M. A. (2009). Permanency for children in foster care: A competing risks analysis. *Journal of Social Service Research, 33*(4), 45–56.

McGowan, B. (2005). Historical evolution of child welfare services. In G. P. Mallon & P. McCartt Hess (Eds.), *Child welfare for the 21st century: A handbook of practices, policies, and programs* (pp. 10–48). New York: Columbia University Press.

Milner, J., Mitchell, L., & Hornsby, W. (2005). Child and family service reviews. In G. P. Mallon & P. McCartt Hess (Eds.), *Child welfare for the 21st century: A Handbook of practices, policies, and programs* (pp. 10–48). New York: Columbia University Press.

National Resource Center for Child Welfare Data and Technology, 2006 State Data Profile Toolkit Version: 7/19/06. Available at http://www.nrccwdt.org/cfsr/cfsr_toolkit.html.

Poertner, J., Moore, T., & McDonald T. (2008). Managing for outcomes: The selection of sets of outcome measures. *Administration in Social Work, 32*(4), 5–22.

Reilly, T. (2003). Transition from care: Status and outcomes of youth who age out of foster care. *Child Welfare, 82*(6), 727–746.

Shih, W. J. (2002). Problems in dealing with missing data and informative censoring in clinical trials. *Current Controlled Trials in Cardiovascular Medicine, 3*:4. Available at www.trialsjournal.com/content/3/1/4. Last accessed September 1, 2009.

Shlonsky, A., Festinger, T., & Brookhart, M. A. (2006). Is survival the fittest? A post hoc evaluation of event history estimations in an experimental design. *Children and Youth Services Review, 28*(7), 841–852.

Testa, M. (1988). Data necessary to support national policy functions in foster care and adoption. *Technical appendix to the report of the advisory committee on adoption and foster care information.* Washington, DC: Administration for Children, Youth and Families, USDHHS.

Testa, M. F. (2002). The gift of kinship foster care. *Children and Youth Services Review, 24*(1/2), 79–108.

Testa, M., Koh, E., & Poertner, J. (2008). Can AFCARS be rescued: Fixing the statistical yardstick that measures state child welfare performance. University of Illinois at Urbana, Champaign, School of Social Work, Children and Family Research Center. Available at: http://www.cfrc.illinois.edu/pubs/Pdf.files/CAN_AFCARS_BE_RESCUED_final.pdf

U.S. Department of Health and Human Services Administration for Children and Families "Title IV–E Foster Care Eligibility Reviews and Child and Family Services State Plan Reviews." *Federal Register* 65:16 (January 25, 2000), 4024–4025.

U.S. Department of Health and Human Services Administration for Children and Families "Invitation To Comment on Proposed Data Composites and Potential Performance Areas and Measures for the Child and Family Services Review." *Federal Register* 70:214 (November 7, 2005), 67479–67489.

U.S. Department of Health and Human Services Administration for Children and Families "The Data Measures, Data Composites, and National Standards To Be Used in the Child and Family Services Reviews." *Federal Register* 71:135 (June 7, 2006), 32986–32987.

U.S. Department of Health and Human Services Administration for Children and Families "Chafee National Youth in Transition Database." *Federal Register* 71:135 (July 14, 2006), 40346–40382.

U.S. Department of Health and Human Services Administration for Children and Families. (not dated). *Child welfare outcomes: 2002-2005: Report to Congress.* Washington, DC: Author. Available at www.acf.hhs.gov/programs/cb/pubs/cwo05/index.htm.

Zeller, D. E., & Gamble, T. J. (not dated). *Improving child welfare performance: Retrospective and prospective approaches.* South Portland, ME: Hornby Zeller Associates.

5

DATA FOR POLICY PLANNING AND ANALYSIS

Mark F. Testa

Results-oriented accountability in child welfare builds on the valid construction and reliable measurement of statistical indicators that systematically vary with the desired outcomes of safety, permanence, and well-being. The purposes of this chapter are to provide an overview of the *statistical validity* of observed associations between child welfare interventions and outcomes and to illustrate how greater *transparency* can be brought to the analysis of these relationships through statistical risk-adjustment analysis for variations in child demographic characteristics, family needs, and other conditions of the populations served by the child welfare system.

The principal sources of data about child welfare populations come from case files, survey interviews, standardized assessments, physical tests, and computerized administrative records. From these sources, statistical indicators can be constructed at various scales of measurement, e.g., dichotomous (safe, unsafe), multinomial (reunification, adoption, and guardianship), ordinal (less to more restrictive placement), counts (frequency of runaways), proportions (percentage of children reentering foster care), continuous measures (Child Behavior Checklist), and time-to-event (time to termination of parental rights). Ideally we try to draw child welfare data from a variety of sources and to measure as validly and reliably as possible the various facets of any single outcome, such as the incidence, type, severity, time to occurrence, and substantiation of child maltreatment. In practical applications, however, data analysis must rely on a narrower set of sources and statistical indicators than what most child welfare professionals would consider optimal, such as counts of repeat child maltreatment reports or administrative data on times to reunification with birth families.

This chapter focuses primarily on the analysis of data from computerized administrative records and case review samples. Advances in automated data-tracking systems, sampling methods, and computer-assisted interviewing have greatly expanded the types of information that can be collected and analyzed by child welfare practitioners, managers, evalua-tors, and researchers. The interest of federal and state governments in using these data for improving policy planning and analysis encourages the development of new statistical methods for distinguishing genuine program impacts from spurious associations. Normally there is some time lag between advances in data collection and the diffusion of new methods for drawing statistically valid conclusions about agency performance and quality improvement. This is certainly the situation in child welfare, where data analysis methods originally developed to test hypotheses about point-in-time data do not adequately mirror the substantive process of change that longitudinal surveys and automated data systems are now able to track (Coleman, 1980). Traditional statistical methods provide a useful summary of whether program and policy objectives have been met, but they do not offer much insight into why progress is being made or how agency performance might be improved.

Longitudinal data analysis aims to model how change occurs and how agency performance can be improved as a result of planned child welfare interventions. A corpus of statistical methods originally developed for engineering and medical applications to analyze mechanical or biologi-cal systems is now routinely applied to child welfare systems to model longitudinal outcomes, such as length of stay, time to reunification and adoption, placement disruption, and reentry back into foster care (Testa, 1984; Goerge, 1991; Wulczyn, 1991; Testa & Slack, 2002; Guo & Wells, 2003; Wulczyn, Chen, & Orlebeke, 2008). Known variously as failure-time, event-history, hazards regression, or survival analysis (Kalbfleisch & Prentice, 1980; Blossfeld, Hamerle, & Mayer, 1989; Hosmer & Lemeshow, 1999), these methods track case processes prospectively from some origi-nation time, for example, the date of case opening, to the date of occur-rence of an outcome of interest, such as family reunification, to evaluate the impact of program and policy inputs as the processes of program and policy implementation are unfolding.

The following sections provide an overview of the current state of data analysis in child welfare with a primary focus on the federal oversight of state child welfare systems. Although the chapter may sometimes sound overly critical of current federal review efforts, the intention is to not to slight the very real accomplishments that federal investments in state computerized data systems, child welfare demonstrations, and child and family services reviews have made in laying down the foundation for a results-oriented system of accountability in child welfare. Current federal data systems, despite their limitations, are capable of providing statistical descriptions that are far richer than the aggregate counts previously reported by the states in the 1970s and 1980s. Fortunately, many of the limitations are correctable by making minor changes in the way states report and encrypt child and family level information. Significant pro-gress has been made in identifying the alterations needed to improve data quality and comparability since these issues were first brought to national attention (Martin Bishop, Grazian, McDonald, Testa, & Gatowski, 2002; Courtney, Needell, & Wulczyn, 2004; Testa, Koh & Poertner, 2008). The Administration for Children and Families (ACF) released its notice of proposed rule-making (NPRM) in 2008, which would modify the state reporting requirements along the lines recommended for longitudinal data analysis. Retooling the guidelines for states' collection and reporting of child welfare data to the federal government not only preserves the sizable investments already made in the existing system but could potentially open the way for impressive advances in child welfare knowledge, program accountability, and quality improvement.

Longitudinal Child Welfare Data

The preferred solution to the problems of censoring, truncation, and selectivity described in Chapter 4 is to collect data on child welfare cases by tracking children prospectively from their date of entry into foster care to their date of exit and for a long enough period afterward so that longer-term outcomes of interest can be observed, such as continued safety, family permanence, and transition to self-sufficient adulthood. This is how the most sophisticated child welfare administrative databases are currently structured as represented by the Illinois Integrated Database on Children and Family Services (Goerge, Van Voorhis, & Lee, 1994) and the Multistate Foster Care Data Archive (Wulczyn, Chen, & Hislop, 2007). These databases provide sufficient information for calculating prospective measures, such as the odds of reunification within a year, median lengths of stay in foster care, rates of placement disruption, and relative risks of reentry into foster care. They can also be linked to follow-up, in-person surveys to learn how youth are faring after exiting the child welfare system (Kessler et al., 2008).

As discussed in Chapter 4, the federal Adoption and Foster Care Analysis and Reporting System (AFCARS) departed from this best practice standard (Fanshel, Finch, & Grundy, 1987; Testa, 1987) and instead opted for the more familiar cross-sectional design that was patterned after point-in-time counts of foster children in institutional facilities, public custody, and as part of the decennial U.S. census. Unique child identifiers were purposely masked to obstruct the linkage of AFCARS records across reporting periods. Fortunately the USDHHS has since altered its stance and has been encouraging states to encrypt child identifiers consistently so that it is now possible to reconstruct longitudinal files from AFCARS submissions. Special software, available in the public domain from Fostering Court Improvement and Hornsby Zeller Associates, stitches together 6-month files into fully longitudinal records at the removal level and partially longitudinal records at the placement level. This allows for the calculation of prospective measures of outcomes that track children's safety, permanence, and well-being forward in time. Prospective measures provide more valid and useful feedback to administrators than retrospective measures (Martin Bishop et al., 2002). They also are less susceptible to manipulation than retrospective measures from exit cohort data because no cases are selectively dropped from follow-up.

The calculation of prospective measures of outcomes from AFCARS data requires the conversion of 6-month AFCARS submissions into long-itudinal data records. Table 5.1 shows how this is done with the Hornsby Zeller software. The program first sorts the 6-month records by case record number, last removal date, and current reporting period as shown in the top panel of Table 5.1. It then substitutes the last reported values for fields expected to remain constant, such as race, gender, and birthdates, and imputes missing date fields that are inferable from adjacent records. Finally it aggregates the biannual records into unique removal episodes as listed in the bottom panel of Table 5.1.

This particular method of rolling up 6-month AFCARS files works well at the removal level, but it can only partially reconstruct the longitudinal record at the placement level. As shown in Table 5.1, AFCARS picks up only the last placement setting during a reporting period, which can leave large gaps in the placement history. In this example of fictitious Case C2424, placement 1 is missing for the first and third removal episodes, and place-ments 2, 5, and 6 are missing for the second removal. If the first placements happened to be institutional care, the incidence of institutionalization would be underestimated. An incomplete history of placement changes can greatly limit the ability to track and analyze not only the restrictiveness of care but foster care stability and other placement-related issues.

Retooling AFCARS to accommodate the reporting of complete place-ment histories can be easily accomplished. Instead of reporting only one record per child, multiple records could be transmitted as is currently the practice with the National Child Abuse and Neglect Data System (NCANDS). Whether the multiple records pertain to just foster care place-ments or to all living arrangements needs to be considered. AFCARS guidelines draw a distinction between foster care placements and tempor-ary living conditions, noting that "there are certain temporary living conditions that are not placements, but rather represent a temporary absence from the child's ongoing foster care placement."[1] These tempor-ary absences include (1) visitation with a sibling, relative, or other care-taker, (2) hospitalization for medical treatment, acute psychiatric episodes, or diagnosis, (3) respite care, (4) day or summer camps, (5) trial home visits, and (6) runaway episodes. Reporting AFCARS records at the foster care placement level would provide the necessary detail to analyze foster care stability. Including temporary living conditions as well would pro-vide the fullest detail needed for longitudinal data analysis.

Gap Analysis

Gap analysis involves assessing whether the difference between an observed outcome and a desired state of affairs is important and statistically valid

TABLE 5.1 Conversion of AFCARS Standard 6-Month Submissions into Removal-Level Longitudinal AFCARS Records

Reporting Period	Record Number	First Removal	Total Removals	Last Discharged	Last Removal	Placement Date	Number of Placements	Placement Setting	Discharge Date	Reason
					Standard AFCARS 6-Month Submissions					
1998 03	C2424	11/15/1996	1		11/15/1996	11/18/1996	2	Relative	3/6/1998	Reunified
2000 03	C2424	11/15/1996	2	3/6/1998	3/17/2000	3/17/2000	1	Relative		
2000 09	C2424	11/15/1996	2	3/6/1998	3/17/2000	9/18/2000	3	Relative		
2001 03	C2424	11/15/1996	2	3/6/1998	3/17/2000	10/24/2000	4	Relative		
2001 09	C2424	11/15/1996	2	3/6/1998	3/17/2000	7/26/2002	7	Relative		
2002 03	C2424	11/15/1996	2	3/6/1998	3/17/2000	10/26/2001	8	Relative		
2002 09	C2424	11/15/1996	2	3/6/1998	3/17/2000	10/26/2001	8	Relative		
2003 03	C2424	11/15/1996	2	3/6/1998	3/17/2000	10/26/2001	8	Relative	5/29/2003	Reunified
2003 09	C2424	11/15/1996	2	3/6/1998	3/17/2000	10/26/2001	8	Independent Living		
2004 03	C2424	11/15/1996	3	5/29/2003	1/23/2004	3/11/2004	2	Independent Living		
2004 09	C2424	11/15/1996	3	5/29/2003	1/23/2004	3/11/2004	2	Independent Living		
					Removal-Level Longitudinal AFCARS Records					
1998 03	C2424	Omitted	1	Omitted	11/15/1996	Omitted	2	Relative	3/16/1998	Reunified
2003 09	C2424	Omitted	2	Omitted	3/17/2000	Omitted	8	Relative	5/29/2003	Reunified
2004 09	C2424	Omitted	3	Omitted	1/23/2004	Omitted	2	Independent Living	Censored[a]	

[a] Censored means that the case is still open as of the last reporting period. All that is currently known about the future discharge date is that it is later than 9/30/2004.

enough to warrant taking corrective action. These differences can be derived
from comparisons with history, another part of the organization, a different
geographic area, an established standard, or a designated target. Describing
the magnitude of the gap can be done with time-to-outcome data or with
simpler derivations such as differences in probabilities or the ratios of odds.

Time-to-outcome data can be characterized in terms of a dichotomous
or multinomial indicator of the occurrence of an outcome and its competing events as well as the time to the occurrence of the outcome and the
other events. From time-to-outcome data, it is possible to estimate the
difference in the *probability* of an outcome within an interval of time, the
relative odds of an outcome's occurrence, and the "instantaneous probability" of an outcome within a very small interval of time, more accurately
described as a *hazard rate* (Allison, 1997)

Both probabilities and odds can be computed from time-to-outcome
data. For example, tracking the times to reunification for foster children for
a year after their initial removal from the home solves the selectivity
problem associated with the federal measure that looks only at exits.
Times less than 366 days are coded 1, indicating reunification within a
year. Discharges to other settings, reunifications after 1 year, and censored
times due to a child turning 18 years old can be coded 0, indicating no
reunification within a year. Figure 5.1 illustrates the differences between
this prospective coding scheme and the retrospective method used during
round 1 of the federal Children and Family Services Review (CFSR) for
measuring timeliness of reunification.

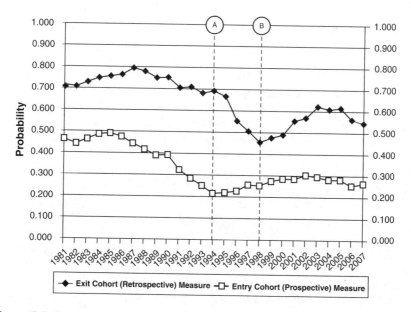

Figure 5.1 Retrospective and prospective measures of family reunification.

As shown in Chapter 4 for the calculation of median lengths of stay, prospective and retrospective measures can give quite different readings of system performance. The federal retrospective measure shows a sharp drop in the proportions of reunifications that occurred in less than a year from removal between points A and B, whereas the alternative prospective measure indicates a slight rise in the probability of reunification within a year of entry during this same period. Likewise after point B, the federal retrospective measure shows Illinois making some progress toward attaining the national standard before regressing backward, whereas the alternative prospective measure shows a less volatile pattern of change.

Table 5.2 presents the data on which the calculations of the probabilities of reunification in Figure 5.1 are based. The frequency of reunifications within a year for each entry cohort is listed in column 1. The next column is the frequency of all the other outcomes for children who entered foster care during that year including adoption, guardianship, emancipation, as well as reunifications after more than a year. Dividing the number of reunifications within a year (Y) by the sum of reunifications and all other outcomes ($Y + N$) provides an estimate of the probability that a child entering foster care for the first time will return home within a year. A closely related measure in column 4 is the odds of reunification within a year. This is calculated by dividing the number of reunifications (Y) by all other outcomes (N). This gives a ratio of 1:1 when the chances are even or 50% in terms of probabilities. Odds are usually expressed in abbreviated form so that 1:1 odds are expressed simply as 1. Odds smaller than 1 indicate a less than even chance and larger odds indicate a greater than even chance. For example, the odds of reunification within a year of initial entry into foster care declined from 0.856 in federal fiscal year 1981 to a low of 0.268 in federal fiscal year 1994. The corresponding probabilities are 0.461 and 0.211, respectively.[2]

A simple way of calibrating the magnitude of the performance gap between an observed and desired level is in terms of the difference between the probability of an outcome compared to a comparison or reference group. Federal fiscal year 1994 serves this purpose in Table 5.2. This year was chosen because it was the year prior to the implementation of HMR reform (see Chapter 3, this volume). The differences in probabilities can be estimated by subtracting the probability for each entry cohort from the probability of reunification for the comparison entry cohort. Column 5 contains the results of this calculation. The column is labeled LPM for linear probability model (Aldrich & Nelson, 1984) because the same results can be obtained by performing a linear regression analysis with a binary outcome indicator that is coded either 1 for reunification within a year or 0 otherwise (see Technical Appendix 5A). These binary outcomes are then regressed on a set of fiscal year (dummy) indicators with 26 values (FFY81 to FFY93 and FFY95 to FFY07) that are all coded 0 except for the federal fiscal year the child initially entered foster care.

TABLE 5.2 Family Reunification Trend Lines: Probabilities, Odds, and Hazards Rates

| Entry Cohorts | Reunified in 1 Year | | Probability | Odds | LPM | Logistic Regression | | Proportional Hazards | | | |
| | Yes (1) | No (2) | Y/(Y + N) (3) | Y/N (4) | Coeff (5) | Coeff (6) | e^{Coeff} (7) | Unadjusted | | Adjusted[a] | |
								Coeff (8)	e^{Coeff} (9)	Coeff (10)	e^{Coeff} (11)
FFY81	3,691	4,311	0.461	0.856	0.250	1.162	3.195	0.888	2.430	0.595	1.813
FFY82	3,582	4,523	0.442	0.792	0.231	1.084	2.955	0.872	2.391	0.589	1.803
FFY83	3,627	4,206	0.463	0.862	0.252	1.169	3.218	0.883	2.419	0.631	1.880
FFY84	3,944	4,166	0.486	0.947	0.275	1.262	3.533	0.946	2.576	0.687	1.988
FFY85	4,105	4,278	0.490	0.960	0.278	1.276	3.581	0.901	2.463	0.642	1.899
FFY86	4,007	4,433	0.475	0.904	0.263	1.216	3.373	0.888	2.430	0.649	1.913
FFY87	4,435	5,565	0.444	0.797	0.232	1.090	2.974	0.783	2.187	0.581	1.787
FFY88	4,303	6,028	0.417	0.714	0.205	0.980	2.664	0.681	1.977	0.530	1.699
FFY89	4,139	6,534	0.388	0.633	0.176	0.860	2.364	0.582	1.789	0.452	1.572
FFY90	4,220	6,528	0.393	0.646	0.181	0.881	2.412	0.591	1.806	0.467	1.595
FFY91	3,961	8,407	0.320	0.471	0.109	0.564	1.758	0.310	1.364	0.274	1.315
FFY92	3,776	9,643	0.281	0.392	0.070	0.379	1.461	0.156	1.169	0.146	1.157
FFY93	3,290	9,993	0.248	0.329	0.036	0.206	1.229	0.106	1.112	0.082	1.085
FFY94 (Comparison)	3,379	12,610	0.211	0.268	b	c	d	0	1	0	1
FFY95	3,263	11,862	0.216	0.275	0.004	0.026	1.027	0.062	1.064	0.064	1.066
FFY96	2,693	9,386	0.223	0.287	0.012	0.068	1.071	0.123	1.131	0.081	1.084
FFY97	2,606	7,675	0.253	0.340	0.042	0.237	1.267	0.208	1.231	0.149	1.161
FFY98	2,313	6,977	0.249	0.332	0.038	0.213	1.237	0.205	1.228	0.118	1.125
FFY99	2,167	5,840	0.271	0.371	0.059	0.326	1.385	0.258	1.294	0.121	1.129
FFY00	1,880	4,780	0.282	0.393	0.071	0.384	1.468	0.346	1.413	0.169	1.184

(continued)

TABLE 5.2 (Continued)

| | Reunified in 1 Year | | Probability | Odds | LPM | Logistic Regression | | Proportional Hazards | | | |
| | | | | | | | | Unadjusted | | Adjusted[a] | |
Entry Cohorts	Yes (1)	No (2)	$Y/(Y+N)$ (3)	Y/N (4)	Coeff (5)	Coeff (6)	e^{Coeff} (7)	Coeff (8)	e^{Coeff} (9)	Coeff (10)	e^{Coeff} (11)
FFY01	1,907	4,868	0.281	0.392	0.070	0.380	1.462	0.294	1.341	0.128	1.136
FFY02	1,925	4,502	0.300	0.428	0.088	0.467	1.596	0.355	1.427	0.198	1.218
FFY03	1,857	4,501	0.292	0.413	0.081	0.432	1.540	0.375	1.455	0.186	1.204
FFY04	1,683	4,366	0.278	0.385	0.067	0.364	1.439	0.340	1.405	0.136	1.145
FFY05	1,695	4,370	0.279	0.388	0.068	0.370	1.447	0.358	1.430	0.146	1.158
FFY06	1,345	4,020	0.251	0.335	0.039	0.222	1.249	0.296	1.344	0.069	1.072
FFY07	1,423	4,020	0.261	0.354	0.050	0.278	1.321	0.246	1.279	0.032	1.032

[a] Adjusted for baseline population conditions of race, Hispanic origins, age at removal, residence in Cook County, and kinship care placement.
[b] 0.211.
[c] −1.317.
[d] 0.268.

The reason that FFY94 is left out of the set of dummy indicators is because children who entered care during that period serve as the comparison group.[3]

The estimated LPM coefficients listed under column 5 in Table 5.2 are interpretable as differences in probabilities. These differences are measured against the coefficient for the FFY94 comparison cohort. This coefficient is also called the constant or intercept-term in a LPM because it is the estimated probability when all of the explanatory variables are 0. In this case, the constant equals the estimated probability of reunification for the FFY94 cohort (compare $b = 0.221$ to the FFY94 probability in column 3). The LPM coefficients for the remaining entry cohorts are interpretable in reference to this constant. Thus the coefficient of 0.250 is the difference in probability of reunification in FFY81 compared to FFY94. Adding together this difference and the constant of the LPM yields 0.461, which is the probability of reunification within a year for fiscal year 1981 listed in column 3.

Although useful for descriptive purposes, the LPM has certain undesirable properties from a statistical point of view (see Technical Appendix 5A). Many of these difficulties can be sidestepped by expressing the probabilities in terms of odds and conducting a logistic regression analysis of the odds (usually reexpressed as logs of odds or *logits* to simplify the math). The logistic regression coefficients listed in Table 5.2 are interpretable as odds ratios or effect sizes after they have been transformed by taking their antilogarithms.[4] Again starting with the constant for the comparison FFY94 cohort, the antilog of the constant, $c = -1.317$, is $d = 0.268$. This is the estimated odds of reunification when all of the explanatory variables are 0 (compare to column 4). The remaining antilogs are interpretable in reference to this comparison cohort. Thus the odds of reunification in fiscal year 1981 were nearly 3.2 times the odds of reunification in fiscal year 1994. We can recover the FFY81 odds from this odds ratio or cohort effect size simply by multiplying it by the constant of 0.268. This calculation yields 0.856, which is the odds of reunification within a year for FFY81 listed in column 4.

Despite the statistical attractiveness of logistic regression, expressing reunification outcomes in terms of a dichotomy of 0 or 1 is arbitrary and discards useful information by truncating time-to-outcome data for children reunified in less than a year and censoring data for children reunified beyond a year. Instead of a 1-year cut-off, for example, a cut-off of 17 months after removal might be the better choice since AFSA instructs states to initiate termination-of-rights petitions on parents whose children have been in foster care longer than this time. But why limit time-to-outcome data to a single cut-off? It is probably important to distinguish between children who are returned to parental custody within a week of removal from those who are reunified after 9 months or 2 years of permanency planning.

A better method for analyzing time-to-outcome data comes from the engineering and biomedical sciences, in which outcomes are expressed in terms of the likelihood that an individual will experience an event of interest in a small interval of time given that the individual has not yet experienced the event up to that moment. This expression is called the *hazard rate*. In the current example, the reunification hazard rate can be thought of as the likelihood of returning home within the next small interval of time for children who are still in foster care. The hazards regression coefficients listed under column 8 in Table 5.2 display the crude cohort differences in reunification hazards rates as of September 30, 2007. Again to facilitate interpretation, the hazards coefficients are transformed into relative risk ratios by using antilogarithms. The relative risk for the comparison group is 1, which stands for the fact that the underlying hazard curve arbitrarily takes the shape observed for FFY94. Thus if children had a high likelihood of being reunified shortly after removal in FFY94 and this likelihood declined the longer the children remained in foster care, the shape of the underlying hazard curve would start out high and gradually tapper off. Because this shape is defined by numerous duration-specific hazard rates, the 1 serves as a reference standard for interpreting the remaining relative risk ratios for different fiscal years. Whatever the underlying shape of the FFY94 hazard curve, the relative risk ratio for other entry years indicates the proportionate amount that the hazard rate at a particular time since removal shifts the hazard curve upward or downward. For example, as shown in column 9 of Table 5.2, foster children who were removed from their homes during federal fiscal year 1981 were about 2.4 times as likely to be reunified at any time after removal compared to children removed during the comparison year of 1994.

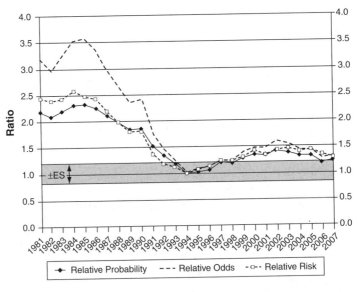

Figure 5.2 Comparison of the relative probability, odds, and risk of family reunification in Illinois.

Figure 5.2 charts the three estimates of the cohort (unadjusted or crude) effects based on reunification probabilities, odds, and hazards rates. Even though the three estimates are calculated differently, they yield somewhat similar pictures of reunification trends in Illinois. Beginning in the mid-1980s, reunification rates declined to a low point in FFY94 before rebounding slightly and then declining again after FFY02.[5] This picture differs considerably from the trend line based on federal exit cohort measures (see Fig. 5.1), which showed reunification performance declining precipitously after FFY94 and then rebounding from 45% in FFY98 to 61% in FFY05 before leveling off and declining again. Child welfare administrators in Illinois would be hard pressed to provide any plausible account for the rollercoaster performance conveyed by the federal measure. Case tracking based on prospective entry-cohort measures shows modest but steady improvements in reunification rates after HMR Reform in 1995 until progress stalled after FFY2002 (see Fig. 5.2).

Assessing Practical and Statistical Significance

The increase in reunification odds by close to 60% for children entering Illinois foster care between FFY94 and FFY2002 suggests that the policies the state pursued with respect to HMR reform, performance contracting, and subsidized guardianship may not have had as dampening an effect on reunification rates as some observers of those policies once feared.[6] On the other hand, the much higher rates in the 1980s suggest that there may be additional room for improvement if DCFS and the courts were to take a less risk-adverse approach to family reunification, particularly with drug-involved parents (Testa and Smith, 2009), and invest resources in postreunification services to ensure child safety and to hold down reentry rates.

In whatever way the comparison is set for assessing agency performance, e.g., in reference to history, another part of the organization, a different geographic area, an established standard, or a designated target, the next important consideration is deciding on the minimum difference or effect size (ES) that would be of practical importance to warrant taking corrective action or judging whether adequate progress is being made. The choice of a minimum difference or ES is a qualitative judgment that ideally takes into account the gravity of the outcome, the costs and benefits of the intervention, the potential side effects, and any other considerations of a political or ethical nature. So for example, a child protection intervention that reduces child mortality by 1% may merit serious consideration, whereas an expensive drug treatment program that increases the odds of reunification by 20% may be judged as inconsequential. In Figure 5.2, the shaded band brackets a minimum ES of ±0.2, i.e., any change less than 20% in either direction relative to the FFY94 baselines for relative probabilities and relative risks is considered negligible. Separate effect size estimates would need to be calculated for relative odds to account for the same amount of proportionate change.[7] Although practitioners and administrators may sometimes look to evaluators to make such determinations, these choices are best made in consultation with individual principals, key agents, sponsors, and other stakeholders.

One of the least satisfactory solutions to the problem of assessing practical importance is to rely on statistical tests of significance to settle the issue of what is clinically significant or substantively important. In 2001, the U.S. Administration for Children and Families issued an information memorandum (ACYF-CB-IM-01-07) that provided guidance on the amount of improvement that states needed to show in meeting the national standards through an approved program improvement plan (PIP). It stated:

> We will consider the sampling error for each indicator as a minimum percentage of improvement for a State to make over the course of a PIP. For example, if a State's recurrence of child maltreatment is 10% at the time of the review, at a minimum we would expect the State to improve by at least .90% on this indicator as part of an approved PIP, thus reducing the incidence of recurrent maltreatment to 9.1%, in order to consider that improvement has been made. We believe that using the sampling error as a framework is appropriate because where a State's improvement exceeds the sampling error, we can conclude that a statistically significant improvement has been made.

Aside from the issue of whether it is appropriate to calculate sampling errors for child welfare outcome statistics based on a nonprobability (convenience) sample of states, the relevant question is what role, if any, null hypothesis significance testing (NHST) should play in establishing performance standards or judging progress toward improvement. Almost all statistical packages in use today test the null hypothesis that the size of improvement in the population of interest is zero. NHST calculates the probability (from 0 to 1) that an observed difference could have arisen by chance if the null hypothesis of zero difference was exactly true in the population from which the probability sample was derived (Thompson, 1996). However, as numerous scholars and statisticians have repeatedly pointed out (Meehl, 1978; Tukey, 1991), there is a certain sense in which the null hypothesis is never exactly true. Agency performance varies from day to day, groups differ on average by small amounts, and patterns of association are seldom exactly zero. The ability to detect such differences is mostly a matter of the size of the sample with which we have to work. The larger the sample size, the more likely it is that the null hypothesis will be rejected. At the extreme, if we were able to collect data on the entire population, any amount of difference or improvement would be detectable as "statistically significant" no matter how trivial the change. In the case of the PIP standards cited, the ACF could have decreased the sampling error and thereby reduced the improvement margin simply by including more AFCARS reporting periods in its calculation of confidence limits. Conversely, it might have enlarged the margin by adjusting the limits for the clustering of data points by state. All and all, backing into a decision about what is important based solely on NHST seems ludicrous or arbitrary at best.

As stated previously, the better approach to choosing a minimum difference or ES is to base the decision on some combination of clinical experience, expert assessment, costs/benefit analysis, political calculation, and ethical judgment. In the case of the Wisconsin subsidized guardianship waiver experiment, for example, it was decided, drawing from the Illinois experience, that it would be important to detect at least a 10 percentage point boost in the permanency rate for the intervention group that is offered the guardianship option over and above the rate for the comparison group from whom this offer is withheld. Projecting that the combined permanency rate of reunifications, adoptions, and legal guardianships (without subsidies) would reach 55% by the mid-point of the demonstration (2.5 years), a sampling allocation plan was developed that would be sufficiently "powered" to detect a combined permanency rate of 65% or more in the intervention group. Expressed in terms of an odds ratio, the magnitude of the corresponding ES is 1.52. In other words, the availability of subsidized guardianship was expected to boost the overall odds of permanence by slightly more than 50%.[8]

Statistical power is a concept that should be commanding greater attention in child welfare research and accountability reviews. It refers to the probability that a real difference, effect size, or pattern of association of a certain magnitude in a population will be detectable in a particular study (Rossi, Lipsey, & Freeman, 2004). Conventionally it is defined as the probability that a statistical test will reject the null hypothesis when the hypothesis of no effect is false (Shadish, Cook, & Campbell, 2002). Although the use of double negatives can get confusing, the language is intended to reinforce the idea that all scientific knowledge is tentative in the sense that hypotheses can be rejected but never conclusively affirmed (see Chapter 2, this volume).

Child welfare practitioners and administrators are all too familiar with findings of "no significant difference." What is often overlooked is that sometimes such findings are in error, that is, an important difference in the population is overlooked because the study design was not sufficiently powered to detect the true difference. Whenever information is based on a sample derived from a larger population, there is always a chance that the decision to reject or not reject a null hypothesis will be wrong due to the lack of complete information about the population. Sampling theory provides a basis for evaluating the chances of error and for taking those risks into account when designing a study.

Sampling statisticians speak of two types of errors: (1) the error of rejecting a hypothesis when it is actually true (referred to as a type I or α error); and (2) the error of failing to reject a hypothesis when it is actually false (referred to as a type II or β error). By convention, the hypothesis is stated in such a way that the rejection of the hypothesis when it is actually true (type I error) is thought to be the more important error to avoid (Neyman, 1950). For example, it is frequently noted that physicians as a profession prefer to avoid type I errors of not treating a patient who is actually ill over type II errors of treating a patient who is actually well, whereas lawyers as a profession prefer to avoid type I errors of convicting a person who is actually innocent over type II errors of acquitting a person who is actually guilty (Scheff, 1999). The goal of results-oriented accountability, however, is not to favor one type of error over another but rather to weight the probabilities of both types and to take these probabilities into consideration in deciding on an appropriate study design.

Statistical power is a function of the magnitude of the ES we think is important to detect, the amount of type I error we are willing to tolerate, and the size of the sample on which data collection is based. Returning to the example of the Wisconsin subsidized guardianship demonstration, stakeholders deemed it important to be able to detect an ES of 1.52, i.e., the odds ratio corresponding to the difference between the permanency rate in the intervention group of 65% and the rate in the comparison group of 55%. Now if we were to depend on the same sized sample of 50 cases that the federal government drew for its Round 1 CFSR reviews, power analysis indicates that only one out of every nine studies that could have been done would have yielded a significant result (at the conventional 0.05 level) of rejecting the null hypothesis that the reunification odds were the same (ES = 1.0) when in fact the true ES was 1.52 in the population. In other words, roughly eight out of every nine studies would fail to reject the null hypothesis that subsidized guardianship was ineffective even though the option was actually successful in boosting permanency odds by 52% in the population as a whole. A casual listener on hearing that the results of the demonstration were not statistically significant might mistakenly assume that the experiment was a failure, when in reality the study was just not powerful enough to detect the real effect of the new permanency option.

One way out of the problem of insufficient power is simply to increase the tolerance for Type 1 error. This would be analogous to withholding medical treatment from more persons who are actually ill or relaxing the rules of evidence so that more innocent people are convicted. In the guardianship example, increasing the chances to 10 out of 100 of getting a significant result (0.10 significance level) when in actuality the program is ineffective nearly doubles the statistical power from 11% to 19%. Applying a one-sided test because it is unlikely that a supplementary permanency option would reduce overall permanence further raises the power to 29%. This is still not much of a gain. But rather than engaging in such tradeoffs, the preferred solution is to increase the sample size. In general, a larger sample size gives more statistical power. For the Wisconsin subsidized guardianship demonstration, using a two-sided test and retaining the 0.05 significance level would necessitate increasing the sample size from 50 children to 752 in order to boost the chances to 8 out of 10 of rejecting the null hypothesis when the hypothesis of no effect is actually false (power = 80%). Adding another 254 children would boost the power to 90%. Of course the desire to get as large a sample as possible has to be balanced against the competing interest of conserving resources. Thus the trick is to decide in advance on an ES that is important enough to justify maintaining or expanding the program and then choosing a sample size that is just large enough to ensure that the ES has a fair chance of being detected statistically.[9]

The procedure for choosing an adequate sample size with sufficient power to detect an ES of practical importance sheds new light on the sample size problems associated with the federal CFSR onsite review. As noted in Chapter 4, each of seven outcomes must be determined to be substantially achieved in 95% (90% during the first round) of the cases reviewed for a state to achieve substantial conformity with CFSR standards. The onsite case review at round one relied on a sample consisting of 50 cases, half of which were in-home services cases and the other half foster care cases. If the 90% threshold was the smallest shortfall that would be important to detect, then the state would need to show a near perfect score (98%) in each of the outcome areas to run a fair chance (80% power) of rejecting the null hypothesis that performance is below 90%. If the threshold were set to the round 2 level of 95%, performance would have to be 99% or better to have a fair chance of achieving substantial conformity. Conversely allowing states to pass the CFSR if the onsite review scores just above 90% increases the risk of type I error to unacceptably high levels, that is many more poor quality systems would erroneously be given passing marks. Onsite statewide samples of 50 or even 75 cases are adequate only for detecting "zero tolerance" for less than perfect performance in most states. As Noonan, Sabel, and Simon (2008) explain the rationale for Quality Service Review (QSR)—a case review process similar to CFSR:

> The system should strive for superior performance in every case, and every substantial failing should be regarded as a problem worth remedying. Thus, the . . . sampling goal is to get a sufficient number of cases that any systemic problem will show up in at least one of the cases reviewed. (Noonan, Sabel, & Simon, 2008, 31)

The authors go on to acknowledge that once the process identifies areas of inferior performance then it becomes important to pinpoint with greater statistical precision those specific areas of agency performance that are in need of correction. For example, the Round 1 CFSR found the state of Maryland to be deficient in ensuring that children have permanence and stability in their living situation. The outcome was rated as substantially achieved in only 8 out of the 30 cases reviewed (27%) in which this outcome was applicable. If the state decided to make a policy change or implement a training program to improve agency performance in this area by at least a third, then a sample of 160 cases would need to be reviewed in order to have a decent chance at rejecting the null hypothesis of no improvement. If the minimum improvement deemed important was set at 50%, then only 70 cases would be needed for review. In general, the narrower the margin of improvement is for assessing performance, the larger the sample size must be to determine whether meaningful progress is being made.

Statistical precision becomes especially important when the minimally acceptable margin of improvement is in the 15% to 20% range the federal government has established for the national outcome standards for safety and permanence. In these cases, however, the issue of random error due to sampling is of much less concern as the comparisons are based on performance measures derived from administrative data on the entire population of children in the child protection system. Instead the greater concern has to do with the nonrandom or systematic sources of variation in the outcomes. Even if a difference or ES is judged to be both important and statistically significant, that is no guarantee that the change represents a genuine improvement in agency performance. Simple differences in probabilities, odds, and hazards rates capture only crude or gross differences between comparison groups. These gross differences embody both the net influences that are directly attributable to program and policy improvements as well as all the other systematic and random influences that can also affect child welfare outcomes.

For example, during the years that reunification rates were falling and then rising slightly in Illinois, the composition of the child welfare population was also changing in ways that could have impacted reunification outcomes. As can be calculated from Table 5.2, the number of children taken into foster care in Illinois between federal fiscal years 1981 and 1994 doubled from about 8000 to 16,000 annual removals. The proportion removed from homes in the city of Chicago and its surrounding suburbs in Cook County increased from 37% to 62% of all removals statewide. The rise was fueled, in part, by increased hospital surveillance of the intrauterine cocaine exposure of infants (Testa & Smith, 2009), which helped to lower by 2 years the average age of foster children at removal. Because of the heavier concentration of African-Americans in Chicago neighborhoods than statewide, the racial composition of foster care entry cohorts changed from 56% white to 68% African-American. It is very likely that these large demographic changes exerted an impact on reunification trends. Therefore before rendering a summary judgment of the importance and statistical significance of a cohort effect or policy change, it would be important to remove the confounding nonprogrammatic influences from the comparison. The statistical methods by which this is accomplished can be grouped under the heading of *risk-adjustment* analysis.

Risk-Adjustment Analysis

The easiest way to comprehend the logic of risk-adjustment analysis is by way of an example. The 2003 *Child Welfare Outcomes Annual Report* issued by the federal government examined the proportion of children who enter foster care at age 12 years or younger at the time of their latest removal and who are placed in a group home or institution. Although no national standard has been set for this outcome, best practice favors placing foster children, particularly younger ones, in the least restrictive, most family-like setting that meets their social, behavioral, and health needs. Progress is assessed by comparing institutionalization rates for an entry cohort of children with its historical controls.

The 2003 *Annual Report* noted that institutionalization rates for young children increased by 50% or more between 2000 and 2003 in five states (Arkansas, Colorado, Utah, Washington, and Wisconsin). Three states (Illinois, Michigan, and Tennessee) experienced a decrease of 50% or more during this period. Using the *PICO* framework, we can label the institutionalization rate as the outcome (O), the 2003 entry cohort of children aged 12 years and under as the intervention group (I), and the 2000 entry cohort as the comparison group (C). Any important programmatic change that might have impacted O between 2000 and 2003 would be captured by the cohort effect, i.e., the difference in the institutionalization rates between I and C.[10] The substantial decline in institutionalization rates among the three states of Illinois, Michigan, and Tennessee raises the possibility that the other five states might have something to learn from the experience of the former states. Before reaching any conclusion, however, the problem of "confounded effects" must be addressed. What must be established first is the amount of gross change ($I - C$) in institutionalization rates (O) that can be directly attributed to the net effects of program or policy changes and the amount that is due to all other population and other systematic influences, which we can label P. This is what is generally meant by risk-adjustment analysis, which adjusts comparison groups for differences in demographic characteristics, special needs, and other preexisting conditions of the population that affect the outcome of interest.

For illustrative purposes, Table 5.3 displays hypothetical AFCARS data for an imaginary bellwether state in the United States. The data show the aggregate numbers of total foster care entrants and the subset of entrants placed in shelters, institutions, and group homes (IGH). To simplify comparisons, the hypothetical number of entrants in 2003 has been kept the same as the total number of 2000 entrants, which is based on a 10% random sample of U.S. foster children who entered care between October 1, 1999 and September 30, 2000. The IGH rate per 100 children is computed by summing up all of the IGH placements for each age group and then dividing this sum by the total number of children aged 12 years and younger who entered foster care during the reporting period. This ratio is then

TABLE 5.3   Institutionalization Rates for Children Entering Foster Care at Ages 12 Years and Younger in a Hypothetical Bellwether State, 2003 and 2000

	Entry Cohort					
	October 2002 to September 2003 (*I*)			October 1999 to September 2000 (**C**)		
		IGH[a] (**O**$_I$)			IGH (**O**$_C$)	
Age at Placement (**P**)	Entrants	*N*	Rate per 100	Entrants	*N*	Rate per 100
All ages	18,470	1,320	7.1	18,470	1,800	9.7
0 < 1 year old	6,750	280	4.1	3,430	125	3.6
1 year old	2,410	100	4.1	1,620	80	4.9
2 years old	1,820	100	5.5	1,450	75	5.2
3 years old	1,260	70	5.6	1,300	70	5.4
4 years old	1,210	75	6.2	1,190	70	5.9
5 years old	880	50	5.7	1,150	80	7.0
6 years old	640	60	9.4	1,230	110	8.9
7 years old	570	50	8.8	1,260	130	10.3
8 years old	610	70	11.5	1,190	130	10.9
9 years old	600	70	11.7	1,240	160	12.9
10 years old	590	95	16.1	1,100	160	14.5
11 years old	540	120	22.2	1,080	200	18.5
12 years old	590	180	30.5	1,230	410	33.3
Age standardized	18,470	2,008	10.9	18,470	2,010	10.9
Average age	3 years old			5 years old		

[a] IGH, institutions and group homes.

multiplied by 100 to obtain a rate per 100 children. This gross rate, or what demographers also call a crude rate, is the outcome measure that HHS tracks in its *Annual Report*.

Comparing the IGH rates for the entry cohorts shows a reduction in institutionalization rates from 9.7 per 100 children entering care in 2000 to 7.1 per 1000 children entering care in 2003. This difference of −2.6 per 100 entrants translates into a 27% reduction in institutionalization rates, which corresponds to a 31% reduction in the odds of institutionalization or an ES (odds ratio) of 0.69.[11] This effect size represents the gross amount of change in the institutionalization of young children during this period. The intervening policy or practice change that may have fostered this improvement might indeed be worthy of replication if such a change were genuinely due to improvements in the diversion of young children from institutional and group care.

A potential confounder of the relationship between entry cohorts and institutionalization rates, however, is the average age of children entering foster care (*P*). Table 5.3 shows that the institutionalization rate increases with each age group. Although there are some slight differences in age-specific rates between time periods, the pattern of association with age stayed approximately the same. Furthermore, the age-specific differences between periods fluctuate in both positive and negative directions. This suggests that diversion from institutional and group care is an unlikely source of lowered institutionalization rates. Overall, children were nearly as likely to be institutionalized in 2003 as they were in 2000. What changed instead was the age composition of the cohorts of children coming into foster care. More young children entered care in 2003 than in 2000. As a result, the average age of entrants decreased from 5 years old in 2000 to 3 years old in 2003. Although a large demographic shift such as this is unusual, similar demographic changes in child welfare have occurred in the past. A major shift in the age composition of the foster care entrants happened, for example, during the 1980s when societal reactions to the crack-cocaine epidemic in the United States swept thousands of infants and toddlers into the foster care system (Wulczyn, 1991).

The same conclusion can be reached by "standardizing" the comparison of the 2000 and 2003 IGH rates for the differences in the age structures of the two entry cohorts. Age standardization applies the same hypothetical age distribution to each group being compared so that no one group has disproportionately more infants or adolescents than the other group. A common method of standardization (called "direct standardization") involves applying the equivalent set of compositional weights for each age group in Table 5.3. For example, treating each age group as identical in size reduces the rate difference in the top row of Table 5.3 from a crude difference of −2.6 (= 9.7 − 7.1) to an age-adjusted difference of 0 (= 10.9 − 10.9) in the next to the last row.[12] If all 18,470 children were distributed equally into the different age groups, there would be about 2008 to 2010 IGH placements in both reporting periods. This lack of difference demonstrates again that there was no important cohort effect on the institutionalization rate during this period.

This hypothetical case illustrates how the absence of a direct intervention effect can easily be mistaken for a genuine effect when outcomes monitoring is done naively without subjecting the comparison to risk-adjustment analysis. As mentioned previously, the problem is often characterized as one of *selection bias* because of the different ways that principals learn about, apply for, and decide whether to participate in a program (principal selection), agents recruit and screen potential participants (agent selection), and numerous other ways of nonrandom selection (Bloom, Michalopoulos, Hill, & Lei, 2002). Statisticians and econometricians have developed a variety of methods of handling selection biases to uncover the genuine causal effect of an intervention on an outcome in observational studies. Appendix 5.1 of this chapter illustrates how linear regression analysis, the most popular risk-adjustment method for disentangling confounded effects from observational data, can be applied to the data in Table 5.3 to arrive at the same conclusions. The advantages of linear and other regression methods over simpler rate standardization methods is that it allows for multiple potential confounders, such as geographic

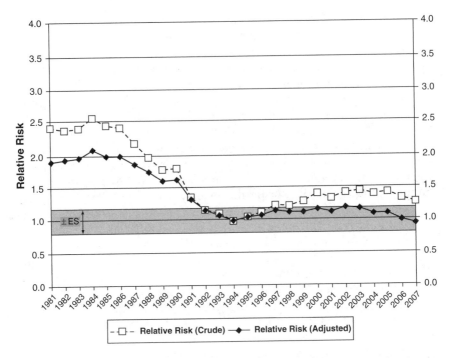

Figure 5.3 Comparison of the crude and adjusted risks of family reunification in Illinois.

residence, ethnicity, gender, and age, to be "adjusted out" of the comparison. To give some indication of the utility of applying regression methods of risk-adjustment analysis, Figure 5.3 compares the relative risks (RR) of reunification in Illinois before (crude) and after adjusting for changes in the gender, geographic, ethnic, and age profile of the children entering foster care (adjusted).

Several tentative conclusions may be drawn from the comparison of crude and adjusted relative risks of reunification. First, in keeping with a cohort ES of less than ±0.2 as substantively negligible (shaded area), there appears to have been no undesirable or desirable impact of HMR reform (see Chapter 3, this volume) on reunification trends in Illinois after adjusting for changes in demographic composition. Second, the entire decline in reunification rates occurred prior to the implementation of subsidized guardianship, performance contracting, and the Illinois permanency initiative. Third, the success of efforts to restore reunification rates back to the levels of the early 1980s will need to be assessed after making appropriate risk adjustments for the characteristics of future cohorts of children entering foster care. The fact that the federal CFSR process does not routinely make such risk adjustments for changing population conditions greatly limits its utility for assessing the effectiveness of program improvement plans.

The above conclusions are described as tentative because they are based entirely on observational data. Although longitudinal data, risk adjustment, and attention to practical and statistical significance bring greater transparency to the "whys" behind important variations in agency performance, actual progress may still be obscured by unmeasured and unobserved influences that could affect in profound ways the outcomes for which child welfare agents are held accountable. Such threats to the internal validity of any causal inferences drawn about agency efficacy and effectiveness are discussed in Chapter 7. Before grappling with these complexities, Chapter 6 by John Poertner explains how careful research review prior to program and policy implementation can help put the evaluation phase of results-oriented accountability on a firmer evidentiary foundation.

Technical Appendix 5A: Regression Method of Risk Adjustment

Regression is a versatile statistical method of fitting lines and curves to relationships between outcomes and interventions and adjusting for the confounding effects of population conditions or risk factors. The problem of confounding is illustrated in Figure 5A.1 using *PICO* terms. It is an adaptation of a figure originally presented by Howard Bloom and his colleagues at the Manpower Demonstration Research Corporation (Bloom et al., 2002).

The figure partitions the influences on an outcome, O, into an intervention component, I, and an error component, ε, which summarizes all the other unobserved systematic and random influences that effect changes in O. The node for ε is represented by a hollow circle in order to distinguish these unmeasured influences from the solid node for the measured influence of I on O. The causal influence of I on O is represented by an arrow, whose size and directional impact, δ, is gauged relative to some

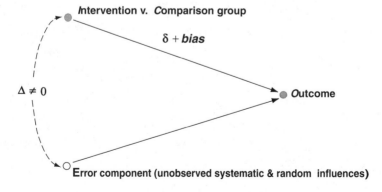

Figure 5A.1 Problem of confounding.

comparison group, *C*. The curved and dashed double-arrow line linking *I* with ε indicates that the unobserved influences on *O* are associated in some fashion with *I* (Δ ≠ 0), which results in these unmeasured influences being mixed up with the measured impact of *I* on *O* (δ + bias).

The regression method of purging selection biases from the estimate of the intervention effect involves separating important systematic influences from the error component, measuring them, and estimating the lines or curves that summarize the relationship between these systematic influences and the intervention and outcome variables. This method is diagrammed in Figure 5A.2. Lines for predicting outcome variables (*O*) from population conditions and risk factors (*P*) are called regression lines. If *P* exerts a genuine effect on *O* (β ≠ 0), the line shows the values of *O* to which all intervention cases would "regress" if random influences on *O* were removed (Heise, 1975). If *P* is trivially associated with *O*, the values would regress all the way to the mean of *O* after random and all other confounding influences have been removed. In this case, the regression line would run horizontal to the mean of *O*, which means that *P* is of no help in predicting or explaining *O* (β = 0).

These ideas are illustrated in Figure 5A.3. The data are the hypothetical institutionalization rates for children entering foster care at ages 12 years and younger in FFY 2000 and 2003 from Table 5.3. Panel A shows the "observed" institutionalization rates for each age group (open circles) relative to a line and curve predicted from the regression of the institutionalization outcome on the age of the child at foster care entry for both cohorts combined. Panel B plots the observed proportions of each age group that entered foster care during FFY 2003 relative to a line and curve predicted from the regression of the year of entry on the child's age.

Panel A shows that age at entry is positively associated with institutionalization rates. The regression line shows that the institutionalization rate increases the older the child is at entry. The intercept of this line is 2.35 (where the line crosses the *y*-axis) and the slope (β) is 1.51 (i.e., the number that is multiplied by the *x*-value). The regression equation, $= 2.35 + 1.51X$,

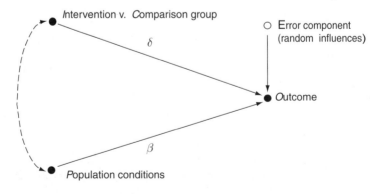

Figure 5A.2 Regression method.

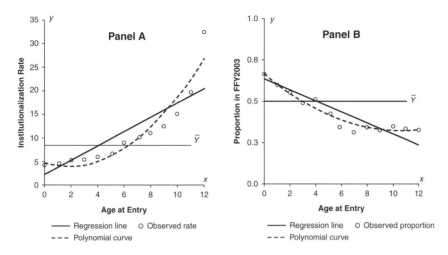

Figure 5A.3 Regression of institutionalization rate (Panel A) and FFY2003 proportion (Panel B) on age at entry.

means that the predicted institutionalization rate for infants is 2.35 per 100 ($= 2.35 + 1.51 \cdot 0$) and the predicted rate increases by 1.51 per 100 for every additional year of age at entry. So for 4 year olds, the predicted institutionalization rate is 8.39 per 100 ($\hat{Y} = 2.35 + 1.51 \cdot 4$). Panel B shows that age of entry is negatively associated with the federal fiscal year the child entered care. The equation of this regression line is $\hat{Y} = 0.632 - 0.03X$. In other words, of all the children taken into foster care during the two periods, infants were more likely to enter in FFY2003 than in FFY2000 whereas older children were less likely to enter in FFY2003.

The intercept and β of the regression line are chosen so as to minimize the sum of squares of the vertical differences (residuals) between the observed rates and the values predicted from the regression line. Panel A of Figure 5A.3 shows that the observed institutionalization rates start out close to a straight line at younger ages but depart from linearity at the middle years and overshoot the line at the age of 12 years. The linear fit is a little better for year of entry but still is far from optimal. Visual inspection of the two graphs suggests that the fit to the observed rates could be improved by bending the regression lines. This can be accomplished by fitting a polynomial curve of the second degree, which includes the square of age as an additional term in the regression equation. The sign of the squared age term is positive for institutionalization rates, which results in a polynomial curve that rises more steeply for older ages, and is negative for cohorts, which results in a flattening out of the curve. In both cases the polynomial curve provides a better fit (smaller residual sum of squares) to the observed data than the linear regression line.

Regression analysis shows that age at entry is associated with both the outcome of institutionalization and the selection into the 2003 cohort.

Therefore it is important to remove the confounding influence of age before rendering a summary judgment about the magnitude of the cohort effect on institutionalization rates. This can be done by regressing the residuals obtained from the regression analysis depicted in Panel A of Figure 5A.3 on the residuals obtained from the regression analysis depicted in Panel B. This provides a "risk-adjusted" estimate of the intervention effect, δ, i.e., what is left over after the systematic effects of the baseline population conditions have been removed from both the outcome and intervention indicators.

Figures 5A.4 shows the results of the regression analysis of the cohort effect on institutionalization rates before and after risk adjustment using residuals. Panel A shows the regression of the indicator variable of institutionalization on the indicator variable of FFY2003. Because both indicators are binary variables coded 0 or 1, the intercept of the regression line (9.7) is the rate of institutionalization of children entering foster care in 2000 (cohort = 0) and the slope is the difference between the intercept and the rate of institutionalization in 2003 ($\beta = -2.6$). This is identical to the crude cohort effect calculated from Table 5.3. After the systematic effects of age are removed from both the outcome and intervention indicators by regressing the residuals from the linear regression of the two variables on age, the net cohort effect diminishes to 0.49 (solid line, Panel B). The regression of the residuals from the polynomial curve further reduces the cohort effect to 0.028 (dashed line). If the age effects are allowed to vary freely with the age-specific rates by assigning age groups to no/yes (0,1) categories, the cohort effect drops to zero, which is consistent with the result obtained from the direct standardization of institutionalization rates by age shown in Table 5.3.

In practical applications of regression analysis, the two-step residuals or "adjusted variables" method is collapsed into a single-step, *multiple*

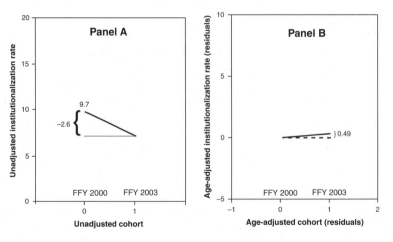

Figure 5A.4 Unadjusted (Panel A) and risk-adjusted (Panel B) estimates of cohort effect.

regression approach that regresses the outcome indicator simultaneously against the intervention indicator and baseline population conditions. The full multiple regression yields the same results as adjusted variables regression. This arises from the "remarkable fact" (Chambers, Cleveland, Kleiner, & Tukey, 1983) that the fitted regression line to the adjusted variables yields a simple regression coefficient that is identical to the corresponding partial regression coefficient from the full multiple regression.

For the linear regression model, the gross difference in institutionalization rates of -2.6 per 100 between FFY2000 and FFY2003 (Fig. 5A.3) is composed of two components: (1) the direct effect, δ, of cohort membership on institutionalization rates (0.49) controlling for age (see Fig. 5A.4) and (2) the effect of age on institutionalization rates ($\beta = 1.53$) multiplied by the difference in the average ages of the two cohorts ($\Delta = -2$ years). The sum of the direct cohort effect and the indirect age effect ($0.49 + 1.53 \cdot -2$) is equal to the gross difference in crude institutional rates of -2.6 per 100. In other words, even though the underlying utilization of institutions and group homes for young children is estimated to have increased slightly between 2000 and 2003, the entrance of more young children in 2003 drove the rate down because younger children face a lower risk of being institutionalized than older children. Thus the change in age composition rather than improvement in diversion accounted for the entire decline in the institutionalization of younger children.

Although useful for descriptive purposes, a major weakness of estimating regression lines for outcomes that are measured on a dichotomous (0,1) scale, such as institutionalization and reunification, is its violation of a variety of statistical assumptions of ordinary-least-squares (OLS) analysis, such as normal distribution of residuals and constant residual variance, which yields inefficient estimates of intervention effects and biases hypothesis tests. Also linear regression can produce predictions that fall outside the 0 to 1 range. For example, predictions of institutionalization rates sometimes fall in the negative range for certain combinations of demographic variables, which obviously makes no sense.

As noted, these violations of the assumptions of the linear regression can be sidestepped by expressing rates, proportions, and probabilities in terms of odds and assuming that the log of the odds, called a *logit*, is a linear function of the set of explanatory variables. Statistical routines for estimating logistic regression coefficients are available in most statistical packages such as SAS, SPSS, and Stata. Applied to the data in Table 5.3, the unadjusted logistic regression coefficient for the FFY03 cohort effect is -0.338, which when transformed into antilogarithms yields an odds ratio of 0.71 or a 31% reduction in the odds of institutionalization between FFY2000 and FFY2003. When age at entry is included in the logistic model, the coefficient for the FFY03 cohort effect diminishes to 0.007 for an odds ratio of about 1.0. In other words, the odds of institutionalization are the same for both entry cohorts after controlling for age at entry.

With the growing availability of logistic regression routines in standard statistical software packages, there is less need for using linear regression to analyze child welfare outcomes when the scale of measurement is dichotomous. Not only do these methods avoid the statistical problems associated with linear regression analysis of dichotomous outcomes, they also open the doorway to newer matching methods of risk adjustment as discussed in Chapter 7. Despite these advantages, it merits repeating that while logistic regression methods of risk adjustment are useful for refining statistical estimates of intervention effects, the utility of both logistic and linear regression for drawing casual inferences is still limited. Internal validity depends on how thoroughly important baseline population conditions and risk factors are specified in the regression models. Only after all confounding effects have been "subtracted out" from the intervention and outcome variables so that just random noise is left over in the error component is it valid to infer a causal relationship between interventions and outcomes. The circumstances under which we can make the assumption that there is no residual association between an intervention and error component so that we can feel confident that risk-adjustment analysis gives valid insight into the causal impact of the intervention on the outcome will be addressed more fully in Chapter 7.

Notes

1. Social Security Act—section 479; 45 CFR 1355.40 & appendices; Child Welfare Policy Manual Sections 1.2B.7 and 1.3 (AFCARS Toolkit: User's Guide, September 2003).
2. Odds are easily convertible into probabilities and vice versa. The formula for converting odds into probabilities is p = Odds/(1 + Odds). The formula for converting probabilities into odds is Odds = p/(1 − p).
3. To perform the regression calculation, the FFY94 comparison cohort must be omitted from the list of regressors so that the explanatory variables are not exact linear combinations of one another.
4. The natural logarithm has a base number of e (= 2.71828...), where $\ln(e^{coeff})$ = coeff, so the antilog of the logistic regression coefficient is $e^{coeff.}$
5. Although the relative odds suggest the greatest decline, this is an artifact of the ratio calculation because odds grow exponentially larger the nearer they approach a probability of 100%. Both trend lines are telling the same story but on different scales.
6. The concerns expressed in the *Report of the Task Force on the Illinois Department of Children and Family Services to Governor Rod R. Blagojevich* are illustrative of those fears: "Given the declining rate at which kinship care leads to adoption of African-American children, DCFS should reexamine the incentive structure that favors adoption over reunification in performance contracting. Currently, the incentive structure pays an equal bonus to private agencies for adoption or reunification. The Department, however, does not fund many of social service and mental health treatment services needed by biological parents to achieve reunification. As a result, most

private agencies find it more cost effective to pursue the termination of parental rights and aggressive promotion of adoption. This rational (and self-interested) behavior of private agencies may eliminate a legitimate path out of the child welfare system for African-American children. DCFS must develop policies and procedures that remove this perverse incentive structure for private agencies, while also fulfilling its obligations under ASFA" (Governors Task Force on the Illinois Department of Children and Family Services, 2003: 33).

7. See discussion in footnote 2 in Chapter 7.
8. The ES of 1.52 is the ratio of the expected permanency odds in the intervention group (65/35) to the odds in the comparison group (55/45). Subtracting 100% from ES·100 yields 52%, which is the expected boost in permanence attributable to the offer of subsidized guardianship.
9. In the case of the Wisconsin demonstration, it was decided to raise the type I error to 0.10 and to rely on a one-tailed test of statistical significance for permanency comparisons. This resulted in a recommended sample size of 600 children after allowing for a design effect of 1.3 for sibling clustering.
10. This comparison does not take into account the use of shelter care as a temporary placement or diagnostic setting for children entering foster care. Because shelter care is often classified as group care in AFCARS, the construct validity of combining shelter care, group care, and institutional care into a measure of institutionalization and comparing rates across states pose additional complications.
11. The ES is calculated by converting probabilities into odds: $0.071/(1 - 0.071) = 0.076$ and $0.097/(1 - 0.097) = 0.11$. Then the ratio of the two odds is calculated: $0.076/0.11 = 0.69$. The odds ratio represents the ES in terms of how much smaller (or greater) the odds of institutionalization are for the later entry cohort than for the earlier entry cohort.
12. The adjustments in Table 2.1 were done by making each age group equivalent in size (weight $= 1/N$ of age groups). Other possible choices include using the average age distribution for the two groups, selecting one group as the standard for comparison (e.g., the 2000 age structure), or referencing some external standard such as the age structure of all children entering foster care in the United States (Clogg, Shockey, & Eliason, 1990). Whichever weighting approach is used, the adjusted rates would end up equal to one another as long as the underlying rates stayed the same across groups.

References

Aldrich, J. H., & Nelson, F. D. (1984). *Linear probability, logit, and probit models.* Beverly Hills, CA: SAGE Publications.

Allison, P. D. (1997). *Survival analysis using the SAS® system: A practical guide.* Gary, NC: SAS Institute, Inc.

Bloom, H. S., Michalopoulos, C., Hill, C. J., & Lei, Y. (2002). *Can nonexperimental comparison group methods match the findings from a random assignment evaluation of mandatory welfare-to-work programs.* New York: MDRC.

Blossfeld, H., Hamerle, A., & Mayer, K. U. (1989). *Event history analysis: Statistical theory and application in the social sciences.* Hillsdale, NJ: Lawrence Erlbaum Associates.

Chambers, J. M., Cleveland, W. S., Kleiner, B., & Tukey, P. A. (1983). *Graphical methods for data analysis*. Belmont, CA: Wadsworth International Group.

Clogg, C. C., Shockey, J. W., & Eliason, S. R. (1990). A general statistical framework for adjustment of rates. *Sociological Methods and Research, 19*(2), 156—195.

Coleman, J. S. (1980). *Longitudinal data analysis*. New York: Basic Books.

Courtney, M.E., Needell, B., & Wulczyn, F. (2004). Unintended consequences of the push for accountability: The case of national child welfare performance standards. *Children and Youth Services Review, 26*(12), 1141—1154.

Fanshel, D., Finch, S. J., & Grundy, J. F. (1987). Collection of data relating to adoption and foster care. Technical Appendix to the Report of the Advisory Committee on Adoption and Foster Care Information. Washington, DC: U.S. Department of Health and Human Services.

Goerge, R. M. (1991). The reunification process in substitute care. *The Social Service Review, 64*(3), 422—457.

Goerge, R., Van Voorhis, J., & Lee, B. J. (1994). Illinois's longitudinal and relational child and family research database. *Social Science Computer Review, 12*(3), 351—365.

Governor's Task Force on the Illinois Department of Children and Family Services. (2003). *Report of the task force on the Illinois Department of Children and Family Services to Governor Rod R. Blagojevich*. Springfield, IL: Author.

Guo, S., & Wells, K. (2003). Research on timing of foster care outcomes: One methodological problem and approaches to its solution. *The Social Service Review, 77*(1), 1—24.

Heise, D. R. (1975). *Causal analysis*. New York: John Wiley & Sons.

Hosmer, D. W., & Lemeshow, S. (1999). *Applied survival analysis: Regression modeling of time to event data*. New York: John Wiley & Sons.

Kalbfleisch, J. D., & Prentice, R. L. (1980). *The statistical analysis of failure time data*. New York: John Wiley & Sons.

Kessler, R. C., Pecora, P. J., Williams, J., Hiripi, E., O'Brien, K., English, D., & Sampson, N. A. (2008). Effects of enhanced foster care on the long-term physical and mental health of foster care alumni. *Archives of General Psychiatry, 65*(6), 625—633.

Martin Bishop, P., Grazian, L., McDonald, J., Testa, M., & Gatowski, S. (2002). The need for uniformity in national statistics and improvements in outcome indicators for child and family services reviews: Lessons learned from child welfare reform in Illinois. *Whittier Journal of Child & Family Advocacy, 1*(1), 1—36.

Meehl, P. E. (1978). Theoretical risks and tabular asterisks: Sir Karl, Sir Ronald, and the slow progress of soft psychology. *Consulting and Clinical Psychology, 46*(4), 806—834.

Neyman, J. (1950). *First course in probability and statistics*. New York: Holt.

Noonan, K. G., Sabel, C. F., & Simon, W. H. (2008). *Legal accountability in the service-based welfare state: Lessons from child welfare reform*. Columbia Law School Public & Legal Theory Working Paper Group (08—162). New York: Columbia University Law School.

Rossi, P. H., Lipsey, M. W., & Freeman, H. E. (2004). *Evaluation: A systematic approach (7th edition)*. Thousand Oaks, CA: SAGE Publications.

Scheff, T. J. (1999). *Being mentally ill: A sociological theory (3rd edition)*. New York: Alidine de Gruyter.

Shadish, W. R., Cook, T. D., & Campbell, D. T. (2002). *Experimental and quasi-experimental designs for generalized causal inference*. Boston: Houghton Mifflin Company.

Testa, M. F. (1984). *Child placement, deinstitutionalization, and social change*. Retrieved from Dissertations and Theses database (AAT T-28874).

Testa, M. (1987). Data necessary to support national policy functions in foster care and adoption. Technical Appendix to the Report of the Advisory Committee on Adoption and Foster Care Information. Washington, DC: U.S. Department of Health and Human Services.

Testa, M., Koh, E. & Poertner, J. (2008). *Can AFCARS be rescued: Fixing the statistical yardstick that measures state child welfare performance*. Urbana, IL: Children and Family Research Center.

Testa, M., & Slack, K. S. (2002). The gift of kinship foster care. *Children and Youth Services Review, 24*(1/2), 79—108.

Testa, M., & Smith, B. (2009). Prevention and drug treatment. In C. Paxson & R. Haskin (Eds.), *The Future of Children: Preventing Child Maltreatment, 19*(2), 147—168.

Thompson, B. (1996). AERA editorial policies regarding statistical significance testing: Three suggested reforms. *Educational Researcher, 25*(2), 26—30.

Tukey, J. W. (1991). The philosophy of multiple comparisons. *Statistical Science, 6,* 100—106.

Wulczyn, F. (1991). Caseload dynamics and foster care reentry. *The Social Service Review, 65*(1), 133—156.

Wulczyn, F., Chen, L., & Hislop, K. B. (2007). *Foster Care Dynamics 2000–2005: A Report from the Multistate Foster Care Data Archive*. Chicago: Chapin Hall Center for Children.

Wulczyn, F., Chen, L., & Orlebeke, B. (2008). Evaluating contract agency performance in achieving reunification. *Children and Youth Services Review*. doi:/10.1016/j.childyouth.2008.10.006.

6

RESEARCH REVIEW OF EVIDENCE IN CHILD WELFARE

John Poertner

The Adoption and Safe Families Act of 1997 (ASFA) specified the accountability concerns for public child welfare and codified the outcomes for children served in these systems as safety, permanence, and well-being. The drive to define, measure, report, and manage these results has dominated the field for many years, even prior to the passage of ASFA. However, some people suggest that the outcome movement has so skewed attention to results that the practices that produce them have been lost. This chapter outlines an approach toward assessing the *external validity* of child welfare practices through research reviews of *evidence-supported* practices and policies across variations in populations, settings, interventions, and outcomes. This is the third phase of the cycle of research-oriented accountability. Child welfare policies based on the best available research evidence balance concerns for process and outcomes and improve agent effectiveness in achieving safety, permanence, and well-being on behalf of abused and neglected children.

Child Welfare Policy and the Context of Decision Making

Selecting and implementing effective child welfare policy is a complex task. One difficulty is that the decision-making context is exceedingly complex, with multiple agents including caregivers, caseworkers, lawyers, and judges. Child welfare decision making is also driven by external conditions including public policy, social values, agency policy and program, and organizational climate.

ASFA is the most recent example of public policy that shapes decision making. Not receiving federal funds by not performing as intended on the outcome measures as implemented by the Department of Health and Human Services (DHHS) is a powerful incentive for a state. As a result, most states rely on these measures regardless of their shortcomings (see Chapter 4, this volume). Social values also play an important role in child welfare decisions (see Chapter 2, this volume). ASFA expresses values when it clarifies reasonable efforts by stating that the child's health and safety shall be the paramount concern [Sec. 101 (a)]. Agency policy that promotes "family-centered practice" is another example of a value that influences decisions. Organizational climate can be a powerful force guiding decision making (see Glisson, 2008). This climate influences workers' decisions through the attitudes and actions of co-workers and supervisors. Community interests also influence the climate of child welfare offices and resulting worker decisions. Child welfare policy based on the best available evidence does not ignore this complex context. It is concerned with one facet of this puzzle.

The Nature of Research Evidence in Public Child Welfare

Another difficulty is the quality and quantity of child welfare research, which varies widely. Child welfare policy based on the best available evidence means identifying interventions that are evidence-supported by research that shows they are causally linked to outcomes. This means foremost that interventions have been demonstrated to produce the intended outcomes through controlled experiments or clinical trials that include random assignment of participants to an intervention group and a comparison group that does not receive the intended intervention. Replication of these experiments and trials builds confidence that the intervention has the intended effect.

However, this rigorous level of empirical support is not always available. Consequently, the term "best available evidence" is used to guide policy decisions. Selection of policy based on the best evidence requires a method for rating or ranking research evidence. This has led to the concept of levels of evidence.[1] Technical Appendix 6A presents three ways of categorizing levels of evidence. One is from medicine, one is transplanted to child welfare from psychology, and one is from mental health. At this point there is no consensus in child welfare on the criteria for different levels of evidence.

Each of the three examples of levels of evidence could be discussed at length, including their strengths and weaknesses. That is beyond the scope of this chapter. The important point is that there are various types of research evidence, with some better able to indicate a cause and effect relationship. Some system of levels of evidence is needed for selecting policy interventions supported by the best available evidence. It is rare in child welfare or its related fields to find policy interventions supported by multiple, high-quality clinical trials. In some cases a problem facing children and families is so recently recognized that there is little research on its amelioration. This may require shaping policy from practice wisdom and subjecting it to more rigorous research. This is also a way for the field to build its research base (see Chapter 8, this volume).

Making Policy Decisions Based on the Best Available Evidence

The process of making child welfare policy decisions based on the best available evidence involves the following steps, which can occur between the data analysis and evaluation stages of results-oriented accountability:

1. Exploring and refining the child welfare intervention and population under consideration.
2. Formulating a well-built question that hypothesizes the key causal relationship between the intervention and outcome for particular populations.
3. Identifying, synthesizing, and classifying the available empirical evidence in support of the efficacy and effectiveness of the intervention.
4. Choosing the intervention based on the best available evidence.
5. Integrating the intervention within the context of clients and community.
6. Implementing the intervention through policy and practice.

Step 1: Exploring and Refining the Child Welfare Intervention and Population under Consideration

The search for an evidence-supported child welfare policy frequently begins with dissatisfaction or a concern about some children or families not achieving desired outcomes. For example, a need to decrease the number of children who are experiencing placement disruptions might be identified as a concern. Although it is tempting to go to the Internet or library and begin to search for a solution to this problem, there is great value in learning more about the problem and refining the statement. Consistent with the conceptual framework for understanding child abuse and neglect that is used in this book, the following steps will produce a much more focused and useful question for collecting evidence.

1. Identify the desired outcome for children or families.
2. Identify the populations of children most at risk of not achieving the desired outcome or experiencing the problem.
3. Identify the agency policy related to the problem.

Desired Outcome

In the example of placement disruption, the desired outcome is identified in the statement of concern. That is a need to decrease the number children experiencing placement disruptions. However, not all children experience placement disruptions.

Risk Analysis

As discussed in Chapter 5, some children are more at risk of experiencing a particular problem than others. Identifying the population conditions and factors that place children or subgroups at greatest risk of placement disruption is best done by analyzing data from the agency using the statistical methods previewed in Chapter 5. However, existing research can also assist the process of risk analysis.

A good literature review is a helpful starting point. For purposes of illustration consider the frequent problem of placement stability. A literature review identifies the child's age, behavioral health needs, and physical and sexual abuse as important risk factors (http://www.rom.ku.edu/ebp_stab.asp).

CAUTION: A research review contains only those variables of interest to or available to the researcher. It is never the entire story!

In addition to the above caution, research on any single factor can be somewhat mixed and confusing. For example, several studies have suggested that the age of the child is linearly associated with placement instability (Hartnett, Falconnier, Leathers, & Testa, 1999; James, Landsverk, & Slymen, 2004; Smith, Stormshak, Chamberlain, & Whaley, 2001; Pardeck, 1984). That is, older children experience less placement stability than younger children. However, Wulczyn, Kogan, and Harden (2003) found that rather than a linear relationship it was curvilinear with younger and older children experiencing more moves. The group with the highest number of moves was youth from 11 to 13 years of age. Among the many possible reasons for mixed findings are the different model specifications that were used and the agency or community context that may moderate the relationship. For the purpose of guiding an investigation of risk factors in the agency with the concern, the finding that age is an important variable is the key point and should be used to identify the age of those children served by the agency who are most likely to experience placement disruption.

Child behavior problems is another identified risk factor in the literature review. It is relatively easy to explore the relationship between age and placement stability within an agency context because of administrative datasets that include the child's date of birth and number of placements. However, these datasets seldom include indicators of child behavior. However, the more that can be learned about the children experiencing the problem within the agency context the better the policy decision is going to be, that is, the better the match between the target population and the chosen intervention. This suggests that the use of other data within the agency and the use of special studies are worth the investment. Data on child characteristics such as behavior problems may exist in other systems such as quality assurance case reading files.

Conducting a small case-control study within the agency can help identify additional risk factors. In case-control studies people who already have a certain condition are compared with people who do not. In this context, this would be comparing a group of children who experienced placement disruption to a group who did not to identify factors that seem to place some children at risk of this event. The benefits of this type of study can far exceed its cost.

The literature review also found that victims of physical or sexual abuse were more likely to experience placement disruption. This indicates that the risk analysis should include studying the association between the types of abuse or neglect experienced by the children served by the agency and placement disruption. The risk analysis should include whatever child characteristics appear to be relevant.

The risk analysis aids thinking about populations of children who might ultimately be the target of a different agency policy. This is an important consideration in later identification of evidence-supported practices. For example, if the risk analysis finds that substantial proportions of children who experience placement disruptions have an unmet behavioral health need, then one type of intervention may be identified. If, on the other hand, a large number of children experiencing the problem are victims of sexual abuse, then a different intervention is likely to be appropriate. It may also be that both of these groups are large and that different interventions are targeted at different groups of children. It may be that current agency policy or normal practice plays an important role.

Agency Policy Context Analysis

It is likely that current agency operations have some association with the problem being examined. Agency policy may even be the most important factor that explains the problem. The agency may have a policy, formal or informal, that may make the problem more pronounced. It may be that changing this policy would alleviate the problem. A thoughtful examination of this may yield powerful policy intervention strategies.

For example, the placement stability problem might be the focus of attention in an agency because of the federal DHHS placement stability standard of no more than two placements for children in care less than 12 months. This agency may routinely place children in emergency placements followed by short-term living arrangements for purposes of evaluating the child to identify the type of care that best meets the child's needs. James et al. (2004) found that many agencies first placed children into shelter care and then emergency foster care before moving them to their intended placement. This agency has now failed the federal measure for many of the children served. Redesigning the initial placement routines in this agency is more likely to have the desired results than identifying new intervention programs.

There may also be agency policies that increase placement stability. For example, an agency may emphasize relative placements. The literature on relative placements has found them to be more stable than nonrelative placements (Koh & Testa, 2008). However, if the child has multiple placements due to agency policy before a relative caretaker is located, this positive feature may be lost.

These are just some of the examples of agency policies and practices that contribute to stability. Others include foster parent selection, training, and support services. The key idea is that a careful examination of agency policy is essential for a more complete understanding of the problem.

> HINT: A change in an agency policy or reinforcement of a current policy may have a substantial impact on the problem.

Step 2: Formulating a Well-Built Question That Hypothesizes the Key Causal Relationship between the Intervention and Outcome for Particular Populations

The risk and policy analysis result in a variety of possible explanations of the problem. These ideas can be formulated in terms of a well-built question that will be examined through targeting a population, implementing an intervention, and assessing its impact on an outcome in reference to a comparison group. To be most useful the well-built question at a minimum should

1. Identify the at-risk population (P);
2. Specify the desired outcome (O); and
3. Hypothesize the direction and strength of the casual relationship between the outcome and intervention (I) relative to a comparison condition (C).

The placement stability example leads to the following well-built questions:

- Are children and youth who have been victims of sexual abuse (P) more likely to have more stable living arrangements (O) if the effects of the abuse were alleviated (I) compared to sexual abuse victims who did not receive this treatment (C)?

- Do older youth exhibiting difficult to manage behaviors (*P*) have more stable living arrangements (*O*) if their caregiver could learn different responses to the behaviors (*I*) compared to caregivers in the *status quo* condition(*C*)?
- Might young children who are placed into emergency placements (*P*) have more stable placements (*O*) if policy were changed to reduce the use of these arrangements (*I*) compared to the existing policy (*C*)?

One or all of these questions could be explored in the next step of identifying potential interventions. To choose between alternatives, first consider the size of the target population. Having maximum impact on the problem might lead to selecting the alternative with the largest risk group. On the other hand the cost of the intervention also needs to be considered. A potentially cost-neutral intervention for the largest risk group is ideal. On the other hand testing a more costly intervention on a smaller risk group might be a good choice.

Step 3: Identifying, Synthesizing, and Classifying the Available Empirical Evidence in Support of the Efficacy and Effectiveness of the Intervention[2]

This is both a rewarding and frustrating step in the process of identifying evidence-supported policy. It is rewarding because of the vast array of ideas and research findings that exist in libraries and on the Internet. It is frustrating because it is difficult to find exactly what you are looking for. You are looking for an intervention with the best available evidence of producing the desired outcome for the identified target population. This leads to another caution.

CAUTION: Don't review and synthesize intervention research yourself! Get help.

The process of evidence identification, review, and synthesis is difficult, time consuming, and technical. There are individual scholars and groups who have dedicated themselves to bringing research literature together so that you don't have to. Three highly respected groups that are dedicated to synthesizing research on interventions are the Campbell Collaboration, The Agency for Healthcare Research and Quality, and the Cochrane Collaboration:

> *The Campbell Collaboration* (C2) is a nonprofit organization that aims to help people make well-informed decisions about the effects of interventions in the social, behavioral, and educational arenas. C2's objectives are to prepare,

maintain, and disseminate systematic reviews of studies of interventions. We acquire and promote access to information about trials of interventions. C2 builds summaries and electronic brochures of reviews and reports of trials for policymakers, practitioners, researchers, and the public [http://www.campbellcollaboration.org].

The Agency for Healthcare Research and Quality (AHRQ) is a part of US DHHS and examines what works and does not work in health care. Its mission includes both translating research findings into better patient care and providing policymakers and other healthcare leaders with information needed to make critical healthcare decisions [http://www.ahrq.gov/news/focus/index.html].

The Cochrane Collaboration is an international nonprofit and independent organization dedicated to making up-to-date, accurate information about the effects of health care readily available worldwide. It produces and disseminates systematic reviews of healthcare interventions and promotes the search for evidence in the form of clinical trials and other studies of interventions [http://www.cochrane.org/docs/descrip.htm].

However, none of these resources is likely to answer every question on intervention efficacy and effectiveness. They do not define their domain as child welfare, and they are largely focused on synthesizing only clinical trials. The California Evidence-Based Clearinghouse (http://www.cachildwelfareclearinghouse.org/) is a recent resource that is devoted to providing up-to-date information on evidence-based child welfare practices. As this Web site continues to develop it should be an extremely valuable source for child welfare professionals. Notice that the definition of levels of evidence used by this clearinghouse is different from any of those referenced in this chapter. You will find it under the tab labeled ratings and scientific rating scale. Like the others, these levels are not without their strengths and weaknesses.

In addition to using the child welfare-specific California Evidence-Based Clearinghouse, it is helpful to examine the other resources. For example, 26 of the current C2 social welfare reviews related to child welfare are listed in Table 6.1. Not all of these topics have completed reviews. Many are in the process of being completed and will appear in the future. They do, however, provide a source of information with names of people conducting the reviews. Contacting these reviewers to find out the status of their preliminary findings is useful.

If you are forced to search the literature yourself, look for research reviews. For example, Chaffin and Friedrich (2004) and Thomlison (2003) have written useful articles summarizing interventions for child maltreatment. Given the emphasis on the use of intervention with the best available evidence more of these types of reviews are emerging. In fact, there is now a journal titled the *Journal of Evidence-Based Social Work*. Review articles are seldom perfect but are useful until groups such as the California Clearinghouse and the Campbell Collaboration complete more systematic reviews.

TABLE 6.1   Campbell Collaboration Social Welfare Reviews Related to Child
Welfare

Behavioral and cognitive-behavioral training interventions for assisting foster carers in
the management of difficult behavior
Case management for persons with substance use disorders
Cognitive-behavioral therapy for parents who have physically abused their children
Cognitive-behavioral treatment for antisocial behavior in youths in residential treatment
Cognitive-behavioral interventions for children who have been sexually abused
Cognitive-behavioral training interventions designed to assist foster carers in the
management of difficult behavior
Effects of school-based cognitive-behavioral anger interventions on child and adolescent
aggressive behavior
Empowerment-based after-school programs for improving self-efficacy and positive
connections for adolescents (aged 10–19 years) in Organization of Economic
Cooperation and Development (OECD) countries
Exercise to improve self-esteem in children and young people
Families and Schools Together (FAST) for improving social, psychological, and
educational outcomes in children aged 4–13 years and their families
Family and parenting interventions for children and adolescents with conduct disorders
and delinquency aged 10–17 years
Family group conferences for children at risk of abuse and neglect
Functional family therapy for families of youth (ages 11–18 years) with behavior
problems
Group-based parent-training programs for improving emotional and behavioral
adjustment in children aged 0–3 years
Independent living programs for improving outcomes for young people leaving the care
system
Individual and group-based parenting for improving psychosocial outcomes for teenage
parents and their children
Interventions for the secondary prevention and treatment of emotional abuse of children
by primary carers
Interventions intended to reduce pregnancy-related outcomes among adolescents
Kinship care for the safety, permanency, and well-being of children removed from the
home for maltreatment
Mentoring to prevent tobacco use by children and adolescents
Mentoring to prevent use of illegal drugs and alcohol by children and adolescents
Multisystemic therapy for social, emotional, and behavioral problems in children and
adolescents aged 10–17 years
Parent-training programs for improving maternal psychosocial health
School-based education programs for the prevention of child sexual abuse
The recurrence of child maltreatment: predictive validity of risk assessment instruments
Treatment foster care for improving outcomes in children and young people

---

Source: http://www.campbellcollaboration.org, last accessed March 1, 2009.

Do not forget all of the areas of a child's life that make child welfare so
complicated. Health, mental health, developmental disabilities, and substance abuse are just a few domains about which child welfare agencies
must be knowledgeable since they all affect children. In addition to various journals in these fields there are organizations that sponsor research

conferences that are another good source for the latest evidence-supported practices. For example, the Florida Mental Health Institute at the University of South Florida holds an annual research conference that is an excellent source for the latest mental health research.

There is good reason for the child welfare agency to establish a knowledge base in these many fields. Not only is the agency responsible for effective treatment for children in their custody but professionals in other fields are not always up to date on practices supported by the best available evidence in their area. A visit to the AHRQ Web site is a bit overwhelming, yet it can yield important information. For example, a child welfare agency is likely to be serving a large number of children with chronic asthma. The AHRQ Web site includes a report on the management of chronic asthma (http://www.ahrq.gov/clinic/epcsums/asthmasum.htm). This report summarizes the research evidence for the management of this condition and this can serve as a policy guide for a child welfare agency's response to this important problem.

Step 4: Choosing the Intervention Based on the Best Available Evidence

For most child welfare managers the selection of an intervention has as much to do with cost as with the level of evidence. These considerations include questions such as: What is the ratio of clients to workers with this intervention? What qualifications will the staff need? What training and supervision are required to implement the intervention? These questions are important because if it is not possible to fund the policy with the best evidence, this becomes an academic exercise. In this section the reader is encouraged to consider the issue of funding the intervention after examination of the evidence.

The ideal situation is to find an intervention that has external validity by virtue of being repeatedly shown to have a large impact across variations in populations, settings, and outcomes. Such a high level of generalized effectiveness is difficult to find. It is more likely that the best that can

---

Looking for Intervention Research?

1. Have someone in the agency develop search skills such as those identified by Gray (2001).
2. Check out the Campbell Collaboration.
3. Look for articles that review evidence-supported interventions.
4. Attend research conferences.
5. Don't forget how interdisciplinary child welfare is and check out the:
   a. Cochrane Collaboration and
   b. Reviews of empirically supported interventions in other fields.

be done is to identify a promising intervention that has been tested less rigorously and try it. This means that evaluation of the intervention with the target population is a critical step. This is also an important way for the evidence base of child welfare to be built.

To illustrate the process of selecting interventions consider the question regarding placement disruption that involved victims of sexual abuse:

> Are children and youth who have been victims of sexual abuse (*P*) more likely to have more stable living arrangements (*O*) if the effects of the abuse were alleviated (*I*) compared to sexual abuse victims who did not receive this treatment (*C*)?

Begin by visiting the Campbell Collaboration Web site and the Cochrane Collaboration to see if someone has reviewed this intervention research. Fortunately the same review of cognitive-behavioral interventions for sexually abused children is listed in both places. Unfortunately, it took 6 years from the date the protocol was first published (2000) to the date of the first published review (Macdonald, Higgins, & Ramchandani, 2006). Ten trials, including 847 participants, were included in this review. The data suggested that cognitive-behavioral therapy (CBT) may have a positive impact on the sequelae of child sexual abuse, but most results were statistically nonsignificant. The reviewer confirmed CBT's potential as a means of addressing the adverse consequences of child sexual abuse, but emphasized the tenuousness of the evidence base and the need for more carefully conducted and better reported trials. A quick search of the bibliographic databases finds that both the Chaffin and Friedrich (2004) and the Thomlison (2003) reviews identify a trauma-focused CBT as a well-tested intervention.

Researchers involved with the Campbell Collaboration have a rigorous protocol for conducting a meta-analysis that involves many questions about how the experiment was conducted (http://www.campbellcollaboration.org/Fraguidelines.html). It is useful for someone in the agency to acquire the skills to carry out a similar type of review. The result of this type of review is needed by a manager to make a decision about selecting an intervention. However, until this type of rigorous review is available there are five questions that a child welfare manager can ask of child welfare researchers when examining the results of intervention research.

1. What were the populations or groups studied?
2. To what was the intervention compared?
3. What were the outcomes examined in the study?
4. How large were the effect sizes of the intervention?
5. How many studies of the intervention are there using the strongest research design?

What Were the Populations or Groups Studied?

It is important to examine the populations studied to determine how well they match the target population in your agency. Some studies may be conducted with populations that are drawn directly from child welfare agencies and others may be community referrals using vague criteria. A research review yielded the six clinical trials summarized in Table 6.2. The table shows that two of the first four studies drew on populations directly from child welfare agencies with one of these requiring substantiated sexual abuse by child protective services (CPS). The third study group was a mix of children drawn from child welfare and from pediatricians and prosecutors. The fourth study was conducted in Australia so it is difficult to determine how similar these children would be to those in the United States. However, because the condition studied is sexual abuse and this was confirmed before children were included in the study this study was included. The ages of the children in the four studies were 2 to 8, 4 to 8, 7 to 13, and 5 to 17 years. The participants in two studies were younger and in two were older. A manager may want to pay closer attention to the studies in which the age of the participants is closer to that of the target population. However, the studies with participant age closest to the population of interest may not be of the highest quality, which would argue against its use. Even if there is not a perfect fit between the age of the target population and the age of the studied group, a manager might still want to explore the use of a cognitive-behavioral intervention, although cautiously.

The number of children included in the studies is another important consideration. Although there are many caveats, in general studies that include more people have greater statistical precision and power (see Chapter 5, this volume). The studies reported in Table 6.2 range from 28 to 89 children. The Australian study had smaller groups of 9 and 10 participants. Because the other studies had reasonably sized groups, we can have more confidence in their results. It should be noted, however, that these numbers represent only those who completed the study. All studies suffer attrition to some extent as some people do not comply or are unable to complete the requirements of the study. In general, we need to be cautious about the validity of findings from studies that do not fully account for all of the people who are assigned intervention even if they do not fully receive the intended treatment. Chapter 7 discusses the importance of intent-to-treat (ITT) analysis and describes a method of adjusting effect size estimates when there is incomplete compliance with the intended treatment in randomized clinical trials.

To What Was the Intervention Compared?

If an intervention is compared to what is usually provided to those in the target population and it demonstrates superior outcomes, then we have added confidence in its effectiveness. In the example of CBT summarized in Table 6.2, two studies compare this to supportive counseling. One

TABLE 6.2 Cognitive-Behavioral Treatment for Victims of Sexual Abuse[a]

Study	Sample	Intervention Groups	Outcomes Assessed	Effect Size Results[b]
Deblinger, Stauffer, & Steer (2001)	44 children between 2 and 8 years of age and their nonoffending maternal caregivers from child welfare system (17), prosecutors offices (14), and pediatricians (12)	Cognitive-behavioral compared to supportive counseling	PTSD Impact of events on intrusive thoughts and avoidance of thoughts Parent emotional reaction, social support, parental practices, CBCL Child sexual behavior What if situations	Comparing posttest scores between groups found that most effect sizes were nonsignificant (ns) or small
King, Tonge, Mullen, Myerson, Heyne, Rollings, Martin, & Ollendick (2000)	28 sexually abused children (groups of 9, 9, and 10) aged 5–17 years referred from sexual assault centers, Department of Health and Community Services, mental health professionals, medical practitioners, and school authorities in Australia	Cognitive-behavioral therapy 1. Children only 2. Child and nonoffending mother compared to those on the waiting list	PTSD symptoms Fear thermometer for sexually abused children Coping questionnaire for sexually abused children Revised children's manifest anxiety scale Children's depression inventory CBCL–PTSD CBCL–internal CBCL–external Global assessment functioning	Large effect size for parent and parent/child Medium effect size for child and small for parent/child Small effect size for child and ns for parent/child Small effect size for child and large for parent/child Small effect size for both groups Small effect for PTSD child and large for PTSD parent/child Small effect size on internalizing behavior for parent/child, ns for child Negative effect size for both groups on externalizing behavior Medium effect size for child only, large for parent/child

Cohen & Mannarion (1997)	43 sexually abused preschool children (4 to 8 years of age) with abuse substantiated by CPS	Cognitive-behavioral therapy for sexually abused preschoolers compared to nondirective supportive therapy	Child behavior Checklist parent version Child sexual behavior inventory Weekly behavior report	Medium effect sizes for total behavior problems, internalized behavior, child sexual behavior inventory, and weekly behavior report Small effect sizes for social competence, externalized behaviors
Deblinger, Lippmann, & Steer (1996)	89 sexually abused children between 7 and 13 years of age from child welfare or prosecutors office	Cognitive-behavioral 1. Children only 2. Parent only 3. Child and parent compared to standard community treatment.	CBCL internalized CBCL externalized Child depression STAIC state STAIC trait PTSD Parenting behaviors	Effect small or ns for all three groups Effect large for parent-only group, medium for parent and child group, and ns for child group Effect medium for parent-only and parent and child groups and small for parent group Effect medium for child group and ns for other two groups Effect small for all three groups Effect large for parent and child and child-only groups and medium for parent-only group Effect medium for parent-only group and ns for the other two groups

(continued)

TABLE 6.2 (Continued)

Study	Sample	Intervention Groups	Outcomes Assessed	Effect Size Results[b]
Berliner & Saunders (1996)	65 sexually abused children between the ages of 4 and 13 years referred by parents, DPS, criminal justice, health, and mental health providers with sexual abuse either substantiated or not unfounded by CPS or law enforcement	Groups of children were randomly assigned to "conventional sexual abuse-specific group therapy" and the same treatment with sessions added regarding fear, gradual exposure, and stress inoculation	Fear survey schedule for children Sexual abuse fear evaluation scales Revised children's manifest anxiety scale CBCL Children's depression inventory Child sexual behavior inventory	ns effect size ns effect size ns effect size Small effect size for total, social, and internalized Medium effect size for externalized ns effect size Small effect size
Celano, Hazzard, Webb & McCall (1996)	32 girls aged 8 to 13 years and their nonoffending female caretakers; all reports of sexual abuse had been substantiated by the appropriate statutory child protection agency	Treatment based on Finkelhor and Browne's theoretical model of sexual abuse compared to treatment as usual	CBCL Children's impact of traumatic events Children's global assessment scale Parent's reaction to incest disclosure scale Parental attribution scale	Medium effect size for externalizing, ns for internalizing and social Medium effect size for self-blame and powerlessness, small for betrayal, traumatic sexualization PTSD Small effect size Small effect size Small effect size on child blame, perpetrator blame, negative impact, ns of self-blame

[a] PTSD, posttraumatic stress disorder; CBCL, child behavior checklist; CPS, child protective services; STAIC, State-Trait Anxiety Inventory for Children; DPS, Department of Public Safety.

[b] Effect sizes are calculated by comparing posttest results between groups. Effect is judged to be small if ES is less then 0.5, medium if ES is between 0.51 and 0.79, and large if ES is 0.8 or larger (Cohen, 1988). Effect sizes are in favor of the intervention unless noted as negative.

compared three different intervention groups with standard community treatment. The three groups were (1) only children receiving the intervention, (2) only a parent receiving the intervention, and (3) both child and parent receiving the intervention. This study is particularly interesting because of the increased knowledge it can yield. In addition to demonstrating the efficacy of CBT it also has the potential of showing the most effective method of delivery (child, parent, or both). Following the lead of this study, the Australian experiment compared a child-only group to a parent and child group and to a waiting list group.

What Were the Outcomes Examined in the Study?

An exact match between the outcomes of the study and the desired outcomes of the intervention is unlikely. In the example used in this chapter, if the risk group is sexually abused children and the desired outcome is placement stability we would like to see this be the outcome of the tested interventions. This is not the case. As Table 6.2 demonstrates, none of the tested interventions targeted placement stability as an outcome. Child behavior, posttraumatic stress symptoms, and parenting behavior are the major outcomes reported in these studies. However, one hypothesis is that placement stability is related to a child's problematic behavior, which results from being a victim of sexual abuse. In that case, if an intervention demonstrates improvement in behaviors, stability may result. Although the studies in Table 6.2 all report positive results on some of the behavioral outcomes, how much of a change results is open to question.

How Large Were the Effect Sizes of the Intervention?

Results of clinical trials are typically reported in terms of statistical significance. This refers to the test of the null hypothesis that the observed difference between the intervention and comparison group on the outcome of interest is statistically indistinguishable from zero. As discussed in Chapter 5, it is preferable to calculate an effect size (ES) that indicates the magnitude of the difference and can be assessed for practical significance. Effect sizes are particularly useful for combining the results of many clinical trials into something like an average effect size. An ES can be negative, zero, or positive for differences or less than one, one, or greater than one for ratios. If an outcome is measured so that higher or larger implies better, a negative difference or a ratio less than one means that the intervention was worse than the comparison, a zero difference or a ratio of one means that there was no difference, and a positive difference or ratio greater than one means that the intervention group demonstrated better outcomes than the comparison group.

Unfortunately it is still rare that an article reporting the results of a study will report the effect size, although usually enough information is included so that it can be estimated. There are effect size calculators that are available on the World Wide Web.[3] Because there are also many ways to calculate effect size, effect sizes reported in different reports may not be comparable. In addition, researchers debate the merits of each type of effect size and this can be confusing (Hunter & Schmidt, 2004). Effect sizes are sometimes classified as small, medium, and large. For example, Cohen (1988) developed what is called Cohen's d, which is defined as the difference between two means divided by a standard deviation of the data. Therefore d represents an intervention effect in standard deviation units. Cohen proposed that a d between 0.2 and 0.5 be considered small, from 0.5 to 0.8 medium, and greater than 0.8 large. Although other effect size measures exist with various proposals for differentiating small, medium, and large, they can all be compared to Cohen's designation, which is still considered to be useful. For example, when comparing odds ratios, a ratio of 1.25 is considered small, 1.66 is considered medium, and 2 or higher is considered large.

For the CBT example in Table 6.2 Cohen's small, medium, and large designations are reported for each outcome. An average effect size calculated by combining all of the studies was not done because such a small number of studies used the same outcome measures. The study of Deblinger, Stauffer, and Steer (2001) that compared CBT to supportive counseling resulted in nonsignificant, small effect sizes for all outcomes. The study by Cohen and Mannarion (1997) found small to medium effects. The study by Deblinger, Lippmann, and Steer (1996) yielded mixed results but did find some large effects. In general, given the difficulty of matching existing research to agency problems as well as problems of implementation, a manager will be most interested in large effects. In this study large effects were found for two outcomes. These were (1) child externalizing behavior for children in the parent only intervention group and (2) symptoms of posttraumatic stress for children in the parent and child treatment group as well as the child-only group.

The Australian study (King et al., 2000) followed the Deblinger et al. (1996) design but did not include parenting behaviors. This study found large effects for the intervention on PTSD symptoms for both the child-only and the parent/child groups. They also found large effects for children's anxiety and overall level of functioning for the parent/child group. Interestingly, in opposition to the study of Deblinger et al. (1996), King et al. (2000) found nonsignificant changes but negative effect sizes for child externalizing behavior. It is not possible to determine why this was the case, but it may be due to the smaller number of children who participated in this study.

An examination of the best available intervention research for the population of victims of sexual abuse and the outcome of placement stability yields the following conclusions.

1. Four randomized studies testing CBT were found representing a beginning body of research.

2. In two studies, the children included in the study were primarily drawn from child welfare populations. One study was conducted in Australia, which makes comparison of the population difficult, although it appears to be similar to the other studies.
3. None of the studies used placement disruption as an outcome. However, the outcomes of child behavior and parenting behavior may be linked to placement disruption.
4. Most effects were small to medium, with one study yielding large effects for child externalized behavior and two finding large effects for symptoms of posttraumatic stress.

A child welfare manager might conclude that for a group of young children who are victims of sexual abuse and who may experience placement disruption linked to problematic child behavior, the type of cognitive-behavioral intervention tested in the experiment of Deblinger et al. (1996) is worth a closer look.

The above example explored interventions tested through randomized clinical trials. For situations in which the studies were observational, i.e., subjects were not randomly assigned to the intervention and comparison groups, the process is similar. The research literature at the next highest level of evidence is collected and synthesized in a similar manner and promising interventions are identified for further evaluation. Careful implementation and testing of selected interventions are essential regardless of the level of evidence with which it is identified. Faulty implementation can render the most powerful intervention powerless. Only careful testing of the intervention can determine if it is effective in a particular context.

How Many Studies of the Intervention Are There Using the Strongest Research Design?

When there are multiple studies using strong research designs with similar results we gain confidence in the efficacy and effectiveness of the intervention. A single study may produce positive results but additional trials may show that this situation was unique. In addition, results from multiple trials make it possible to estimate the size of the effect of the intervention.

Thomlison (2003) includes three references for the trauma-focused CBT, and Macdonald et al. (2006) included 10 studies and excluded three studies. A current review of abstracts should also be conducted to identify more recent research. As each study is obtained, checking the research base used by the author may also identify additional research that has been missed by other search methods. In this case a search of *Psychological Abstracts* using sexual abuse and cognitive-behavioral as key words, Thomlison's references and studies mentioned in each of the articles yielded the six clinical trials summarized in Table 6.2.

As expected, these studies vary as to the intervention tested. Although most of them are identified as CBTs, they are not all defined in the same way. The study by Berliner and Saunders (1996) was not included in Macdonald's review of cognitive-behavioral interventions and this may be due to the belief that their subsequent research better fits this category. If a cognitive-behavioral intervention is ultimately selected to be tested, a closer look at similarities and differences between interventions and identification of those that are most effective is needed.

Step 5: Integrating the Intervention within the Context of Clients and Community

Table 6.2 summarizes the clinical trials of cognitive-behavioral treatment of victims of sexual abuse and identifies the populations that participated in the studies. Each study included a different group of clients. One was conducted in Australia. With only six studies it is impossible to cover a broad range of clients or communities. How this intervention might fit a particular community is an important question.

To gain insight into how the policy might fit, it is useful to engage the potential client group and community in examining the intervention and how well it fits the particular context. For the example of sexual abuse it is unlikely that it would be possible to engage victims. However, engaging a diverse group of community members will indicate how well the intervention fits the community. An intervention that is selected but is unacceptable to the community is likely to fail.

Step 6: Implementing the Intervention through Policy and Practice

Implementation of the intervention involves a number of considerations. Among these are the specifics of how the intervention is operationalized, the costs of implementation, funding sources, and other organizational supports. These include consideration of training, organizational norms, and other systems that support the use of evidence.

The child welfare agency is clearly a knowledge organization. Child welfare policy, training, and workers' interactions with children and families are driven by knowledge as well as by values and organizational resources. Just as organizations have elaborate systems to manage the various types of resources that exist, organizations need systems to manage knowledge.

Gray (2001) devotes considerable attention to what is needed to create an organization that systematically uses the best available evidence and points out that this requires a culture that includes

- Managers using the best available evidence.
- Systems that provide evidence—the evidence center.
- Systems that promote the use of evidence.

Evidence-Guided Managers

A manager who is guided by the best available evidence is someone who is continually learning and challenging others to test their opinions and beliefs. Friedman, Lipshitz, and Overmeer (2001) describe this person as someone who will produce action strategies such as combining advocacy with inquiry, making statements that can be disconfirmed, openly testing their own inferences, and inquiring into the reasoning of others. This is a seemingly curious combination of self-confidence and doubt.

For these managers to flourish, an organizational climate needs to be cultivated that fosters both critical inquiry and agency integrity. One the one hand, there needs to be an "ethos of science" (Merton, 1996) that legitimizes universalism, collaboration, disinterestedness, and organized skepticism in the development of valid knowledge. On the other, there needs to be an "ethos of accountability" that reinforces a diffuse scope of interest in the welfare of principals, transparency, empirical research, experimentation, and the reflexive use of results to improve agency performance. The overriding orientation is that managerial judgments be guided by evidence.

Evidence Center

The example of research review and analysis of promising interventions to address the problem of placement stability is illustrative of the work of an evidence center. An evidence center is a collection of staff with the skills and resources to conduct this process for specific child and family outcomes that are of concern to principals and agents. For purposes of presentation in this chapter the process was simplified, but resources such as the Campbell Collaboration and books such as those by Gray (2001) and Hunter and Schmidt (2004) describe important tasks and skills needed by staff of an evidence center.

A real world example of this idea was implemented by Jess McDonald when he was Director of the Illinois Department of Children and Family Services. He established a "Best Practices Committee" composed of people who were responsible for the major divisions within the agency including policy, training, permanence, and protection. The purpose of this committee was to examine the research base for all proposed policy, training, and practice guides.

It is difficult for an agency that devotes its time and attention to the daily work pressures of helping vulnerable families and children to operate an evidence center. However, many universities are familiar with this type of work. Establishing an evidence center through a partnership with a university brings together the strengths of both organizations (see Chapter 11, this volume).

Promote the Use of Evidence

In addition to managers guided by evidence and an evidence center, results-oriented accountability requires organizational mechanisms to promote the use of evidence. The healthcare field has demonstrated that even when there is evidence that a particular treatment is effective, it still might not be widely adopted (Gira, Kessler, & Poertner, 2004). Researchers identified many factors that hinder implementation including variations in making clinical decisions, gaps between what is known and what is practiced, and the knowledge revolution as problems for the healthcare field (Gray, 2003). Going from a rapidly growing knowledge base to practice is a substantial problem. A report by AHRQ states:

> Recent studies indicate an average of 17 years is needed before new knowledge generated through research, such as randomized clinical trials, is incorporated into widespread clinical practice—and even then the application of the knowledge is very uneven. (Agency for Healthcare Research and Quality, 2004)

This emphasizes the need for organizations to have mechanisms that promote the use of evidence. Adoption of policy based on the best available evidence is one dimension of the problem. Another is implementation of the intervention in a way that is the same as was used in the clinical trial. This is called treatment or model fidelity. It is not uncommon for a well-tested intervention to produce positive results in an experimental situation but not produce the same results when implemented in the field.

For example, the Washington State Institute for Public Policy conducted an evaluation of "research-based" programs for juvenile offenders (Washington State Institute for Public Policy, 2004). A judgment about the degree to which the intervention was implemented as intended was included in this evaluation and called "competent" or "not competent." One of their findings is that when a program called Functional Family Therapy was competently implemented it resulted in a 38% decrease in recidivism, but when it was not competently implemented the result was a 16% *increase* in recidivism. One of their conclusions was that "for these programs to achieve success . . . the program must be delivered in a competent manner that follows the programs specifications" (p. 3).

In the placement stability example in this chapter the organization may want to improve its competence in the delivery of the cognitive-behavioral intervention. In this case the organization would want to obtain the manual that Deblinger et al. (1996) used to define and test their intervention. This manual should answer important questions regarding qualifications of staff, staff-to-client ratios, type of training required, etc. It is the manual that should operationalize the intervention with sufficient specificity that most or all questions regarding implementation can be answered.

Get the manual. It is the manual that the researchers used to train staff and monitor the implementation of the new practice that operationalizes the intervention. Beware of vague manuals.

Training is also useful in promoting the use of evidence. However, frequently the knee-jerk response to implementing a new idea is to offer training, but the content and delivery of training materials seldom accomplish the intended goal. For example, a review of continuing education in the healthcare field showed that traditional continuing education using didactic lectures was not effective in promoting evidence-based practices (Gira et al., 2004).

Despite such limitations, training does have an important role in promoting the use of evidence. When implementing an evidence-guided policy, training content should be drawn from the manual used by those who tested the intervention. For this training to be effective it is not just the content of training that is important it is also the methods of delivery. The review of continuing education in the healthcare field found that when training included a practice component it was more likely to be effective. There have also been studies of the transfer of training that identify important design considerations for promoting the use of training (Wehrmann, Shin, & Poertner, 2002). Aspects of training that are important to the use of skills on the job are similar to those used by researchers to ensure consistent implementation of the intended intervention.

Researchers who conduct clinical trials go to extraordinary lengths to ensure that the intervention that is tested is in fact what is delivered and training plays a central role in these efforts. For example, Deblinger et al. (1996) describe the process that they used, which included training the therapist using a session-by-session detailed treatment manual, implementing the intervention with one pilot case before treating study participants, and intensive supervisory oversight that included review of audio-taped treatment sessions. This type of attention, which ensures that those who are supposed to deliver the intervention have detailed behavioral training in the intervention, demonstrate these skills, and receive feedback on their application, is not only essential to clinical trials but also to the implementation of a well-tested intervention.

An agency's quality assurance system is still another mechanism to promote evidence-guided policies. Audits and sample case readings can focus on those items that evidence shows are linked to the desired child or family outcome. The Washington State study that found that program models that had positive effects were delivered as intended, but those that were not demonstrated negative results, led to guidelines for delivering these programs as well as quality assurance measures to monitor their delivery (Washington State Institute for Public Policy, 2004).

This is the concept of treatment or model fidelity. Fidelity is monitored through questionnaires that assess the degree to which an intervention is being implemented as intended. These fidelity instruments were developed because of findings similar to those of the Washington State evaluation of programs for juvenile offenders. If a decision was made to pilot test CBT for victims of sexual abuse, in addition to carefully designed training, it is important to use mechanisms such as fidelity instruments to better ensure that the intervention is delivered as intended.

For example, the developers of multisystemic therapy (MST)[4] developed several fidelity instruments including a supervisor adherence measure (SAM) and a therapist adherence measure (TAM). The TAM allows consumers to report their experience with their work with therapists. This includes items such as:

- The therapist recommended that family members do specific things to solve our problems.
- Family members and the therapist agreed on the goals of the session.
- There were awkward silences and pauses during the session.
- The therapist's recommendation required family members to work on their problems almost every day. (Henggler, Schoenwald, Liao, Ketourneau, & Edwards, 2002)

By obtaining periodic consumer feedback through fidelity instruments it is possible to determine if critical aspects of the intervention are occurring as intended. This feedback is then used as part of a quality assurance system. This provides feedback so that managers can make decisions to reinforce what is occurring or take corrective action through supervision or retraining.

The steps outlined for guiding the selection and implementation of decisions concerning child welfare practices and policies based on the best available evidence require significant organizational commitment and resources. These preparatory steps help ensure that the most promising interventions are implemented as intended. This sets the stage for the evaluation of the new practice to determine if the intervention is having the intended effect on client outcomes. In addition to determining if the policy is having the intended effect, careful evaluation also helps build and refine the knowledge base of child welfare. Chapter 7 takes up this next stage in the cycle of results-oriented accountability.

Technical Appendix 6A: Ways of Categorizing Research Evidence

Level 1: Well-supported, efficacious treatment with positive evidence from more than two randomized clinical trials.

Level 2: Supported and probably efficacious treatment with positive evidence from two or more quasi-experimental studies, or where researchers found positive evidence from only one clinical trial.

Level 3: Supported and acceptable treatment with positive evidence from comparative studies, correlation studies, and case control studies; one nonrandomized study; or any type of quasi-experimental study.

Level 4: Promising and acceptable treatment with evidence from experts or clinical experience of respected authority or both (Thomlison, 2003).

Figure 6A.1 Child welfare.

Level 1: At least 5 published studies with scientifically rigorous designs (randomized clinical trials, well-controlled quasi-experimental designs) using a variety of meaningful outcome measures.

Level 2: Less than five published scientifically rigorous studies and /or studies using single outcome measures or less rigorous dependent variables.

Level 3: Published studies of less rigorous design (e.g. pre/post designs with no control group, client self-report of perceived changes following receipt of services).

Level 4: Multiple organizational "case studies" with reported outcomes published in peer-reviewed journals.

Level 5: Expert panel recommendations based upon empirical research evidence but NOT including expert consensus (e.g., based on "surveys" of expert clinicians, surveys of consumer preferences, unpublished program evaluations, etc.). (Cook, Toprac & Shore, 2004).

Figure 6A.2 Mental health.

TABLE 6A.1 Evidence-Based Medicine Levels of Evidence[a–f]

Level	Therapy/Prevention, Etiology/Harm	Prognosis	Diagnosis	Differential Diagnosis/ Symptom Prevalence Study	Economic and Decision Analyses
1a	SR (with homogeneity*) of RCTs	SR (with homogeneity*) of inception cohort studies; CDR† validated in different populations	SR (with homogeneity*) of Level 1 diagnostic studies; CDR† with 1b studies from different clinical centers	SR (with homogeneity*) of prospective cohort studies	SR (with homogeneity*) of Level 1 economic studies
1b	Individual RCT (with narrow confidence interval†)	Individual inception cohort study with >80% follow-up; CDR† validated in a single population	Validating** cohort study with good††† reference standards; or CDR† tested within one clinical center	Prospective cohort study with good follow-up***	Analysis based on clinically sensible costs or alternatives; systematic review(s) of the evidence; and including multiway sensitivity analyses
1c	All or none§	All or none case series	Absolute SpPins and SnNouts††	All or none case series	Absolute better-value or worse-value analyses††††
2a	SR (with homogeneity*) of cohort studies	SR (with homogeneity*) of either retrospective cohort studies or untreated control groups in RCTs	SR (with homogeneity*) of Level >2 diagnostic studies	SR (with homogeneity*) of 2b and better studies	SR (with homogeneity*) of Level >2 economic studies
2b	Individual cohort study (including low quality RCT; e.g., <80% follow-up)	Retrospective cohort study or follow-up of untreated control patients in an RCT; derivation of CDR† or	Exploratory** cohort study with good††† reference standards; CDR† after derivation, or validated only on split-sample§§§ or databases	Retrospective cohort study, or poor follow-up	Analysis based on clinically sensible costs or alternatives; limited review(s) of the evidence, or single studies; and

2c	"Outcomes" Research; ecological studies	validated on split-sample§§§ only "Outcomes" research		Ecological studies	including multiway sensitivity analyses Audit or outcomes research
3a	SR (with homogeneity*) of case-control studies		SR (with homogeneity*) of 3b and better studies	SR (with homogeneity*) of 3b and better studies	SR (with homogeneity*) of 3b and better studies
3b	Individual case-control study		Nonconsecutive study; or without consistently applied reference standards	Nonconsecutive cohort study, or very limited population	Analysis based on limited alternatives or costs, poor quality estimates of data, but including sensitivity analyses incorporating clinically sensible variations
4	Case series (and poor quality cohort and case-control studies§§)	Case series (and poor quality prognostic cohort studies***)	Case-control study, poor or nonindependent reference standard	Case series or superseded reference standards	Analysis with no sensitivity analysis
5	Expert opinion without explicit critical appraisal, or based on physiology, bench research, or "first principles"	Expert opinion without explicit critical appraisal, or based on physiology, bench research, or "first principles"	Expert opinion without explicit critical appraisal, or based on physiology, bench research, or "first principles"	Expert opinion without explicit critical appraisal, or based on physiology, bench research, or "first principles"	Expert opinion without explicit critical appraisal, or based on economic theory or "first principles"

a From Centre for Evidence-Based Medicine (May 2001). Last accessed 10/10/2008 from http://www.cebm.net/index.aspx?o=1025.

b Produced by Bob Phillips, Chris Ball, Dave Sackett, Doug Badenoch, Sharon Straus, Brian Haynes, and Martin Dawes since November 1998.

c Notes: Users can add a minus sign "−" to denote the level that fails to provide a conclusive answer because of

- EITHER a single result with a wide confidence interval (so that, for example, an ARR in an RCT is not statistically significant but whose confidence intervals fail to exclude clinically important benefit or harm)
- OR a systematic review with troublesome (and statistically significant) heterogeneity.
- Such evidence is inconclusive, and therefore can generate only Grade D recommendations.

(Continued)

* By homogeneity we mean a systematic review that is free of worrisome variations (heterogeneity) in the directions and degrees of results between individual studies. Not all systematic reviews with statistically significant heterogeneity need be worrisome, and not all worrisome heterogeneity needs to be statistically significant. As noted, studies displaying worrisome heterogeneity should be tagged with a "−" at the end of their designated level.

† Clinical Decision Rule. (These are algorithms or scoring systems that lead to a prognostic estimation or a diagnostic category.)

‡ See Note 2 for advice on how to understand, rate, and use trials or other studies with wide confidence intervals.

§ Met when all patients died before the Rx became available, but some now survive on it; or when some patients died before the Rx became available, but none now die on it.

§§ By a poor quality cohort study we mean one that failed to clearly define comparison groups and/or failed to measure exposures and outcomes in the same (preferably blinded) objective way in both exposed and nonexposed individuals and/or failed to identify or appropriately control known confounders and/or failed to carry out a sufficiently long and complete follow-up of patients. By a poor quality case-control study we mean one that failed to clearly define comparison groups and/or failed to measure exposures and outcomes in the same (preferably blinded) objective way in both cases and controls and/or failed to identify or appropriately control known confounders.

§§§ Split-sample validation is achieved by collecting all the information in a single tranche, then artificially dividing this into "derivation" and "validation" samples.

†† An "Absolute SpPin" is a diagnostic finding whose specificity is so high that a positive result rules in the diagnosis. An "Absolute SnNout" is a diagnostic finding whose sensitivity is so high that a negative result rules out the diagnosis.

‡‡ Good, better, bad, and worse refer to the comparisons between treatments in terms of their clinical risks and benefits.

††† Good reference standards are independent of the test and are applied blindly or objectively to all patients. Poor reference standards are haphazardly applied, but still independent of the test. Use of a nonindependent reference standard (where the "test" is included in the "reference" or where the "testing" affects the "reference") implies a Level 4 study.

†††† Better-value treatments are clearly as good but cheaper, or better at the same or reduced cost. Worse-value treatments are as good and more expensive, or worse and equally or more expensive.

** Validating studies test the quality of a specific diagnostic test, based on prior evidence. An exploratory study collects information and trawls the data (e.g., using a regression analysis) to find which factors are "significant."

*** By a poor quality prognostic cohort study we mean one in which sampling was biased in favor of patients who already had the target outcome, or the measurement of outcomes was accomplished in <80% of the study patients, or outcomes were determined in an unblinded, nonobjective way, or there was no correction for confounding factors.

**** Good follow-up in a differential diagnosis study is >80%, with adequate time for alternative diagnoses to emerge (e.g., 1–6 months acute, 1–5 years chronic)

^dGrades of Recommendation

A Consistent Level 1 studies

B Consistent Level 2 or 3 studies *or* extrapolations from Level 1 studies

C Level 4 studies *or* extrapolations from Level 2 or 3 studies

D Level 5 evidence *or* troublingly inconsistent or inconclusive studies of any level

^eIn "Extrapolations" data are used in a situation that potentially has clinically important differences from the original study situation.

^fSR, systematic review; RCT, randomized clinical trials; CDR, clinical decision rule; ARR, absolute risk reduction.

Notes

1. The concept of levels of evidence is controversial. However, the author's position is that it is necessary for selection of policy that has the best available evidence of its effectiveness.
2. An excellent reference for identification and development of the skills of searching the evaluation research literature is *Evidence-based practice for the helping professions: A practical guide with integrated multimedia* by Leonard E. Gibbs (2003) or *Evidence-based healthcare* by J. A. M. Gray (2001).
3. Effect size calculator was last accessed March 30, 2007 at http://web.uccs.edu/lbecker/Psy590/escalc3.htm.
4. Although the effectiveness of MST is much debated, it is used as an example because of its well-developed fidelity instruments.

References

Adoption and Safe Families Act of 1997, Pub. L. No. 105-89, 42 USC 1305, 111 Stat 2115 (1997).

Agency for Healthcare Research and Quality. (2004). *Closing the quality gap: Fact sheet—a critical analysis of quality improvement strategies.* Online: available at http://www.ahrq.gov/clinic/epc/qgapfact.htm.

Berliner, L., & Saunders, B. E. (1996). Treating fear and anxiety in sexually abused children: Results of a controlled 2-year study. *Child Maltreatment, 1*(4), 294—309.

Chaffin, M., & Friedrich, B. (2004). Evidence-based treatments in child abuse and neglect. *Children and Youth Services Review, 26,* 1097—1113.

Cohen, J. (1988). *Statistical power analysis for the behavioral sciences (2nd edition).* Hillsdale, NJ: Lawrence Erlbaum.

Cohen, J. A., & Mannarion, A. P. (1997). A treatment study for sexually abused preschool children: Outcome during a one-year follow-up. *Journal of the American Academy of Child and Adolescent Psychiatry, 36*(9), 1228—1235.

Deblinger, E., Lippmann, J., & Steer, R. (1996). Sexually abused children suffering posttraumatic stress symptoms: Initial treatment outcome findings. *Child Maltreatment, 1*(4), 310—321.

Deblinger, E., Stauffer, L. B., & Steer, R. A. (2001). Comparative efficacies of supportive and cognitive behavioral group therapies for young children who have been sexually abused and their nonoffending mothers. *Child Maltreatment, 6*(4), 332—343.

Friedman, V. J., Lipshitz, R., & Overmeer, W. (2001). Creating conditions for organizational learning. In M. Dierkes, A. B. Antal, J. Child, & I. Nonaka (Eds.), *Handbook of organizational learning and knowledge.* Oxford: Oxford University Press.

Gibbs, L. E. (2003). *Evidence-based practice for the helping professions: A practical guide with integrated multimedia.* Pacific Grove, CA: Brooks/Cole-Thomson Learning.

Gira, E. C., Kessler, M. L., & Poertner, J. (2004). Influencing social workers to use research evidence in practice: Lessons from medicine and the allied health professions. *Research in Social Work Practice, 14*(2), 68—79.

Glisson, C. (2008). Organizational climate and culture. In R. Patti (Ed.), *The handbook of human services management.* Thousand Oaks, CA: SAGE Publications.

Gray, J. A. M. (2001). *Evidence-based healthcare (2nd edition).* London: Churchill Livingston.

Hartnett, M. A., Falconnier, L., Leathers, S., & Testa, M. (1999). *Placement stability study*. Urbana, IL: Children and Family Research Center.

Henggler, S. W., Schoenwald, S. K., Liao, J. G., Ketourneau, E. J., & Edwards, D. L. (2002). Transporting efficacious treatments to field settings: The link between supervisory practices and therapist fidelity in MST programs. *Journal of Clinical Child Psychology, 31*(2), 155—167.

Hunter, J. E., & Schmidt, F. L. (2004). *Methods of meta-analysis: Correcting error and bias in research findings (2nd edition)*. Thousand Oaks, CA: SAGE Publications.

James, S., Landsverk, J., & Slymen, D. J. (2004). Placement moves in out-of-home care: Patterns and predictors. *Children and Youth Services Review, 26*, 185—206.

King, N. J., Tonge, B. J., Mullen, P., Myerson, N., Heyne, D., Rollings, S., . . . Ollendick, T. H. (2000). Treating sexually abused children with posttraumatic stress symptoms: A randomized clinical trial. *Journal of the American Academy of Child and Adolescent Psychiatry, 39*(11), 1347—1355.

Koh, E., & Testa, M. F. (2008). Propensity score matching of children in kinship and non-kinship foster care: Do permanency outcomes still differ? *Social Work Research, 32*, 105—116.

Macdonald, G., Higgins, J., & Ramchandani, P. (2006). Cognitive-behavioral interventions for Children who have been sexually abused. *Campbell Systematic Reviews*. The Campbell Collaboration. Available at: http://www.campbellcollaboration.org/library.php.

Merton, R. K. (1996). The ethos of science. In P. Sztompka (Ed.), *Robert K. Merton: On social structure and science* (pp. 267—276). Chicago: The University of Chicago Press.

Pardeck, J. T. (1984). Multiple placement of children in foster family care: An empirical study. *Social Work, 29*, 506—509.

Smith, D. K., Stormshak, E., Chamberlain, P., & Whaley, R. B. (2001). Placement disruption in treatment foster care. *Journal of Emotional and Behavioral Disorders, 9*(3), 200—205.

Thomlison, B. (2003). Characteristics of evidence-based child maltreatment interventions. *Child Welfare, 82*(5), 541—569.

Washington State Institute for Public Policy. (2004). *Outcome evaluation of Washington State's research-based programs for juvenile offenders*. Online: available at http://www.wsipp.wa.gov.

Wehrmann, K. C., Shin, H., & Poertner, J. (2002). Transfer of training: An evaluation study. *Journal of Health and Social Policy, 15*(3/4), 23—37.

Wulczyn, F., Kogan, J., & Harden, B. J. (2003). Placement stability and movement trajectories. *Social Service Review, 77*(2), 212—236.

7

EVALUATION OF CHILD WELFARE INTERVENTIONS

Mark F. Testa

Results-oriented accountability seeks to strengthen the validity of child welfare knowledge and improve agency performance by rigorously evaluating the efficacy and effectiveness of promising interventions for attaining the outcomes valued by families, administrators, policymakers, and the public at large. Whereas progress is steadily being made in cataloguing evidence-supported interventions (ESI) and the generalizability of their impact (see Chapter 6, this volume), addressing our nation's critical child welfare challenges requires much more than a *few* examples of research-proven programs. It demands a veritable explosion of innovations, rigorous verification of hypothesized solutions, and the systematic dissemination of ESI that can foster accountability and improve child welfare policy and service delivery.

The purpose of this chapter is to lay out an evaluative framework for assessing the *internal validity* of promising interventions, which is sufficiently robust to withstand credible challenges to inferences about *causality*, such as the average causal effect of an intervention on outcomes. A key claim is that randomized controlled experiments should be and can be implemented more routinely in child welfare than is currently the practice. Uncontrolled experimentation on vulnerable children and families by well-meaning child welfare agents is no more ethical than controlled experimentation that seeks to improve the validity of knowledge and the efficacy of practice and policy. This is especially important when empirical support is as tenuous as it is currently for many existing practices and policies in child welfare.

Child welfare lags farther behind its sister disciplines of psychology, education, criminology, public health, and medicine in the routine use of randomized controlled experiments. But, when investments in rigorous child welfare experimentation and evaluation are occasionally made, the results are sometimes as unexpected and often as clarifying as, for example, what medical researchers have since learned about the once supposed public health benefits of preventative medical treatments, such as hormone-replacement therapy (Writing Group for the Women's Health Initiative Investigators, 2002) and breast self-exams (Gaskie & Nashelsky, 2005).

The family preservation experiments, which Congress mandated in the mid-1990s, illustrate the value of basing policy decisions on rigorous experimental designs. At the time, observational studies that monitored children's removal from their homes (but often lacked comparison groups) heralded the promise of intensive family preservation services (IFPS) programs. More than 80% of children who received IFPS avoided removal from their homes. Many private foundations and child welfare administrators seized upon these early findings as the way to preventing more costly foster care. In fact, hundreds of millions of dollars were devoted to this very purpose under the 1994 Family Preservation and Support (since renamed Promoting Safe and Stable Families) provisions of the Social Security Act. This was, however, before the results of the IFPS experiments, which were mandated by the U.S. Congress, became more widely known.

The multi-site studies that Westat, the Chapin Hall Center for Children, and James Bell Associates conducted in the late 1990s showed that IFPS were no more effective in preventing out-of-home placement or in reducing the recurrence of abuse than regular, less costly in-home services (Westat, Chapin Hall Center for Children, & James Bell Associates, 2001). The absence of randomly assigned comparison groups in many of the early IFPS studies had obscured the fact that removal rates were also generally low among children in regular in-home programs. Although these results are sometimes misinterpreted as indicating that family preservation services don't work (MacDonald, 1994), the correct message is that in-home services appear to be just as effective (or no less ineffective) as IFPS in preventing the removal of children from the home.

Federal Subsidized Guardianship Experiments

The benefit of randomly assigning clients, caseworkers, siblings, families, or other units of analysis to a promising, but still unconfirmed, intervention is that it greatly simplifies causal inference. By leaving the assignment process to chance, such as when flipping a coin, drawing a lottery ball, or consulting a table of random numbers, the laws of probability help to ensure that the intervention and comparison groups are statistically equivalent within the boundaries of chance error on both observable and unobservable characteristics before the start of the intervention. If, after the intervention is fully delivered, significant differences in outcomes emerge, it is reasonable to infer that the cause is the intervention itself rather than any preexisting dissimilarities between the groups. Crude or gross effect sizes can be used as valid estimators of the intervention's genuine causal impact on outcomes. Risk adjustment of the sort discussed in Chapter 5 is usually unnecessary. Although regression methods are sometimes used to adjust for significant differences that remain after randomization, there is disagreement about the appropriateness of such procedures (Freedman, 2008; Victoria, Habicht, & Bryce, 2004).

One of the largest randomized controlled experiments in child welfare is the subsidized guardianship demonstration, which the state of Illinois implemented under a federal IV-E waiver granted by the U.S. government in 1996 (Testa, 2002). The purpose of the demonstration was to test the impact of removing monetary disincentives to exit the foster care system by providing subsidies to relative and foster caregivers who become the permanent legal guardians of the children formerly under their foster care. The waiver authorized the state to draw on federal dollars to fund guardianship subsidies in amounts similar to the subsidies given to caregivers such as licensed foster or adoptive parents.

Figure 7.1 displays the subsidized guardianship logic model that guided the implementation of Illinois' waiver demonstration. One of the external conditions that prompted Illinois' application was the rapid growth in the state's Home of Relative (HMR) program as detailed in Chapter 3 of this volume. Although the HMR reform plan that the state instituted in 1995 reduced the number of children entering foster care, the reforms did little to alleviate the large backlog of children in long-term kinship foster care. Around the time Illinois applied for waiver

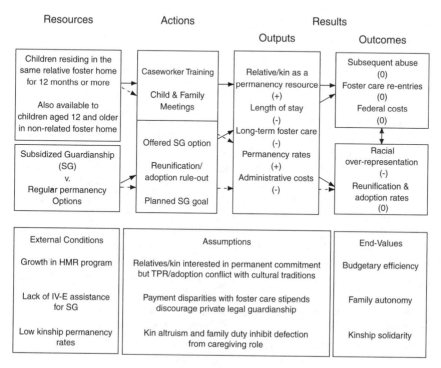

Figure 7.1 Subsidized guardianship logic model.

authority, the state registered the highest per-capita rate of foster care in the nation—17.1 foster children per 1000 children (Petit & Curtis, 1997).

Much of the need for substitute care in Illinois was accommodated at the time by placing foster children in the homes of their relatives. A court order, *Reid vs. Suter* (1992), prohibited state officials from diverting relatives caring for foster children to less costly Aid to Families with Dependent Children (AFDC) programs or summarily discharging them to relatives without first offering families the benefits of foster care licensing and financial support. Although legal guardianship was recognized as a permanency option under the Adoption Assistance and Child Welfare Act (AACWA) of 1980, the lack of federal IV-E assistance for guardianship, as the law had authorized for adoption, made this permanency option difficult to afford for most relatives. With federal subsidies limited to long-term foster care or adoption, permanency rates plummeted, leaving a growing backlog of children in long-term kinship foster care.

After HMR reform proved inadequate to alleviate the backlog, Illinois searched for alternative ways to support children in extended family care without retaining them in state custody. Focus groups conducted a few years earlier in Chicago indicated that many of these children in relative foster care were, for all practical purposes, "already home" (Testa, 1997). Reunification with birth parents had been ruled out, and many of the children had formed life-long attachments to their caregivers. A survey of families found that most relatives believed that the best plan for the children was for them to remain in their care until the children were fully grown (Testa, Shook, Cohen, & Woods, 1996). A sizeable share of the relative foster parents expressed a willingness to adopt, but few had been informed of this option by their caseworkers. Practice wisdom at the time held that kin don't adopt their own family members (Burnette, 1997; Thornton, 1991). The focus groups in Chicago suggested, however, that this reluctance wasn't necessarily born of kin's unwillingness to make permanent legal commitments. Rather, some kin felt that termination of parental rights needlessly severed family ties and that adoption forced extended family relations into the nuclear-family mold of parent and child. They preferred, instead, to retain their family identities as grandparents, aunts, and uncles rather than become their grandchildren's, niece's or nephew's mom and dad by adoption.

The Illinois survey of kinship caregivers suggested that family permanence might be boosted if kin were allowed to retain their foster care subsidies and become, instead, the private guardians of their young relatives for whom the state was spending far more money by keeping them in long-term foster care. Subsidized private guardianship appears tailor-made to address some families' concerns about adopting, because it transfers legal guardianship without severing parental rights. As noted in Chapter 3, it also preserves a role for the birth parents in their children's upbringing, as visitation rights, consent to adoption, and child support liabilities remain with the parents. The one major hitch at the time was that the federal IV-E program did not recognize guardianship subsidies as a federally reimbursable expenditure the way it did for adoption subsidies. Families suffered a sizeable drop in financial assistance if they assumed legal guardianship of the children under their foster care.

With Congress' authorization of IV-E waivers in 1994, Illinois found an affordable way to subsidize legal guardianship without losing federal reimbursement. In October 1996, the state received waiver authority to permit a five-year demonstration of subsidized guardianship with federal funds from the title IV-E program. The availability of federal guardianship assistance under a IV-E waiver promised to facilitate the conversion of safe and stable kinship placements into permanent homes, reduce lengths of stay in foster care, and reap savings from lower administrative costs. The hope was that all of this could be accomplished without jeopardizing the outcomes of child safety, home stability, and federal cost-neutrality. A potential positive side effect was a reduction in the overrepresentation of African-American children who dominated the numbers of foster children in long-term kinship foster care.

To achieve these desired outcomes, legislation first had to be passed to establish subsidized guardianship as a supplementary permanency goal, caseworkers had to be trained and family meetings convened. The terms and conditions of the federal waiver required the rule-out of reunification and adoption before subsidized guardianship could be pursued to ensure that guardianship didn't simply substitute for reunification and adoption. Even though the logic model depicts the null hypothesis of no difference, there was the concern that a negative side-effect of subsidized guardianship could be a decline in reunifications and adoptions.

The Illinois demonstration was implemented in May 1997. A decade after their initial assignment, more than 11,000 children were discharged through subsidized guardianship under the demonstration. Two follow-up interviews were completed with caregivers on a probability sample of 2425 children enrolled in the demonstration who were randomly assigned to intervention and comparison groups.[1] As of December 30, 2008, there was a 5.5 percentage point difference in overall permanency rates (reunification, adoption, and guardianship) between sibling groups (clusters) randomly assigned to the intervention (88.6 %) and comparison (83.1%) groups. This difference corresponds to an effect size (OR = 1.58, 95% CL = 1.19 − 2.01, sig. < 0.001, one-tailed test adjusted for clustering), which is slightly smaller than the 6.1 percentage point difference (OR = 1.38), which was reported in the final evaluation report filed with the U.S. Department of Health and Human Services (HHS) (Testa, Cohen, Smith, & Westat, Inc., 2003).[2] Although the difference in proportions was small, the boost in overall permanence, combined with the court's ability to transfer guardianship without first terminating parental rights, reduced the intervention group's average length of stay in foster care by 209 days. This produced a net administrative IV-E cost savings of $2294 per child, which, when multiplied by the 40,000 children assigned to the intervention group, yielded Illinois a net surplus of approximately $90 million federal dollars that the state was able to reinvest in subsidies for non-IV-E eligible children and other child welfare improvements.

These findings on greater family permanence, shorter lengths of stay, administrative savings (Testa et al., 2003), and subsequent positive results for child safety and well-being (Testa, 2005), convinced the federal government to renew the Illinois waiver for another 5 years (U.S. Department of Health and Human Services, 2004). The evidence was compelling enough for the Pew Commission on Children in Foster Care (2004) to recommend amending title IV-E of the Social Security Act to fund guardianship assistance. Congressmen Danny Davis (D-IL) and Timothy Johnson (R-IL) acted on the Illinois findings and the Pew Commission recommendations by introducing bipartisan legislation, the Kinship Caregiver's Support Act (H.R. 2188), which authorized all states to offer federal guardianship assistance payments to relatives who assume legal guardianship of children under their foster care. These provisions were subsequently incorporated into the Fostering Connections to Success and Improving Adoptions Act that President Bush signed into law on October 7, 2008 (P.L. 110–351).

One of the reasons that the USDHHS, the Pew Commission, and the U.S. Congress found the Illinois findings so compelling was the demonstration's use of random assignment. Table 7.1 shows that randomization

TABLE 7.1   Differences in Sample Characteristics of Children and Caregivers Enrolled in the Illinois Subsidized Guardianship Demonstration from 1997 to 1999

Items	Intervention	Comparison	Difference
Child characteristics			
Age at interview	9.9	10.1	−0.2
Age at removal	4.8	4.8	0.0
Female	49.5%	49.7%	−0.2%
White	9.9%	9.4%	0.5%
African-American	83.6%	85.3%	−1.7%
Caregiver characteristics			
Age at interview	51.2	51.8	−0.7
White	10.7%	10.8%	−0.1%
AfricanAmerican	82.5%	83.2%	−0.8%
Married	32.5%	32.2%	0.3%
Less than high school	40.0%	39.9%	0.1%
High school graduate	17.2%	19.3%	−2.1%
Some college	28.5%	24.8%	3.7%
Full-time employment	34.8%	34.2%	0.6%
Not in labor force	47.6%	48.7%	−1.1%
Intend to raise child to adulthood	78.7%	79.6%	−0.9%
Caregiver—child relationships			
Grandparent—grandchild	43.4%	48.3%	−4.9%
Aunt/uncle—niece/nephew	18.0%	18.1%	−0.1%
Foster parent—foster child	18.5%	17.2%	1.3%
Unmatched ethnic backgrounds	2.8%	3.3%	−0.5%
Sample N	1,197	1,228	

was largely successful in balancing the characteristics of children and their caregivers assigned to the intervention and comparison groups.[3] This statistical equivalence at baseline strengthens the internal validity of the claim that the observed boost in family permanence and the reduction in days in foster care was attributable to the offer of subsidized guardianship rather than to observed or unobserved differences with the comparison group at baseline or any co-occurring changes in policy. During this time period, there were many related policy changes that also had an impact on family permanence and length of stay, such as HMR Reform, performance contracting, and the federal ASFA legislation. Because these changes affected both groups of children assigned to the intervention and comparison conditions, any net difference in outcomes could plausibly be attributed to the effects of the waiver rather than to other contemporaneous influences.

Although the demonstration's rigorous evaluation design bolstered confidence in the validity of Illinois' results, there was still some uncertainty about the generalizability of the findings beyond the state's unique historical circumstances and its distinctive policies on kinship foster care. As discussed in Chapter 3, the state had implemented a controversial Home of Relative (HMR) Reform Plan in 1995 that supported non-licensed relative caregivers at a lower subsidy level than what relatives could receive as licensed foster or adoptive parents (Gleeson, 1996; Testa, 1997). This helped create a financial incentive for the majority of caregivers enrolled in the Illinois HMR program to leave the foster care system for higher subsidies under the new subsidized guardianship program or the existing adoption assistance program. The question that this unique circumstance raised was whether there would be as large an effect of subsidized guardianship on permanency rates across other populations and in other settings where such a financial incentive didn't exist.

The final set of subsidized guardianship waivers that the HHS awarded prior to the expiration of federal waiver authority in 2006 offered the opportunity to test the external validity of Illinois' results. Two of the demonstration sites, Milwaukee, Wisconsin, and the state of Tennessee, operated under terms and conditions that were similar to Illinois'. Both demonstrations utilized random assignment to ensure statistical equivalence between the intervention and comparison groups. Although the sizes of the Milwaukee and Tennessee demonstrations were much smaller, the results proved to be even more compelling than the Illinois findings.

At the mid-point of the five-year demonstrations, Milwaukee showed a 19.9 percentage point difference in overall permanence between the intervention (58.6%) and the comparison groups (38.7%). This difference corresponds to a large effect size (OR = 2.25, 95% CL = 1.18–4.30, sig. < 0.008, one-tailed test adjusted for clustering). Tennessee showed a 15.1 percentage point difference between the intervention (83.0%) and the comparison group (67.8%). This also corresponds to a large effect size (OR = 2.31, 95% CL = 1.32–4.04, sig. < 0.002, one-tailed test adjusted for clustering).

Cognizant of these successful replications of the Illinois results, the U.S. House Ways and Means Committee moved forward with federal legislation that added subsidized guardianship as a supplementary permanency option to the federal IV-E foster care program.

Ethical Issues and Agency Risks

In retrospect, the ethics of randomly assigning sibling groups to intervention and comparison groups under the subsidized guardianship demonstration may appear questionable to some. In all of the demonstration sites, a significant portion of caseworkers, court personnel, and other child welfare agents objected to or chaffed at the idea that any family would arbitrarily be denied the benefits of subsidized guardianship simply because of a sibling group's assignment to the control group. It is easy to overlook, however, that a decade ago subsidized guardianship was viewed by many state and federal officials as a potentially costly and risky undertaking.

There were doubts left over after Congress' repeal of the AFDC program about the wisdom of adding another uncapped entitlement to the federal child welfare program. Even though subsidized guardianship looked cost effective on paper, that is, the transfer of guardianship closes the foster care case so that administrative expenses are no longer shouldered by the state, there were concerns that any savings could become deficits in the long run because of the possible lengthier reliance of families on state assistance than if the children were reunified with their birth parents. Would family reunification suffer as a result of subsidized guardianship? Similarly, there were concerns about agency risks to adoption. Because guardianship is a quicker and less adversarial process than adoption, there were concerns that caseworkers and the courts might take the shorter route and stop initiating termination of parental rights proceedings. Would guardianship simply displace adoptions rather than boost family permanence? Finally, there was the worry that the withdrawal of public agency oversight would leave children in harm's way because birth parents would have unregulated access to the home and caregivers would be left to fend for themselves if problems arose. Would guardianship result in higher levels of maltreatment and re-entries back into foster care?

Addressing such concerns requires imagining what would have happened to reunifications, adoptions, and removal rates if the same families that were offered guardianship were also simultaneously denied this option. If such an experiment could be done, figuring out the downside of offering guardianship would simply be a matter of comparing what happened when these families were offered guardianship to what happened when these same families were denied this option. This is known as *counterfactual* reasoning. But, such empirical knowledge is of course unattainable. It is impossible for an identical group of people simultaneously to both receive and not receive the intervention. The best that can be done is to create high-quality approximations to this impossible counterfactual and to describe how the potential outcomes might differ on average (Shadish, Cook, & Campbell, 2002)

Approximating the Counterfactual in Experimental Research

Counterfactual reasoning makes explicit what evaluators and policymakers would really like to know: Is there an important difference between what actually happened (the factual) and what could have happened (the counterfactual). Even though such a difference is unobservable, randomization offers a method for creating high-quality empirical approximations to the desired counterfactual. Although not exactly clones of each other, randomized groups are similar enough on average that, under certain assumptions, the difference between the averages of the observed outcomes for the intervention and comparison groups can be taken as good approximations of the unobservable average difference between the potential outcomes under intervention and comparison conditions (Rubin, 2004).

Table 7.2 compares the difference in averages (rates) between the observed outcomes of reunification, adoption, and removal for the intervention group to the observed outcomes for the comparison groups in all three demonstration sites in Illinois, Tennessee, and Wisconsin. The differences in the rates of reunification and living with relatives between the intervention and comparison groups are negligible across all three sites. This suggests that the financial worries often expressed about subsidized guardianship's costing more in the long run appear to be unfounded. The concern that children would be dependent on guardianship assistance until their 18th birthday, whereas if denied this option they might have instead been reunified or discharged to the custody of kin, is not borne out by the data. Although one may wish reunification rates to be higher, the reality is that the children who are denied guardianship assistance are no more likely to be reunified than children who are afforded this option.

The answer to the concerns over the potential loss of adoptions appears less clear-cut. Although in Milwaukee the increase in guardianships came on top of the comparison group's proportion of adoptions, in both Illinois and Tennessee guardianships cut into the share of adoptions, which might have otherwise occurred as can be approximated by the higher adoption rates in the comparison group. Because adoption assistance is just as costly as guardianship assistance in terms of subsidies, the loss of potential adoptions is not a fiscal concern. Rather, there was and still is a belief among many that guardianship substitutes a "lasting," but potentially breakable, permanency promise for a "binding" and unbreakable adoption commitment (Testa, 2005). When asked to react to the statement that

TABLE 7.2   Differences in Outcomes for Children Randomly Assigned to Subsidized Guardianship Demonstrations in Illinois, Tennessee, and Wisconsin

	Intervention Group	Comparison Group	Difference
Illinois N (10-year follow-up)	1,197	1,228	
Combined permanency outcomes	88.6%	83.1%	5.5%*
Reunification	5.1%	7.7%	−2.6%
Adoption	60.2%	74.9%	−14.7%*
Subsidized guardianship	23.2%	0.5%	22.7%*
Removed from assigned home	29.5%	32.2%	−2.7%
Tennessee N (2-year follow-up)	264	227	
Combined permanency outcomes	83.0%	67.8%	15.1%*
Reunification	3.4%	4.0%	−0.6%
Adoption	31.8%	56.4%	−24.6%*
Living with other relatives	3.8%	4.0%	−0.2%
Subsidized guardianship	43.9%	3.6%	40.4%*
Removed from assigned home	11.4%	13.7%	−2.3%
Wisconsin N (2-year follow-up)	157	163	
Combined permanency outcomes	58.6%	38.7%	19.9%*
Reunification	9.6%	8.6%	1.0%
Adoption	31.2%	28.8%	2.4%
Living with other relatives	0.0%	0.6%	−0.6%
Subsidized guardianship	17.8%	0.6%	17.2%
Removed from assigned home	na	na	na

*p < 0.05

"Guardianship is just as permanent as adoption," 30% of Tennessee case-workers said they disagreed or strongly disagreed, as did 35% of Illinois caseworkers, and 56% of Milwaukee caseworkers.

Although it is true that birth parents can seek to vacate guardian-ship orders (and some are successful), in reality, the long-term stability of living arrangements are practically equivalent in both the intervention and control groups. After two and one-half years, there was a trivial, statistically insignificant difference (in favor of the intervention group) between the proportions of children removed from homes assigned to the Tennessee demonstration even though only 32% of children had been adopted in the intervention group compared to 56% in the comparison group (see Table 7.2). Likewise, after 10 years, there was a small percentage point difference (also in favor of the intervention group) between the proportions of children removed from homes assigned to the Illinois demonstration, even though only 60% of children had been adopted in the intervention group compared to 75% in the comparison group. Although the stability data are missing for Wisconsin, it doesn't affect the debate because there were no losses of adoptions in Milwaukee.

If adoption truly conferred greater stability on permanency commitments, one would expect fewer children to have been removed from comparison-group homes than intervention-group homes. Because no important differences were found after a decade of follow-up in Illinois, it may be concluded that the safety and stability of children had not been compromised as a result of discharging children to subsidized guardianship. But, is this the appropriate comparison if only 23% of the intervention group went to guardianship? The counterfactual one really wants to approximate is: What would have happened to these 23% if their caregivers had been denied this permanency option? Because children were not randomly assigned to subsidized guardianship, but were only encouraged by virtue of their random assignment to the intervention group, to approximate the desired counterfactual, it is necessary to employ a quasi-experimental design to conduct the comparison. This is the topic of the next section.

Approximating the Counterfactual in Observational Research: Matching Methods

Results-oriented accountability proceeds on the premise that any promising child welfare intervention has potential outcomes that could conceivably range from the beneficial to the trivial to the downright harmful. Unless carefully tested in randomized controlled experiments, incorrect causal inferences may be drawn from intuitions about what the differences between potential outcomes might be. For example, some state officials still believe that subsidized guardianship preempts family reunification, even though three federal waiver demonstrations now show this not to be the case. Intensive family preservation was once believed to prevent unnecessary child removal until experiments showed it to be no more effective than regular in-home services. Performance contracting is generally accepted as improving agency performance in Illinois (see Chapter 10, this volume), but experiments in Michigan raise doubts about generalizing this claim (Meezan & McBeath, 2008). All in all, responsible agency stewardship demands greater use of randomized controlled experiments than is currently the practice in child welfare. At the same time, there are situations in which controlled experimentation is inadvisable, unethical, or just plain impossible.

For example, it is imprudent to assign children randomly to crowded or less crowded foster homes just to study the effects of crowding on placement stability given preliminary findings from observational studies (Testa, Fuller, & Nieto, 2007). Likewise, it is unethical to deprive a random group of families the financial benefits of existing adoption assistance benefits to refine assessments of the impact of adoption assistance on the observed nationwide slowdown in rates of family reunification (Wulczyn,

Chen, & Hislop, 2006). Finally, it is impossible to assign children randomly to densely or sparsely populated extended family networks to determine the genuine benefits of kinship foster care. For a variety of political, ethical, and practical reasons, therefore, results-oriented accountability must continue to rely on historical cohorts, geographical divisions, and other observational comparisons for drawing inferences about the efficacy and effectiveness of child welfare interventions.

In Chapter 5, the method of linear regression was introduced as a way of handling selection biases to separate out the net causal effect of an intervention on an outcome from confounding influences. Another method for handling selection biases concentrates on balancing the observed mean characteristics of the intervention and comparison group. Two studies of kinship foster care help to illustrate the application of matching methods in child welfare research: Barth, Guo, Green, and McCrae (2007) and Koh and Testa (2008).

As Barth and his colleagues noted, the century-old debate over the value of foster family care versus institutional child care has since evolved into a debate over the merits of kinship care versus foster family care. In the language of agency theory, the issue is whether primordial agents recruited from extended family networks are more responsible benefactors of neglected and abused children than bureaucratic agents whom the state selects and licenses as foster parents. There are potentially large selectivity differences between these two groups of substitute caregivers. Extended family members typically have more foreknowledge about the parents and children when deciding whether to accept or reject the caregiving role than licensed foster parents who are usually strangers to the families. This differential knowledge as well as other factors can result in large differences in the types and characteristics of children who are taken into kinship versus non-kinship care at the time of removal (Grogan-Kaylor, 2000). One approach to narrowing these differences involves matching cases that are similar in the two groups. One particular matching method, known as "propensity score matching" (PSM), attempts to balance the mean characteristics of the two groups by incorporating as many measured predictors of the intervention (in this example, placement with kin) as is practical into a regression-like model to select matched samples of children in kinship and non-kinship care.

Table 7.3 shows the differences in the characteristics of children before and after matching from the study by Koh and Testa (2008). The study used PSM to match a random sample of 1,500 children from a population of 10,908 non-kin placements with similar children in a population of 21,914 kin placements. Comparing the percentage distributions for the unmatched populations shows that kin placements in Illinois are quite different from those of non-kin placements. Children in kinship foster homes are older, more likely to be African-American and to have African-American caregivers, less likely to have disabilities and to be removed because of abuse, and are more heavily concentrated in Cook

TABLE 7.3   AFCARS Data for Children Initially Placed in Kin and Non-kin Foster Homes in Illinois, Federal Fiscal Years 1998 to 2004, Unmatched and Matched Samples

Variables	Unmatched Kin (n = 21,914)	Unmatched Non-Kin (n = 10,108)	Matched Kin (n = 1500)	Matched Non-Kin (n = 1500)
Population Conditions				
Child age at entry				
0 year	25.98*	48.10	46.33	44.87
1—2 years	17.82*	14.10	15.27	16.00
3—5 years	19.81*	13.42	13.40	14.00
6—8 years	15.22*	9.49	9.27	9.60
9—12 years	14.21*	8.50	10.00	9.73
13 years and older	6.95	6.40	5.73	5.80
Child race				
African American	73.76*	54.21	53.73	54.20
White	20.00*	38.57	38.93	38.60
Others	6.24*	7.21	7.33	7.20
Child disability				
Mental retardation	2.36*	6.00	5.87*	7.73
Mental disorder	4.50*	8.84	8.20	9.13
Other disability	2.10*	7.61	6.33	7.00
No disability	91.03*	77.55	79.60*	76.13
Reason for removal				
Abuse	15.77*	22.27	22.20	22.87
Neglect	64.89*	71.41	73.33	71.20
Child-related problem	2.62*	1.71	1.27	1.67
Others	16.80*	4.64	3.20	4.27
Foster caregiver race				
African American	75.03*	44.48	45.96	46.39
White	20.67*	49.37	50.73	50.79
Others	4.30*	6.15	3.31	2.82
Locality of services				
Cook County	70.19*	37.52	38.27	38.13
Others	29.81*	62.48	61.73	61.87
Outcomes				
Within three years of entry				
Reunification	19.7*	30.3	29.5	31.6
Adoption	12.7*	26.3	21.4	24.9
Legal guardianship	6.2*	1.4	3.2	1.8
Initial placement disruption	24.8*	38.8	28.8*	37.1

* $p < 0.05$

County, Illinois, than children in non-kinship foster home. After matching, most of the differences between kinship and non-kinship placements become statistically negligible. The lone exception is child disability. Slightly higher rates of mental retardation and the presence of a disability persist for children in non-relative foster homes than children in relative foster homes.

The outcomes reported at the bottom of Table 7.3 for the unmatched groups replicate differences typically reported in the child welfare literature: Children in kinship foster care are less likely to achieve legal permanence through reunification and adoption and are more likely to be discharged into legal guardianship. When the analysis is based on the matched samples, however, these permanency differences diminish to statistical insignificance. This suggests that it is largely the characteristics of children initially placed with kin that account for their lower rates of reunification and adoption rather than any properties of the kinship placement, such as financial needs or cultural barriers to legal permanence (Burnette, 1997; Thornton, 1991). With regard to placement stability, however, the advantages that accrue to children placed initially with kin appear to persist even after the children are matched on demographic characteristics.

A major limitation of studies that rely heavily on administrative data like Koh and Testa (2008) is the small set of predictors that can be incorporated into the regression model for matching purposes. Because the specification of conditioning variables can have a significant impact on the results of the analysis that makes use of propensity scores (Guo, Barth, & Gibbons, 2006), it is best to include the most relevant variables in the calculation. Barth, Guo, Green, and McCrae (2007) were able to draw on a rich assortment of social and psychometric data from the National Survey of Child and Adolescent Well-Being (NSCAW) to match children in non-kinship and kinship foster care. After matching, the authors found few differences in the developmental progress of children in kinship care compared to children in non-kinship care. But, they did find that children in kinship care seemed to experience greater reductions in externalizing and total problem behaviors as measured on the Child Behavior Check-List (CBCL) than children in non-kinship care.

With this basic understanding of propensity score matching, we can now return to the counterfactual question left unanswered at the end of the previous section: Would children, discharged to guardianship, have as long-lasting family relationships as they might have if their permanency options were restricted to the more legally binding commitment of adoption? The first impulse might be to compare the stability of guardianships with adoptions, but this would misstate the counterfactual because some of the children taken into guardianship would not have been adopted and instead would have remained in foster care and possibly moved to other homes. Additionally, the kinds of children who are adopted tend to differ

TABLE 7.4   Average Characteristics of Guardianship Cases Compared to Matched Controls, Adoption Cases, and all cases in the Comparison Group, Illinois Subsidized Guardianship Demonstration

Characteristics	Guardianship Cases	Comparison Group		
		Matched Controls	Adoption Cases	All Cases
Sample size	307	307	915	1,580
Female child	47.6%	44.6%	49.0%	49.0%
Child's race				
African American	88.6%	87.6%	82.8%*	88.0%*
White	10.1%	8.5%	11.1%	11.3%
Other	1.3%	3.9%	6.1%*	0.7%
Child's age (years)	11.9	11.7	8.7*	9.4*
Caregiver's age (years)	53.4	54.0	50.4*	50.0*
Caregiver working	39.7%	36.8%	44.2%	46.2%*
Caregiver high school	52.1%	55.4%	52.1%	53.5%
Relationship to child				
Grandparent	53.3%	56.4%	40.2%*	37.7%*
Aunt or uncle	22.2%	19.2%	14.8%*	14.7%*
Other relative	15.4%	17.9%	13.5%	13.8%
Foster parent	9.1%	6.5%	31.5%*	33.8%*
Affection scale	0.179	0.295	0.160	−0.044
Family duty scale	0.526	0.585	−0.106*	−0.030*
Prior years with caregiver	5.5	5.5	5.1*	4.0*
Intend to raise to adulthood	95.4%	97.1%	98.0%*	79.3%*

*p < 0.05

in age, ethnicity, and in other ways from those who are taken into guardianship. Propensity score matching can be used to arrive at a better approximation of the counterfactual to address "what-if" concerns about subsidized guardianship.

Table 7.4 compares the characteristics of the 307 children discharged to subsidized guardianship in the Illinois demonstration with their matched controls in the comparison group, all adopted children, and all children assigned to the comparison group as of date of the second round of follow-up interviews. The data show that adopted children are two years younger on average than children taken into guardianship arrangements. Their caregivers are older, less often related to them, and spent fewer years looking after them prior to discharge. Also, the adoptive parents were less likely to agree that families have a moral duty to take care of their own kin regardless of whether government helps pay for the cost of care (duty scale), but just as likely to admit to displays of affection and encouragement (affection scale).

Comparing the stability of guardianship and adoption arrangements seven years after the interview date without making risk adjustments for the differences in child and caregiver characteristics shows that the risks of disintegration are 81% greater for guardianship arrangements than adoptive arrangements (hazard ratio $= 1.81$, 95% CL $= 1.16 - 2.82$, sig. < 0.009, two-tailed test). This conforms to the impression that many caseworkers and court personnel have formed about the greater fragility of guardianship commitments. When risk-adjustments are made for the child and caregiver characteristics listed in Table 7.4 with hazards regression methods, the hazard ratio diminishes to statistical insignificance (hazard ratio = 1.14, 95% CL $= 0.649 - 2.00$, sig. < 0.651, two-tailed test). Finally, when the comparison is restricted to the matched cases from the comparison group, the hazard ratio dips below 1.0, but still to an insubstantial effect size (hazard ratio $= 0.86$, 95% CL $= 0.509 - 1.49$, sig. < 0.581, two-tailed test). Children discharged to guardianship experience no less lasting family relationships than if their permanency options were restricted to the more legally binding commitment of adoption.

The reason that matched cases from the comparison group provide a better approximation of the counterfactual than looking only at adopted cases is that PSM picks up those guardianship cases that would otherwise have stayed in foster care. In fact, the permanency plans that caregivers of the matched cases voiced at round 2 of the interview closely approximate the substitution effect on adoptions that can be estimated by comparing the combined share of adoptions and guardianships in the intervention group to the proportion of adoptions in the comparison group: 68% of guardianships might have eventually resulted in adoption, 1% might have been reunified, and 29% would have likely remained in foster care until they aged out. Once allowances are made for these potential non-permanency outcomes, the instability rates for the two groups are about the same. A reasonable conclusion is that little is gained in terms of stability from denying guardianship assistance in the hopes of encouraging more lasting family relationships though adoption.

The growing appeal of propensity score-matching methods and the enduring popularity of regression adjustment methods in child welfare research suggest that administrators and policymakers will need to gain greater familiarity with both approaches to stay current with the latest developments in evidence-supported practice and policy. A major limitation of both types of analysis, however, remains the assumption that all systematic influences that have an impact on both the outcome and selection of subjects into the intervention group have been accurately measured and correctly specified in the statistical prediction models. Because of the difficulties of satisfying this requirement in observational research, the "gold standard" for overcoming specification errors and selection biases is still the random assignment of subjects to intervention and comparison groups.

Refining Treatment Effect Estimates: Instrumental Variable Methods

Randomization, in and of itself, however, provides no guarantee of construct or statistical validity. Sample attrition, failure to receive the intended intervention, and crossovers from the comparison to the intervention group can result in misestimates of the actual treatment effect. Many randomized controlled experiments in child welfare are what Paul Holland calls "encouragement designs" (Holland, 1988). These are designs that involve the randomization of principals or their agents to an encouragement condition, which is intended to induce compliance with an intended plan of treatment by manipulating one or more sources of social influence, for example, enforceable trust (authority ranking), feelings of bonded solidarity (communal sharing), a sense of generalized responsibility (equality matching), or price incentives and penalties (market pricing). See Chapter 1 for a definition of terms.

Like all cooperative relationships, there are risks that some principals or their agents will "defect" from the intended course of action. Whereas encouragement designs are experimental at the start, they can end up being "quasi-experimental" at the end because of differential principal/agent selection into alternative compliance states. For example, the subsidized guardianship experiments authorized under IV-E waivers are encouragement designs in the sense that they offer price incentives in the form of guardianship subsidies to a randomly selected subset of caregivers (agents) to become the permanent guardians of the children (principals) under their foster care. Not all caseworkers will choose to present this permanency option to caregivers. Some caseworkers will withhold the information from foster parents because they do not think them suitable guardians or hope to persuade them to adopt. Even when the option is offered by caseworkers, the caregivers, guardians *ad litem*, juvenile court judges, and children aged 14 years and older may agree or decide to make an alternative choice.

The differential selection by population units into alternative treatment conditions is what differentiates encouragement designs from randomized controlled trials in which treatment selection is entirely under the control of the researcher, as was the case with the Salk vaccine trials. All children randomized to the intervention group received the vaccine and all children randomized to the comparison group received a placebo injection of saline solution. Knowledge about which children were treated with the vaccine was kept from both the injected and the injector. By contrast, such double-blinded precautions, let alone 100% treatment, are impossible to ensure in most social experiments.

In the past, incomplete compliance might have been handled by restricting comparisons to only those population units that actually received the intended treatment. In the example of subsidized guardianship, this would mean limiting the comparison to only those children in the intervention group whose caregivers were informed by caseworkers about the program. The problem with this approach is that the subset of informed families may no longer be a random sub-sample of all the families of children who were initially assigned to the intervention. Such an analysis could bias the estimate of the guardianship treatment effect. Because of the various principal/agent choices involved with the actual receipt of the intended treatment, child welfare researchers often must fall-back on the same statistical methods for dealing with selection biases on observable and unobservable conditions (to the researcher) that are employed in non-experimental studies.

Cross-classifying whether or not the researcher controls assignment to the intervention group and the selection of treatment and control conditions yields a typology of common evaluation designs as follows:

TABLE 7.5   Typology of Evaluation Designs

Assignment Control	Treatment Selection	Evaluation Design	Example
Researcher	Researcher	Randomized controlled	Salk vaccine
Researcher	Other	Randomized encouragement	Subsidized guardianship
Other	Other	Quasi-experimental	Kinship foster care
None	Other	Observational	Gender

Although a simple comparison of means and proportions is all that is necessary to estimate the average causal effect of treatment on the treated in randomized controlled designs with complete control or compliance, special statistical methods are required to disentangle the direct effect of a received treatment from the confounding effects of unobservable influences on treatment selection in randomized encouragement and quasi-experimental designs.[4] One such approach makes use of what econometricians call an instrumental variable (IV).

Two of the key assumptions of the IV method are: (1) there exists some important condition of assignment to the intervention that encourages exposure to the intended treatment and (2) the mechanism of assignment itself doesn't have a direct impact on the outcome, except through its effect on the received treatment. One can think of randomized encouragement in experimental designs as a special case of the IV method. Under most circumstances, random assignment satisfies the dual key assumptions: (1) a larger fraction of the intervention group is exposed to or complies with the intended treatment than the comparison group; and (2) the mechanism of random assignment, e.g., coin toss, lottery ball, or table of random numbers, only affects the outcome through its effect on the received treatment.

The economist Joshua Angrist (2006) has summarized the rules for calculating the average causal effect of the treatment when there is

TABLE 7.6   Illinois Subsidized Guardianship Waiver Demonstration, Cumulative Days of Paid Foster Care and Displacement Rates by Received Treatment as of December 2006

Group	Group Size	Days of Paid Foster Care		Displaced from Home	
		Sum	Mean	No.	Rate per 100
Intervention	1197	1,303,784	1089	355	29.7
Offered SG	930	906,685	975	238	25.6
Not Offered SG	267	397,099	1487	117	43.8
Comparison	1228	1,593,580	1298	377	30.7

incomplete treatment and the IV satisfies the key assumptions (see Technical Appendix 7A for details). This approach can be used to refine, for example, estimates of the cost effectiveness of offering families the option of subsidized guardianship on reducing length of stay in foster care. Table 7.6 shows the cumulative amount of paid foster care days for children assigned to the intervention and comparison groups in the Illinois subsidized guardianship demonstration. The difference between all 1197 children assigned to the intervention group and all 1228 children assigned to the comparison group yields an unbiased estimate of the savings resulting from eligibility for guardianship assistance. This comparison ignores the fact that not all of the subjects received the treatment to which they were allocated. This so-called intention-to-treat (ITT) analysis preserves the statistical equivalence of the original group assignments, but it yields an unbiased estimate only of the effects of being assigned to the intervention group and not the effects of actually receiving the intended treatment.

Table 7.6 subdivides the intervention group by whether caregivers reported ever being offered the guardianship subsidy. The response can be considered a proxy for the receipt of the intended treatment. In-person surveys with these caregivers in 1998 found that approximately 22% of caregivers in the intervention group reported that they had never been informed by their caseworkers of the availability of subsidized guardianship. As discussed previously, restricting the analysis to only those children in the intervention group whose caregivers were actually informed about the program could potentially bias the estimate of the effect of the subsidized guardianship offer on the treated. As of December 2006, children in homes that were not offered the guardianship option had higher rates of displacement than other children in the intervention and comparison groups. Perhaps caseworkers withheld information from caregivers whom they perceived to be less suitable as permanent guardians. If this were true, an analysis limited to only the treated would tend to overstate the guardianship effect on stability rates because of the withholding of information from homes likely to disrupt.

An ITT analysis shows an average 209 day difference (1089 days – 1298 days) in length of foster care, ignoring whether families in the intervention were actually offered the SG option or not. This is an understatement of the treatment effect on the treated, but still it represents 16% fewer average days of foster care relative to the comparison group. On the other hand, an analysis that restricts the comparison to only those 78% of families in the intervention who were actually informed about the program shows an average 323 day difference (975 days – 1298 days). This represents 25% fewer average days of foster care. This is clearly an overstatement of the treatment effect. It compares the subset of children whose families received the treatment to all of the families in the comparison group, some of whom would also have not been informed about the new permanency option if they had instead been assigned to the intervention group. An analysis of the effect of the treatment-on-the-treated (TOT) requires taking into account the selectivity biases associated with the actual receipt of treatment.

In the Illinois demonstration, only those families who were encouraged by virtue of their assignment to the intervention group could avail themselves of the guardianship subsidy. Families assigned to the comparison group were excluded from obtaining the subsidy by the automated restrictions built into the computer system that short-circuited attempts to process such orders through the court. This reduced the numbers of crossovers from the control to the treatment condition to practically zero. Under such circumstances, Angrist (2006) shows that the TOT effect can be estimated by dividing the ITT effect of −209 foster care days by the rate of treatment compliance in the intervention group (77.6%). This yields an average treatment effect on the treated of −269 days. It is important to note that this treatment effect applies only to the subset of children whose caseworkers would change their permanency planning approach from not discussing the SG option to offering the option because of the family's assignment to the intervention group.[5]

The estimation of the TOT effect from the ratio of the ITT effect to the compliance rate provides a segue to the two-stage-least-squares (2SLS) method, which economists have long employed to solve the variety of omitted-variable and simultaneity biases in economic research (Foster & McLanahan, 1996). The 2SLS method involves first regressing the compliance indicator against the IV (i.e., assignment indicator) as well as any other explanatory predictors, and second, substituting the predicted rate from the compliance model for the assignment indicator. In the Illinois demonstration, the probability of treatment is 0 when the family is assigned to the comparison group and 77.6% when the family is assigned to the intervention group. In the second step, the days of foster care are regressed against the predicted treatment rate. In our example, the intercept term without additional covariates is 1244 days, which is the approximated average length of stay for treated families under the counterfactual condition. The regression coefficient is −269, which is the TOT effect on the predicted days of care as the treatment indicator changes from 0 to 1. Substituting the predicted compliance rate of .776 for the treatment indicator scales the average treatment effect on the treated back to the standard ITT estimate of 209 days (see Technical Appendix 7A for additional details).

IV Methods for Adjusting for Unobserved Selection Effects

The utility of the IV method extends beyond the analysis of encouragement designs and other experiments with incomplete compliance. It can be applied to quasi-experimental designs in which some of the selection biases arise from unobserved influences on the intervention and outcomes. Even in the absence of random assignment, plausible instrumental variables can sometimes be identified which satisfy both the exclusion restriction, that is, the IV affects the outcome only through its effect on the received treatment, and the nonzero causal effect of the IV on treatment, i.e. the probability of treatment changes with the IV level. Examples of non-randomly assigned IVs include Newhouse and McClellan's (1998) use of the additional travel distance from a nearby hospital to another hospital specializing in a certain medical diagnostic procedure as an instrument for the effects of the procedure and associated treatment on the survival of heart-attack victims and Foster and McLanahan's (1996) use of local labor-market characteristics as an instrument for the effect of neighborhood conditions on high-school dropout rates.

There are purposeful ways that child welfare administrators can also help to generate instrumental variables by building quasi-experimental design features into how the implementation of service demonstrations and innovations is rolled out. For example, the rotational assignment of child removal cases to public and voluntary child welfare agencies for placement services is a pseudo randomization device that is already in place in some jurisdictions, which can be put to good use as an instrument for the effect of privatization on permanency rates. Another way of improving program evaluation is to stagger the implementation by geography so that neighboring communities experience program interventions and policy innovations at different times. Also selection into a program can be mechanically determined by the use of some uniform criterion such as birth year, time in care, or a standardized measure of latent need.

An innovative use of non-randomly assigned IVs in child welfare research are Joseph Doyle's studies of the effects of foster care placement on long-term, child well-being outcomes, such as juvenile delinquency, teen parenthood, and employment (Doyle, 2007a) and adult crime (Doyle, 2008). Children who are placed in foster care constitute a non-random subset of all children referred for child protective investigations. The use of regression methods to analyze foster care effects is limited by the likelihood that unobserved population characteristics distinguish the children who are investigated and placed in foster care from those who are investigated, but left in the custody of their parents and offered in-home services. Because the subset of investigated children who are removed from their homes are those at greatest risk for adverse safety and developmental outcomes and probably most likely to benefit from foster care, the unobserved differences between removed and non-removed children could bias the regression-adjusted estimates of foster care effects on long-term, well-being outcomes.

The studies of foster care effects by Doyle (2007a, 2008) attempted to account for the potential selection on these so-called "unobservables" by making use of the pseudo-randomization procedure of rotational assignment of maltreatment reports to child protective investigators with different removal tendencies as an instrument for estimating the probability of entry into foster care. Allegations of child maltreatment are telephoned to screeners at a statewide "hotline," who accept roughly 20% of calls for follow-up investigation. These so-called "reports" are then forwarded to an office nearest the child's residence and assigned to the next available investigator on a rotational basis to even-out the workload. Doyle makes use of the fact that some investigators on the rotational list exhibit a somewhat higher propensity to remove children from their homes than other investigators on his or her team in a given year even if the children's risk of harm profiles similarly. He excludes from his analysis cases that bypass rotational assignment, for example, sexual abuse and repeat maltreatment. Doyle offers compelling arguments that this differential propensity to remove satisfies the two key assumptions of an instrumental variable: (1) it predicts the probability of removal in a non-trivial way; and (2) it affects long-term child well-being outcomes only through its effect on the likelihood of removal. He uses the predicted probability of removal as an instrumental variable to estimate the causal effect of foster care intervention on long-term child welfare outcomes. In this way, Doyle is able to generate plausible estimates of the net impact of foster care on a variety of long-term outcomes, such juvenile delinquency, teenage motherhood, youth employment, and adult crime. Again, it is important to note that these estimates do not apply to all foster children, but only to the subset of cases where investigators may disagree about the necessity or desirability of removal. Given this caveat, Doyle finds that children who are rotationally assigned to removal-prone investigators are more likely to experience adverse outcomes later in life than children assigned to less removal-prone investigators. Specifically, they are estimated to be three times as likely to have a delinquency petition filed with the juvenile court; two to three times as likely to be arrested as adults and significantly more likely to have lower job earnings; and girls are twice as likely to give birth before the age of 20 years than if they had remained at home (Doyle, 2007a, 2008).

Rotational assignment can also serve as an instrument for correcting for sample selection biases in estimating the impact of systemwide policy reforms. An excellent application is Joseph Doyle's (2007b) study of the impact of Illinois' 1995 HMR Reforms on the quality of substitute care (see Chapter 3, this volume). Children who were placed with kin after HMR reform constitute a non-random subset of the kinds of children who were placed with kin prior to the reform. Unobserved characteristics of the children taken into foster care and unobserved propensities of relatives to assume child-caring responsibilities most likely changed in important ways after the implementation of HMR Reform. Again, these unmeasured changes could bias the risk-adjusted estimates of cohort effects on reunification outcomes that were presented in Chapter 5.

As identified in the HMR Reform logic model (see Chapter 3, this volume), two of the most important reforms were the exclusion of children left in the informal care of relatives from the statutory definition of parental neglect and the 30% reduction in the subsidy amount paid to nonlicensed relative foster parents who agree to assume temporary care of a child. The first change diverted children already in informal kinship arrangements from state custody to extended family support services. Fewer children, unlikely to return to parental custody, were entering formal foster care. The second change reduced the financial incentive for kin to take on formal foster care responsibilities. Because administrative data did not contain any reliable information on pre-existing kinship arrangements or the changing propensity of relatives to become foster parents, neither regression nor matching methods adequately addresses the potential selection biases.

Doyle's study of HMR Reform (2007b) attempted to account for the potential selection by also making use of the rotational assignment of abuse and neglect reports to child protective investigators with different removal tendencies as an instrument for estimating the probability of entry into foster care. The assignment process for child protective investigation stayed the same before and after HMR Reform. Each child's predicted removal probability from the selection model is included in the substantive regression model of kinship placement adjusted for baseline population conditions. In this way, Doyle is able to generate plausible estimates of the net impact of HMR Reform on the variety of outputs and outcomes that were diagrammed in the logic model presented in Chapter 3. Again, these estimates apply only to the subset of families whose decision to take a related child into their home would be affected by the lowering of the amount of foster care subsidy offered to the family.

Doyle's study estimates the impact of HMR Reform on the supply of relatives who accepted substitute care responsibility for new cohorts of children entering foster care the year following the July 1, 1995, implementation date. The comparison group is the cohort that entered the previous year. The cohort removed in SFY96 for a substantiated report of neglect by a family member was affected both by the payment cut and the change in neglect definition that diverted children who were already living with kin. This cohort experienced an estimated 20% drop in the proportion placed with kin. The cohort of children removed for a substantiated report of abuse by a non-family member was affected only by the payment cut. This cohort experienced an estimated 10% decline in the proportion placed with kin. Both results are consistent with the logic models' expectations that HMR reform would slow down the expansion of the program by lessening the financial incentives for relatives to join the foster care system.

Doyle's other findings are also consistent with the logic model's assumption that the reduction in HMR payment levels would not increase the rate of placement disruptions. Relatives who still chose to welcome children into their homes despite the payment cut were perhaps more strongly motivated by feelings of kin altruism and family duty than families recruited prior to the reform. The lessening of pecuniary incentives as reinforcement for agency relationships could also explain a key departure from prior expectations that the prospect of receiving higher payments would encourage relatives to become licensed foster parents. Up until the push to license relatives prompted by the passage of the Fostering Connections Act, less than 25% of relative foster parents became licensed, despite the financial advantages. Narrowing the financial disparity between AFDC support and foster care subsidies paid to non-licensed caregivers also did not increase the rate of reunification with birth parents or reduce the rate of foster care re-entry. Reunification decisions appear to be more the choice of administrative and judicial agents than the product of comparative financial calculations within the extended family network. Finally, the worry that lowering foster care subsidies would compromise the well-being of children in kinship care was not borne out in Doyle's analysis.

The threats to the validity of inferences drawn from both quasi-experimental studies and incompletely implemented experimental designs are key reminders of why it is important to have a well developed logic model to identify relevant predictors of outcomes and selection differences. The construct validity of descriptions of why interventions work or don't work clearly depend on how well the actual implementation matches the expectations derived from the logic model and underlying theory of action. In the next chapter, Terry Moore offers practical methods for improving the construct validity of program improvement plans by tracking performance data, acting on the feedback to inform managerial action, and fostering an organizational culture that is open to new strategies for enhancing agency performance.

Technical Appendix 7A: Causal Inference and Counterfactual Reasoning

One of the major assumptions emphasized in this chapter for drawing valid inferences about the average causal effect of an intervention on child welfare outcomes is the assumption of statistical independence between the process of assignment or selection into the intervention group and any unmeasured or unobserved population conditions that are related to the outcomes.[6] As noted by Bloom, Michalopoulos, Hill, and Lei (2002), this assumption is very difficult to satisfy in most non-experimental studies. The large variety of selection factors associated with different types of population conditions and agency relationships in child welfare means that one can never be quite sure if the effect being estimated is the genuine intervention effect or a biased (gross) estimate that mixes up the direct causal effect of the intervention with an indirect "spurious" relationship via unmeasured and unobserved population characteristics and agent choices. The greater the departure from the assumption of independence and the stronger the effects of unmeasured population characteristics and agency selection on the outcome, the larger is the biased component of the observed intervention effect on the outcome.

One of the major breakthroughs in addressing the problem of selection bias was R.A. Fisher's insight that statistical independence can best be obtained by connecting the selection method to some chance process under the control of the researcher, such as flipping a coin, drawing a lottery ball, or consulting a table of random numbers (Fisher, 1935). Because a random draw is unaffected by observed or unobserved population conditions, the causal effect of the intervention is disentangled from population characteristics and agent choices. It is the researcher's control over the selection or assignment method that is one of the defining features of experimental research and distinguishes it from observational research in which the allocation of units to intervention groups is outside the researcher's control (Cox and Reid, 2000).

Researcher control over assignments to an intervention group allows for unbiased estimates to be made about the effects of being assigned to the intervention, but not necessarily about the effects of actually receiving the intended treatment, unless the exposure to treatment is also under the control of the researcher. Most randomized experiments in child welfare research leave room for some degree of selection of intended treatments by clients and their agents and, for this reason, they are better described as randomized encouragement designs (Holland, 1988) instead of randomized controlled trials (RCTs), in which the delivery of the treatment is entirely under the researcher's control, such as the Salk vaccine trial. Only when compliance with the encouraged treatment and comparison conditions is 100% are the results the same as would be obtained from an RCT. But, 100% compliance is seldom achieved in child welfare research for both ethical and practical reasons, and consequently client self-selection, agent selection, and other selection factors can result in a sample that actually receives the intended treatment, which is a non-random sub-sample of the population originally assigned to the intervention group.

Econometricians and statisticians have developed a variety of statistical methods for dealing with non-random assignments and treatment

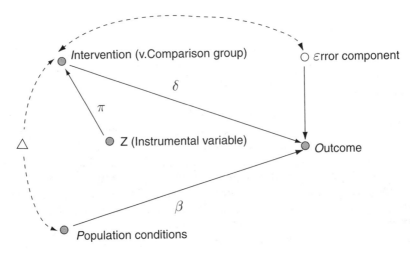

Figure 7A.1 Diagram of alternative strategies for dealing with the problem of confounding in estimating the impact of an intervention.

selections to estimate the average treatment effects in randomized encouragement and quasi-experimental designs. Each of these methods can be conceived as attacking the problem of confounding by dealing with different components of the causal model diagrammed in Appendix Figure 7A.1.

Two new components are added to the *PICO* factors previously identified in Appendix Figure 5A.2 in Chapter 5: Z, an instrumental variable, which affects the outcome only through its impact on the intervention, and is associated with an increased likelihood of exposure to the intervention, and π, the magnitude of the intervention/comparison group difference in the likelihood of exposure to the intervention. These new components can be used in randomized encouragement and quasi-experimental studies to control for unobserved population conditions in the error component, which are correlated with both the outcome and assignment to the intervention group.

The technical appendix to Chapter 5 provided an overview of the method of linear regression that concentrates on estimating linear or curvilinear relationships (β) between measured population conditions (P) and the outcome of interest (O), so that differences between the predicted outcomes and the actual data (residuals) can be computed. The same set of variables is then used to predict the probability of receiving the intended intervention and to create another set of residuals. The coefficient estimated from the simple regression of the outcome residuals on the intervention residuals, i.e., what's left over after the systematic effects of the population conditions are removed from both the outcome and intervention variables, provides a "risk-adjusted" estimate of the intervention effect.

Another approach discussed in Chapter 7 for addressing selection biases concentrates on balancing the mean characteristics of the intervention and comparison group. It involves first fitting a logit, probit, or some other non-linear model to predict exposure to the intervention from the measured population conditions and then computing a probability, commonly called a "propensity score," of being in the intervention group instead of the comparison group. These propensity scores can then be used to link individual participants or other units in the intervention group to their statistical counterpoints in the comparison group that exhibit similar propensity scores. If done properly, balancing the propensity scores so that each group has the same mean score will balance the means of the contributing conditions and narrow the selection bias ($\Delta \approx 0$).

Although practical experience shows that results are often similar when either matching methods or regression adjustment is used, there are certain features of matching methods that make them more attractive for child welfare research than the more typical regression methods of risk adjustment (Rubin, 2001). First, matching helps protect against the "data snooping" (Freedman, 2005), which can occur when researchers are searching for an appropriate specification of a regression model for adjusting the intervention and outcome variables. Because outcomes don't explicitly figure in the specification of matching models, researchers are free to refit the model numerous times until an adequate balance is achieved without compromising the statistical conclusion validity of the inferences about intervention effects, which arises when refitting regression models to predict outcomes. Second, multiple outcomes can be examined after an adequate balance has been achieved unlike regression models that may require different specifications to adjust for each of the separate outcomes. Incorrectly specified regression models can lead to misleading results. Third, insufficient overlap among the intervention and comparisons group in the distributions of population conditions can result in misleading regression estimates of intervention effects. Finally, the results of matching methods are more easily communicated to a general audience because the "apples to apples" comparison most closely approximates the classical experimental design, and intervention differences can be displayed in simple cross-tabular or graphical form.

Despite the advantages, the major difficulty with matching methods as well as with regression adjustment is the requirement that all relevant conditions that affect both the intervention and the outcome must be specified in the statistical prediction model. This is a demanding requirement and a major reason why it is important to have a well developed logic model to identify relevant predictors of change. Some of the latest thinking about the problem of selection bias in randomized encouragement and quasi-experimental designs builds on the "counterfactual" or "potential outcomes" perspective on intervention effects.

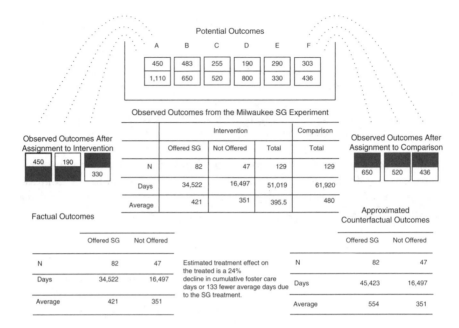

Figure 7A.2 Potential days of foster care (outcomes) for children offered and not offered subsidized guardianship.

To gain an intuitive feel for the power of this perspective, Appendix Figure 7A.2 elaborates on an illustration that Freedman, Pisani, and Purves (2007) used to explain randomized controlled experiments. Figure 7A.2 depicts a group of six foster children who are imagined to be carrying numbered tickets hidden somewhere in their pockets. On the top half of each child's ticket is the number of additional days he or she would remain in foster care if his or her family were offered the option of guardianship; on the bottom half is the number of foster care days the child would spend in care if this information were withheld from the family. The average of the differences between the two quantities printed on the tickets of all the persons in the population, if it could be observed, would provide an estimate of the average causal effect of the intervention of subsidized guardianship in reducing children's length of stay in foster care. Making this hypothetical calculation for the six children in the playpen yields an average of 328.5 days for the top half of all the tickets and 641 days for the bottom half for a difference of −312.5 days. This is the causal effect of the intervention for this hypothetical population of children. But, such a simple calculation cannot be done because children can be allocated to only one of the two treatments at a time. Hence, only one of the two potential outcomes can be observed as illustrated by the darkening of top or bottom half of the tickets after allocation to the intervention or comparison condition (see Figure 7A.2).

Now, first let's consider that the allocation process is outside of the control of the researcher and that caseworkers have considerable discretion in deciding which families receive the offer of subsidized guardianship and which ones do not. Although unobservable, caseworkers probably have some intuition about the different number of days on each of the children's tickets, that is, the times each would spend in care under different permanency options. They decide to withhold information from the families of those children whom they believe would be better off being adopted even if it adds to the days spent in foster care. They extend the guardianship offer only to the families of children who otherwise would age out of care. Under these conditions, only the families of children A, C, and D would be offered guardianship assistance. whereas the information would be deliberately withheld from the families of children B, E, and F, even if guardianship assistance would shorten their time in foster care. The difference in the observed average days of foster care for the two caseworker-selected groups is −173.7 days, which is considerably less than the average of the individual treatment effects of −312.5 days. Mindful of the possible biases that can arise from leaving the allocation of the guardianship treatment to the discretion of caseworkers, all of whom believe they are acting in the best interests of each child, the administrator of the program decides that a more accurate estimate could be obtained by allowing his research department to assign families randomly to the intervention and comparison groups. Even though the administrator recognizes that caseworkers will exercise their discretion after randomization, it is expected that these unobservable (latent) tendencies will be evenly distributed in both intervention and comparison groups. Furthermore because the guardianship subsidy can be denied to all families in the comparison group, non-compliance is limited to only caseworkers serving families in the intervention groups. This asymmetry can be used to refine the estimate of average treatment effect on the treated.

The following illustration draws from interpretations of the counterfactual framework offered by Schwartz and Ash (2003). As shown in Appendix Figure 7A.2, the top half of the ticket is unobserved for the children assigned to the comparison group, but a complication arises for the children assigned to the intervention group. One of the assigned children does not receive the intended treatment because his caseworker decided to withhold the information in anticipation that his extended family would adopt him. Even though the caseworker expects that the relatives would take subsidized guardianship if informed of their eligibility for the program, he decides that adoption would be in the best interests of the children, despite the longer time the child would remain in foster care. For this child, the top half of the ticket is unobserved just as if he had been assigned to the comparison group. To estimate the guardianship effect on the remaining two who actually received the treatment, it is necessary to estimate the amount of days on the missing bottom-half of their tickets.

Switching from the hypothetical scenario to the actual data collected on children assigned to the Milwaukee subsidized guardianship demonstration (center panel), the missing counterfactual data can be approximated in the aggregate by calculating the days of foster care. that the intervention group would have accumulated if the offer of guardianship had been withheld from all of them. This can be done by multiplying the 480 average days of foster care observed for the comparison group by the 129 children assigned to the intervention group. This yields a counterfactual estimate of 61,920 days that all 129 children would be expected to spend in foster care in the absence of the guardianship program. Because randomization makes the two groups statistically equivalent with respect to the kinds of children likely to be offered subsidized guardianship, the counterfactual for the 82 children (63.6%) who were treated as intended can be approximated by subtracting from this total the 16,497 cumulative days of foster care recorded for the 47 children (36.4%) in the intervention group who went untreated. This leaves a remainder of 45,423 foster care days or an average of 554 days when divided by the 82 children whose families were offered the guardianship option under the intervention condition. On the basis of this counterfactual reasoning, it can be inferred that the SG treatment reduced the average length of foster care by 133 days in Milwaukee from 554 to 421 days or by 24% for this group of treated children whose caseworkers complied with the assigned intervention and offered their caregivers the SG option.

The use of the counterfactual framework to estimate the average treatment effect of subsidized guardianship on the treated (TOT) can be considered a special case of the instrumental variable approach to causal inference. Angrist (2006) gives the following formula for calculating the TOT effect when compliance with the intended treatment is incomplete:

$$TOT = ITT/\pi,$$

where, ITT is the intention-to-treat effect and π is the predicted increment in the received treatment that is associated with the instrumental variable, Z (see Appendix Figure 7A.1).

The ITT estimate is the observed average for all children assigned to the intervention group (395.5 days), regardless of whether they actually received the intended treatment, minus the observed average for all children assigned to the comparison group (480 days). Dividing this difference of 84.5 days by the increment in the probability of received treatment because of random assignment (.636) yields the same TOT result of −133 days derived from the counterfactual simulation above. The result can be also obtained by using two-stage least squares (2SLS), which entails substituting the predicted rate of received treatment from a selection model, which includes the random assignment indicator, into a behavioral model of the outcome, which excludes the indicator. Using the linear probability model, the predicted probability of SG treatment in the Milwaukee demonstration is as follows:

$$\hat{T} = \alpha + \pi Z,$$

where $\alpha = 0$ and $\pi = .636$. Thus, the predicted treatment rate is 0 when $Z = 0$ (comparison group) and 63.6% when $Z = 1$ (intervention group). Inserting the predicted treatment rate of .636 into the linear regression of days in foster care on the predicted treatment rate as follows:

$$\hat{O} = \alpha + \delta \hat{T},$$

where $\alpha = 554$ days and $\delta = -133$ days from the counterfactual simulation above, scales the estimate of the average treatment effect on the treated back to the standard ITT estimate of -84.5 days. 2SLS also allows for the addition of other population conditions as predictors of both the probability of treatment and the outcome of interest. Multiple OLS regression can be used in both steps but, generally, the standard errors of the estimates will be incorrect. Many software packages, such as SPSS, SAS, and Stata can handle 2SLS when the outcomes are continuous, such as days of care and service expenditures. Appendix Table 7A.1 shows the estimated impact on days of foster care and expenditures of the offer of SG on the treated with additional covariates included the 2SLS model. The standard errors have been corrected for sibling clustering by using replicate weights to generate the appropriate estimates.

The results show that for the two-thirds of families who were offered subsidized guardianship as intended, Milwaukee would have spent an average of $4601 in maintenance payments, for an additional 4.4 months of foster care in the absence of the IV-E waiver. The difference between the 2SLS estimates of TOT effect with and without additional covariates is minimal for days of care but about $929 lower for expenditures. Although

TABLE 7A.1   2SLS Estimates of TOT Effects on Foster Care Days and Expenditures

Covariates	Foster care days			Foster maintenance payments		
	Coeff.	Sig.	Std. Err.	Coeff.	Sig.	Std. Err.
Offered SG	−133	0.01	57	−$4601	0.01	$1922
Male	−5	*	27	$2768	0.01	$1228
African American	110	0.00	42	$2679	0.02	$1323
Age of child (years)	9	0.00	3	$472	0.00	$131
IV-E eligible	58	0.04	34	−$217	*	$1284
Relatedness	14	*	21	$1208	*	$852
Paternal side	30	*	37	−$1440	*	$1478
Constant	238	0.00	81	$553	*	$2791

*p > 0.05

the other coefficients and their associated standard error estimates are fixed prior to the intervention and should not be considered causal, the patterns are consistent with some previously known statistically significant associations.

First, even though boys are no more likely than girls to have longer lengths of stay, the cost of their care tends to be significantly more expensive usually because of placement in more restrictive placement settings. African-American children are also more likely than white and children of other races to run up higher average costs, but this is primarily associated with the longer time African-American children stay on average in foster care. Also, for each year older the child is at the time of assignment to the demonstration, the longer the child stays in foster care and the more dollars are spent on his or her care. Although IV-E eligibility is also associated with an additional 2 months of foster care, the extra time appears not to translate into higher average costs.

Notes

1. The number of enrolled children is smaller than the total number of children randomly assigned to the demonstration. Enrolled children exclude randomized children aged 11 years and younger who were residing with non-relatives and exited care before the age of 12 years.

2. The seemingly anomalous result of a smaller OR associated with a larger difference in proportions arises from the fact that relative odds increase substantially the greater the odds deviate from 1:1. Thus, a 6.1 percentage point difference in permanence at the end of the initial 5-year demonstration period corresponded to an OR of 1.38 when the permanency rate was 71.8% in the comparison group. After another five years elapsed, the slightly smaller 5.5 percentage point difference corresponded to a larger OR of 1.58 because the permanency rate rose to 83% in the comparison group. Given the sensitivity of odds ratios to how rare ($< 20\%$) or common ($> 20\%$) an outcome is, it is helpful to convert small or large odds ratios into differences in proportions to facilitate interpretation. Because probabilities are more easily interpreted by most people than odds, it is sometimes recommended that relative probabilities (usually called relative risks) be computed instead of odds ratios. Whereas this works well for rare events, the interpretation of relative risks (RR) is less straightforward for more common events. For example, the relative risk of permanence a decade into the subsidized guardianship demonstration was only 6.6% larger (0.885/.830) in the intervention group than the comparison group. However, stated in terms of the opposite probability, the RR of impermanence was 32% smaller in the intervention group than the comparison group (0.115/.170). Odds ratios do not exhibit this property. The relative odds of impermanence (1.57) are simply the inverse of the relative odds of permanence ($0.63 = 1/1.57$). Thus, special care needs to be taken when interpreting relative risks as well as relative odds.

3. The small mean differences in child and caregiver characteristics indicate that the intervention and comparison groups can be regarded as statistically

equivalent. Although the differences with respect to caregiver education and grandparent-grandchild relationship are not as small as for the other characteristics, they are not large enough to threaten the internal validity of the findings.

4. The last row in Appendix Table 7.A1 refers to observational studies in which there is no manipulable control over the assignment process, but there may be some selectivity involved in complying with the assignment, such as gender role. There is a lively debate over whether causal effects can be meaningfully analyzed for nonmanipulable attributes, such as age, race, and sex (Morgan & Winship, 2007; Shadish, Cook, & Campbell, 2002). One of the issues involves the difficulty of approximating the counterfactual when there is no specific procedure for manipulating the cause of interest, such as racial background. Even if compliance with the assigned attribute is changeable, as when some women disguised their sex to enlist as soldiers in the Civil War (Blanton & Cook, 2003), it is likely that the female enlistees differed from female civilians in many ways other than their biological sex. So, the counterfactual inference about what would have happened to female soldiers who retained their "femaleness" is more difficult to make. On the other hand, it is possible to conceive of an analogue experiment in which the sex of job seekers is randomized on their employment applications to assess how sex is related to hiring practices. But, in this case, the nature of the gender effect is different from the effect of changing a woman into a man.

5. In the statistical literature, the subset of agents that comply with the assigned treatment are called "compliers." The estimated causal effect of assignment for the compliers is called the complier average causal effect (CACE) in some writings (Rubin, 2004) or the local average treatment effect (LATE) in others (Angrist, 2006). In general, the average treatment effect on the treated (ATET) does not equal CACE, because some agents will always accept treatment regardless of assignment. In the special case where the agents randomly assigned to the control group are prohibited from accepting treatment, as in the subsidized guardianship demonstration, CACE equals ATET because there can be no crossovers in the control group and non-compliance is a possibility only in the intervention group.

6. There are other important assumptions that are not discussed in this chapter, such as the stable unit treatment value assumption (SUTVA), which requires that the potential outcomes of persons be unaffected by potential changes in the intervention assignments of other persons. For example, because SUTVA was likely to be violated in the guardianship experiments if siblings were assigned to different groups, it was decided that the sibling group was the appropriate unit of randomization. For a good description of the major assumptions of causal inference in experimental and observational studies, see Rubin (2004).

References

Angrist, J. D. (2006). Instrumental variables methods in experimental criminological research: What, why and how. *Journal of Experimental Criminology*, 2, 23–44.

Barth, R. P., Guo, S., Green, R. L, & McCrae, J. S. (2007). Kinship care and nonkinship foster care: Informing the new debate. In R. Haskins, F. Wulczyn, &

M. B. Webb (Eds.), *Child protection: Using research to improve policy and practice* (pp. 187–206). Washington, DC: The Brookings Institution.

Blanton, D., & Cook, L. M. (2003). *They fought like demons: Women soldiers of the American Civil War.* New York: Random House, Inc.

Bloom, H. S., Michalopoulos, C., Hill, C. J., & Lei, Y. (2002). *Can nonexperimental comparison group methods match the findings from a random assignment evaluation of mandatory welfare-to-work programs?* New York: MDRC.

Burnette, D. (1997). Grandparents raising grandchildren in the inner city. *Families in Society: The Journal of Contemporary Human Services, 78,* 489–501.

Cox, D. R., & Reid, N. (2000). *The theory of the design of experiments.* Boca Raton: Chapman & Hall/CRC Press.

Doyle, J. J. (2007a). Child protection and child outcomes: Measuring the effects of foster care. *The American Economic Review, 97*(5), 1583–1610.

Doyle, J. J. (2007b). Can't buy me love? Subsidizing the care of related children. *Journal of Public Economics, 91,* 281–304.

Doyle, J. J. (2008). Child protection and adult crime: Using investigator assignment to estimate causal effects of foster care. *Journal of Political Economy, 116*(4), 746–770.

Fisher, R. A. (1935). *The design of experiments.* New York: Hafner.

Freedman, D. A. (2005). *Statistical models: Theory and practice.* Cambridge: Cambridge University Press.

Freedman, D. A. (2008). On regression adjustments to experimental data. *Advances in Applied Mathematics, 40,* 180–193.

Freedman, D., Pisani, R., & Purves, R. (2007). *Statistics (4th edition).* New York: W.W. Norton& Company.

Foster, E. M., & McLanahan, S. (1996). An illustration of the use of instrumental variables: Do neighborhood conditions affect a young person's chance of finishing high school? *Psychological Methods, 1*(3), 249–260.

Gaskie, S., & Nashelsky, J. (2005). Are breast self-exams or clinical exams effective for screening breast cancer? *Journal of Family Practice, 54*(9), 803–804.

Gleeson, J. P. (1996). Kinship care as a child welfare service: The policy debate in an era of welfare reform. *Child Welfare, 75*(2), 419–449.

Grogan-Kaylor, A. (2000). Who goes into kinship care? The relationship of child and family characteristics to placement into kinship foster care. *Social Work Research, 24,* 132–141.

Guo, S., Barth, R. P., & Gibbons, C. (2006). Propensity score matching strategies for evaluating substance abuse services for child welfare clients. *Children and Youth Services Review, 28,* 357–383.

Holland, P. W. (1988). Causal inference, path analysis, and recursive structural equation models. *Sociological Methodology, 18,* 449–484.

Koh, E., & Testa, M. (2008) Propensity score matching of children in kinship and nonkinship foster care: Do permanency outcomes still differ? *Social Work Research, 32*(28), 105–116.

MacDonald, H. (1994). The ideology of 'family preservation. *Public Interest* (Spring), 45–60.

Meezan, W., & McBeath, B. (2008). Market-based disparities in foster care outcomes. *Children and Youth Services Review, 30*(4), 388–406.

Morgan, S. L., & Winship, C. (2007). *Counterfactuals and causal inference: Methods and principles for social research.* Cambridge, UK: Cambridge University Press.

Newhouse, J. P., & McClellan, M. (1998). Econometrics in outcomes research: The use of instrumental variables. *Annual Review of Public Health, 19,* 17–34.

Petit, M. R., & Curtis, P. A. (1997) *Child abuse and neglect: A look at the states.* Washington, DC: CWLA Press.

The Pew Commission on Children in Foster Care. (2004). *Fostering the future: Safety, permanence, and well-being for children in foster care.* Washington, DC: The Pew Commission on Children in Foster Care.

Reid vs. Suter, N. 89 J 6195 (Cook Cty. Cir. 1992).

Rubin, D. B. (2001). Using propensity scores to help design observational studies: Application to the tobacco litigation. *Health Services and Outcomes Research Methodology, 2,* 169–188.

Rubin, D. B. (2004). Teaching statistical inference for causal effects in experiments and observational studies. *Journal of Educational and Behavioral Statistics, 29*(3), 343–367.

Shadish, W. R., Cook, T. D., & Campbell, D. T. (2002). *Experimental and quasi-experimental designs for generalized causal inference.* Boston: Houghton Mifflin Company.

Schwartz, M., & Ash, A. S. (2003). Estimating the effect of an intervention for observational data. In L. I. Iezzoni (Ed.), *Risk adjustment for measuring health outcomes (3rd edition)* (pp. 286–295). Chicago: Health Administration Press.

Testa, M. F. (1997). Kinship foster care in Illinois. In J. Duerr Berrick, R. Barth, & N. Gilbert (Eds.), *Child welfare research review* (Vol. 2, pp. 101–129). New York: Columbia University Press.

Testa, M. (2002). Subsidized guardianship: Testing an idea whose time has finally come. *Social Work Research, 26*(3), 145–158.

Testa, M. (2005). The quality of permanence—Lasting or binding? *Virginia Journal of Social Policy and Law, 12*(3), 499–534.

Testa, M., Cohen, L., Smith, G., & Westat, Inc. (2003). *Illinois subsidized guardianship waiver demonstration: Final Evaluation Report.* Springfield, IL: Department of Children and Family Services.

Testa, M., Fuller, T., & Nieto, M. (2007). Placement stability and number of children in home. Urbana, IL: Children and Family Research Center. Last accessed March 1, 2009 at http://www.cfrc.illinois.edu/pubs/pdf.files/Placement_Stability.pdf.

Testa, M. F., Shook, K., Cohen, L., & Woods, M. (1996). Permanency planning options for children in formal kinship care. In D. Wilson & S. Chipungu (Eds.), *Child Welfare Kinship Care: Special Issue. 75*(5), 451–470.

Thornton, J. L. (1991). Permanency planning for children in kinship foster homes. *Child Welfare, 70*(5), 593–601.

U.S. Department of Health and Human Services. (2004) Waiver authority terms and conditions, State of Illinois. Amended October 22, 2004 to extend the implementation date for the enhanced guardianship component from no later than September 30, 2004 to no later than June 30, 2005. Washington, DC: U.S. Department of Health and Human Services.

Victoria, C. G, Habicht, J., and Bryce, J. (2004). Evidence-based public health: Moving beyond randomized trials. *American Journal of Public Health, 94*(3), 400–405.

Westat, Chapin Hall Center for Children, & James Bell Associates. (2001). *Evaluation of family preservation and reunification programs: Interim report.*

Washington, DC: ASPE, U.S. Department of Health and Human Services. Last accessed March 1, 2009 at http://aspe.hhs.gov/hsp/fampres94/index.htm.

Writing Group for the Women's Health Initiative Investigators. (2002). Risks and benefits of estrogen plus progestin in healthy postmenopausal women: principal results from the Women's Health Initiative randomized controlled trial. *Journal of the American Medical Association, 288*(3), 321–333.

Wulczyn, F. H., Chen, L., & Hislop, K. B. (2006). Adoption dynamics and the Adoptions and Safe Families Act. *Social Service Review*, 584–608.

8

RESULTS-ORIENTED MANAGEMENT

Using Evidence for Quality Improvement

Terry Moore

The main objective of public child welfare policy and practice is to promote the achievement of safety, permanence, and well-being for the children and families that come to the attention of child protective agents. The essence of a case or program manager's job is to secure and direct resources, together with other child welfare agents, to optimize positive outcomes for children and families. Quality improvement is one aspect of managing, at whatever organizational level, which involves the use of data on current operations to inform managerial decision making. These efforts initially proceed along the single-loop track of more timely, efficient, and accurate implementation of existing practices and policies. However, if these incremental adjustments prove inadequate or contrary to other general end-values, quality improvement then needs to proceed along the double-loop track of developing a different model of quality improvement or forging a new consensus on alternative goals.

The purpose of this chapter is to provide practical methods for improving the *construct validity* of quality improvement by tracking performance data, acting on the feedback to inform managerial action, and developing new strategies to improve agency performance. These methods extend beyond the single-loop refinements for fine-tuning performance to the shaping of an organizational culture that encourages double-loop learning and *reflexivity*, so that existing practices are regularly critiqued and innovative solutions for achieving desired outcomes are continuously tried and routinely evaluated.

Managing for Outcomes

Managing for outcomes involves a complex set of technical and interpersonal skills as well as knowledge of evidence-supported interventions. It poses special challenges because results-oriented practice is:

- Reliant on a multifaceted, often fragmented, social service delivery system that is often outside of direct management control to address the many public concerns about children and families;
- Embedded within a legal framework and subject to the hierarchical direction and authority of the court;
- Often carried out within large bureaucratic organizations; and
- Under a high level of scrutiny by the public and key stakeholders

Within this environment, child and family outcomes data are central to the managerial task of orienting both individual practitioners and corporate partners towards achieving a balanced-set of outcomes on behalf of children and their families.

The Adoption and Safe Families Act of 1997 (ASFA) changed the way child welfare programs need to be managed. ASFA expects managers to achieve specific results in shorter periods of time while uphold child safety as paramount. The ASFA also established the Child and Family Services Review (CFSR), a federally administered quality improvement program (Federal Register, 2000). The CFSR establishes outcome measures with performance expectations, implements an ongoing process of review and requires quality improvement plans (Milner, Mitchell, & Hornsby, 2005). Although some refinements were made for the second four-year cycle, the basic structure of the CFSR process and the national focus on achieving outcomes was reaffirmed in 2006. Perhaps the most significant changes were a more comprehensive set of measures, and the introduction of the composite measures methodology, which summarizes performance on individual measures into four composites (see Chapter 4, this volume).

The CFSR has led to more robust quality improvement systems at the state and local levels, and has contributed to child welfare managers becoming more focused on improving outcomes. To demonstrate improvement toward meeting these outcomes, managers are encouraged to adopt continuous quality improvement approaches that assess practice in light of performance, use data to effect changes in policy and practice, and engage a broad range of internal and external stakeholders in information gathering (O'Brien & Watson, 2002).

Managers who undertake the task of quality improvement with skill and purpose create learning organizations. They track performance data, take action to improve outcomes, and shape an organizational culture of reflexivity (Holland, 1999), which encourages critical appraisal, learning, and continuous quality improvement. Garvin (2000) offers the following definition of learning organizations:

> A learning organization is an organization skilled at creating, acquiring, interpreting, transferring, and retaining knowledge, and at purposefully modifying its behavior to reflect new knowledge and insights. (Garvin, 2000, p. 11)

Poertner and Rapp (2007) identify three major ingredients for creating learning organizations focused on achieving results: (1) an organizational culture that supports learning, (2) sufficient managerial skills to use information, and (3) an information system to store, retrieve, and report performance information. These three interactive attributes affect how data are interpreted and acted upon to improve outcomes performance (Moore, Rapp, & Roberts, 2000). This chapter uses this framework and presents practical steps aimed at increasing the capacity of managers and other agents to use data reflexively to improve outcomes including:

- Access to data reports
- Analysis and interpretation of data
- Action strategies to improve performance
- Attitudes in the organizational culture

Although using data is unfamiliar to some child welfare managers (Schoech, Quinn, & Rycraft, 2000), problem solving and managing change is not. Many managers were caseworkers or clinicians that engaged in a similar process. When caseworkers have a client with an identifying problem, they undertake an assessment for underlying causes, and then design a case or treatment plan based on that assessment. Throughout the life of a case, the plan is changed in response to additional information and results of the treatment. Improving program performance involves a similar process (Traglia, Massinga, Pecora, & Paddock, 1996). Both managers and line staff identify problems, conduct an assessment (analyze their data) resulting in tentative conclusions, develop and implement an action plan, monitor progress toward goals, and modify the plan accordingly. Chapter 2 presented a framework for results-oriented accountability. Figure 8.1 presents a similar framework for managing change, which applies whether working with people or programs.

Other similarities exist between the casework and quality improvement processes. Even though the diagram in Figure 8.1 implies a linear (step by step) process, in reality, the change process is very dynamic as one is working on many levels of this at once. Assessment never ends and action steps evolve in light of new information. Likewise, there are both short and long range strategies taken.

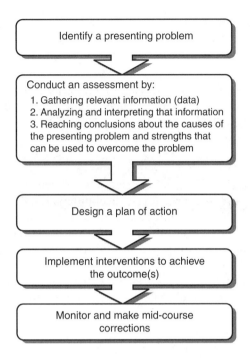

Figure 8.1 The common process for change.

Access to Data in Reports

Management reports enable managers to monitor performance on outcomes and key service processes and make informed program or policy changes (Jamieson & Bodonyi, 1999; Moore et al., 2000). The way performance data are reported affects the extent to which data can and will be used. A number of problems have been identified in reporting systems including information overload, lack of relevant aggregation for multiple audiences, inaccuracy of data, and insufficient analytic tools to aid in hypothesis identification and testing (Bamford, 1996; Fluke, Edwards, Kutzler, Kuna, & Tooman, 2000). The ability to see performance over time and across management units (e.g., region, office, supervisory unit) enhances the ability to target improvement efforts, identify strengths, and evaluate the results of policy and practice actions.

A management report system provides updated data on the extent to which standards or goals are being met. Most report systems provide performance data on achievement of outcomes and service responses. Both types of indicators are needed. It is important for program managers to recognize that process measures (e.g., parent–child visitations) are procedures or practices that are intended to lead to outcomes (e.g., timely reunification), thus creating a hierarchy of interest (Friedman, Garnett, & Pinnock, 2005). Reports systems should strive to balance the use of these different measures and distinguish between the two. An imbalance of service response measures can distract from the focus on outcomes.

Child welfare managers generally have access to a mass of data, however, the format, content, timing, and method of delivering these data has made it difficult for mangers to gain insights, translate findings into action, and generate knowledge. It is difficult to develop electronic reporting systems that are sufficiently simple and sophisticated for meaningful use by non-technical managers at all levels. To accomplish this, effective partnerships between information technology and program staff are necessary. Additionally, partnerships with university researchers can assist in developing sound indicators of the major federal outcomes and introducing analytic strategies (See Chapter 11, this volume).

Guidelines for Effective Management Reports

Management reports need to be user friendly, simple and facilitate interpretation (Chapel & Horsch, 1998; Courtney & Collins, 1994). Convenience and simplicity of getting to the data helps to overcome other barriers to using data, such as lack of available time and expertise. Advanced computer technologies and the increased use of creating longitudinal databases have made useful management reporting systems possible (Webster, Needell, & Wildfire, 2002). Availability of user-friendly web applications, electronic spreadsheets, and powerful desktop computers are providing greater capacity to access and analyze data (Fostering Court Improvement, 2007). Whereas the old style, printed paper reports, can be effective, electronic report systems facilitate the user's ability to access and manipulate data for more in-depth understanding. Promising web-based report systems, such as the ROM Reports system, have been developed and are being implemented across the country (Moore, 2002). Figure 8.2 is a screen shot from ROM Reports that provides an example of a web-based report system. The reports are updated nightly from agency databases.

The following are guidelines for developing effective management reports.

Ease of Use

Staff needs to be able to get to the data quickly and easily. In Figure 8.2, the user can easily look at the graph and immediately compare performance against a set standard. Web-based report systems provide an environment with which most people have familiarity and can use with minimal training. Users need to be able to easily select a report (measure), management unit, and time period of interest, the basic parameters of any report. The ability to change only one of these parameters at a time (outcome measure of interest), while maintaining the others, is more efficient for navigating the report system. The screen shot of ROM Reports in Figure 8.2 displays these controls on the left side of the page allowing the user to easily set the parameters they want for their report.

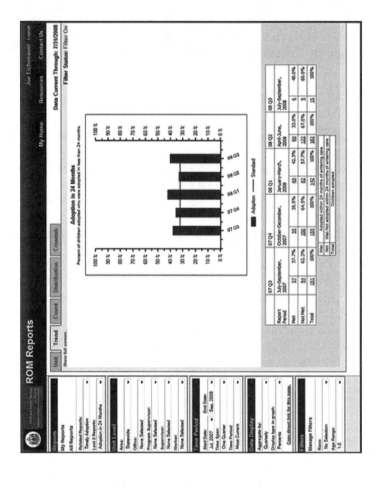

Figure 8.2 An example of a web-based report system.

Facilitate Interpretation

The use of graphs and supporting tables makes data more understandable and useful (Schoech et al., 2000). Graphs provide instant visualization of performance (a picture worth a 1000 words). Establishing and displaying a standard of expected performance or a goal on the graph aids with quick understanding of performance (Poertner & Rapp, 2007). Supporting tables provide additional detail such as the number of cases used to compute a performance rate providing a more realistic perspective on the measure (see Fig. 8.2). For example, 80% reunification in 12 months is not reliable if it is only based on five cases. Presenting data as performance rates or percentages (e.g., percent adopted in less than 24 months) makes comparisons possible. Comparisons between management units (e.g., regions/areas, offices) and change over time are particularly useful (Fluke et al., 2000).

Using rates or percentages that read in the same direction (i.e. positively stated) also aids data interpretation, because the bars or lines on graphs going up consistently reflect more positive results. To achieve this, some commonly used measures/indicators have to be reworded. For example "re-entry" into foster care rate can be re-worded as "maintaining reunification."

Enable Further Analysis

Once managers understand their performance on an outcome measure another set of questions arises (e.g., how does our reunification rate in 12 month vary by age groups)? In ROM Reports, users can select crosstab views and analyze the data by a range of other variables (e.g., age, race, disability, etc.). A report system that allows users to access individual case information (drill down) from an aggregate number (e.g., entered foster care 12 months ago) enables managers to cross tabulate the data by other variables (e.g., age group, case type, etc.) to see how successful they have been with each subgroup (Fluke et al., 2000). In our ROM Reports example (Fig. 8.2), the users can "drill down" on any aggregate number to retrieve a spreadsheet of those cases by using the mouse. By knowing what cases are used for a measure the supervisors or case workers can begin to consider other real-time case information not available from the information system. Some report systems allow the users statistically to test outcome attainment (dependent variable) by a variety of client or case characteristics (independent variables), or perform more sophisticated statistical analysis (see Chapter 5, this volume).

Promote Trust and Accuracy of Data

The more managers believe the data on a performance indicator, the more they are willing to undertake improvement efforts (Bamford, 1996; Schoech et al., 2000). The capacity to view individual cases (drill down) from aggregate numbers in a report, results in increased validation of the data. If there are errors in data entry or how performance was calculated, corrections can be made.

Focus Attention on Fewer Measures

Too many measures/indicators can be overwhelming and lead to confusion. This can lead to inaction because it is difficult for managers to know what is important (Poertner & Rapp, 2007). Limiting the number of measures/indicators to monitor can be done in a couple of ways. Report systems can be set up to allow the users to customize their menu by selecting measures that are most relevant for their management. For example, if the unit is only responsible for child abuse or neglect investigations, the indicators on maintaining child safety (no recurrence of maltreatment) or timely completion of investigations would be more useful than a measure on timely adoption. In ROM Reports, the users set up their own menu of reports from a larger list of reports available. Another way to reduce the number of indicators is to choose the best indicators that have the least amount of redundancy.

Show Progress Toward an Outcome

In addition to knowing if an outcome was achieved (hindsight), providing advance notice (foresight) on achieving outcomes is beneficial. Tracking prospectively the percentage of children reunified by the number of months since entry into foster care can provide advance notice on how well timely reunification is being achieved. Such reports help managers become proactive in achieving performance standards.

Feedback helps us do most skill-based activities better from playing tennis to improving outcome performance. Reports show the extent to which desired results are being achieved. Effective reports are those that lead to increased use of data and achievement of outcomes. This is especially important for the environment of child welfare management, where there are many opportunities to be distracted.

Analyzing and Interpreting Data

Once performance on established measures is known, the next step is to bring meaning to those numbers in a way that informs program or policy actions to maintain or improve performance. With data, managers can postulate causal relationships and seek to uncover patterns and correlations that provide clues upon which action steps can be taken. Data do not provide the "answer" on what is causing performance or what to do about it. Causal relationships are difficult to isolate under less than optimal experimental conditions (Kettner, Daley, & Nichols, 1985). Most real-life situations are too complex and dynamic to be able to determine cause from observational studies alone (see Chapter 7, this volume). However, much can be done to identify contributing factors associated with variations in performance (Friedman et al., 2005; Schoech et al., 2000). Ultimately, the analysis leads to reaching tentative conclusions about the causes (hypotheses) of the presenting problem. Strengths are also revealed, which can provide insights on how to improve performance.

An important part of analyzing data is to understand how a measure is computed. All measures have limitations and some have more than others. Knowing these limitations helps in understanding the meaning of the data. Chapter 4 discussed several limitations of the current CFSR measures. One of these is a commonly used indicator that measures reunification in less than 12 months. The measure is the percentage of children reunified (an exit cohort), who were reunified in less than 12 months. Therefore, if the children were not reunified (e.g., age out of care, entered juvenile justice system), they would not be included. Entry cohort measures provide a more accurate picture because they track all children that entered care during a range of dates (a year) and report the outcome achieved either along a continuum of time or after the end of an observation period (12 months after the children entered care). Point in time (snap-shot) measures for children in foster care (e.g., average length of stay) also over-represent children in care for long periods of time (Webster et al., 2002). In interpreting data, you should also be mindful of the interplay between measures. That is, improving performance on one set of measures can have repercussions on other measures of performance (Usher, Wildfire, & Gibbs, 1999). For example, speedier reunification rates can lead to more children re-entering care.

Managing for outcomes requires the best measures possible. Unfortunately, analysis of administrative data is not commonly taught in schools of Social Work (DiLeonardi & Yuan, 2000). Common sense and critical thinking helps in understanding how measures are computed and their strengths and weaknesses. Because it is difficult for most managers to know the details of measure construction, partnerships with university child welfare researchers can help develop this expertise.

Good report systems provide managers with tools that enable an in-depth analysis of outcomes performance. Regardless of the report system, the following are questions for analyzing performance:

- *How has the performance on this measure changed over time?* Has there been a time when performance has been good? For example, noting that performance got better when the unit was fully staffed may indicate the impact of lower caseloads.

- *Is the percentage of outcome achievement based on a sufficient number of cases?* A common mistake is to pass judgment on a percentage based on too small a sample. This is particularly problematic when using outcome data for evaluating staff performance or the performance of rural counties. Statisticians use "power analysis" to determine the number of cases needed to draw a conclusion (see Chapter 5, this volume). Sometimes, the number of cases can be increased by looking at longer lengths of time or across more case types.

- *How does performance vary among management units?* If some units are doing particularly well on an outcome, they could be consulted to find out how they are achieving this. If the performance problem is across management units, it may reflect more systemic issues (e.g., lack of resources, failing policies). For example, a state may not do well with its placement stability because it has a policy of first processing all children through a 15-day assessment placement.
- *Are there other outcomes that interact with the outcome being analyzed?* Performance rates should be examined in the context of a balanced-set of outcome measures. For example, a management unit might be doing well with time to reunification but less well maintaining reunification (children are re-entering care). A study in Kansas uncovered that one county in the state had the longest time to permanency rate, but had the lowest out-of-home placement rate per 1000 children in the population (Moore et al., 2006). This county was able to successfully divert children from foster care, so those entering care were more complex cases that take longer to achieve permanence. These interactions provide a larger picture of performance.

Exploring Reasons Associated With Performance

Uncovering factors associated with performance helps inform the development of improvement strategies. There are many factors to consider that can help explain performance. If one can identify sub-populations that they are not successful with, that client group can be targeted for improvement strategies. Observing that longer times to achieve permanence are associated with large caseloads, experimental interventions to lower caseloads can be undertaken to assess the impact on permanency rates.

A common problem is the tendency to jump to conclusions before considering an array of factors. For example, if data are aggregated by county offices and performance for an outcome is low, that office becomes the identified problem. Although it may be true that a county office is not performing well, it may also be true that a certain judge, a lack of community resources, a challenging sub-population being served, or staffing vacancies also contribute to lower performance. Managers need to consider and then analyze a variety of factors for their effect on the outcome of interest. The following is a starter list of factors to consider grouped into four major categories (Moore, 2002).

Population Characteristics and Needs

What population characteristics correlate with the outcome performance? Characteristics may include age; race; gender; disabilities; referral reasons, family/parent characteristics, or other special needs (e.g., mental illness, substance abuse, and poverty).

Intervention Factors

Does the quality, quantity, or type of intervention help to explain performance? Are evidence-supported interventions being implemented as intended? This may include type of services provided (e.g., mental health services, respite care, parent training, substance abuse treatment, aftercare services, or any specialized programs or treatment); duration of services; placement types; conformity with policies and procedures (e.g., case plan reviews within time requirements, court recommendations approved by the supervisor); service quantity (e.g., contacts with parents or child, parent–child visitation); or quality of services (e.g., engagement of family, placement proximity).

Organizational Factors

What organizational factors have an impact on the achievement of this outcome? This may include analyzing data by management unit; service providers; changes in policy and procedures; staffing (e.g., caseload size, filling vacancies, staff morale); resources available (e.g., placement, treatment, funding) where they are needed; program design (e.g., the array of services provided to whom under what conditions, use of concurrent case planning); or values and organizational culture.

Community Factors

What is the effect that other child welfare agents and stakeholders have on meeting outcome goals? Managers may consider the effect of the courts (i.e. judges or county/district attorney); child or parent attorneys; court-appointed special advocates; and the availability and cooperation of community resources (e.g., education, housing, employment, child care, mental health providers, and other medical providers).

Multiple Factors Usually have an Impact on Performance

Managers have a better chance of developing solutions to a performance problem by identifying and addressing the major contributing factors. For example, action steps to reduce re-entry into foster care become clearer if managers determine that children that re-enter are more likely to be adolescents with acting-out behaviors who were in care less than 6 months and re-entered care within 60 days of returning home. Having this information allows the managers to target efforts to improve performance. For example, one strategy is to intensify aftercare contacts in the first 60 days to assist with the transition home for this target population rather than for all reunifications. There are certainly more questions about this group of children such as: How do we better prepare these youths and their families for reunification while in foster care; what are evidence-supported treatment strategies; and what kind of supports do we need to provide after they go home, in particular during the first 60 days?

Strategies for Identifying and Verifying Factors Contributing to Achieving Outcomes

A variety of approaches can be taken to uncover factors that may be influencing performance that can be tested and verified using data. Managers most often use their experience, observations, and practice wisdom as well as that of other internal or external stakeholders to develop hypotheses. When asked, people often offer their opinions about the factors affecting outcomes. Sometimes these opinions are offered as solutions that imply casual factors. These solutions can be reframed as contributing factors and verified through data analysis and experimentation. Involving those closest to the work is also informative. However, this is also prone to perpetuating myths and assumptions (e.g., foster parents cannot help with reunification because they don't want contact with biological parents). Involving internal and external stakeholders in this reflexive process can help confront these assumptions as well as engage a wider array of perspectives about what may be affecting outcomes (Kettner et al., 1985). The act of asking the question about what is having an impact on performance not only helps identify what might be affecting performance, but begins to create energy toward improvement.

The process of identifying and validating factors can be informed by reviewing cases in which an outcome was achieved or not (providing confidentiality standards are met). Some report systems offer the capacity to drill down to retrieve information on specific cases. This allows those engaged in the process to bring in information that may not be in the computer system. For example, poverty may be a common theme observed in cases where it takes more time to achieve reunification, even though there are no data elements that capture economic well being.

Another approach in the search for clues and testing hypotheses is to conduct intensive case reviews on a sample of cases that failed to achieve the desired outcome (O'Brien & Watson, 2002, Poertner & Rapp, 2007). Selected cases are put under a microscope by a group of staff members (including the caseworker responsible for the case) to determine what happened and what might have changed the case outcome. These reviews require trust and a non-blaming environment. Creating this environment requires a range of actions, such as setting the proper tone for the process, facilitating the discussion toward solutions, encouraging examination of a wide range of factors (e.g., organizational, community, client population, resources), and selecting a variety of cases for review that does not target any one staff member.

With well developed management report systems, managers can, with a few clicks of a mouse, analyze the database to see if outcomes vary by certain factors. Managers can look at performance on an outcome (dependent variable) by any factor (independent variable) available in the database such as age groups (or other demographic factors), disability types, or the effect of not meeting service response actions such as visitation requirements. Some report systems have built in analytic functions that make this "data-snooping" expedition easier. But, such a search should be regarded as purely exploratory and hypotheses should be subjected to more rigorous and sophisticated forms of testing.

More sophisticated statistical analysis can involve university researchers knowledgeable about working with child welfare databases and statistical analysis (see Chapter 11, this volume). Researchers can conduct bivariate, or multivariate analyses on the relationship between the outcome and one or more independent variables. They can also undertake survival or event-history analysis of time-to-outcome data. This provides a richer view than is offered by a single point on the time continuum (e.g., reunification within 12 months). Accelerated failure time (AFT) and Cox regression models can reveal the statistical likelihood of achieving outcomes for various groups of clients or service responses along that time continuum while controlling for other factors (see Chapter 5 on reunification trends).

Verifying Factors Contributing to Achieving Outcomes

There are a large number of factors and combination of factors to consider when identifying what is contributing to performance. This requires our best critical thinking skills. It is, therefore, useful to narrow the field of ideas or hypotheses to be tested. A variety of statistical tools can produce insights into relationships between outcomes and contributing factors. In addition to quantitative methods to analyze the data, qualitative methods involving interviews and focus groups can help test hypotheses. Each factor by itself, or together with others, provides clues about where the agency can focus improvement efforts.

This data analysis process results in tentative conclusions about what is having an impact on performance. This serves as a basis for an action strategy. The conclusion summarizes your findings and attempts to connect the dots (clues). It may be something like: Adolescents are not achieving timely reunification and are re-entering care more often because of not being able to resolve issues between the youth and the major adults in their home environment (e.g., school personnel, parents), which is complicated by the lack of placement resources for adolescents, requiring placement in more distant locations. Just as in direct practice, conclusions are tentative and additional analysis occurs with new data as it becomes available or new factors become identified.

Involving Stakeholders in the Process

The quality improvement process from analyzing the problem to implementing improvement plans can be undertaken entirely by individual managers or can involve other stakeholders (Bamford, 1996). Making this decision depends on the type and extent of the problem and the level of change needed to improve performance. If there are few factors having an impact on performance and they are easily identifiable, managers can act on their own by testing and verifying their hypotheses and initiating action.

Engaging stakeholders that have the most impact on improving the outcome of interest, increases the chances for successful improvement efforts (McDaniel, 1996). Gaining the perspective of stakeholders can result in an enriched understanding of the problem and speaks to the reality of the interconnectedness of community partners. An example of this level of stakeholder involvement is the Family to Family initiative that developed the capacity for "self-evaluation" among stakeholders as a key strategy of program improvement (Webster et al., 2002). Building these relationships also provides an opportunity to increase understanding of the outcomes being sought, and creates greater ownership of and commitment to the eventual quality improvement strategy (Weiss, 1997).

Stakeholders may be internal or external to the child welfare agency. Internally, managers should consider involving direct service staff, varying levels of management, and those that handle more administrative functions (e.g., human resources, finance, licensing, policy, etc.). Involving direct service workers not only helps them see how their work connects to child welfare outcomes (Sahonchik, Frizsell, & O'Brien, 2005), it also provides an important perspective. Externally, stakeholders may include foster parents, child welfare service providers, court personnel, law enforcement, educators, mental health professionals, or any other group that is relevant to the outcome of interest. Another stakeholder group that is worth considering is consumers such as birth or adoptive parents, relatives, and youth.

Determining whom to involve, how to involve them, and when to seek their involvement depends on the decision-making structure of the agency, the outcome being addressed, community politics, informal leadership, and whomever is needed to improve performance. Involving too many people can get unwieldy. If the list is too long, one can prioritize those identified as key stakeholders (those that must be at the table), important stakeholders (their presence would benefit the process), and helpful stakeholders (those that may be helpful).

Involving stakeholders takes time and resources. However, their involvement may be as little as consulting the stakeholder on the phone or as much as their participation in meetings. Also, some stakeholders can be asked to participate in only part of the process. Those the manager involves can also change depending on the direction that is taken. Participation in the early stages of the improvement process is desirable. Regardless, managers can benefit from maintaining stakeholder involvement throughout the improvement process, even if it is just keeping them informed about actions taken and results achieved.

Action Strategies to Improve Performance

Developing an action plan or logic model is made easier by a good analysis of the problem. Depending how many clues were uncovered, data are frequently more accessible for targeting attention on particular outcomes and population groups (e.g., re-entry rates for adolescents with acting out behaviors who were in care less than 6 months) and less helpful in identifying promising interventions for doing something about the problem. Searching the internet for evidence-supported treatments can be helpful in identifying promising interventions (see Chapter 6, this volume). The intent is to implement a logic model with the highest level of evidence for its efficacy.

Management actions to optimize outcomes can take many forms. For example:

- Taking action on individual cases or group of cases
- Making refinements or changes in program design, policy, or procedures
- Securing needed resources
- Developing staff skills and knowledge
- Influencing internal and external stakeholders

Friedman et al. (2005, p. 250) suggest that logic models make explicit the underlying theory of change. They outlined three questions that can be used to evaluate action strategies:

1. Plausible—Is there a reasonable chance that taking such action would deliver the desired results?
2. Doable—Are the action strategies doable within existing resources?
3. Testable—Are the action strategies and the desired effect measurable?

Logic models need to be specific and answer the questions:

Who will do
What, by
When, to achieve what
Result.

Rarely is all the data available and analysis completed when managers want to take action. So just as in direct practice, it is important to initiate action at the earliest time knowing that more will follow. Although not strictly necessary, diagramming the plan in the *PICO* format of a logic model serves as a useful reference for everyone involved (see Chapter 3, this volume).

Keeping the process simple, efficient, and focused on improving outcomes is important. Undertaking program improvement planning can occur at any level of an organization, including the supervisory unit level. However, it is advantageous to use the limited resources available on delivering better results than on an elaborate planning system or wasting efforts on organizational makeovers that often end up diverting attention rather than directing attention. Overly elaborate planning systems can consume a disproportionate amount of resources. The key is to balance the "thinking" and "doing" aspects of the improvement process. The bias here is on taking action rather than contemplating action.

Operationalizing Goals through Incremental Tasks

One of the important skills needed to lead quality improvement efforts is opening up the "black box" linking interventions to outcomes and breaking down the intermediate tasks, procedures, and outputs into identifiable and manageable components. We do this all the time in our personal lives. Buying a car or house is made more manageable by making monthly payments. Losing that extra 20 lbs. requires one to break down what they do into manageable goals (3 lbs. a week) and tasks (e.g., eating only certain things and exercising 20 minutes a day). Then it takes discipline, motivation, and persistence to carry out the plan.

Breaking down goals into measurable outputs and manageable tasks is the same process that caseworkers go through when developing a case plan. In both casework and management actions for quality improvement:

- Goals and objectives need to be clear, unambiguous, and measurable;
- The principals affected by the plan (clients, staff, or stakeholders) need to be involved in its development and have ownership.
- Tasks should be assigned to specific agents, should be manageable, and be spelled out to the level necessary for the person responsible for the task.

Action plans turn identified problems into desired futures (goals), outline general improvement strategies, develop specific measurable outputs, and articulate tasks as well as who will do them by when (Sahonchik et al., 2005). The following are examples of these components of a plan:

1. Establish the outcome goal (and any intermediate outputs)
   Example: Increase reunification within 12 months of entry into foster care to 80% among adolescents.

2. Determine general strategies.

   Example: Increase the number of adolescents and their parents who are participating in family therapy to resolve areas of conflict. A perceived barrier to participation is that 70% of the adolescents were in placements over 50 miles away from the parent's home).

3. Develop measurable objectives.

   Examples: Develop 12 foster homes in county that will accept and work with adolescents on the assumption that eliminating this barrier will increase family contact. Track number of adolescents and parents who participate in family therapy sessions.

4. Specify tasks, establish responsibilities, and determine timelines.

   Examples: Host three group meetings in January with existing foster parents who do not currently accept adolescents. Discuss the general need for foster homes that accept adolescents and address their particular concerns about caring for adolescents.

There are only a couple of examples for each plan component. However, there are generally several tasks for each objective, several objectives tied to a strategy, and several strategies to achieve an outcome goal. Keeping these components linked helps to keep the improvement process on track. People often lose track of why they are doing something (only see trees not the forest). In the example previously mentioned, the worker needs to know the objective for an additional 12 homes for adolescents so that there can be increased contact between adolescents and their families, which facilitates earlier reunification. The managers also need to continually re-evaluate the improvement process for the impact of the strategies being used.

Standardized planning forms can help link goals, strategies, and tasks. Likewise, these connections can be documented through the use of a logic model as illustrated in Figure 8.3. This is a useful conceptual model for program design and action planning that offers useful tools for making these linkages.

Managers often make the mistake of getting absorbed in and overwhelmed by "fixing everything." After all, everything is connected to everything else. Whereas understanding the entire system is important, the quality improvement process requires discipline and the setting of some parameters around what can be done.

Guidelines for Developing Measurable Objectives

The two areas that managers often struggle with in developing action plans are developing measurable objectives and establishing targets. The following are general guidelines on developing measurable objectives that are needed for action plans.

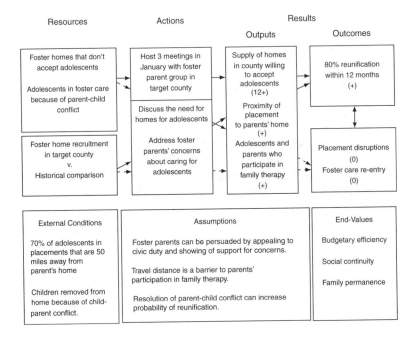

Figure 8.3 Foster home recruitment logic model.

Objectives should be Result Oriented

Establish objectives that are the outputs or outcomes of action rather than an action or task. The result of an action could be:

- A client outcome for all or a smaller group of cases;
- A service output measure (e.g., in-county placement, parent-child visitation);
- The development of a resource (e.g., foster home);
- A change of policy or procedure;
- Increased skills of staff or foster parents;
- A product (e.g., an agreement, a community services directory); or
- Adherence to a policy or procedure (e.g., aftercare contacts requirements met).

Objectives should be Clearly Defined

Everyone needs to agree on what is meant by what is being measured (e.g., in-county placement, placement move) so that everyone will count it the same way, and it is easily understood. Avoid using judgment terms such as "adequate" or "appropriate," and vague terms like "coordination" or "cooperation." If there were an objective to increase coordination between an agency and the school system, it would be difficult to get any two people to agree on what that meant. It is better to state what you wanted to accomplish through better coordination (e.g., the school will notify the foster parent of any disciplinary hearing on children in our custody). Alternately, a memorandum of understanding could be developed that includes any number of understandings. In some cases, objectives are products or are written in such a way that there is no target other then yes or no (e.g., develop an agreement with the school). That is, either the objective is completed or not.

Objectives should Measure What You Mean

Develop measures that get directly at what is important. For example, if one was trying to measure the objective "remain in school" by counting suspensions (rather than counting days of school missed because of suspension or expulsion), one might miss the value of a suspension versus an expulsion. Getting suspended for a few days might actually be an improvement compared to being expelled for the rest of the school term.

Objectives should be Single Focused

A measure should establish one criterion for achievement. Be on the lookout for the word "and." This guideline was not followed in the objective, "Kids are able to remain in school and receive the special services they need." It begs the question, if kids remained in school, but did not receive the special services they needed, would you not count this as a success?

Objectives should be Easy to Measure

Use measures already available. If that is not possible, keep your measures and data collection systems simple. The burden of extra data collection is felt by everyone, especially frontline staff. Measuring progress on your plan is essential and provides a basis for modifying your plan of action.

Set Numeric Targets

Establish a specific numeric target (benchmark, goal) for each objective. A benchmark provides a criterion for success and helps motivate staff. Having a target makes goals real for most staff. Relative terms like "more" or "increase" are not sufficiently informative. Furthermore, they leave the impression that the objective is never ending.

   Much of the time, a target can be calculated for an increase of something needed (e.g., number of foster homes, reunifications within 12 months of removal). If data are not available, estimates can be made. There is some basis for setting the target. For example, of the children that entered foster care 8 months ago, how many more of them would need to achieve reunification in the next 4 months to achieve an outcome goal of 80% reunification in 12 months? If there were 20 children that entered care 8 months ago and 5 (20%) had already been reunified, an additional 11 children would need to be reunified over the 4 months left to achieve an

80% outcome goal. Calculations such as these are easier for caseworkers to do when the work is structured in the form of a performance-based contract (see Chapter 10, this volume)

Objectives are set for many aspects of an improvement plan. For example, a county supervisor was able to figure out that she needed to develop 12 more foster homes in her county to increase the chances for timely reunification. She started by calculating how many more kids in foster care would need to be placed in county foster homes to meet the performance standard and then how many homes it would take to place that many kids. Here is how she figured this:

- **118 kids** (the number of children removed within the last year with reunification as a case goal)
- **times 80%** (the service response to attain reunification goal)
- **equals 95** (kids that would need to be placed in the county to meet the goal)
- **minus 74** (kids already placed in the county)
- **equals 21 more in-county placements needed** (this is the net gain needed for children placed in the county)
- **divided by 1.75** (the average capacity of foster homes)
- **equals 12 additional foster homes** (needed to be recruited)

Targets should be as understandable as possible. This may mean translating percentages into whole numbers for setting targets. For example, when the supervisor told her staff that they needed to develop an additional 12 foster homes, she made the goal more tangible and understandable than if she had said to achieve an 80% reunification rate. She arrived at this by dividing 21 children by an average of 1.75 (average capacity per foster home), which equaled 12 foster homes. Using numbers makes measuring performance, monitoring your progress, and keeping the goal in front of people much easier.[1]

The Dynamic Nature of the Quality Improvement Process

Like the cycle of results-oriented accountability that is the heart of this book, the process of establishing and carrying out an action plan is dynamic. Although there are sequential aspects (i.e., analyze, develop plan, take action), the process is multidimensional because one is reviewing data, planning, and taking action on several fronts at the same time. David Cassafer (1996, p. 177) presents a Plan-Do-Check-Act model to describe the circular nature of the quality improvement process. Managers are continually modifying action plans based on new information, monitoring progress on task completion and obtaining of objectives, analyzing new or additional data, and checking to see of the outcome is being achieved.

As in the clinical casework process, starting to take action often begins before completing an assessment. One continually gathers more information making assessment ongoing rather than a single or static event. Information is gathered, hypotheses formed, tested, and then kept or discarded. The job of managers is to manage this change process until the major outcome objective is achieved.

Fostering a Results-Oriented Culture

Every work environment has a culture that communicates the attitudes, behaviors, and values staff "should" have to work in that environment. The underlining message is that if one holds these attitudes and values and conforms to these behaviors, they have conformed to the norms of the culture and are accepted as a member of the "group." All child welfare organizations have a culture around the use of data, quality improvement planning, and its efficacy in making meaningful change toward improving results for the principals of child welfare services.

In a results-oriented culture, data are used routinely, learning is encouraged, action is taken to improve performance, stakeholders are involved, and rewards are given (Moore et al., 2000). Traglia et al. (1996, p. 96) said that implicit in this approach is ". . . the responsibility of administrators to create and maintain an organizational culture that values excellence in service design, execution, and results." Toward achieving excellence, data is an effective vehicle for organizational change when the culture values open mindedness, confronts issues, engages in participative decision making, and the people involved feel supported and are treated with dignity (Fluke et al., 2000; Garvin, 2000).

Many challenges exist in developing a results-oriented culture in child welfare agencies. Limited resources, high staff turnover, complex and urgent needs presented by families, and the zero tolerance for errors by the public and headlined by the press all contribute to a defensive mentality among child welfare professionals (Scott, Moore, & Ward, 2005). Introducing outcomes and other critical results measures provides even more opportunity for being criticized and subjected to punitive measures. Child welfare agents have, over the years, been subjected to frequent attacks by the press, legislators, judges, attorneys, advocates, and the public. Law suits, newspaper headlines, and continuous scrutiny by the courts all contribute to a "circle the wagons" mentality and blaming culture, which leads to denial and maintaining the status quo. This environment makes it difficult to recognize or accept problems, let alone seek improvements (Vincent, 1997).

It is difficult to fully understand the culture when one is immersed in it. Managers both shape and are shaped by the cultures in their organization. Managers can become more aware of the culture in their unit. They can ask others what they notice about their own units (e.g., attitudes, values, behaviors). Visiting other units (e.g., participate in meetings) or having visitors can offer insights. One can also examine things from a detached researcher perspective seeing what people say and do throughout a day. What do people say about data, or about their ability to make changes? Paying attention to lateral communications between peers, which continually reinforces the established culture, provides valuable information in understanding the culture and how it may be changing.

Organizational culture is communicated and reinforced formally and informally. Here are a few ways in which culture is communicated:

- What is said and done by leaders (e.g., supervisors, directors), peers and mentors
- What is attended to in meetings (performance discussed?)
- What is measured and discussed regularly
- The "official" rationale given for decisions
- The office environment, including what is posted on the bulletin board, how celebrations take place, who gets hired for which jobs
- Who gets rewarded for what
- Content and process of trainings and agency orientation
- What does and doesn't get reported in newsletters
- What is discussed in performance reviews
- The "grapevine" of agency gossip, both theme and volume

Another challenge for managers is isolation from worker culture. Managers may be less aware of certain aspects of the culture of the units they manage by virtue of their exclusion from the peer-to-peer cultures of those they supervise. However, managers play an important role in providing cues to staff for how to behave, what to believe, and what to value.

The culture of an organizational unit is affected by the overall agency, and top management support is vital to establishing a culture of quality (O'Brien & Watson, 2002). However, each management unit (e.g., office, supervisory unit) is a sub-culture. Change is admittedly more difficult to achieve if the larger culture is at odds with that of one unit. Managers often underestimate their ability to affect the culture of their management units. The most skilled managers find ways to preserve what's good about the organizational culture within their units and to shield their workers from negative aspects of the larger agency culture.

The Culture of Blame

It is unfortunate that managers sometimes use performance data to assign blame and take punitive action against those they supervise (Scott et al.,

2005). Taking this approach often leads to defensive and cynical attitudes and reinforces the "us against them" blaming mentality. Perhaps, most importantly, blaming and making excuses blocks learning and taking positive quality improvement action (Poertner & Rapp, 2007).

Most managers and staff are interested in the feedback provided by outcomes data. However, many workers have concerns about these data being used "against them." This may be symptomatic of a blame-oriented culture. In a blame-oriented culture, sub-optimal performance results in finger-pointing and accusations rather than positive action to remedy the problem. For example, it is common for:

- State offices to blame field offices, and field offices to blame state offices.
- Managers to blame caseworkers, and caseworkers to blame managers.
- Legislatures to blame state offices, and state office staff to blame legislators.

In child welfare agencies, blame for underperformance often gets focused on stakeholders such as:

- Judges
- Prosecutors
- Educational systems
- Mental health centers
- Law enforcement

Blaming seems like an easy road to take for many managers. The following are some reasons that blaming is so tempting despite its ineffectiveness.

Blaming Feels Good

Blaming absolves the blamer of responsibility. It feels good to the blamer to believe, "It is their fault, not mine."

Blaming is Simple

Blaming usually comes from being overly simplistic. A management unit's less than stellar performance can be blamed on the deficiency of workers who lack skill, effort, or focus. However, this is only one of many possible explanations. Others include the impact of staff vacancies, inadequate training, too many meetings, resource deficiencies, lack of community resources, etc.

Blaming is Easy

Blaming is much easier than working to figure out effective solutions. The blamer can feel like s/he has done something about the poor performance. In fact, s/he has only complicated the situation. There are many opportunities for blame in child welfare, because child welfare is not only embedded within the legal system, it relies on community resources to resolve the concerns that brought children to the attention of the agency.

Blaming is the Basis for Punishing (Meet the Macho Manager)

Placing blame internally can result in managers taking punitive action against those under them. The "Macho Manager" seems to feel better when s/he can punish someone—even though punitive approaches are mostly counterproductive. Punitive approaches are demoralizing, cause divisiveness, and promote fear and defensiveness. Such approaches also create an environment in which the honest examination of facts cannot take place. Those lower in the organizational hierarchy can also exercise passive aggressive punishment. For example, office staff or caseworkers may engage in constant complaining, slacking off, or cynicism. The attitude is, "We will show them."

Blaming is Contagious

Blaming and punishing creates a chain reaction. The state director chews out the area director, who chews out the county director, who chews out the supervisor, who chews out the caseworkers, who treat their clients with disrespect. On the other hand, positive change occurs when all these levels work together.

Blaming Looks Like Accountability

Blaming is often seen as a part of holding staff accountable. Accountability is one of the pillars of Results-Oriented Management; the key is *how* one holds people accountable. Blaming is not taking responsibility for taking positive action. Managers must first hold themselves accountable by taking responsibility for developing solutions. When it comes to confronting staff performance problems, managers factually confront the situation, work with the staff in identifying the problems and solutions, and assist them with making needed changes. This can be done in a positive manner that holds staff accountable.

Results-Oriented vs. Blame-Oriented Cultures

In a results-oriented culture the staff accepts responsibility and is accountable for achieving positive outcomes for children and families. Outcomes are understood and represent a major focus of the agency. Figure 8.4 provides specific examples of the attitudes and values of a results-oriented culture and provides a comparison with what will be termed a blame-oriented culture.

Behavior	
Results-Oriented Culture	**Blame-Oriented Culture**
Outcomes data are sought out and shared with staff.	Data are seen as being only for managers, and is not shared with other staff members..
Positive action is taken to improve performance (e.g. training provided, policies changed, resources reallocated, and improvement plans developed)	Blame is assigned. If assigned internally, workers (or others deemed responsible) are punished. If assigned externally, nothing is done, as performance is seen as the result of external forces or stakeholders (e.g.judges).
Staff are actively involved in developing strategies for quality improvement.	Managers take control of the situation and make unilateral changes.
Specific performance improvement goals are set.	If established at all, improvement goals are vague (e.g. improve coordination).
Good performance is rewarded.	Only poor performance is recognized.
Community stakeholders are consulted.	Community stakeholders are blamed not consulted.

Attitudes	
Results-Oriented Culture	**Blame-Oriented Culture**
Staff shares optimism about their ability to make changes to improve outcomes.	Staff feels helpless in the face of judges, state office, the legislature, etc.
Staff shares responsibility for making improvements.	Staff members seek to assign blame and punish the identified source, or dismiss the problem as something that cannot be changed.
Actions taken are viewed in light of their impact on outcomes.	Actions are taken to satisfy those in authority or to enhance the stature or status of the manager.
Data are seen as helpful.	Data are used to assign blame.
Staff adapt and innovate to achieve outcomes; they maintain a healthy disrespect for the impossible.	Staff maintain status quo; they don't want to create any waves.
Community stakeholders are seen a partners.	Community stakeholders are seen as "them" in a pervasive "us against them" mentality.
Staff learn from both good and poor performance.	Good performance is expected; poor performance is punished.

Values	
Results-Oriented Culture	**Blame-Oriented Culture**
Top priority is achieving outcomes for children and families.	Satisfying the boss and following all the rules is the top priority.
Staff members who work hard work for kids and families are valued.	Compliant staff are valued.
Community stakeholders are valued as key to success in child welfare.	Stakeholders need to conform to requests and manager's way of thinking.
Innovation and perseverance are valued.	Following the rules without question is valued.
Staff members feel passionate about their work.	Staff members think of their job only as a way to survive.

From "Results Oriented Management in Child Welfare" by T. Moore, www.rom.ku.edu

Figure 8.4 Results-oriented cultures vs. blame-oriented cultures.

Reward & recognize
Encourage learning
Seek involvement
Use data routinely
Lead improvement efforts
Take responsibility
Stimulate positive action

Figure 8.5 What do you get in a results-oriented culture?

Seven Steps to a Results-Oriented Culture

The following is a description of the qualities of a results-oriented culture and actions that can be taken to develop this organizational culture over time.[2] Figure 8.5 is offered as a useful mnemonic for keeping the following material in mind.

Use Data Routinely

The first, and perhaps most important, thing managers can do is to share outcome reports on a regular basis throughout the organization and to stakeholders. Data can create synergy and send an important message to everyone about the common purpose of the collective effort. When all levels of an organization are provided with outcomes data, awareness of the primary outcomes for service principals is increased, which provides an environment in which management and practice reinforces each other (Traglia et al., 1996). Data will need to be seen as central to the work, not as an added responsibility (McDaniel, 1996).

In a culture new to outcome measurement, efforts will have to be made to inform those involved on how data are collected, compiled, and used (e.g., not requirements but goals, used to inform improvement efforts). Data needs to be seen as a barometer of performance and a tool for addressing problem areas rather than a "messenger of bad news or a punitive tool" (Jamieson & Bodonyi, 1999). When the norm is blaming and punishing, staff are at best leery about performance, and at worst, hostile to performance reports. It is challenging to create a safe environment in which performance data can be seen as a tool for improving services and outcomes for clients. Here are a few ideas for using data productively.

- *Start slowly.* When first introducing data to your staff start slowly. Looking at performance data is a little like looking in a three-way mirror; it gives you a lot of information that takes some time to process. Don't rush to make quality improvements before your staff can absorb the information. You can:

- Introduce reports one measure or one report at a time. This allows time for your staff to get used to the report and learn what it is saying about their performance.
- Start with positive results.

- *Be non-judgmental.* Take a non-judgmental approach to reviewing data. No one gets beat up, humiliated, or put on the spot. Approaching the review of data non-judgmentally can:

  - Reduce anxiety.
  - Create a space for people to become more familiar with what the data says and means.
  - Encourage a curiosity about how workers might improve outcomes for children and families.
  - Initiate self-correction—even without a well developed plan of action.

- *Throw a data party.* A fun, non-threatening environment may be just what is needed to introduce data successfully. Establish an informal atmosphere to lessen anxiety. One can hold the meeting somewhere other than the office (e.g., coffee shop) and give prizes (joke of the day; queen for a day; geek of the week). Later, this kind of atmosphere can facilitate brainstorming to improve performance. The only agenda item is to review outcome data. Review performance data non-judgmentally and encourage understanding of the measure. The first parties should probably end here. No action steps are needed. As your data parties progress, the group will want to do something in an organized way to improve performance. The data party can be a good atmosphere for brainstorming solutions and letting the creative juices flow.
- *Establish a routine.* The regularity of seeing data reports makes them less threatening over time. A manager can:

  - Review reports at weekly or monthly staff meetings.
  - Host regular quarterly quality improvement retreats.
  - Post a particular performance report.

- *Do not disclose individuals' performance.* Do not share performance of individual front line workers with others. Share team performance, but individual performance should be shared privately. The numbers of cases are often very small on reports of outcomes of a caseload which leads to misleading assessment of performance. Also, not all caseloads are created equally.

Take Responsibility

Taking responsibility for good performance is easy. Taking responsibility for unsatisfactory or below standard performance is challenging. It is common to identify and discuss possible causes of poor performance. It is important for the manager to take the lead in accepting responsibility for achieving goals and doing something about it when outcomes are not achieved (Poertner & Rapp, 2007). Consider the following actions:

- *Explore results-based data in non-blaming ways.* To move beyond the identification of causes, managers can:

  - Get more specific about the cause. Rather than identify a judge's personality as the problem, identify the judge's reluctance to terminate parental rights. A behavior is easier to change than a personality.
  - Broaden the scope of factors that may contribute to poor performance. Rarely is poor performance due to just one factor.
  - Do not allow the discussion or exploration to stop with the identification of a cause. Approach the process with the idea that there is always something that can be done, even if it is small.

- *Keep the focus on what you can do.* Ask what is within your control to change or influence (however slightly).

  - If the identified problem is not within your direct control to change, ask how you can influence it.
  - If there are a number of strategies from which to choose, choose the ones that are the most within your control or sphere of influence (e.g., one can write a position paper about a policy but may not be able to change the policy).
  - Re-frame the problem.

- Rather than seeing the judge as the problem, perhaps you can frame the problem in terms of what can be done to help the judge make the decision you think is best.

  - Challenge staff without criticizing. Approach poor performance with the future in mind rather than dwelling on the past.

Stimulate Positive Action

The managers' job is to take action toward improving outcomes. Data is most powerful when it is accompanied with a framework for solutions (Jamieson & Bodonyi, 1999). With an orientation toward achieving outcomes as opposed to meeting procedural requirements, an agency can empower those involved to develop creative solutions (Traglia et al., 1996). The following are reminders about how to take action effectively:

- *Understand the performance problem.* Although the message is to do something, it is not to do any old thing. Before taking action, understand and use data to inform improvement actions.
- *Set goals and decide on action to take to achieve those.*
- *Follow through with plans.* Without follow-through, staff and other stakeholders will be less likely to spend their time planning the next time you need to address a performance problem.
- *Dare to think big.* Why not try to change a state policy or seek new resources in the community? Field managers who have great ideas but who do not explore many action options because they perceive that certain barriers are beyond their influence such as state procedures or policy, the lack of resources, a judge or district attorney, or unavailable or uncooperative community resources. Here are some ideas about thinking big:

  - *Document the barrier* that is preventing the achievement of the particular outcome.
  - *Write letters* or memos to the highest level you can.
  - *Invite those you seek to influence to your office* or find another place to discuss the problem and its possible solutions.
  - *Ask for technical assistance* from IT people, from local universities, from state and local government, etc.

- *Innovate and be creative.* When developing action plans, have a little fun. Get outlandish; this sometimes helps you to uncover innovative solutions. A suggestion to bribe the judge can easily turn into giving the judge more frequent reports (or something elses/he may want).
- *Above all, do something.* By taking positive action to improve performance, you are conveying to your staff that you see yourself and your team as influential. Here are a few small but common excuses and possible responses to overcome inaction:

  - *Lack of staff because of hiring freeze.* You cannot hire someone, but you can:

    - Hold fewer meetings and do more by e-mail.
    - Ask for specific kinds of help (e.g., clerical on Mondays to handle weekend traffic).

- ○ Write a memo to state office to request suspension of the new case reviews for the next 2 months until positions can be filled.
- ○ Identify and temporarily suspend low priority activities that take staff time.
- ○ Tap into or develop a pool of community volunteers.

- ○ *Judge places children back in care* at the slightest provocation. Things you can do to change this situation:

  - ○ Share the county's re-entry performance rate with the judge so they can see how s/he might be contributing to the problem. Then engage the judge in the development of a plan for improving performance.
  - ○ Ask what you can do to improve; don't tell the judge that s/he needs to improve.
  - ○ Ask the judge to help you design your new aftercare program, in collaboration with other community stakeholders.
  - ○ Introduce the judge to the home services program and other community emergency resources in the community.
  - ○ Ask the judge for the opportunity to work with the families that come back to her attention so that you can address their problems and connect them with community resources to prevent children from reentering out-of-home placement.

Reward and Recognize

Managers need to create rewards-based environments (Moore et al., 2000; Poertner & Rapp, 2007). A free flow of rewards helps to establish trust, thus enabling data to be evaluated more critically (Scott et al., 2005). We all know how powerful it is to be recognized for doing good work. In our hearts, we're always looking for that gold star on our spelling quiz. Even though everyone knows that positive acknowledgement is a potent behavioral reward, we do not often take the time to do it. Rewards, however small, reinforce those actions, behaviors, and values that you, as a manager, want to encourage. In a rewards-based environment;

- People feel like winners.
- People's need to achieve is met.
- Staff members have ample examples of "good" work.
- Everyone shares in the success of others.
- Everyone participates in providing rewards.
- The focus is on good practice and outcomes more than problems.

Rewards are most effective when they are tied to achieving results or actions that contribute to results (Traglia et al., 1996). Rewards can also help to create a fun atmosphere in which people enjoy their work. Here are a few tips on establishing a rewards-based environment:

- *Use a variety of rewards.* There are a million different ways to reward employees. Many cost nothing. Consider the following:

  o *Verbal.* Giving verbal rewards is simple and straightforward: go to the person's work area, telephone them, speak in the hallway, use a staff meeting to compliment them in front of colleagues and upper level management, etc.

  o *Written.* It takes just a few minutes to handwrite a personal note, send an e-mail, send a memo to agency leadership praising a person, post something on a bulletin board or wall, put a memo in the person's personnel file, etc.

  o *Symbolic.* Consider awarding a worker or team with a certificate, plaque, or trophy. Establish a traveling trophy (e.g., family hero of the week, bright idea award), or give new job tasks that recognize good performance and allow the worker some time away from other tasks (e.g., mentor a new staff person, represent the agency in city or state-wide coalition meetings, etc.).

  o *Attention.* Give staff members some time and attention. This will look different depending on one's position. Have lunch with the person (you don't have to pay); hear out an idea; or simply visit with them. Ask them if they would like to go with you to an important meeting, or ask them to work with another staff person who is having difficulty. In short, acknowledge their worth to you by spending time with them in the way that feels most appropriate.

- *Provide valued rewards.* The reward should be something the recipient values or wants. Everyone has a rewards menu. For example, being asked to represent the agency by making a presentation to a local service club would be a reward for one person, but torture for another.

- *Provide frequent and varied rewards.* Rewards should be an everyday occurrence; however, it is neither possible nor effective to reward a behavior every time it occurs. Actually, rewards are most effective if they are provided on an unpredictable or variable schedule (think of the intermittent rewards involved in gambling).

- *Celebrate good performance.* There is almost always good news in a team's performance data. Point it out, discuss how it was accomplished, do something fun once your team meets a certain performance goal, ring a bell every time a permanency plan is achieved, hand out the Unit Champion of the Month award, bring in a dozen doughnuts, or whatever. There is a lot of room to be creative here.

- *Reward the little things, even effort.* Because big things do not happen as often, it is important to recognize the little things your workers do well. Don't forget to reward effort as well as results. This encourages workers to take new approaches and helps them feel supported.
- *Specify reasons for rewards.* The most effective rewards are specific. When you clearly reward a particular behavior, a certain outcome, or a specific attitude or value unambiguous reinforcement for a desirable outcome has been provided.
- *Provide timely rewards.* The closer the reward is to its precipitant, the better.
- *Encourage reward giving.* To establish a rewards-based environment, a manager should become both a giver of rewards and an instigator for everyone to reward one another.
- *Reward people up and down the organizational hierarchy.* Forget the "brown-nose" accusation; if the boss is doing something helpful, recognize it.
- *Encourage peer-to-peer rewards.* Sometimes peer rewards are the most valuable. Make "Way to Go" note cards from card stock and then have workers send them to anyone they catch doing something right.
- *Reward stakeholders outside the agency* when they do something right or courageous. What is wrong with a little thank you note to a judge or a state official for getting a policy changed?
- *Put others in the reward giver position.* Ask a judge to stop by the office to present an award, or snag the agency director on her tour of the state to recognize someone. Have one of peers present an award to the director of a community agency.

Seek Involvement

Although managers can take action on their own, involving others to improve outcome performance has many advantages. Such advantages include: an enriched understanding of the performance problem, more ideas for how to improve, increased focus on outcomes, and greater ownership and cooperation for carrying out the action plan. For example, one approach taken by the Family to Family initiative was to establish "Self evaluation teams." These groups monitored outcome attainment and worked to make the link between data and program and policy decisions (Webster et al., 2002). Involving others usually means more meetings, but it does not have to. The following are tips on running task oriented groups:

- *Respect the time of others.* Meetings can take an extraordinary amount of time. Make sure that a meeting or series of meetings is worth the investment. Keep the meetings short and to the point, and create some parameters (three meetings or a certain date).
- *Involve key people.* Not everyone needs to be involved in meetings, but everyone needs the opportunity to provide input. Involve stakeholders outside your agency. Involve anyone with resources, ideas, or a perspective that will help resolve the problem. This can include families, children (as age appropriate), community service providers, the legal community, educators, etc.
- *Designate a leader.* This can be you as the manager, or someone that you trust. It is important to identify a point person that can move a task group quickly toward its goal.

One should always consider alternatives to meetings. Instead of having a task group, a key stakeholder can be called or meet with individually or in small groups.

Encourage Learning

The most effective agencies are those engaged in learning and continuous improvement. The regular use of data provides an opportunity for learning to occur. Learning organizations review data regularly, assess its implications, and make changes. Ultimately, organizational intelligence is created when staff and stakeholders share data, learn together, and strive for improvement. (Schoech et al., 2000). Many of the leading management gurus talk about the importance of establishing a learning culture. Peter Senge (1990) in *The Fifth Discipline* describes a *learning organization* best as follows:

> . . . where people continually expand their capacity to create the results they truly desire, where new and expansive patterns of thinking are nurtured, where collective aspiration is set free and where people are continually learning how to learn together.

For organizational learning to flourish, managers establish an atmosphere of openness and curiosity for how they can improve (Poertner & Rapp, 2007). Learning requires continual questioning and repeated evaluation of performance (Garvin, 2000). Given the interdependence that child welfare agencies have on legal and community systems, organizational learning needs to also extend to the stakeholders that comprise the "system." Bringing together the experience, skill, and judgment of these stakeholders, developing evidence for practice effectiveness holds promise for enhancing learning even more.

The following are ways to promote organizational learning:

- *Learn from those who are doing well.* If another management unit or staff person is performing well on a certain outcome, ask them what they are doing to be successful. (Friedman et al, 2000; Poertner & Rapp, 2007)
- *Review successes and failures.* Review cases to learn what was successful and what went wrong.
- *Consult professional literature.* The professional literature is a great resource for managers, but can be overwhelming at times. Search for web sites that exist that seek to simplify and organize the available research. Invite university professors or professional staff to present information in a staff meeting.
- *Provide ongoing training.* Training is often overrated, but it can be helpful in developing specific skills and stimulating new ideas. There are many forms of training; some are formal, some less so. For example, one can consider assigning responsibility for a 30-minute in-service training at monthly staff meetings.
- *Arrange mentoring.* Pair up staff members who have demonstrated competence in certain areas with those who have had less success.
- *Seek input from principals.* Both parents and children have direct experiences that are useful in improving performance. They can be consulted through interviews, focus groups, or participation in meetings or advisory groups.
- *Provide opportunities for staff to share their knowledge.* For unit supervisors, group supervision is a good way of sharing knowledge between staff members.

Lead Improvement Efforts

Building a results-oriented organizational culture requires that managers both "talk the talk" and "walk the walk." This consistency provides staff with needed guidance and direction.

- *Do as you say.* There is no substitution for modeling the behavior, attitudes, and values that managers want their staff members to have. This includes being on time to meetings, recognizing the accomplishments of others, setting specific goals, forging partnerships, and the list goes on and on.
- *Be optimistic.* This is not to suggest that one is Pollyanna, but a can-do attitude can be infectious.

- *Establish your unit's identity.* Managers are in a leadership position and have a platform for articulating the group's wants and needs. They also have to bring everyone along on that journey. In developing a group identity ask your staff the following question: If someone outside our agency were to describe us, what would we like them to say?
- *Follow through on plans.* Following through on plans conveys to those involved that their time and input is valued.
- *Curb your own cynicism.* It is easy to get cynical in this work. However, if you must be cynical, try to do it with someone other than your immediate staff. Not sharing your innermost thoughts is one aspect of being a manager that can be lonely.

Change Takes Time

Changing an organizational culture is hard work. It requires long sustained effort and confronting those forces that work against a manager's efforts to establish the culture they want. Organizational cultures are elusive and are buried in an organization's subconscious. The good news is that subordinate staff pays attention to what their managers say, what they do, and what they believe. Managers have a substantial influence on the culture of their own management unit even though their unit is often part of a larger organization.

An important step is to recognize and give up old habits that are counterproductive to establishing a results-oriented culture. Believing that positive change is possible may be one of the more substantial obstacles. The most agreed to item on a survey to measure the organizational culture on the use of data recently administered in two state child welfare agencies was: "Staff (including managers) see their ability to impact outcomes as greatly diminished by the lack of control/influence they have over forces outside the agency (e.g., judges, community resources, district attorneys)." In both states, the mean response was 3.8 on a four-point scale (Moore, 2006).

Seeking positive solutions, celebrating success, taking a methodical approach using data, and being persistent are certainly important to changing an organizational culture over time. Outcome and other results data provide an objective focus for achievement and moving forward.

Conclusion

Many challenges lie ahead in adopting results-oriented approaches in public child welfare. The federal government has laid the foundation for this by establishing outcomes, and has provided the impetus for developing quality improvement systems to monitor and continually improve outcome attainment. State and local child welfare agencies can build upon that foundation by improving access to good quality data, building analytic capacity of staff to use data, taking action to improve outcomes, and developing a results oriented cultures that seek excellence. Child welfare agencies are encouraged to go beyond the notion of meeting federal expectations and genuinely embrace the use of data to create reflexive learning organizations.

To improve child welfare performance, report systems have to be improved to provide easy access to relevant data and tools to analyze that data. Child welfare professionals need to have skills in understanding data, increasing organizational analytic capacity, and developing action strategies based on the evidence through engaging internal and external stakeholders. Child welfare agency and system cultures need to be orientated positively toward achieving results.

This chapter includes a range of practical actions to address the challenges of increasing the use of data and creating learning organizations. Partnerships with university faculty and professional research staff can also help by providing training, technical assistance, and research. There is much work to do to in providing understandable data, developing skills, and changing the overall culture of child welfare agencies to improve outcomes for children and families.

Notes

1. Additional practical examples of working with data may be found in the Results Oriented Training in Child Welfare on-line training at http://www.rom.ku.edu/.
2. Material in this section has been taken from Module 13: Establishing a Results-Oriented Culture in the Results Oriented Management in Child Welfare web-based training, www.rom.ku.edu.

References

Bamford, T. (1996). Information driven decision making: Fact or fantasy? In A. Kerslate & N. Gould (Eds.), *Information management in social services* (pp. 18–27). Aldershot: Avebury Ashgate Publishers, Ltd.

Cassafer, D. J. (1996). How can planning make it happen? In P. Pecora, W. Seelig, F. Zirps, & S. Davis (Eds.), *Quality improvement and evaluation in child and family services: Managing into the next century* (pp. 175–192). Washington, D.C.: CWLA Press.

Chapel, J., & Horsch, K. (1998). Interview with Patricia McGinnis. *Harvard Family Research Project Newsletter: The Evaluation Exchange: Emerging Strategies in Evaluating Child and Family Services, 4*(1), 8–9.

Courtney, M., & Collins, R. C. (1994). New challenges and opportunities in child welfare outcomes and information technologies. *Child Welfare, 73*(5), 359–378.

DiLeonardi, J. W., & Yuan, Y.-Y. T. (2000). Using administrative data. *Child Welfare, 79*(5), 437–443.

Fluke, J. D., Edwards, M., Kutzler, P., Kuna, J., & Tooman, G. (2000). Safety, permanency, and in-home services: Applying administrative data. *Child Welfare, 80*(5), 573–595.

Fostering Court Improvement. (2007). Last accessed March 30, 2007 at http://www.fosteringcourtimprovement.org/

Friedman, M., Garnett, L., & Pinnock, M. (2005). Dude, where's my outcomes? Partnership working and outcome-based accountability in the United Kingdom. In J. Scott & H. Ward (Eds.), *Safeguarding and promoting the well-being of children, families, and communities* (pp. 245–261). London: Jessica Kingsley.

Garvin, D. A. (2000). *Learning in action: A guide to putting the learning organization to work.* Boston, MA: Harvard Business School Press.

Holland, R. (1999). Reflexivity. *Human Relations, 52*(4), 463–484.

Jamieson, M., & Bodonyi, J. M. (1999). Data-driven child welfare policy and practice in the next century. *Child Welfare, 78*(1), 15–30.

Kettner, P. M., Daley, J. M., & Nichols, A. W. (1985). *Initiating change in organizations and communities: A macro practice model.* Monterey, CA: Brooks/Cole.

McDaniel, N. (1996). Key stages and common themes in outcome measurement. *Harvard and Family Research Project Newsletter: The Evaluation Exchange, 2*(3). Last accessed September 1, 2009 at http://www.hfrp.org/evaluation/the-evaluation-exchange/issue-archive/results-based-accountability-2/key-stages-and-common-themes-in-outcome-measurement.

Milner, J., Mitchell, L., & Hornsby, W. (2005). Child and family services reviews. In G. P. Mallon & P. M. Hess (Eds.), *Child welfare for the twenty-first century: A handbook of practices, policies, and programs* (pp. 707–718). New York: Columbia University Press.

Moore, T. (2002). Results oriented management in child welfare. Retrieved February 27, 2007 http://www.rom.ku.edu/.

Moore, T. (2006). *Results of the organizational culture survey on the use of performance data.* Lawrence, KS: University of Kansas, School of Social Welfare.

Moore, T., McDonald, T., Bryson, S., Holmes, C., Taylor, P., & Brook, J. (2006). *Final report: Children in need of care non-abuse neglect.* Lawrence, KS: University of Kansas, School of Social Welfare.

Moore, T., Rapp, C., & Roberts, B. (2000). Improving child welfare performance through supervisory use of client outcome data. *Child Welfare, 79*(5), 475–497.

O'Brien, M., & Watson, P. (2002). *A framework for quality assurance in child welfare.* Portland, ME: National Child Welfare Resource Center for Organizational Improvement.

Poertner, J., & Rapp, C. (2007). *Social administration: The consumer-centered approach.* Binghampton, NY: The Haworth Press.

Sahonchik, K., Frizsell, B., & O'Brien, M. (2005). Strategic planning for child welfare agencies. In G. P. Mallon & P. McCartt Hess (Eds.), *Child welfare for the twenty-first century: A handbook of practices, policies, and programs* (pp. 719–727). New York: Columbia University Press.

Schoech, D., Quinn, A., & Rycraft, J. R. (2000). Data mining in child welfare. *Child Welfare, 79*(5), 633–650.

Scott, J., Moore, T., & Ward, H. (2005). Evaluating interventions and monitoring outcomes. In J. Scott & H. Ward (Eds.), *Safeguarding and promoting the well-being of children, families, and communities* (pp. 262–273). London: Jessica Kingsley.

Senge, P. (1990). *The fifth discipline: The art and practice of the learning organization.* New York: Doubleday.

Title IV-E foster care eligibility reviews and child and family services state plan reviews; final rule. 65 *Fed. Reg.* 4019.

Traglia, J. J., Massinga, R., Pecora, P., & Paddock, G. B. (1996). Implementing an outcome-oriented approach to case planning and service implementation. In P. Pecora, W. Seelig, F. Zirps, & S. Davis (Eds.), *Quality improvement and evaluation in child and family services: Managing into the next century* (pp. 76–98). Washington, D.C.: CWLA Press.

Usher, C. L., Wildfire, J. B., & Gibbs, D. (1999). Measuring performance in child welfare: Secondary effects of success. *Child Welfare, 78*(1), 31–51.

Vincent, P. (1997). The organizational culture of child protective services. *Family Resource Coalition Report, 16*(2), 19–20.

Webster, D., Needell, B., & Wildfire, J. (2002). Data are your friends: Child welfare agency self-evaluation in Los Angeles County with the family to family initiative. *Children and Family Services Review, 24*(6/7), 471–484.

Weiss, H. B. (1997). Results-based accountability for child and family services. In E. Mullen & J. Magnabosco (Eds.), *Outcomes measurement in the human services: Cross-cutting issues and methods* (pp. 173–180). Washington, D.C.: CWLA Press.

9

FLEXIBILITY, INNOVATION, AND EXPERIMENTATION

The Rise and Fall of Child Welfare Waiver Demonstrations

Mark F. Testa

Results-oriented accountability in child welfare seeks to inform service decisions and budgetary investments in light of incoming information on a service system's progress in attaining child and family outcomes. There is an emerging consensus in public child welfare that the existing federal financing structure imposes a serious stranglehold on program innovation and continuous quality improvement (CQI) by favoring interminable foster care over in-home services and other policy options that could ensure safe and permanent families for children (Cornerstones Consulting Group, 1999; The Pew Commission on Children in Foster Care, 2004). What began as a well-meaning effort to lessen federal financial disincentives to removing needy children from unsuitable homes is now perceived as having created an inflexible, $8.0 billion federal bureaucracy that stifles local reform, strait-jackets innovation, and discourages spending on options other than long-term foster care (McDonald, Salyers, & Shaver, 2004; Office of the Assistant Secretary for Planning and Evaluation, 2005).

Frustration with the existing federal financing structure became so widespread that powerful political leaders and respected blue-ribbon commissions have urged the replacement of some or all of the IV-E entitlement with a simple, flexible funding scheme that is capped much like a block grant. The Bush Administration, for example, proposed a voluntary, flexible funding option (but never sought introduction of legislation) that would have offered states a fixed 5-year allotment of federal dollars, based on a negotiated projection methodology, to spend any way they deem fit to achieve federal child welfare standards. The Pew Commission on Children in Foster Care (2004) recommended a hybrid-funding arrangement that preserves the subsidy entitlement for foster homes and child-caring institutions, but consolidates spending on child placement services, training, and other administrative activities with Title IV-B dollars into a capped indexed grant. House legislation that was referred in 2004 to the Ways and Means Committee (H.R. 4586) went one step further. It proposed capping the IV-E subsidy entitlement into a consolidated block grant along with any remaining IV-E and IV-B federal funds for child placement services, training, data collection, and administration. Although the replacement of open-ended categorical entitlements with capped flexible funding purports to spur innovation and experimentation, it is important to examine closely the promised benefits and the agency risks that can accompany such a trade-off.

Block Grants and Categorical Entitlements

Proposals to consolidate multiple, categorical federal funding streams into flexible, broad-scale grants first surfaced after World War II (Conlan, 1984). But, it was the 1994 Republican *Contract with America* that popularized the concept of the block grant as a solution to the problems associated with excessively fragmented and administratively complex, categorical entitlement programs. The *Contract with America* proposed to cut through bureaucratic red tape and to stop runaway expenditure growth by loosening federal controls and imposing a lid on discretionary spending of federal dollars by the states.

Although block grants are often portrayed as aligned with conservative values and entitlements with liberal ones, the distinction is far too facile. For example, most block-grants proposals favored by conservatives call for the retention of entitlement funding for adoption assistance and other evidence-supported programs that strengthen family autonomy and lessen governmental intrusion into the lives of families. The non-partisan Pew Commission recommended folding subsidized guardianship into the federal IV-E entitlement largely on the basis of rigorous evaluation findings that demonstrated guardianship subsidies were a cost-effective alternative to retaining children in administratively burdensome and more costly long-term foster care (Testa, Salyers, Shaver, & Miller, 2004). Furthermore, block grants are no guarantee that federal dollars will be spent any more wisely or efficiently by local bureaucratic agents. A "no strings" approach to federal revenue sharing can just as easily invite defections from public purposes as encourage responsible state innovations (Rector, 1995).

It should be recalled that it was the widespread defection by states from the fair and equitable administration of federal income maintenance programs in the 1950s that originally prompted federal officials to carve out the foster care entitlement from the Aid to Families with Dependent Children

(AFDC) program in 1961. The so-called "Flemming Rule" (named after the departing HEW Secretary at the time) prohibited states from denying AFDC to otherwise eligible homes that local welfare agents deemed unsuitable because of out-of-wedlock births, non-marital cohabitation, or parental criminal convictions (Bell, 1965). The new rule instead instructed states to continue making AFDC payments while offering the family in-home services to remedy the problems that contributed to the home's unsuitability. If the problems persisted, states could claim AFDC reimbursement for the removal and out-of-home placement of the children into foster care.

Congress enacted the Flemming Rule into law as part of its 1962 Public Welfare Amendments that established the AFDC foster care program. The law also carved-out enhanced funding (75% federal match) for in-home services to protect children and to strengthen family life (Gilbert, 1966). Although the 1962 amendments mandated the coordination of child welfare services with AFDC, the paucity of trained social workers in public welfare administration and the eventual separation of income maintenance from social services in 1967 hampered the coordinated delivery of in-home services to families at risk of child removal. Entitlement funding for in-home services was completely severed from income maintenance under the Adoption Assistance and Child Welfare Act (AACW) of 1980. AACW created a separate IV-E title under the Social Security Act, which excluded in-home and child protective services from the child placement costs and other administrative expenses that could be claimed for federal reimbursement.

With the separation of federal child welfare financing into an open-ended IV-E entitlement for foster care and a capped IV-B funding for in-home services, the balance of concern over agency risks shifted from the arbitrary denial of a family's welfare rights to the paternalistic over-reliance on foster care at the expense of in-home services. Both risks represent different types of defections from responsible public policy. Whereas the entitlement solution imposes tighter controls on agent discretion to minimize opportunistic defections from public purposes, the block-grant solution delegates greater discretion in anticipation of local agents' acting authoritatively (hierarchical agency) or benevolently (fiduciary agency) on behalf of their principals.

The promised flexibility that block grants extend to local agents accounts for much of the appeal of flexible funding options to child welfare professionals who historically have favored less categorical and more individualized approaches to child and family problems. The downside is that most of the proposals that Congress has considered in recent years impose a funding cap on federal spending, which necessitates projecting several years in advance how many children will enter and leave foster care state by state. Given the wide error-band of long-term social forecasts, flexible-funding proposals can create unforeseen agency risks for abused and neglected children whose best interests may not be adequately served at fixed levels of projected funding. If a state were to experience an unexpected rise or fall in the number of children requiring foster care, the barometric formula of categorical entitlements at least ensures that the right amount of money goes for spending on foster care. Instead of imposing a lid on discretionary spending, a more efficient and equitable solution is a federal financing structure that permits greater state flexibility, but within a solid accountability framework that aligns financial incentives with the child welfare outcomes desired by elected officials, families, children's other agents, and the citizenry at large.

Results-Oriented Accountability and Evidence-Supported Practice

Results-oriented accountability means more than simply the flexibility to innovate. It also involves controlled experimentation and systematic evaluation of alternative courses of action. Innovation and experimentation are best built upon a solid foundation of evidence-supported practices and policies that are embedded within an evaluative framework that routinely tests both the internal and external validity of existing programs and promising innovations using well-defined outcomes standards and scientific methods.

An alternative to "no strings" block grants became available to states in 1994 under the child welfare waiver demonstration program. It offered states greater flexibility in the spending of IV-E dollars, without sacrificing the funding guarantees of entitlements or the cost neutrality afforded by block grants. The idea first surfaced in 1990 legislation proposed in the U.S. House of Representatives (H.R. 5011). It was modeled after a similar section 1115 of the Act, which authorized HHS to approve public assistance experiments and service demonstrations under the AFDC program (Harvey, Camasso and Jagannathan, 2000). The legislation was reintroduced several times before Congress passed it in 1994, and President Clinton signed it (P.L 103-432). The law established a new section, 1130, of the Social Security Act. It permitted as many as ten states per year to conduct demonstration projects by waiving certain requirements of titles IV-B and IV-E to facilitate the demonstration of new approaches to the delivery of child welfare services. The IV-E child welfare waiver process relaxed federal constraints on state innovation and mandated external evaluations to test promising programs and to firm up the evidence base for child welfare policy and practices. Since 1996, 24 states have implemented 34 demonstration components through 30 IV-E waiver agreements (see Table 9.1). The mechanics of the waiver demonstration process is best illustrated by considering the service innovations and field experiments, which occurred in the two states that received the most child welfare waivers during this period (three apiece)—Illinois and Maryland.

TABLE 9.1   Summary of Child Welfare Waiver Demonstrations

State	Demonstration Component	Evaluation Design	Implementation Date	Scheduled End Date
Arizona	Intensive Service Options	Matched Case Comparison	4/15/2006	3/31/2011
California	Intensive Service Options	Experimental	12/1/1998	12/31/2005
California	Capped IV-E Allocations/ Flexibility to Local Agencies	Time Series Analysis	7/1/2007	6/30/2012
Colorado[1]	Managed Care Payment Systems	Experimental	10/26/2001	6/30/2003
Connecticut[1]	Managed Care Payment Systems	Experimental	7/9/1999	10/31/2002
Delaware	Assisted Guardianship/ Kinship Permanence	Comparison Site	7/1/1996	12/31/2002
Delaware	Services for Caregivers with Substance Use Disorders	Pre-Post Comparison	7/1/1996	12/31/2002
Florida	Capped IV-E Allocations/ Flexibility to Local Agencies	Time Series Analysis	10/1/2006	9/30/2011
Illinois	Assisted Guardianship/ Kinship Permanence	Experimental	5/1/1997	12/31/2008
Illinois	Services for Caregivers with Substance Use Disorders	Experimental	4/28/2000[3]	12/31/2011
Illinois[1]	Enhanced Training for Child Welfare Staff	Experimental	1/1/2003	6/30/2005
Indiana	Capped IV-E Allocations/ Flexibility to Local Agencies	Matched Case Comparison	1/1/1998	6/30/2010
Iowa	Managed Care Payment Systems	Experimental	7/1/2008	
Iowa	Assisted Guardianship/ Kinship Permanence	Experimental	2/1/2007	1/31/2012
Maine	Post-Adoption Services	Experimental	4/1/1999	12/31/2004
Maryland	Assisted Guardianship/ Kinship Permanence	Experimental	3/1/1998	9/30/2004
Maryland[1]	Managed Care Payment Systems	Experimental	1/1/2000	12/31/2002
Maryland[1]	Services for Caregivers with Substance Use Disorders	Experimental	10/1/2001	12/31/2002
Michigan	Managed Care Payment Systems	Experimental	10/1/1999	9/30/2003

(continued)

TABLE 9.1   (Continued)

State	Demonstration Component	Evaluation Design	Implementation Date	Scheduled End Date
Michigan	Intensive Service Options	Matched Case Comparison	1/1/2008	12/31/2012
Minnesota	Assisted Guardianship/ Kinship Permanence	Experimental	11/16/2005	8/30/2010
Mississippi[1]	Intensive Service Options	Experimental	4/1/2001	9/30/2004
Montana	Assisted Guardianship/ Kinship Permanence	Experimental	6/21/2001	5/1/2007
New Hampshire	Services for Caregivers with Substance Use Disorders	Experimental	11/15/1999	11/30/2005
New Mexico	Tribal Administration of IV-E Funds	Comparison Site	7/1/2000	12/31/2005
New Mexico	Assisted Guardianship/ Kinship Permanence	Experimental	7/1/2000	12/31/2005
North Carolina	Assisted Guardianship/ Kinship Permanence	Comparison Site	7/1/1997	6/30/2009
North Carolina	Capped IV-E Allocations/Flexibility to Local Agencies	Comparison Site	7/1/1997	6/30/2009
Ohio	Capped IV-E Allocations/Flexibility to Local Agencies	Comparison Site	10/1/1997	9/30/2009
Oregon	Assisted Guardianship/ Kinship Permanence	Comparison Site	7/1/1997	3/31/2009
Oregon	Capped IV-E Allocations/Flexibility to Local Agencies	Comparison Site	7/1/1997	3/31/2009
Tennessee	Assisted Guardianship/ Kinship Permanence	Experimental	12/1/2006	11/30/2011
Virginia[2]	Assisted Guardianship/ Kinship Permanence	Experimental	7/1/2008	6/30/2013
Washington[1]	Managed Care Payment Systems	Experimental	3/27/2002	6/30/2003
Wisconsin	Assisted Guardianship/ Kinship Permanence	Experimental	10/14/2005	8/30/2010

[1]Terminated early.
[2]Not yet implemented.
[3]Date in source corrected.
Source: U.S. Children's Bureau, Summary Table of the Child Welfare Waiver Demonstrations as of May 2007. Last accessed January 31, 2008, at http://www.acf.hhs.gov/programs/cb/programs_fund/ cwwaiver/2007/summary_table2007.htm.

As noted in Chapter 7, around the time Congress authorized child welfare waivers in 1994, Illinois registered the highest per-capita rate of foster care in the nation—17.1 foster children per 1000 child population (Petit & Curtis, 1997). Maryland ranked eighth highest with 8.8 foster children per 1000 child population. Much like the *Reid vs. Suter* (1992) consent decree in Illinois, the *L.J. vs. Massinga* (1988) consent decree in Baltimore, Maryland prohibited officials from discharging children to the custody of relatives without first offering families the benefits of foster care licensing and financial support. Both Illinois and Maryland searched for alternative ways of supporting children in extended family care without retaining them in state custody.

With the availability of IV-E waivers, Illinois and Maryland found an affordable way of subsidizing legal guardianship without losing federal reimbursement. Both states submitted applications to HHS requesting waiver authority to permit a 5-year demonstration of a federally subsidized private guardianship as a permanency option under the title IV-E program. Maryland's started its program a year after Illinois began its demonstration in 1997, and at the end of the initial 5-year demonstration period, Maryland courts were able to transfer over 300 children from state custody to legal guardianship, whereas Illinois courts were able to transfer approximately 6800 children under the IV-E waiver demonstration.

The two demonstrations closely paralleled one another with some exceptions. Illinois established 12 months as the minimum time a child must continuously reside with a caregiver before becoming eligible for subsidized guardianship, whereas Maryland set the bar at 6 months. Illinois also extended the option to children aged 12 years and older who resided in the home of non-related foster parents. Maryland restricted eligibility to children in kinship homes. Although both programs shared the assumption that kinship altruism and family duty solidified permanency commitments, they differed in their suppositions about the impact of the financial disparity between foster care and guardianship subsidies on a caregiver's willingness to make the transition to subsidized guardianship. Maryland's guardianship subsidy was set much lower than its foster care rate, which made it financially advantageous only for non-licensed kin to accept subsidized guardianship. Illinois' guardianship subsidy, by contrast, was set at the same basic level as both the adoption subsidy and the foster care payment.

During the first 10 years of the demonstration, Illinois' foster care program shrank from 51,000 children in 1997, to less than 16,000 in 2007. This was partly the result of the waiver, but it was also an outgrowth of related statutory changes and administrative initiatives such as performance contracting, which boosted both adoptions and guardianships (see Chapter 10, this volume). Maryland's foster care program also turned a corner declining from 13,500 children in 1999, to below 12,000 children. The impact of the waiver was less far-reaching in Maryland than in Illinois because of the limited appeal of Maryland's program to relatives who were already licensed as foster parents. Because in Illinois there was no loss in basic subsidy payments to licensed foster families and non-licensed kin stood to gain additional help, adoptions and guardianships soared and the number of children in assisted adoptive and guardianship homes surpassed for the first time the number of children remaining in public foster care.

Rewarding Innovation While Limiting Federal Financial Risk

The subsidized guardianship waivers enabled Illinois and Maryland to claim IV-E reimbursements for otherwise unallowable child welfare costs and services. Illinois recouped millions in IV-E reimbursements for reinvestment in system improvements that would otherwise have been foregone in the absence of the waiver. Maryland also was able to realize administrative savings and to maintain cost neutrality, even though non-licensed kin who became legal guardians were paid $133 more per child in monthly assistance than they would have received under TANF in the absence of the waiver.

The cost-savings from the waiver program were calculated using a formula that built upon the random assignment of families and children to the intervention and comparison (cost-neutrality) groups. Assignment to the intervention offered relative foster families the new guardianship subsidy that was hypothesized to increase family permanence at no additional cost to federal expenditures, family stability, or child safety compared to the cost-neutrality group from whom the offer was restricted to the regular permanency options of reunification, adoption, and independent living.

Random assignment not only improves the internal validity of causal inference, but it also provides a cost-neutral method of financially rewarding states for efficacious demonstrations while limiting the federal financial risk for ineffective experiments. As detailed in Chapter 7, by the end of the observational period, 23.2% of the intervention group in Illinois was eventually discharged to subsidized guardianship. The combined permanency rate of guardianships with reunifications and adoptions was 5.5 percentage points higher in the intervention group than in the comparison group. Because of the overall permanency difference, and the shorter time it takes to finalize legal guardianships as opposed to adoptions because parental rights do not need to be terminated, children assigned to the intervention group spent an average of 209 fewer days in foster care than children assigned to the cost-neutrality group.

The fewer average days in foster care figures into the cost-neutrality formula as follows: Instead of claiming IV-E reimbursements for the 1089 days spent in foster care by the children in the intervention group on average, the waiver generates IV-E claims by basing bills on the average 1298 days spent in foster care by the children in the cost-neutrality group. In this way, spending on the cost-neutrality group, who receives the regular federally eligible services, approximates the counterfactual reimbursements that the state would have received for the children assigned to the intervention group in the absence of the waiver. Because IV-E administrative claims for foster care in Illinois ran approximately $11 per day higher at the time than the IV-E administrative costs for guardianship and adoption, multiplying this unit cost by the additional, on average, 209 days spent in foster care in the cost-neutrality group yielded a net administrative IV-E cost savings of $2294 per child assigned to the intervention group. Multiplying this imputed per-child savings by the total 40,000 children ever assigned to the intervention group in Illinois produced a surplus claim of approximately $90 million dollars that the state was able to reinvest in guardian subsidies for non-IV-E eligible children and other child welfare improvements.

Under the waiver's cost-neutrality formula, if a state is correct in hypothesizing that a service innovation achieves the desired outcomes at a lesser cost, it is rewarded with the difference (i.e. savings) between the lower actual costs and the higher imputed IV-E costs. On the other hand, if the proposed innovation does not prove to be cost effective, then the federal government's financial liability is limited because IV-E reimbursements cannot rise above the amount of money it would have spent in the absence of the waiver (i.e., as fixed by the per-child spending in the cost-neutrality group). The federal government spends no more than it would have spent in the absence of the waiver. Whereas block grants and other flexible funding options also accomplish this goal of limiting federal financial risk, they differ from waivers in the sense that they do not guard against federal investments in politically appealing, but ultimately inefficacious, innovations. Although some proposals call for continued outcomes monitoring by federal officials, states typically gain wide discretion in spending block-grant dollars as they deem fit (Conlan, 1984). The waiver's cost-neutrality formula of reimbursement also avoids the block grant's complication of having to forecast future trend lines and payment ceilings. Instead, imputed claims are processed quarterly, based on the actual costs incurred in the cost-neutrality group, which can rise or fall with the changing conditions and needs of children and families. The transferability of savings creates a financial incentive to squeeze efficiencies out of remediation expenses so that child welfare agents can spend more on prevention services. A similar incentive does not exist with block grants (Friedman, 2005) and operates with other flexible funding options only when external conditions are conducive to falling foster care rates. Waivers allow for savings transferability independent of whether children's need for foster care is rising or declining.

Falsifiabilty of Promising Interventions

It has often been said that the IV-E waiver program was not very successful because so many of the demonstrations failed. But, this is precisely what evidence-supported child welfare policy is all about. Not all waiver demonstrations will be as successful as the guardianship demonstrations were in Illinois and Maryland in achieving the intended outcomes and in capturing IV-E savings. The potential falsifiability of promising interventions is the key strength of waiver demonstrations as compared to block grants and other flexible funding mechanisms. But, the failure of a particular demonstration doesn't necessarily mean that a promising practice or policy generally should be abandoned altogether.

Both Illinois and Maryland received second waivers to address the treatment needs of parents with substance abuse problems. At the time, it was estimated that between 50% and 80% of foster children were taken from families with substance abuse problems (Government Accounting Office, 1994). Illinois' second waiver, which began in 2000, permitted the state to use the cost-neutrality formula to fund drug "recovery coach" services to parents that are otherwise disallowed under existing IV-E guidelines. Maryland's second waiver, which was implemented in 2001, permitted the state to fund family support team to assist parents in overcoming their addiction.

Illinois targeted its recovery coach services on parents whose children were already in state custody in the hopes of boosting treatment completion and family reunification rates. Maryland targeted its substance abuse services both on parents with children in out-of-home care and on intact families in the hopes of preventing children from being taken into protective custody as a result of parental drug relapse or recurrence of abuse. In this latter instance, if substance abuse services proved successful in engaging parents in treatment and helping them stay drug free, fewer children in the demonstration group would come into foster care than children in the cost-neutrality group. Because foster care is more costly in the long run than funding drug recovery services and maintaining children in parental custody, both the children and the state stand to gain if substance abuse services prove efficacious in preventing removal. If successful, the demonstration can yield significant net savings when the per-child cost in the cost-neutrality group is applied to the cost claims for children in the demonstration group. However, if the hypothesized differences in removal rates fail to materialize, the state absorbs the extra cost and either discards the once promising innovation (single-loop learning) or retools the program to fix suspected errors in the logic model (double-loop learning).

Both Illinois and Maryland ran into implementation problems, which resulted ultimately in Maryland's abandoning its substance abuse demonstration and in Illinois' substantially shifting implementation gears to focus greater attention on co-occurring problems, such as mental health, domestic violence, and housing problems, and on the role of the courts (Marsh, Ryan, Choi, & Testa, 2006). The findings that reunifications in Illinois failed to keep pace with the demonstration group's greater success in connecting birth parents to treatment raised questions about the adequacy of the logic model's assumption that affording parent's better access to drug treatment was sufficient to turn around state's declining rates of family reunification (see Fig. 9.1). Both states also encountered lower than expected enrollment, which raised questions about past estimates of the percentage of birth parents in the system with substance abuse problems.

The double-loop learning that arises from the testing of hypotheses about service delivery assumptions and expected outcomes is what distinguishes IV-E waivers from other flexible funding options. Although in principle block grants may be used to support experimental evaluations, it

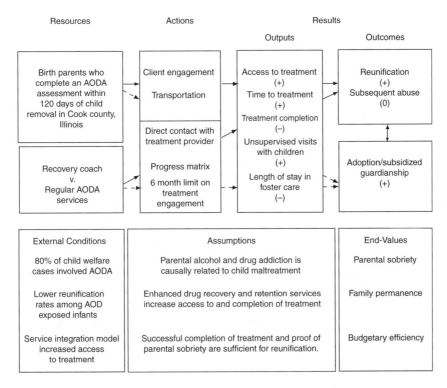

Figure 9.1 Illinois alcohol and other drug abuse (AODA) waiver demonstration logic model.

is seldom done in practice. For example, funds for research and evaluation dried up after the TANF block grant replaced the waiver provisions of the former AFDC entitlement program. Waivers emphasize random assignment and provide for a 50% match-rate (without regard to eligibility) for independent evaluations. Without these provisions and financial incentives, many state and local administrators find it difficult under block grants or other flexible funding options to devote the necessary resources to research and evaluation.

Challenges to Randomized Controlled Innovations

The motivations behind the child welfare waiver program were to encourage service innovations and to reward states for demonstrations that could be scientifically validated as effective in attaining desired child welfare outcomes. For example, the experimental evidence from Illinois was compelling enough for five other states to apply for waivers to replicate the state's subsidized guardianship demonstration. If similar results could be reproduced, the process is supposed to culminate in Congress' authorization of scientifically-proven programs for IV-E reimbursement. The process worked in the case of subsidized guardianship. The positive findings from the state demonstrations encouraged the re-introduction of the Kinship Caregiver Support Act (S. 661) in the Senate and companion legislation (H.R. 2188) in the House. These provisions were subsequently incorporated into The Fostering Connections to Success and Improving Adoptions Act of 2008, which authorized the use of federal IV-E dollars to fund guardianship subsidies for children living with relatives who agree to care for them permanently. The legislation was signed into law on October 7, 2008 (P.L. 110-351).

The expiration of the child welfare waiver program in 2006 brings to close a decade-long experiment in evidence-supported policy-demonstration and legislation of promising innovations in child welfare. Prior to this, Congress had periodically renewed HHS' authority to grant waivers. The first came in 1997, when the Adoption and Safe Families Act (ASFA) raised the cap on the number of waivers that HHS could grant from a total of ten to as many as ten new demonstration projects per fiscal year from 1998 to 2002. HHS' authority to grant new waivers lapsed briefly at the end of federal fiscal year 2002, but was reinstated when Congress included provisions in its TANF reauthorization legislation to extend the waiver program through federal fiscal year 2003 and again through 2005. House Ways and Means staff had prepared legislation in 2004 that would have again extended the program through 2008. The bill also proposed several changes to fix problems that stakeholders had identified as weaknesses in the program (Waldman, 2000). These included the elimination of the cap on the number of new waivers that HHS could approve, a streamlined process for amendments and extensions, and authorization for states to implement multiple waivers and to replicate demonstrations that had already been implemented on the same topic, Many of these changes were later echoed in the waiver recommendations made by the Pew Commission on Children in Foster Care (2004).

Although the House bill originally considered in 2005 (H.R. 4241) contained language to extend the waiver program through 2010 and expand it along the lines recommended by the Pew Commission, these provisions were inexplicably dropped from the legislation that was signed into law in 2006 (P.L.109-171). Although HHS retains authority to renew existing waivers, its ability to grant new waivers ended. The reasons behind the choice to terminate the program are not entirely clear. The evaporation of political support appears to have been bipartisan. Enthusiasm for waivers in general eroded among liberals who had come to view the earlier AFDC waiver program as paving the way for the dismantlement of the federal AFDC entitlement (Williams, 1994). Conservative support also waned as key administrative and legislative staff came to perceive child welfare demonstrations as diverting attention away from block grants and other flexible funding options for containing federal social services spending. Even state administrators cooled to the idea after HHS restricted the number of flexible-funding demonstrations that could be replicated and tightened evaluation requirements to favor experimental over non-experimental designs.

Much of the early excitement over child welfare waivers arose from the frustrations states experienced with the IV-E categorical funding structure, which limited their use of federal dollars for preventive and treatment services. Although states could claim IV-E funds for casework services to so-called foster care "candidates," that is, children who were at risk of removal, the amounts states could spend on the prevention and treatment of conditions that necessitated children's removal in the first place were meager in comparison to the amounts they could claim after the children were taken into foster care. Child welfare advocates joined state and local officials in arguing that the IV-E restrictions discouraged states from fully developing services that could facilitate maintaining these children in their own homes (U.S. Department of Health and Human Services, 2005). Many embraced the idea of waivers as a means of gaining greater flexibility in the spending of federal dollars especially at the front-end of the child protection system.

Of the first five child welfare waivers granted to states in 1996 and 1997, three authorized flexible spending on a wide array of services, including child and family counseling, substance abuse treatment, and temporary housing assistance. Because these flexible-funding demonstrations were "full-coverage programs" in the sense that they encompassed entire geographical regions (Rossi, Freeman, & Lipsey, 1999), evaluators had to rely on historical controls or geographical comparison groups to estimate program impacts. Although non-experimental methods, such as regression adjustment, matched comparison groups, and instrumental variable analysis (see Chapter 7, this volume), can sometimes yield impact estimates similar to those that would result from a randomized field experiment (Aiken, West, Schwalm, Caroll, & Hsiung, 1998; Heinsman & Shadish, 1996), external evaluators of these flexible-funding demonstrations found it difficult to distinguish the unique impact of the waiver from the broader social, economic, and demographic influences operating in these regions (U.S. Department of Health and Human Services, 2005). Even when a flexible-funding effect on outcomes could plausibly be detected, the opaque nature of the black-box evaluation left unclear the precise logical links between the intervention, mediating services, and the desired child welfare outcomes. The HHS summed up its view of the limitation as follows: "The fact that States' waiver evaluations did not link specific services or interventions to observed changes in child welfare outcomes seriously limits their ability to assess the effects of the flexible funding demonstrations" (U.S. Department of Health and Human Services, 2005, p. 12).

The uncertainty over the efficacy of flexible-funding demonstrations and the lack of clarity about the effectiveness of specific model

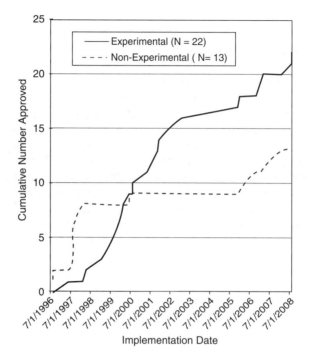

Figure 9.2 Cumulative number of IV-E waivers approved by evaluation design.

components prompted HHS officials to issue policy guidance that tilted away from full-coverage, flexible funding demonstrations. Instead, the focus was put on previously untested, service innovations that could "contribute to the national evidence base on effective strategies for serving children and families coming to the attention of child welfare agencies" (Administration for Children and Families, 2003). Figure 9.2 charts the impact of this shift in orientation on the cumulative number of non-experimental and experimental designs approved by HHS for the evaluation of state waiver demonstrations.

The first wave of evaluations was heavily weighted toward non-experimental methods that relied on historical controls, geographical comparisons, and matched cases for drawing causal inferences. Most of these were undertaken in conjunction with the flexible-funding demonstrations conducted in North Carolina, Ohio, Oregon, and Indiana. In subsequent years, the balance shifted toward experimental designs as HHS approved service demonstrations on subsidized guardianship (Maryland, Montana, Tennessee, and Wisconsin), managed care (Colorado, Connecticut, Michigan, and Washington), drug treatment (Illinois and Maryland), and other targeted interventions, which were more amenable to randomized assignment at the child, family, worker, or service provider level than full-coverage programs. During the period from March 1998 to November 2005, only one non-experimental evaluation design was approved. This was done in conjunction with New Mexico's demonstration on the benefits of delegating greater control of the administration of title IV-E programs to Tribal government authorities. Just prior to the waiver program's demise in 2006, HHS approved another set of non-experimental designs in conjunction with the Administration's efforts to generate enthusiasm for its flexible-funding option. Both Florida and California received IV-E waivers to conduct full-coverage, flexible funding demonstrations that rely on historical controls to monitor improvements among successive cohorts of children entering or at risk of entering foster care.

The swing back toward flexible-funding demonstrations and non-experimental designs toward the tail-end of the waiver program may be taken as evidence of the struggle between two competing perspectives on the fundamental purpose of waivers (Cornerstone Consulting Group, 1999). Many state administrators, legislative staff, and child welfare advocates initially embraced the idea as a tool for testing how financial flexibility could promote broad-scale system reform to improve outcomes for children and families. This perspective helps account for the large share of full-coverage waivers awarded to states for flexible-funding demonstrations at the beginning of the program. It was later superseded by the alternative perspective that reaffirmed the primary purpose of waivers as a method for evaluating the efficacy and effectiveness of well-defined service interventions that were amenable to random assignment at the child, family, worker, or service-provider levels. This alternative view steadily took hold of the waiver approval process as a technical community of federal managers, evaluation consultants, and child welfare researchers were called upon to account for the contributions of waiver demonstrations to the empirical evidence base for informing future directions in national policy and program development.

The split between perspectives on the basic purpose of child welfare waivers and the failure to reconcile these tensions may help explain some of the reasons for the tepid support from legislative staff, state administrators, and child welfare advocates for the renewal of the program in later years. Critics found fault with the program's apparent downplaying of full-coverage reform in favor of targeted service demonstrations. Many state administrators and child welfare workers chaffed at the random assignment stipulations that they perceived as cumbersome or unethical. Others feared that the 5-year funding limitation on demonstrations would stick states with the entire bill for successful policies and programs that would be politically difficult to revoke. So, when the time came to show support for extending the waiver program as part of the Deficit Reduction Act of 2005, few of the original backers were willing to stand up.

Reconciling Different Perspectives on Waivers

Congress' authorization of child welfare waivers in 1994 gave states a powerful incentive for testing promising innovations to improve child and family outcomes. It offered them the flexible use of categorical IV-E dollars to experiment with novel approaches to service delivery. It rewarded them with savings for successful demonstrations and limited the federal risk for failed experiments. By encouraging rigorous evaluations to identify valid models and to eliminate erroneous hypotheses, waiver demonstrations promised to advance best practice and contribute to the evidence base of what works best for children and families. If the opportunity were ever to arise again to reinstate federal waiver authority, it would be important to reconcile the tensions that eroded political support for this evidence-based approach to policy development.

One of the alleged inadequacies of the expired IV-E waiver program was that it was ill-suited for encouraging the broad-scale comprehensive reforms that many administrators and advocates perceived as critical for meaningful change. But, as has been already noted, many states applied for and received waivers to operate full coverage, flexible funding demonstrations that functioned very much like a block grant. The problem was not that the waiver process precluded such demonstrations, but rather that the underlying logic models were not always fully articulated and evaluators had difficulty ascertaining with any confidence that the results or lack thereof resulted from the intervention rather than from other causes.

As discussed in Chapter 7, the classical experimental design that randomly assigns subjects to treatment and control conditions is the best way to determine causal connections between interventions and outcomes. Because random assignment helps to ensure that the comparison groups are statistically equivalent in both observed and unobserved characteristics at the start of the intervention, if there are statistically significant differences in outcomes at the end of the intervention, a reasonable inference is that the intervention itself rather than any pre-existing disparities or concurrent influences is responsible for the result. The waiver program's endorsement of random assignment for both evaluation and savings-recovery purposes and the federal government's shared funding of evaluation costs gave state administrators powerful incentives to cooperate with the study plan that offered the best opportunity to measure the actual results of their programs in a credible and straightforward fashion.

Randomized field experiments are notoriously more difficult to implement than observational studies. They require enumerating eligibility lists of potential clients, relinquishing control over whom actually receives the intervention, training key personnel in the logic of the intervention while encouraging workers to withhold the treatment from randomly selected groups, and, finally, explaining to some groups and to their agents why a certain treatment is available to others in similar circumstances, but not to them. Ordinary routines are interrupted and usual agency relationships must be constrained for the sake of experimentation. It is little wonder that many child welfare administrators pushed for less disruptive observational evaluations that simply compare the outcomes for a new policy or practice to the outcomes for a comparison site, a waiting list, or set of "historical controls," that is, subjects treated the old way in the past (Waldman, 2000).

The problem with historical controls, geographical comparison sites, or clients relegated to a waiting list, as statisticians and methodologists have repeatedly pointed out (Cook & Campbell, 1979), is that the intervention group may systematically differ from the comparison group in other important ways than just the intervention. In their introductory textbook *Statistics*, Freedman, Pisani, and Purves (2007) cited studies that compared the outcomes from medical investigations using randomized controlled trials (RCTs) to those using historical controls. On average, the historical-control studies suggested more favorable health outcomes than the RCTs because it appears that physicians select healthier patients (agent selection) whom they believe are most likely to benefit from the intervention.

The more units that a researcher has available for assigning to treatment and control groups, the more precise the statistical inference that the experimenter can draw. As units are clustered into higher levels of aggregation (e.g., siblings, families, neighborhoods, counties, and regions) or organization (e.g., caseworkers, teams, private agencies, public departments, counties, and court jurisdictions), the less precise are the inferences that can be drawn. Still, broad-scale change at the level of an agency or county can be reliably tested using place-based experimental methods so long as there are a sufficient number of agencies or counties available to randomly assign to different experimental conditions (at least ten per group).

Given sufficient numbers of organizational units, random assignment poses no insurmountable barrier to the evaluation of systemic reforms. In fact, Illinois' "recovery coach" waiver successfully implemented randomization at the level of private agencies. But, even when randomization proves difficult, there are recognized alternative evaluation designs, which may not have all the merits of a classical experiment, but can still yield valid inferences. For example, North Carolina evaluated its flexible funding waiver by matching 19 demonstration counties to 19 comparison counties based on size and demographics. The evaluators found that the probability of placement for children in the demonstration counties declined more than for children in the comparison counties (Usher, et al., 2002).

But, what if the level of aggregation extends all the way up to the state level and leaves no units that can be randomly assigned? Again, the challenge is really one of evaluation design rather than an inherent limitation of waivers. For example, a workable quasi-experimental design for evaluating single-site demonstrations, particularly in large states or counties, includes staggering implementation so that sub-units (e.g., counties, field offices, supervisory teams) are brought in randomly at different times. This often occurs naturally as new policies and training are gradually rolled out. Randomized implementation helps rule out the possibility that other contemporary influences (e.g., economic, political, or policy) account for the effect, which is harder to do if a single pre-post comparison is done on the entire site. For example, Illinois staggered the implementation of performance contracting to occur in downstate counties a year after it was implemented in Cook County (see Chapter 10, this volume). The fact that downstate caseloads declined a year later than Cook County helped to strengthen the inference that the introduction of performance contracting was responsible for the change. If other factors were actually responsible, such as an improved economic climate or federal policy changes, the decline should have occurred at approximately the same time in both sites.

Quasi-experimental designs are less burdensome to implement than classical experimental designs. There are times that they make sense even though they offer less credible evidence than a random assignment experiment. This is particularly true when a state wants to replicate a promising innovation that has already been shown to be efficacious in prior experimental studies. In these cases, the waiver approval process could be simplified and structured as a sequence of phases. For example, a Phase I could continue to require random assignment for untested innovations, and a new Phase II could allow alternative quasi-experimental designs for the replication of previously tested innovations. Further simplification could provide for a Phase III that could make the service innovation an allowable IV-E expense in all states after all experimental and quasi-experimental testing requirements have been satisfied. This would give states the flexibility to spend categorical dollars on evidence-supported demonstrations by requesting waivers, perhaps as part of a state plan amendment. Under current rules, states must develop and submit state plans before they may receive funding for child welfare activities under the Social Security Act.

Encouraging Innovations to Achieve Child Welfare Outcomes

The real test of the utility of waivers or any other financing mechanism is how well it advances the capacity of child welfare systems to achieve the outcomes valued by families, children, and society at large. As detailed in Chapter 2, there is broad consensus around the general aims of child welfare intervention with respect to safety, continuity, stability, well-being, and permanence. Both the prevention of a child's removal (continuity) at the front end of child protective intervention and the expedited discharge of a foster child to birth, adoptive, or guardianship homes (permanence) at the back end have the potential to directly reduce IV-E costs below cost-neutrality thresholds. For example, previously approved waivers that authorize wrap-around services to shore-up family stability (California), hasten reunification through drug rehabilitation services (Illinois and New Hampshire), subsidize private guardianships (Delaware, Illinois, Maryland, Montana, New Mexico, North Carolina, and Oregon) and fund post-adoption services to reduce re-entry (Maine) carry the greatest opportunity for earning IV-E savings.

Safety innovations offer a smaller potential for earning savings, because success is rewarded indirectly only if the safety improvement ultimately reduces rates of entry or re-entry into foster care. Prevention of recurrence in and of itself doesn't directly yield IV-E savings because child protective services are unallowable expenses under existing guidelines. Thus, IV-E waivers directed towards improving safety profited the most by targeting those circumstances, such as drug addiction, parental mental illness, or domestic violence, which in the absence of ameliorative services have a high likelihood of precipitating an out-of-home placement. Waivers that authorized services to substance-abusing parents (Delaware and Maryland) are examples of the sorts of demonstrations that target high-risk factors to prevent placement into foster care.

Continuity innovations also present some potential for generating IV-E savings even though they are primarily concerned with reallocating IV-E funds to conserve sibling, kinship, and community ties. For example, Mississippi's intensive service waiver funded new services, such as respite care and other support services, to encourage relative placements, placements with siblings, and placement in the community of origin. New Mexico's waiver allowed Tribes to administer IV-E funds to protect and care for their children directly without state supervision. If the goals of safety and permanence can be accomplished at a lower cost by preserving continuity, such waivers can also generate significant savings.

The principle of well-being has been less successfully promoted through IV-E waiver demonstrations since success is rewarded indirectly only if improvements in health, education, and psychological well-being ultimately result in less costly care, for example, by enabling "step-down" to less intensive settings or preventing more restrictive placements. Improvements in health status, grade-point average, and psychological tests don't directly lower costs because none of these services are currently fundable under IV-E. States would be hard pressed to maintain cost neutrality if they were to undertake innovations to enhance child well-being alone. This is demonstrated by the fact that no state was approved for a waiver demonstration that focuses exclusively on the improvement of child well-being. This is an outcome area that could potentially benefit from the establishment of federal challenge grants.

The utility of child welfare waivers is reflected in the fact that all of the federal financing reform proposals advanced over the past decade—the Administration's flexible funding option, the Pew Commission's recommendations, and the Ways and Means block grant—each sought to extend or simplify and strengthen the waiver provisions. The Pew Commission (2004) recommended eliminating the cap on the number of waivers HHS may approve, permitting HHS to approve waivers that replicate waiver demonstrations that have already been implemented in other states, and urging states to solicit waiver applications from their counties and cities to encourage and support practice innovation at the local level. The only practical wrinkle is that the folding in of IV-E child placement activities and administration into a capped, indexed grant lessens the ability of states to reap savings from foster care reductions, as administrative costs would no longer be claimed as part of the cost-neutrality group. This reduced financial incentive to innovate could be offset by challenge grants or by giving states the option of removing child placement activities from the consolidated grant and continuing to claim these particular expenses in the cost neutrality calculation. Although the Ways and Means proposal also called for the expansion and improvement of the federal child welfare waiver process along the lines recommended by the Pew Commission, it is difficult to see the incentive for states to obtain waivers if the capped block grant already gives them the flexibility they would ordinarily seek through the waiver process. Furthermore, the consolidation and capping of foster care maintenance expenses together with child placement and administrative costs obviates the need for cost-neutrality groups and prevents states from realizing savings from any cost efficiencies achieved in the demonstration group.

Much of the momentum behind eliminating the IV-E entitlement in favor of block grants appears to have slowed down. This creates an opening for reinstituting an improved IV-E waiver program that would give states greater flexibility while maintaining accountability for achieving desired outcomes. The rigorous evaluation requirements could be retained for untested ideas, but be relaxed for those innovations that have already accumulated a firm evidence base for their internal and external validity. Cost-neutrality calculations would apply only to untested programs to reward states for successful innovations and limit the federal risk for failed experiments. Funding for the replication of empirically-tested programs would require Congress' periodically acting on the results from successful waiver demonstrations by making them a statutorily allowable IV-E expense for all states as it did for subsidized guardianship. In this way, Congress can ensure that best practice and successful innovations routinely get woven into the institutional fabric of our nation's child welfare systems.

REFERENCES

Administration for Children and Families. (2003) *Information memorandum: Child welfare demonstration projects for fiscal year 2004*, ACFY-CB-IM-03-06, November 24.

Aiken, L. S., West, S. G., Schwalm, D. E., Caroll, J. I., & Hsiung, S. (1998). Comparison of a randomized and two quasi-experimental designs in a single outcome evaluation: Efficacy of a university-level remedial writing program. *Evaluation Review, 22*, 207–244.

Bell, W. (1965). *Aid to dependent children*. New York: Columbia University Press.

Conlan, T. J. (1984). The politics of federal block grants: From Nixon to Reagan. *Political Science Quarterly, 99*(2), 247–270.

Cook, T. D., & Campbell, D. T. (1979). *Quasi-experimentation: Design and Analysis issues for field settings*. Chicago: Rand-McNally.

Cornerstones Consulting Group. (1999). *Child welfare waivers: Promising directions, missed opportunities*. Houston, TX: The Cornerstone Consulting Group, Inc.

Freedman, D., Pisani, R., & Purves, R. (2007). *Statistics (4th edition)*. New York: W.W. Norton & Company.

Friedman, M. (2005). *Trying hard is not good enough*. Victoria, BC: Trafford Publishing.

Gilbert, C. E. (1966). Policy-making in public welfare: The 1962 amendments. *Political Science Quarterly, 81*(2), 196–224.

Government Accounting Office. (1994). *Foster care: Parental drug abuse has alarming impact on young children* (Rep. No. HEHS-94-89). Washington, D.C.: Author.

Harvey, C. H., Camasso, M. J., & Jagannathan, R. (2000). Evaluating welfare reform waivers under section 1115. *The Journal of Economic Perspectives, 14*(4), 165–188.

Heinsman, D. T., & Shadish, W. R. (1996). Assignment methods in experimentation: When do nonrandomized experiments approximate the answers from randomized experiments? *Psychological Methods, 1*, 154–169.

L.J. vs. Massinga, 838 F. 2nd 118 (4th Cir. 1988).

Marsh, J. C., Ryan, J. P., Choi, S., & Testa, M. F. (2006). Integrated services for families with multiple problems: Obstacles to family reunification. *Children and Youth Services Review, 28*, 1074–1087.

McDonald, J., Salyers, N., & Shaver, M. (2004). *The foster care straightjacket: Innovation, federal financing and accountability in state foster care reform*. Urbana-Champaign, IL: Fostering Results, Children and Family Research Center, School of Social Work, University of Illinois. Available online at http://www.fosterin-gresults.org/.

Office of the Assistant Secretary for Planning and Evaluation. (2005). Federal foster care financing: How and why the current funding structure fails to meet the needs of the child welfare field. *ASPE Issue Brief* (June). Washington, D.C.: U.S. Department of Health and Human Services.

Petit, M. R., & Curtis, P. A. (1997). *Child abuse and neglect: A look at the states*. Washington, D.C.: CWLA Press.

The Pew Commission on Children in Foster Care (2004). *Fostering the future: Safety, permanence and well-being for children in foster care*. Washington, D.C.: The Pew Commission on Children in Foster Care.

Rector, R. (1995). Stringing along. *National Review* (April 17), 50–53.

Reid vs. Suter, N. 89 J 6195 (Cook Cty. Cir. 1992).

Rossi, P. H., Freeman, H. E., & Lipsey, M. W. (1999). *Evaluation: A systematic approach (6th edition)*. Thousand Oaks, CA: SAGE Publications.

Testa, M., Salyer, N. S., Shaver, M., & Miller, J. (2004). *Family ties: Supporting permanence for children in safe and stable foster care with relatives and other caregivers*. Urbana-Champaign, IL: Fostering Results, Children and Family Research Center, School of Social Work, University of Illinois. Available online at http://www.fosteringresults.org/.

U.S. Department of Health and Human Services. (2005). *Synthesis of findings: Title IV-E flexible funding child welfare waiver demonstrations.* Washington, D.C.: U.S. Government Printing Office

Usher, C. L., Wildfire, J. B., Brown, E. L., Duncan, D. F., Meier, A., Salmon, M. A., Painter, J., & Gogan, H. C. (2002). *Evaluation of the title IV-E waiver demonstration in North Carolina.* Chapel Hill, NC: Jordan Institute for Families, the University of North Carolina.

Waldman, W. (2000). Statement of William Waldman, Executive Director, American Public Human Services Association. H.R. 5292, The flexible funding for child protection act of 2000. *Hearing before the Subcommittee on Human Resources of the Committee on Ways and Means, House of Representatives, 106th Congress, 2nd Session,* January 3, 8–13.

Williams, L. A. (1994). The abuse of section 1115 waivers: Welfare reform in search of a standard. *Yale Law & Policy Review, 12*(8), 8–37.

10

PERFORMANCE-BASED CONTRACTING

Aligning Incentives with Outcomes to Produce Results

Ken Taylor and Michael Shaver

The idea of performance contracting or performance-based contracting (PBC) has become increasingly popular in public child welfare. This isn't surprising given that it comes on the heels of two very powerful shifts in the provision of child welfare services since the early 1990s: a rapid growth in privatization and the emergence of major accountability efforts from the federal government in the form of the Child and Family Services Review (CFSR). The CFSR, in turn, reflects the general trend towards more results-oriented accountability as represented at the federal level in the Government Performance and Results Act of 1993. Unfortunately, too often the label "performance contracting" gets applied to efforts that are either strictly about privatization or strictly about accountability As will be discussed later in this chapter, the privatization of child welfare services and mechanisms designed to ensure accountability are both important strategies in the effort to ensure better results for children and families. But, unless these ideas are leveraged appropriately in performance contracts that align incentives with outcomes, they are less likely to drive significant improvements in agency performance.

This is a chapter with a distinct point of view; it is not a neutral summary of ideas.[1] After laying out a theoretical framework and a common definition of terms, it proposes a particular way to approach PBC, which has been implemented in two heavily privatized child welfare systems in two large U.S. cities: Chicago and Philadelphia. Drawing on a detailed discussion of the problems and opportunities faced by each jurisdiction, this chapter will illustrate the common elements underlying their design of a PBC system and the results of that system.[2] This chapter and the underlying theoretical foundation illustrate that there are likely other strategies that could be useful for designing and implementing PBC for child welfare services. However, in keeping with the general tenor of this book, this chapter does not attempt to be all inclusive. Rather, we describe the underlying theoretical basis for PBC in general and offer for the reader's consideration one model for which there is some evidence that it has contributed to improved outcomes for children and families.

Analytical Framework

In Chapter 2, the concept of the "principal–agent" problem was introduced in the context of family relations. This problem refers to the agency risks that arise from adult-agents' imperfectly fulfilling their responsibilities for ensuring the best interests of their child-principals. Principal–agent theory was originally developed in economics and has been applied to the challenges of contracting in general. In both contract theory and practice, the principal–agent problem arises when a principal compensates an agent for performing certain acts in a world of conflicting interests, information asymmetry, uncertainty, and strategic action. The main concern is that principals are not fully informed about whether (or to what extent) contractual expectations are being satisfied by their agents. This information does tend to be known by the agents themselves; hence the information asymmetry. In addition, if the interests of the agent are in conflict with those of the principal, the agent may not always act in the way that is beneficial to the principal.

A related concept that bears some similarity to the problem of agency risk is the notion of "street-level bureaucracy." In his book by the same name, Michael Lipsky (1980) posits that "the policy making roles of street-level bureaucrats are built upon two interrelated facets of their positions: relatively high degrees of discretion and relative autonomy from organizational authority" (p. 13). He goes on to say: "One can expect a distinct degree of noncompliance if lower level workers' *interests* differ from those at higher levels, and the incentives and sanctions available to higher levels are not sufficient to prevail" (p. 17). This is another formulation of the principal–agent problem.

A possible solution to these types of problems is to shift from an input and process driven contracting model[3] to one that is based on the clear definition of measurable outcomes. Using this method, incentives are aligned with outcomes so that agents are more inclined to achieve what the principals wish them to accomplish. This involves changing the rules of cooperation so that the self-interested rational choices the agent is likely to make fulfill the outcomes that the principal desires. In the child welfare case, the goal is to reduce the risk of defecting from the norms of safe and reliable care and elevate the probability of agents' contributing to the well-being of the principals (the child and family). The intention is to discourage strategic behavior of the agent in "gaming" the contract by making self-interested choices that increase the payout from the contract without adequately satisfying the interests of the principals (Baker, 1992, p. 600). One of the challenging aspects of creating appropriate incentives is that incentives work differently for different types of agents. Because certain types of contractual frameworks are more or less attractive to certain types of vendors; principals influence the type of agents they recruit by the form of contract they offer (Kiser, 1999). PBC attempts to take all of these issues into account.

An interesting aspect of the child welfare system is that most participants are both principals and agents. For example, public child welfare agencies are the agents of elected officials, but they are also the principals when contracting with private agencies (agents) that deliver many of the services to children and families. In turn, the workers in the field are the agents of the private agency principals, and the foster parents are agents of the worker-principals as well as the children. Because of the interlocking nature of principal–agent relationships within child welfare, it is important to structure the principal–agent relationship in a way that minimizes agency risk, information asymmetry, and incentives to defect from cooperative action.

The typical bureaucratic solution to these principal–agent problems is to increase direct monitoring of agent performance by principals through direct supervision, on-site visits, routine reporting, and other types of agency surveillance. Such monitoring approaches tend to focus heavily on service inputs and sometimes performance outputs, such as number of service contacts, timeliness of the submittal of paperwork, deviations from best practice, and cost over-runs. They also tend toward micro-management of agency relations, which can greatly increase the transaction costs of performance monitoring to the point that the costs exceed the benefits of the delegation of discretion. PBC helps to reduce these costs by shifting the focus of monitoring from outputs to outcomes. The transaction costs of contract monitoring are significantly decreased by shifting from intense supervision and procedural oversight to one of outcomes monitoring, which has very tight expectations on measurable outcomes, but delegates discretion to agents and allows them flexibility in the choice of means for achieving those outcomes. PBC is intended to facilitate this shift.

It is useful at this point to contrast the PBC model with the fiduciary model of principal–agent relationships, which have been presumed to underlie child welfare and other human services interventions in the past. The model of fiduciary agency assumes that agents are motivated by internalized norms of personal probity, ethical obligation, or professional duty to act in the best interests of principals. This has been the dominant model in patient–doctor relationships, in which physicians are expected to invest their skills and resources on behalf of the well-being of patients, who in turn trust that the physicians will faithfully and equitability fulfill their responsibilities to themselves and other patients in similar circumstances. This is not to say that physician behavior is unilaterally altruistic or that their interests always align with their patient's. Rather the expectation is that physicians will subordinate their interests in remuneration or conflicting purposes to their dominant interest in the well-being of their patients (Buchanan, 1988).

The patient–doctor model of fiduciary agency has served as a model for client-professional relationships in child welfare and other human services. The fiduciary model uses professional prestige, educational credentials, word-of-mouth reputation, and other symbolic tokens of reliability as substitutes for performance incentives and outcome measurement to reduce the risks that service agents will inadequately fulfill the interests of their principals. To some degree, faith or trust in the fiduciary agency of child welfare experts and service providers is essential. Otherwise, the massive public investments required for ensuring the reliability of purely contractual forms of bureaucratic agency with respect to direct surveillance, performance measurement, and quality control of output production would overwhelm any benefits from the delegation of discretion and responsibility to child welfare experts and service providers. Because of this, we believe that performance-based contracts might best be thought of as supplementing the fiduciary model, rather than replacing it, and that the two models in combination ensure better outcomes for children and families than either on their own.

PBC has arisen alongside results-oriented accountability as a method of holding fiduciary agents accountable for their decisions and choices and for subjecting their arguments and claims to verification by obtaining information on outcomes and evaluating actual results. Interest in these new results-oriented methods is tied up with the general trend toward "reflexive modernization" of social relations, which calls into doubt all inherited and settled patterns of behavior deriving from authority, tradition, and faith (Beck, 1992). Interest in applying these new methods to child welfare also arises because of the perceived and actual deterioration in the prestige, professionalism, and expertise of the child welfare workforce (see Chapter 11, this volume).

Both contractual and fiduciary relationships can be distinguished from affine relationships by the fact that the former are voluntary whereas the latter are largely ascribed based on common solidarities, such as the relationships between child and birth parent, relative, and tribal elders (see Chapter 1, this volume). Another difference is that affine agents are assumed to act in the best interests of principals because their interests directly overlap, whereas contractual agents are assumed to be motivated by self-interest and fiduciary agents are trusted to act in the interests of principals because they are ethically responsible or expert in realizing client interests (e.g., physical health, emotional reassurance, spiritual comfort, and educational well-being) more efficiently than lay persons. It is probably more than coincidental that interest in PBC has grown at the same time that public confidence in these other forms of managing agency risks has declined.

Most illuminating in this respect is the dwindling percentage of the population that expresses "a great deal of confidence" in the institution of medicine, which plummeted from the high 50% range in the early 1970s to below 40% in the early 2000s (Shott, 2007). Confidence in religious institutions also dropped sharply from the mid-40s to the mid-20s. This trend is perhaps best represented by the percentage of the population that agreed that, "generally speaking, people can be trusted" declined from 45% in the early 1970s to 35% in the early 2000s (Shott, 2007).

Performance-Based Contracting

Before describing what PBC is, it may be helpful to describe what it is *not*. There are a number of terms used in the previous section (privatization, accountability), which are sometimes used as synonyms for PBC. In some cases, these terms are components of PBC, but should not be considered to be PBC in their own right. Another way to characterize them is necessary, but not sufficient. *Privatization* is not PBC because private contracts can be (and usually are) focused on the delivery of inputs and outputs rather than on the achievement of outcomes. *Performance measurement* and *performance management* are both components of PBC, but lack important characteristics in terms of incentives for improved performance. *Capitation* is beginning to be applied to child welfare, but most of those attempts have not been successful in part because of the fact that for the child welfare population, there is insufficient knowledge about the needs of children served and the cost to meet those needs At the point this chapter was written, the authors were unaware of any examples where *managed care* was successfully implemented in the child welfare arena.[4]

So, if none of these things are PBC, what is PBC, and why is it necessary? PBC is a form of contract between the government and private sector that exchanges increased performance for the necessary resources and flexibility needed to achieve the higher performance benchmarks. It aligns the financial incentives in the contract with the outcomes the system should achieve on behalf of children and families. In the examples discussed in this chapter, it redirects resources from decisions that expose children to risks by keeping them in care, for example, multiple moves, uncertain futures, and emotional insecurity, toward concerted efforts to find children permanent homes and improve their safety and well-being while they await family permanence or prepare to emancipate from the system. It inserts quasi-market competition into a historically non-competitive service environment. It shifts provider agency accountability from "Did you do what you were told to do?" to "Did what you did work?", and, "What difference did it make in the outcomes for children?" (Schorr, 1994). Finally, under PBC, contractual agents are given as much freedom as possible to figure out how to meet their performance objectives. In sum, PBC shifts contract oversight away from surveillance of processes to service management through incentives, shifting from a focus on inputs and outputs to a focus on outcomes.

For PBC in Chicago and Philadelphia, the contractual outcomes were permanence (reunification, adoption, or guardianship) and stability (the number of placement moves to a higher level of care or out of the agency). One could argue that these are also outputs and that the true outcome is a well functioning adult who promotes the well-being of their own family. Although that may be true, it is not practical to build those sorts of long-term outcomes into a contract. So, for the purposes of this chapter, we draw the following distinctions between inputs, outputs, and outcomes (see Chapter 3, this volume).

1. Inputs: services that are paid for (e.g., counseling, care management, parenting classes, or foster care)
2. Outputs: services that are actually received (e.g., counseling sessions attended, % clients who graduated from a parenting education class, or days of foster care provided)
3. Outcomes: impacts of the services provided (e.g., family permanence achieved for children and placement stability while they are in care).

PBC represents an important tool in the current child welfare environment because—at least for the foreseeable future—child welfare will be constrained by fiscal limitations that necessitate restraint in the use of resources. Although the federal government has slowed down the process of retreating from historic funding commitments in child welfare, it is unlikely that it will significantly increase funding levels. The willingness of states and counties to fund child welfare activities varies, but it is unlikely there will be significant increases in child welfare spending given the current economic downturn, and more likely there will be cuts in many places. The PBC model examined in this chapter addresses the challenge that child welfare officials face in securing the additional resources they need to improve outcomes in an environment where there is, at best, no additional funding or, perhaps more likely, shrinking resources. The PBC response to that challenge is the design of a results-oriented contracting system that can generate the additional resources it needs through increased performance. This is not to say that the field should give up its attempts to acquire additional and more appropriately configured resources, it should not. But, PBC is a way to use the resources it does have more efficiently and effectively.

The more conventional model for child welfare contracts is based on a per-diem model (an amount paid for each day of care) that specifies mainly outputs (children served and days of care) and contains financial incentives that run contrary to systems goals (i.e., providers get paid if children remain in foster care but don't get paid if children go home).

Under a per-diem model, taxpayers, families, and children bear much of the costs and consequences of agency risk because providers are contracted to provide days of care, not outcomes. This creates an incentive structure that favors spending on foster care rather than helping children and families attain permanence. PBC creates an environment where the costs of agency risks and defections from responsible child-caring are not borne exclusively by the taxpayer-principals or child-principals, but are distributed between principals and agents by structuring financial incentives to achieve desired child and family outcomes, and by breaking down the barriers to achieving improved outcomes at a systemic level.

The flip side of cost is reward. Through the more appropriate sharing of responsibilities, PBC creates the opportunity for rewards. Rewards can come in a number of forms, including increased payments that are earned through improved agency performance and increased market share for high performers. PBC raises the performance benchmarks above the current system average, budgets the savings obtained from improved performance, and reinvests these savings in additional program improvements and specifically targeted purposes. The difference between current performance levels and the higher performance benchmarks yields surplus resources that the system can re-invest—mostly back into the contract. If agencies out-perform these new, higher performance expectations, they get to keep those savings and reinvest them in ways they choose: in lower caseloads, additional pay, or any number of other supports for staff and agency. If they underperform they, in effect, lower their payment rate by serving more children for the same amount of money. In addition, they run the risk of their contract being decreased or canceled, and those services being transferred to higher performing agencies.

One very powerful aspect of PBC is the process of reviewing, discussing, and agreeing to outcomes; benchmarking the level of outcomes achievement; and determining the resources needed to achieve outcomes. This should be done in open forums that give some say, at a minimum, to the contractual service providers and ideally also to the children and families and their affine agents, who are the subjects of these policies. In both Chicago and Philadelphia, the conversations between the government and provider agencies enabled both sides to think differently about outcomes, how to measure them, and the power of leveraging resources in targeted ways. In Chicago, public forums organized by local community groups enabled clients to voice their dissatisfactions and to demand straightforward explanations and accounts of changes. PBC drives improved outcomes performance by addressing three interlocking concepts: (1) Investments, (2) Participation, and (3) Incentives. These work best in concert. If one leg of the stool is missing, the level of performance improvement will not be as significant.

Whereas child welfare jurisdictions typically have no shortage of areas where performance improvements are desirable, the use of the contracting process as a primary tactic for reducing agency risks and improving results requires some analysis to determine whether or not a contractual strategy fits the conditions to enable the improvement of agency performance. For example, targeting a particular issue, like shortening the time between the termination of parental rights and the finalization of adoptions, reduces to the old fiduciary model if there is only one private service provider responsible for processing all legally free children headed for adoption. Similarly, using performance contracts to reduce the number of children who disrupt from intact family placements and require a foster care stay would be a poor fit for a system where all in-home services to at-risk families are provided by a single union of public service workers. These examples—although admittedly very basic—point to an important step in developing performance contracts for child welfare services: understanding whether or not contracts can be a tool for reducing agency risk and driving agency performance. Performance contracts are not the answer to all performance problems; it is important not to try to force a square peg into a round hole. That said, performance contracts can be very effective in addressing certain types of challenges. In the following section, we analyze the core components of designing a PBC framework and the resulting contract, and how to determine whether or not linking performance benchmarks to the contracting process is likely to produce the desired results.

Design Components of a Performance Framework

As previously discussed, a contract with performance expectations is not an especially new concept in social service delivery. At some level, a contract must always communicate performance expectations. Even if the contract consists of a series of inputs or process expectations, the idea that the contracted provider must "perform" the prescribed activities should be explicit. A performance contract, however, is different in a number of important ways. This difference begins with understanding the performance framework.

Creating a performance framework means asking and answering a series of questions designed to determine whether or not, and how, using contracts to drive performance will yield better results. The framework is similar to the logic models presented in previous chapters, which detail several key areas, including:

1. An evaluation of whether or not conditions are conducive to using contracts to drive performance (Environmental Scan of External Conditions);
2. A determination of specific outcomes, whether they can be measured and used to distinguish superior performance from inferior performance (Outcomes Determination);

3. A full discussion of the link between performance expectations and the work needed to produce specified results (Investing in Results/Theory of Action); and

4. Clearly articulated benefits for exemplary performance and consequences for failing to perform (Performance Incentives).

Environmental Scan of External Conditions

Despite the reality that government generally expects good performance from contractual agents, using a contract to drive specific performance expectations (especially where significant improvements are sought) necessitates finding the right fit between the needs of the system and the structure for securing those results. An important first step in this process is an evaluation of the environment in which the contracting process is expected to play a part. Within the child welfare context, this environmental scan should involve not only a careful review of the service area (prevention services, foster care, residential treatment, or post-adoption services, for example), but also an examination of how services within each of these areas are provided.

To illustrate how this environmental scan can develop, it's useful to examine the origins of performance contracts in Chicago and Philadelphia. In both jurisdictions, the idea of using performance-based contracts was preceded by a careful monitoring of performance trends and data analysis of the underlying factors that drove each system's case flow dynamics. In the case of Chicago, data analyses indicated that low rates of children exiting from relative foster care to permanent placements were contributing to a bloated system.

As illustrated in Figure 10.1, the quarterly cross-sectional count of children in kinship foster care in Chicago and the surrounding Cook County suburbs climbed steeply in the early 1990s as entries into relative care greatly exceeded exits out of relative care. It was projected that more than half of the children would end up remaining in care for more than 8 years (Illinois Department of Children and Family Services, 2006). The line marked (A) shows the impact of Home of Relative (HMR) reform in Illinois on case flow dynamics, which diverted children formerly taken into care by providing relative caregivers extended family support to prevent removal. Although entries into relative care declined in anticipation of the passage of the legislation, exits of existing cases did not rise above entries into care as anticipated.

Similarly, administrative data in Philadelphia pointed to exit rates for children to permanent homes, which were far below comparable urban child welfare systems. An evaluation of system performance in Philadelphia suggested that securing more timely permanence for children was essential for addressing the lengthening time spent by youths entering the foster care system.

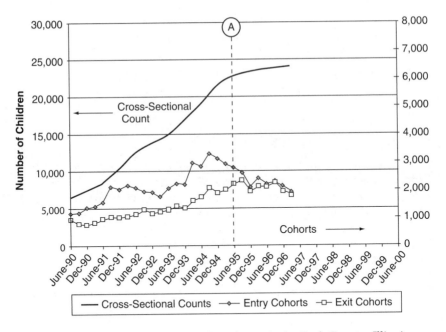

Figure 10.1 Kinship foster care case flow dynamics in Cook County, Illinois.

Understanding the underlying case flow dynamics driving system performance is a critical first step in the environmental scan. A thorough assessment of the setting and context in which relevant services are provided is crucial for identifying those services thought to have a direct bearing on the performance area(s) of interest. The kinds of questions asked during this part of the environmental scan include:

1. Are the relevant services delivered by the public sector, the private sector or both?
2. Are privatized services delivered by a large number of providers or a small number of providers?
3. Is there a wide range of performance on important measures, or do most providers perform at a similar level?
4. Are the current service providers unique with respect to geography, specialized training or certification, equipment, or facilities?

Although this is not a complete list of relevant questions, the point to emphasize is that the environmental scan, in addition to the analysis of performance trends, should also include a thorough analysis of how services are organized and delivered.

Continuing with the performance contracting examples in Chicago and Philadelphia, both jurisdictions operated foster care systems where the bulk of services provided to children that directly affected time to permanence were organized and delivered by a diverse set of private agencies. Both jurisdictions also included providers that were in close proximity to one another, were similarly organized with respect to service capacity, but performed quite differently on important measures. Both systems retained public sector responsibility to investigate cases of alleged maltreatment, and, in each system, the public sector made determinations about the level of service a child needed and made assignments to private agencies. Taken together, these factors proved to have direct relevance for the performance framework that was ultimately developed.

Admittedly, the environmental scan can be a time consuming and challenging undertaking. Still, the examples of where performance contracts have been successfully implemented highlight the importance of this activity in generating the performance framework that will ultimately guide the specifics of doing the work. Without significant effort at the outset to understand why a system is underperforming, the solutions that emerge are less likely to be designed and targeted in a way that will be successful in turning performance around. This seems obvious, but there are many examples where systems did not accurately assess their problems and, as a result, built ill-suited solutions that ultimately did not improve outcomes.

In both Chicago and Philadelphia, another part of the environmental scan was something that came to be known as "interest-based negotiations." These discussions between the public and private sector were different from the traditional positional negotiating framework, because each side was focused on improving the system as a whole as opposed to simply maximizing their positions. This is important, both to agree on the problems and to come up with solutions. Improved performance will not just occur because it is demanded. Leadership, public and private, must give staff/agencies the capabilities necessary for achieving desired outcomes. So, the negotiations that led up to PBC included long discussions between the public and private sectors to review, discuss, and agree to outcomes; set benchmarks for achieving outcomes; and determine the resources needed to achieve outcomes.[5] In both Chicago and Philadelphia, the conversations between the government and provider agencies required both sides to actively listen to each other, enabled both sides to think differently about outcomes and how to measure them, and demonstrated the power of leveraging resources in targeted ways.

One question that always needs answering is: "Who knows how to improve performance?" The answer depends on a variety of contextual factors, but it is almost certain that few of the answers reside solely with either the public sector or the private sectors. So, it is incumbent on those who are interested in, or responsible for, performance improvement to engage the proper mix of interested parties, regardless of affiliation, in interest-based discussions about performance improvement. These strategies will then need to be translated into the language of performance contracts.

Identifying areas of leverage only occurs as a result of deep understanding of the systems and how they work. Our logic models of how systems work will never be complete or entirely accurate, and we can't predict the future. But, we must find ways to work within the limits of our knowledge and use what we do know to our best advantage (Hirsch, 1994, p. 93). Interest-based negotiations, or true partnership, between the public and private sector is one way to develop more sophisticated, accurate, and shared mental models.

Another important aspect of successful performance contracts is that they do not just include bonuses for good performance.[6] As important as it is to align financial incentives with outcomes, successful performance improvements usually require significant system reforms as well. Some of the barriers to improved agency performance are beyond the control of individual private agencies or for that matter, the public agency. That means that the system as a whole must work together to break down those barriers. There will likely be less performance improvement if agencies are left on their own to address the barriers. It takes interest-based negotiation to figure out what the system level barriers are and how best to address them.

Outcomes Determination

In the Koran it is said "If you don't know where you are going, any road will take you there." Over a thousand years later, management guru Steven Covey said "Begin with the end in mind." PBC applies this sage advice in the child welfare context. Starting with the outcomes the system wants to achieve on behalf of children, PBC then focuses attention on strategies to achieve those outcomes and on the barriers to their achievement. However, agreeing on outcomes may be more complex than it sounds.

Earlier in this chapter, we discussed some of the basic terms frequently used when discussing performance contracting, and, in previous chapters, areas were presented, which are frequently the target of performance strategies within child welfare settings, specifically, the areas of safety, continuity, stability, permanence, and well-being. Of course at the macro level, there is no real disagreement as to the relevance and appropriateness of these outcomes for children served by the child welfare system. When it comes to the development of a performance framework, however, sorting through the details of what constitutes good performance and how that is measured prompts a number of important questions.

First, the models of performance contracting used in Chicago and Philadelphia shared a key characteristic: contract expectations that focused on outcomes rather than the service inputs and outputs discussed earlier in the chapter. The performance framework must necessarily ask the basic (although never easy) question: What are the observable, valid results of doing the work well? Valid here refers to demonstrating how the outcomes for children served through these contracts would be better than under the (counterfactual) pre-existing contracts. Specifically, this requires verifying that PBC actually improves permanence[7] and stability while the children are in foster care and the changes were not the result of other extraneous factors (e.g., changes in the kinds of children entering care, general improvements in the economic climate, or sweeping policy changes that affect all programs regardless of the intervention).

This of course assumes an important requirement when considering outcomes: Are they observable and measurable? Einstein said: "Not everything that can be counted counts, and not everything that counts can be counted." This is true, but for a contract to be effective, its expectations must be clear and its anticipated outcomes must be able to be reliably measured. This is quite different from the more subjective aspects of social work practice that require an interpretative understanding of the motives, impulses, wishes, and desires of clients. Social workers make judgments every day based on their qualitative interpretations of client intention and meaning. Performance management also depends on qualitative information as discussed in the interest-based negotiations phase of PBC. But, full implementation of PBC requires that information be based on objectively verifiable, quantitative data; otherwise it is vulnerable to distortion through "gaming" and will not adequately address the principal–agent problem discussed at the beginning of this chapter. This is very important because with performance-based contracts financial incentives are attached to outcomes. Therefore, the assessment of outcomes cannot be based on subjective measures that could be inconsistently implemented or vulnerable to manipulation.

For an outcome to be considered appropriate for PBC it should be:

- Objectively measurable
- Comprehensible by workers and managers
- Definable by an agreed upon operational indicator
- Equally attainable by all providers
- If possible, have a direct impact on the agency's bottom line.

In both Chicago and Philadelphia, children were moving to permanent placements prior to PBC. The problem for both jurisdictions proved to be the tempo of permanency planning and finalization, which were taking longer and longer. Measuring the change in tempo proved straightforward, in this case, because the "facts" of permanence are established through legal processes: either the court returns a child home, awards private guardianship, or finalizes an adoption. To ensure that the increased tempo indeed translated into lasting outcomes, only those permanencies that endured for at least one year without disruption were counted as meeting performance benchmarks. Of course, getting the public sector data systems to reflect these facts proved to be challenging in both jurisdictions. Other areas of performance, particularly in the arena of child well-being, can make choosing the right measure more complicated.

Take, for example, a child welfare jurisdiction's decision to target placement stability for PBC. Although a placement change is a distinct event, careful programming of administrative data has to be done to ensure that transaction dates for payment changes are not mistaken for actual placement moves, (sometimes referred to as "paper moves"), temporary absences are taken into account (e.g., trial home visits, respite, or hospitalizations), and allowances are made for provider status change (e.g., from regular to specialized foster parent or pre-adoptive home). Besides getting the counts correct, there are additional evaluative questions about whether or not a particular placement change should be considered undesirable or desirable for the child. For example, suppose the placement change moves a child from a more restrictive to a less restrictive setting (e.g., from institution to foster family home) or from an unrelated foster home to a (more family-like) relative foster home. Existing federal policy regards both types of moves in a positive light, but the federal CFSR stability standard currently makes no distinctions between these desirable moves and those less desirable moves. Efforts to draw such distinctions pose some challenges. For example, there may be some local jurisdictions that would want to reduce certain forms of "policy-driven" instability, such as moves to relatives after a certain length of time in a non-relative home, or jurisdictions that would want to allow for certain types of moves, such as routine placements in a diagnostic home prior to movement to a stable setting. Such situations in which there can be either a positive or negative value attached to various types of countable events create additional, although not insurmountable, challenges for the performance measurement required by PBC.

The PBC model implemented in both Chicago and Philadelphia contained a partial solution to the complication of value ambiguity in certain types of placement changes. The contracts created an allowable level of movement based on the premise that some moves were in the best interest of the child. There was also the general assumption that moves should be kept to a minimum,[8] and that the pre-existing level of aggregate movement was too high. Therefore, the benchmarked level of movement allowed by the contracts was roughly half the level of movement in the previous year. For this purpose, movement was defined as a "step-up" to a more restrictive level of service (e.g., from foster home to residential treatment center), or movement from one agency to another agency. The problem of placement instability at the same level of restrictiveness within a particular agency's array of placement resources was not originally addressed. However, the number of within-agency moves was monitored for outliers. In subsequent years, as PBC continued to evolve in Chicago, all child placement moves were counted.

Ensuring that outcomes were equally attainable by providers is a particularly important aspect of the PBC model implemented in Chicago and

Philadelphia. A crucial feature of the model was the assurance of a "level playing field," so that no agency had an unfair performance advantage. This was addressed in the following ways: (1) data analysis showed that agencies had a similar client caseload mix at the start of PBC; (2) every agency received a similar mix of clients as referrals; (3) each agency was provided with the same level of resources within the contract; and (4) every agency was held to the same benchmark of performance as all other agencies. Holding each agency accountable for the same high performance expectations was seen as essential in both Chicago and Philadelphia. It would be considered unfair for a child to be placed with an agency that is allowed under contract to perform to a lower benchmark of performance than other agencies. In addition, in the sometimes charged political environment of child welfare, protecting against charges of bias or unfair advantage given to some providers is paramount. Having the same performance expectation for each provider makes it easier to demonstrate a level playing field.

Traditionally the public sector has attempted to minimize agency risk by first matching the needs of children to qualified providers deemed competent to service those needs and then relying on the fiduciary model of bureaucratic agency to control agency risks. The problem that PBC confronts is that many traditional child welfare practices, such as specialized services matched to client needs, uncapped spending for individualized services, and unquestioned deference to professional expertise, no longer fit well with the tenor of the times or the realistic conditions of public child welfare practice. Better mechanisms of system coordination between public and private sectors must be developed to blend the fiduciary model with the new contractual requirements of PBC, such as otational assignment of cases, capitated funding of services, and financial incentives and sanctions to motivate performance improvement.

In both Chicago and Philadelphia, the public sector contracted out the generation of the performance data to local university partners. This helped to instill confidence that the data were not being manipulated to the advantage of either the public principal or the provider agencies. A significant amount of time was spent reconciling these data with providers to make sure they were accurate.

The Performance-Based Contracting Theory of Action

Child welfare jurisdictions exploring a PBC framework are likely to encounter system deficits (whether resources, infrastructure, policy or practice), which play a major role in undermining performance. Child welfare jurisdictions where performance contracting models have been successfully implemented demonstrated not only a commitment to identifying and securing specific outcomes, they also showed a willingness to think about and respond to barriers to success. Harvard Professor and government performance expert Robert Behn thinks about addressing these barriers as a multi-step process, including:

- Determining the elements of operational capacity that are critical for vendors to produce results;
- Providing critical resources so vendors have the necessary assets to produce results; and
- Assisting in the transfer of effective ideas, better practices, and essential technologies (Behn, 2004,p. 8)

In Chicago, a substantial problem was inherent in the existing contracting structure that had not adequately invested in permanence, either financially or as a primary outcome. Providers agreed that the contracts invested in the wrong results; revenue was based upon the retention of children in foster care. Contracts based upon a fee-for-child payment undermined family permanence by rewarding continued placement of children in care by only paying for children who remained in care, whereas moving a child to a permanent home entailed the loss of revenue. Additionally, children headed for adoption were served under a separate contract, often involving a transfer to another agency because only a select group of specialized providers had adoption contracts. Taken together, this dynamic resulted in work being focused on maintaining children in care rather than aggressively pursuing permanence. Although it cannot be said that providers were strategically defecting from their fiduciary responsibilities to maximize their revenue streams by keeping children in care, it was generally acknowledged that achieving permanence was made more difficult by the existing payment structure.[9] PBC reverses this dynamic.

The performance contracting model developed for Chicago also sought to address these system deficits by investing in permanency-planning activities. These investments provided new staff positions in the form of permanency workers; enabled providers to initiate services more quickly upon placement of children; carved out resources for supporting children reunified with birth parents; and created flexibility in the use of administrative funds to support different models of child welfare service provision. Importantly, the contract realigned financial incentives to reinforce the importance of achieving outcomes over maintaining children in care. This was accomplished by developing a contract where payment was driven by investing in the capacity to do the work (staff, supervisors, and supportive services) rather than counting children and child care days.

In Philadelphia, prior to PBC there were similar obstacles in the contracts and resource allocation, resulting in a lack of emphasis on permanence as a core part of foster care work. The system had not adequately invested in permanence for children. The supports made available to providers for returning a child home from foster care were minimal and not especially useful in ensuring a stable reunification. Similarly, providers were ill-equipped to support the additional work that would be needed to bolster an increase in permanence through adoption and guardianship. Having successfully confronted these challenges in Chicago, it was agreed that investing in provider contracts to allow for permanency workers and putting flexible and adequate funding in place to foster successful reunifications would also be useful strategies in Philadelphia.

In both jurisdictions, the change to PBC represented a major shift for providers, who had seen their job as providing foster care placements for children, not securing permanence. In retrospect, this should not have been surprising because providing foster care placements was precisely what providers were paid to do. Unfortunately, this was in direct conflict with a primary stated goal in both systems—permanence—and it serves to highlight a prime example of the misalignment between existing contracts and the goals of the system that can account for a failure to perform. The central lesson in both Chicago and Philadelphia is that the expectation for improved performance must be accompanied by a real investment in resources leveraged to ensure the desired results.

Many of the investments listed in earlier paragraphs clearly required additional funding, and those dollars were built into the contracts through specific enhancements. Investments also went beyond dollars, into streamlined processes so that workers could be freed to focus more of their time on achieving outcomes for clients. Additional, non-contractual investments were also made, including: changing the referral process, creating clarity in level of care decision making and streamlining consents required for services. Still another area of emphasis was improving the relationship with court and legal personnel, decreasing their frustration with the child welfare system and allowing them to devote more of their efforts to achieving better outcomes for children and families.

Just as it is important to understand the context in which a particular performance framework must operate, it is also important to have a clear understanding of how responsibilities are divided up between the agent under contract and the principal issuing the contract. Specifically, it means having clarity about where the lines of authority and responsibility are and whether or not the agent has the necessary resources to achieve the principal's interests.

The barriers to the implementation of PBC in both Chicago and Philadelphia should not be understated. Prior to PBC, both shared a per-diem payment structure that financially rewarded maintaining children in care. There were unique differences with respect to staffing and activities designed to bolster permanence that needed to be dealt with specifically in each location. Failing to invest in a contracting and support structure geared to the specific challenges and outcomes in a particular jurisdiction can undermine any effort to drive serious changes in performance. Certainly, any agreement around performance improvement that includes specific outcomes and benchmarks is an important accomplishment. But, failing to invest in the structures and processes necessary to secure these results leaves contractual agents without the necessary vehicles for driving change. Too often, service providers and government come together only to agree on performance improvements without advancing the conversation enough to seriously address the specifics of how best to achieve those improvements. The performance contracting models from Chicago and Philadelphia each highlight examples of the need to bring together performance expectations and the investments necessary to deliver on these expectations.

Performance Incentives

Once the performance framework has been sufficiently developed to address the outcomes and the necessary investments for securing those outcomes, all parties need to be clear about the rewards for success and the consequences of performance failure. Linking performance expectations with clear consequences is at the heart of the performance contracting strategy. This is why performance contracts are not synonymous with privatization, performance measurement, or performance management. Articulating the consequences of success and failure and embedding those consequences in the payment structure ensures performance contracts are not simply the business-as-usual contract with a separate appendix on expected outcomes attached.

To be most effective, performance contracts should leverage a set of self-enforcing financial incentives to ensure a targeted level of performance improvement. Simply put, when providers exceed specific performance expectations, they can expect to benefit financially. When providers fail short of benchmarks, they can expect to lose financially. In this way, they share the financial risk with the public investor. In Chicago and Philadelphia PBC models, this happens automatically through the case flow mechanism, without additional action by the principal to pay a bonus for high performance or take funding away from an agency that is not meeting performance benchmarks.

This kind of direct link between performance and payment is missing from contracts that call only for generic performance improvements or contracts that include a long laundry-list of expected outcomes. In such contracts, the only instrumental interest driving performance is the implied or sometimes even stated threat of the cancellation or non-renewal of the contract. Despite clear language articulating benchmarks for providers, there are countless examples of public principals' renewing contracts with provider agencies year after year without evidence of even marginal progress in performance improvement. Why? Because such contracts continue to pay for the production of outputs, for example, days of care, number of visits, and client contacts, rather than performance outcomes, for example, stable placements, least restrictive care, and legal permanence for children.

PBC is different from usual payment-for-service contracts because the benefits of success or the consequences of failure are built into the structure of the PBC. Agencies are not paid for days of care, but for a minimal set of performance standards, which includes a starting caseload, a flow of new cases into the caseload (referrals), and a flow of existing or new cases out of the caseload (outcomes), which result in caseload balance or equilibrium, i.e. ending caseload level equals starting caseload level. Agencies are paid a flat amount for maintaining the caseload at equilibrium.[10] If the agency discharges more children to permanence than they receive in referrals, the ending caseload falls below the starting caseload (see Fig. 10.2). In this circumstance, the agency ends up spending resources on fewer total days of care, but receives a fixed level of funding (in effect increasing their rate per day) which reinforces the drive to exceed performance benchmarks.[11] On the other hand, as illustrated in Figure 10.3, if the agency moves fewer children to permanence than they receive in referrals, they will see their ending caseload rise above starting levels. This will require the agency to spend resources on additional days of care above the fixed funding level, but at their own expense rather than passing the costs back to the principal. The financial risk to the agent creates an incentive for focusing on managing outcomes.

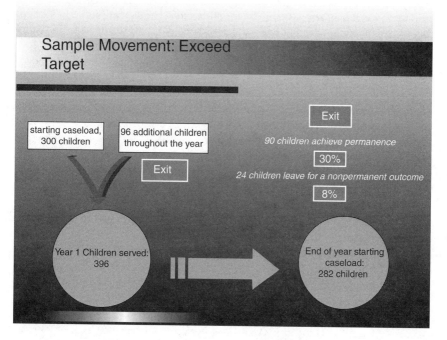

Figure 10.2 Reward structure of PBC. The key here is that the agency continues to get paid for 300 children, even though by the end of the year they are only serving 282 children.

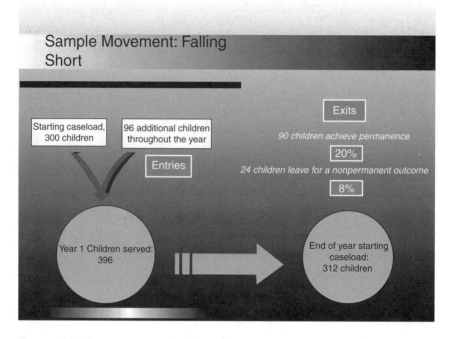

Figure 10.3 Cost structure of PBC. In this scenario, the agency continues to get paid for 300 children, even though by the end of the year they are serving 312; thus they have to provide uncompensated care because they did not meet the performance benchmarks.

A major concern about performance contracting is that it might create agency risks for moving too many children to permanence prematurely without adequate assurances that they will be secure and safe. To guard against these risks, the expectation was included in the contracts that permanencies needed to last one year to ultimately "count." If a permanency placement disrupts within a year, the case comes back to the agency with no additional administrative funding attached to it. Along with significant new investments in post-permanency supports for families, this incentive structure was aligned with the best interests of children to keep them secure and safe.

The mechanism of establishing equilibrium caseload benchmarks creates a PBC in which performance expectations are self-enforcing. Such contracts do not rely on bonuses at the end of the year to reward performance above the benchmarks. Instead, the financial benefits of superior performance materialize throughout the year whenever performance outpaces contract expectations. Additional encouragement to exceed performance benchmarks is created by making future referrals conditional upon the prior year's record of performance, which ties the provider's future market share directly to its performance success.

Success with any performance framework requires contracts that authorize public principals either to reduce capacity or eliminate the agent's contract for inferior performance. Such decisions are never easy. First, they have significant impact for the staff of the affected agencies. Second, these decisions often carry political implications, which can slow, delay, or even prevent the government from taking action. Third, acting on these decisions can also represent major transaction costs for the government agency associated with shifting services from one provider to another. However, the failure to abide by market pricing principles in responding to poor providers is usually enough to undermine any sustainable improvement in performance and to raise suspicions about cronyism and the integrity of the process.

Evaluating Success

The unique aspects of the PBC model developed for Chicago and Philadelphia are the specific set of strategies that aligned desired outcomes with financial incentives for providers to do the work. In previous sections, we've discussed the theoretical basis for structuring contractual relationships to share risk and improve performance; the need to fit PBC within a framework that recognizes broader system objectives; and the operational importance of choosing desired outcomes, investing in success, and specifying in advance the consequences of performance success and failure. In this section, we examine the extent to which the performance contracting model used in Chicago and Philadelphia delivered on the outcomes identified and reinforced in the contract design. Although both jurisdictions have operated foster care programs using performance contracts for several years (Chicago since 1997 and Philadelphia since 2003), the focus of our evaluation is on the first 3 years after implementation of PBC in each system.

In Illinois, the Department of Children and Family Services (DCFS) was able to stagger the implementation of PBC in the rest of the state approximately a year after its implementation in Chicago. Using this approach of observational research improves our confidence in the *internal* validity of PBC as a child welfare intervention (see Chapter 7, this volume). In addition, the replication of the PBC model in another city increases our confidence in the *external* validity of the model by comparing the before-and-after results of the results-oriented system in different policy contexts and at different time-periods.

Before and After: Chicago

As discussed earlier in this chapter, the permanency outlook for a child entering the foster care system during the early 1990s in Chicago was

bleak. Systemwide data for the city and surrounding Cook County suburbs pointed to a growing length of stay for children, suggesting that
approximately half of the children could expect to spend nearly 8 years
in the system before achieving permanence or aging out of the system. Put
in other terms, the rate of annual permanency discharges to children ever
served during 1997 was 11% (this includes both relative care and family
foster care). Previous years hovered in the same range. The permanency
rate in 1996 was 9% and in 1995 it was 10% (Illinois Department of
Children and Family Services, 2002). It was this kind of anemic performance at the back-end of the foster care system that made it difficult to
"right-size" the system back to the relatively stable caseload levels of the
mid-1980s.

Contributing to the costs of an over-subscribed foster care system was
the growing fiscal pressure from the more restrictive and high-priced
parts of the substitute care system including specialized or therapeutic
foster care and residential care. During fiscal year 1997, approximately
15% of children in foster care placements moved to these higher-end and
more costly placements (Illinois Department of Children and Family
Services, 2001). The inability of the foster care system to stabilize the care
of children within relative or family foster care threatened to impose an
enormous financial liability on an already resource-strained child welfare
system.

Contract Objectives

As previously discussed, the performance contract designed for foster
care in Chicago sought two basic outcomes: an increase in the number of
children leaving relative care and family foster care for permanent placements (either through reunification, adoption, or subsidized guardianship[12]) and a reduction in the number of children moving from relative
care and family foster care to higher levels of care such as therapeutic
foster care, group homes, or residential care. The permanence benchmark
was fixed at 25% and the contract limited moves to higher levels of care to
8% of the beginning caseload. In numerical terms, the expectation for
every caseload of 24 children was 6 permanencies and 2 step-ups or
step-outs. The key stipulation was that each provider was also obligated
to accept a total of 33% of their contracted caseload in new referrals. This
translated into 8 new referrals for each 24 children in the starting caseload.
This referral agreement was the key element driving the incentive to meet
the performance benchmarks designated in the contract. In this way, the
flow out of the contract through permanence (6 children) and through
movement (2 children), was balanced with the flow into the contract
(8 new referrals), to attain equilibrium. If benchmarks were not met,
agencies began to lose money because more children entered care than
exited.

Savings Reinvestments

The basic assumption underpinning the Chicago and Philadelphia contracting structures is that the alignment of financial incentives with desired results will drive improvements in overall child welfare service delivery. Although initial investments are made in anticipation of real improvements in system performance, it is important to understand how the contracting structure permits both up-front investment and the potential for both the public and private sectors to recoup savings associated with improved performance.

There is a fairly complex interplay between the savings generated by various aspects of performance-based contracting, but for explanatory purposes, it is best to break it down into three parts:

- *Permanence increases from baseline to contracted standards.* By using the PBC mechanism, both the Illinois DCFS and the Philadelphia Department of Human Services (DHS) were able to calculate and capture the savings from improved permanence, which could then be reinvested in more services in a richer contract structure. The public agency could be confident in the savings calculations because the private agencies were at risk for not performing up to required levels: the cost of failing to improve performance would not be absorbed by the public agency with additional administrative funding.
- *Permanence increases above contracted standards.* Although private agencies took on the risk of performing up to the new contracted levels, they also gained the benefit from performing above those levels. If they beat performance targets, they effectively received additional funding for each child remaining on their caseload (they served fewer children, but the administrative payments remained unchanged from the original contracted caseload).
- *Intake changes:* Although the public sector had reduced its risk by shifting some of it to the private sector for performance on permanence and stability, it remained at risk for intake (which it controlled through the decisions to investigate, substantiate maltreatment and, if necessary, place the child in foster care). If intake increased, performance contracts would cost the public sector more (as would be the case under per diem payments). However, if intake decreased, PBC presented the public sector with a straightforward mechanism to capture savings from that decrease. As illustrated previously in Figure 10.1, even with a considerable drop in the number of new relative care cases following HMR reform in 1995, the cross-sectional caseload remained constant because the number of children achieving permanence fell

as the number of new entries fell. PBC, with its emphasis on managing case flow and outcomes, allowed Illinois DCFS to contract with an expectation that if intake declined, less capacity would be required by the end of the fiscal year, and contracts would shrink accordingly over the course of the year. This is another way the public sector can capture savings.

Table 10.1 illustrates the case flow dynamic from Cook County's relative foster care program—the first wave of PBC in Illinois—which was implemented in fiscal year 1998 (FY98). As can be seen, the FY98 standards for permanence were significantly higher than the FY97 actual performance. This difference generated the savings that were re-invested back into the contracts in the form of increased resources. Although the private agencies as a whole did not meet their permanency performance targets in the first year, they did significantly increase permanence over FY97 and some agencies did exceed their targets and capture additional savings. In subsequent years, more and more agencies beat their goals and, as a result, nearly doubled their payment rate.

Even though the agencies did not meet their permanency goals in aggregate for FY98, for the first time in a decade the overall caseload decreased. This was because of the combination of intake decreases and permanency increases and as a result, the public sector captured savings. By beginning the following year with a caseload of 2500 fewer children, Illinois DCFS generated annualized administrative savings of approximately $12.5 million. PBC continues to drive results in Illinois. By September 2008, the relative foster care caseload in Cook County had dropped to 2584. This generated millions in savings that were used to further reduce caseload standards in the private sector (from 25 children per 1 case manager to 15:1) and redeployed into other services within the child welfare system.

Association or Causation

After PBC was announced in March 1997 for children in relative care (see B in Figure 10.4), the number of children exiting the relative care program in

TABLE 10.1   Caseflow Dynamic from Cook County HMR Program

			Contracted Exits				
	Beginning Caseload	New Referrals	Permanent	Step-ups	Other Exits	Total Exits	Ending Caseload
FY97 Actual	23,987	5875	2209	3094	700	6003	23,859
FY98 Standards	23,859	7632	5724	1908	N/A	7632	23,859
FY98 Projections	23,859	5875	5724	1908	N/A	7632	21,335
FY98 Actual	23,851	4218	4036	1955	878	6869	21,200

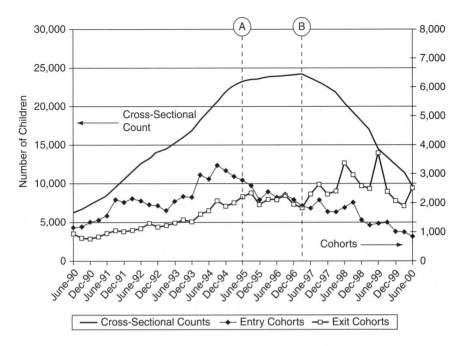

Figure 10.4 Post-PBC caseflow dynamics in relative care program, city of Chicago and surrounding Cook County suburbs.

Cook County exceeded the number entering relative care for the first time. After 3 years, the relative foster care program in Cook County had dropped from 24,195 children in March 1997 to 11,484 in March 2000. The permanency rate during this period increased from 7% for the four quarters preceding March 1997 to 32% for the four quarters preceding March 2000. Some private agencies experienced remarkable gains in performance, with one agency going from zero permanencies in 1997 to 20% by the end of 1998. Another agency achieved similar gains moving from 3% in 1997 to 23% by the end of the 1998 state fiscal year. Although only fully observable several years later, the median length of stay for children entering care after the implementation of performance contracting was cut from 44 months in FY94 to 26 months by FY 2000 (Illinois Department of Children and Family Services, 2001). Although these examples show agencies falling short of the contract benchmark of 24%, most agencies more than doubled previous performance, and many met the 24% standard the first year (thus tripling the previous year's average performance) proving that the targeted level of performance was achievable.

Private agencies and the system as a whole saw similar success with respect to placement stability. The number of children leaving relative care contracts to higher levels of care was cut nearly in half—a drop from 15% to 8% by the end of 1998. In part resulting from PBC, although not exclusively, in the 10 years since the inception of PBC, relative care caseloads have declined in Chicago by 89%, from 24,000 in 1996 to under 3000 in 2007. Although the association between PBC and caseload decline is strong, the question of causation cannot be confidently answered with these data alone.

Internal Validity: Staggered Implementation

The sharp upsurge in permanencies after the announcement of PBC for relative care is strongly suggestive of a cause-and-effect relationship. But, many other changes were underway during this time, such as the passage of the Adoption and Safe Families Act (ASFA) of 1997 and the implementation of the Illinois subsidized guardianship waiver demonstration (see Chapter 7, this volume). These other initiatives are competing explanations for the turnaround in caseload and permanency trends in Illinois. Perhaps the rise in permanence after the announcement of PBC is only a coincidence. But, confidence in the internal validity of PBC as a causal factor in performance improvement is bolstered by the staggered implementation of PBC a year later for the relative care program in downstate Illinois and non-related foster care in Chicago.

Figure 10.5 displays the caseload dynamics for the relative care program in the downstate Illinois counties. Though not as dramatic as in Cook

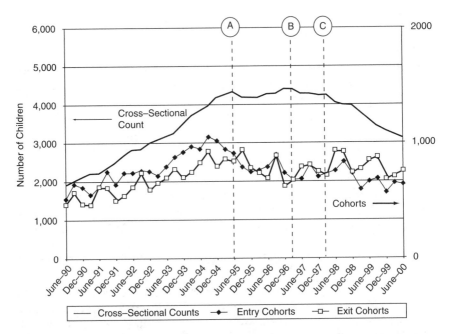

Figure 10.5 Pre- and Post-PBC case flow dynamics in the relative foster care program, downstate, Illinois.

County, the decline in entries into relative care in anticipation of the implementation of Relative Care Reform (A) is also discernable in the trend lines. But unlike the trend lines for the relative care program in Chicago, there is no sustained jump in exits during the four quarters following the Chicago announcement of PBC (B). Only after the implementation of PBC for the relative foster care program in downstate counties (C) do we see evidence of an excess of exits over entries. If federal or other statewide policies or other changes such as the state economy were driving relative care trends in Chicago, we should have seen an analogous response in downstate counties. The fact the relative care caseload did not decline until after the implementation of PBC in downstate counties provides compelling evidence for the internal validity of the efficacy of PBC in improving permanency performance.

Similarly, Figure 10.6 shows no evidence of a drop in the non-related foster care caseload in Chicago between points B and C when the relative foster care program in Chicago declined precipitously. Again, it is only after PBC was implemented for the non-related foster care program (C) that we see a change, albeit delayed, in caseload dynamics. The Illinois DCFS' decision to stagger implementation of PBC by geographical site and program type enabled state policymakers to evaluate the efficacy of the intervention in a way that across-the-board implementation would have left up in the air.

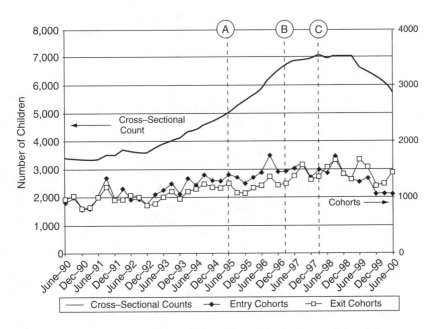

Figure 10.6 Pre- and Post-PBC case flow dynamics in the traditional foster care program, Cook County, Illinois.

External Validity: Philadelphia

Unlike Chicago, the Philadelphia DHS did not face a set of immediate pressures related to caseload growth and runaway budget deficits. Still, an examination of their data revealed performance opportunities similar to Illinois' in terms of permanence and placement stability that Philadelphia's leadership was interested in pursuing through a new contracting arrangement with providers.[13] On the permanency front, existing data from 2003 revealed that nearly one third (28%) of all children in care had been in care for more than four years. Data from 2001 to 2003 also showed that the over-all permanency performance for the system had flat-lined below 30%. Strikingly, even with permanence rates well above Illinois[14]; performance levels for adoption and the lack of a permanency option similar to subsidized guardianship suggested that with changes, better performance was possible. On the stability front, Philadelphia faced dynamics similar to those in Illinois. Data on the frequency moves of children leaving foster care placements for higher levels of care showed rates that were higher than what the provider community or DHS were comfortable with. The similarity in performance opportunities created an opening for the replication of the PBC model in Philadelphia, albeit with different permanency benchmarks.

Contract Objectives

The contract sought to increase the number of children leaving relative care and family foster care for permanent placements lasting a year or longer (either through reunification, adoption, or permanent legal custody[15]) and to reduce the number of children moving from foster care to higher levels of care, such as therapeutic foster care, group homes, or residential care. Because of historically high performance in the area of reunification and a new permanence option (permanent legal custodianship), the benchmark for permanency was fixed at 38%, meaning 38% of the contracted caseload was expected to move to permanent placements during the fiscal year. The contract also limited moves to higher levels of care to no more than 15% of the contracted caseload (the level for allowed movement was twice as high as in Chicago). Finally, the contract stipulated that each provider was obligated to accept a total of 46% of their contracted caseload in new referrals.

Results

- Philadelphia very quickly registered increased performance. As can be seen in Figure 10.7, in the first full year of implementation, permanency was almost double the FY02 rate (the last full fiscal year before PBC) and instability was down 47%. In the first three full years of implementation, the rate of permanencies increased 124%.

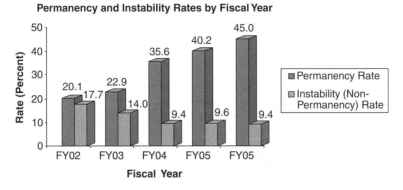

Figure 10.7 Pre- and Post-PBC permanency and instability in Philadelphia foster care (relative and unrelated). PBC was implemented midway through FY03.

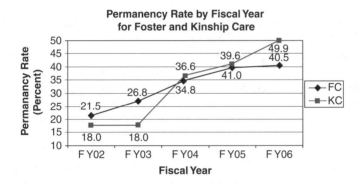

Figure 10.8 Permanency rate for foster and kinship care in Philadelphia, PA.

It is also interesting to note that under PBC, performance was higher in relative foster care than non-related foster care, both for permanence and for instability. This runs counter to the often held notion that relative care performs at a lower level than non-related foster care. These differences can be seen in Figures 10.8 and 10.9.

Results Beyond the Outcomes

From a system management perspective, the structure of performance contracting in Chicago and Philadelphia was invested with a very powerful tool to motivate those providers who failed to perform. In Chicago, by the middle of the first year, data on referrals for relative care made it clear that there would be too few referrals to keep all contractual agents open for new intake. Although shrinking the size of the foster care system is a stated goal of policymakers, shrinking private agencies or eliminating public sector service jobs is a difficult undertaking. The Illinois DCFS

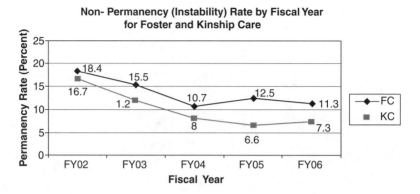

Figure 10.9 Instability rate for foster and kinship care in Philadelphia, PA. PBC was implemented midway through FY03.

announced that referrals for the second half of the contract year would be awarded to the top performers in the system and remaining providers would see their contracts decreased. Using the market pricing (achievement) principle (see Chapter 2, this volume) in this way enabled the system to adjust capacity instantly to meet the decreased service need. Moreover, providers affected by this hold on new referrals were able to make program adjustments appropriate to the size of their contract reduction. Why is this important? One of the biggest challenges in right-sizing a child welfare system is preserving the provider base of exemplary performers and concentrating the reduction in capacity on the least performing parts of the system. Many jurisdictions must deal with political strong-arming and cronyism that stymie plans to implement such reductions, which slow down shrinkage of the system as a whole. Often times, if cuts are made at all, they are across the board cuts where each provider is cut by the same percent. This means good providers face the same risk as poor providers in getting smaller as the system declines. In our opinion, this is not in the best interest of either groups of principals—taxpayers or children.

Limitations

Despite these gains, the performance-based contracts used in Chicago and Philadelphia were criticized (then and now) on three primary fronts: (a) failing to evaluate placement stability more inclusively; (b) using the same permanency benchmark for each provider; and (c) using a rotational referral system for quasi-randomization of new cases.

Stability

The performance contracts used in Chicago initially looked at placement stability through the lens of moves to a higher level contract or to a new agency rather than any new placement. From a child perspective, it was fair to criticize the contract's failure to discourage lateral placement moves within the agency. It merely measured these types of placement moves, and in this regard PBC was like other contracts. The process of deciding what to reward, and what to penalize is a fundamental part of any performance framework. But, the success of the contract necessarily entails prioritizing the range of outcomes and making decisions about how best to balance what is possible with what would be ideal. Through the negotiating process, it was decided to hold agencies accountable for moves outside the PBC contract, but to allow them the flexibility to change the placements of children within the contract. As PBC evolved over the years in Chicago, agencies were held accountable for all placement moves.

Consistent Benchmarks

The directive that one simple permanency benchmark should apply to all providers highlights an important question: Is the work too complex and individuated to be reduced to a common permanency or stability standard? This was addressed during the interest-based negotiations with providers in a few ways. First, an analysis was done on an agency-by-agency basis about the characteristics of children in their caseloads. The private agencies agreed that the differences between their caseloads for the levels of care covered by PBC (relative and traditional foster care) were not significant. Second, through rotational assignment, every agency would get a representative mix of children as new referrals, that is, no agency would have an unfair advantage through creaming the "easy" cases. Third, the concept of a level-playing field was very important to providers, particularly for minority owned agencies, some of which felt they had not been treated fairly in the past. Having different performance expectations for different agencies, for any reason,[16] was a non-starter for many participating in the negotiations. In addition, the benchmarks that were used were relatively easy to understand, an important consideration for a field that has historically been numbers averse.

Rotational Assignment

There has also been some criticism of the model that referrals are made to agencies on a no decline basis and that the entire system is not searched for the best placement "match." There are a few different aspects of this issue to consider. First, for relative care, which is where PBC started, there is no placement matching because the children are already placed with a relative prior to agency assignment. Second, as stated in the previous point, it was important that the referral system was fair to all providers; it was agreed through negotiation with the agencies that a quasirandomized referral system was fairest system of case allocation. Furthermore, in a system that was overwhelmed and did not have sufficient foster care capacity, the idea of placement matching was more illusory that real.

Third, for the first time, agencies were able to select the areas of the city/ county from which their referrals would come. Fourth, also for the first time, siblings who came into care at different times were assigned to the same agency to facilitate placing siblings together and consolidate case management responsibilities. Fifth, resources were put in foster care contracts so they could begin to serve children right away, thus limiting the need to place children at the shelter upon entry. Sixth, a web-based system was created to confidentially list children who needed placements to help facilitate placement matching among foster homes in different agencies. We would not propose that the PBC referral system is perfect or that it cannot be improved upon, but, for the reasons just listed, it is clear to us that it is better than the system it replaced.

Ongoing Discussions

It is important to note that signing a performance-based contract is more a beginning than an end. In Chicago and Philadelphia, the interest-based negotiations that contributed to the design of PBC continued after its implementation. This was very important because there was a great deal of system learning that was necessary, and problems to solve, to ensure PBC was a success. In his article "Goal-Based Learning and the Future of Performance Management," Donald Moynihan states:

> The weakness of most state MFR[17] systems lies between the points of dissemination of the data (which is done well) and use (the ultimate purpose, which is done poorly).... The gap between dissemination and use occurs partly because of an absence of routines in which data are examined and interpreted—learning forums. Learning forums are routines that encourage actors to closely examine information, consider its significance and decide how it will effect future action. (Moynihan, 2005, p. 205)

The use of performance data and the resolution of problems, some of which were highlighted by the data, others which came forward through other channels, was an important component of the coordination of different agency models and the reconciliation of contrasting management philosophies. The usual resistance of fiduciary models to the use of data and incentives to manage agency risks was overcome in PBC because the performance data was all of a sudden very important. In addition to the tie to dollars, published rankings of providers' performance were important because peer-reputations were at stake. Another problem that attention to data overcame was the typical underinvestment made by agencies (public and private) in getting the data accurate and reliable. Again, because dollars are attached to the performance data, it quickly became very important to both provider agencies and public sector contract managers that the data were valid. Because of this, a great deal of time was spent reconciling the data to make sure it accurately reflected agency performance.

Drawing from management expert Peter Senge, Moynihan identifies the elements of learning forums as follows:

- Routine event
- Ground rules to structure dialogue
- Non-confrontational approach to avoid defensive reaction
- Collegiality and equality among participants
- Diverse set of organizational actors responsible for producing the outcomes under review
- Dialogue centered, with dialogue focused on organizational goals
- Quantitative knowledge that identifies successes and failures, including goals, targets, outcomes, and points of comparison, is shared
- Experiential knowledge of processes and work conditions that explain success, failures and the possibility for innovation is shared
- Members wiling to raise the most pressing organizational issues for dialogue

Although not referred to as "learning forums" at the time, in practice these are the characteristics of the interest based negotiations, ongoing implementation, and performance management discussions for PBC.

Summary

The conversations around results-oriented accountability and performance-based contracting in child welfare will likely continue to develop and shape the work well into the future. Indeed, as more and more jurisdictions confront the challenges of changing caseloads, increased oversight, financial constraints, and the ever-present expectation of doing more with less, the need for innovative ideas which bind pay and performance will likely expand. The model used in Chicago and Philadelphia highlight some important lessons in this pursuit.

First, the right performance framework needs to be paired with the right environment. The simple idea that performance needs to improve seems to do little to actually drive outcomes that lead to real improvement. The successes in Chicago and Philadelphia point to the importance of linking a broader set of system goals to very clear outcomes. This is a very basic point, but it bears emphasis because it is often missed. Understanding the performance opportunities for a particular jurisdiction and figuring out exactly what success means for the system as a whole is an important part of pairing the right strategy with the right context.

Second, incentives matter. Prior to PBC, public and private service providers saw themselves as diligent, effective advocates for children. However, in relation to outcomes the providers agreed were paramount (permanence and stability), the data told a different story. More than this, conversations about data evolved into conversations about system barriers and underresourced activities (such as a limited number of judges to hear permanency petitions and a lack of permanency workers and reunification services), which proved vital in building a system capable of improved performance. What had been accepted limitations shrugged off under the old system, became unacceptable once performance on outcomes mattered. This resulted in the system collectively addressing and resolving challenges that had been left to fester for years. Once the requisite capacity was developed to take on the work, PBC reinforced performance in an important way: explicitly linking the consequences for failing to perform and the benefits for exceeding performance expectations in the contract and payment structure. In this way, PBC in Chicago and Philadelphia was able to align incentives and outcomes in way that fundamentally changed the work undertaken in the field.

Although PBC is examined in this chapter with a distinct point of view—namely that performance improvements in foster care need a powerful engine to drive change—the broader lessons have potential implication in a vast array of contracting relationships between government agencies and social service providers. Ideally, these ideas can give sufficient power to as yet untested strategies designed to produce results in other aspects of services to children and families.

Notes

1. For references to other performance contracting models, see Quality Improvement Center on the Privatization of Child Welfare Services (2006); Westat & Chapin Hall Center for Children (2002); Wulczyn (2005); Friedman (1995); and Hollingworth and Roth (2006). For additional information about performance contracting efforts in specific locations, see Figgs and Ashlock (2001) on Kansas, and Meezan and McBeath (2003) and Meezan and McBeath (2008) on Michigan.
2. In the interest of full disclosure, it is worth noting that the authors had significant involvement in the design and implementation of the PBC models used in Chicago and Philadelphia. This chapter is based on that experience. The model was conceived of by Joe Loftus in 1996, who was then the Executive Deputy Director of the Illinois Department of Children and Family Services.
3. Most contracts in child welfare are input and process oriented with payments based on units of service provided. For placement services (foster care) these are often called per diems.
4. Two papers that discuss the challenges of applying managed care in child welfare are Malloy (1995), and Feild (1996).
5. All the data generated by the public sector was shared with the private sector so they could make choices based on the best data available. This sort

of transparency builds trust and is an important component of the successful design and implementation of PBC.

6. A problem with most bonus structures is that they are usually distributed at the end of the year. This is problematic because: (1) it does not facilitate upfront investment in the capacity to improve performance; (2) it creates incentive to achieve outcomes at the end of the year as opposed to the beginning; and (3) they are often structured in a way that holds agencies harmless for not improving performance. In combination, this means that agencies are less likely to invest their own resources up front for the possibility of securing bonus payments at the end of the year. It is less risky for them to do nothing different. The incentives built into Chicago's and Philadelphia's PBCs were designed to address these problems.

7. Permanence is defined in order of preference as reunification, adoption, or subsidized guardianship, but each carries equal weight contractually.

8. This is important for the well-being of the child, but also has an impact on the likelihood of achieving permanence for a child because children who have less stable placement experiences are less likely to find permanent homes, in part because some types of permanent arrangements (adoption and guardianship) are most likely to come from foster caregivers with whom the child has bonded.

9. The contract structures that existed prior to PBC in Chicago and Philadelphia were very similar to those that exist today in most systems.

10. The payments to foster parents fluctuate based upon days of care.

11. The length of stay of children in the system can be set shorter by increasing the case flow ratio of new cases to starting caseload or set longer by decreasing the ratio. In addition, this creates an incentive to move children to permanence early in the timeframe so as to capture as much savings as possible. For per-diem contracts with traditional bonus payments, there is incentive to achieve permanency at the end of a review period to get payment most of the year for the child in care, but still get credit for permanence. This contributes to the tendency in many jurisdictions to have a rush to permanence at the end of the year.

12. Through a federal IV-E waiver project, Illinois was able to use IV-E dollars to provide subsidies for children leaving substitute care to permanent legal guardianship (see Chapter 7, this volume).

13. The Illinois PBC model was awarded the Innovations in American Government Award in 2000. With that award came funding to replicate the model. This was used as seed funding, matched by Philadelphia DHS, to facilitate the analysis of the system in Philadelphia to determine the applicability of the model

14. In part, this might result from the fact that worker caseload was about half the level of Chicago's at the start of PBC.

15. Similar to legal guardianship, permanent legal custodianship (PLC) allows the child welfare case to be closed once a caregiver agrees to assume full responsibility for the child. The caregiver receives a subsidy of the same amount they received as a foster parent.

16. Statistical analysis of caseload characteristics and/or past performance have been used to set differential agency performance targets in other locations.

17. MFR = Managing For Results

References

Baker, G. (1992). Incentive contracts and performance measurement. *Journal of Political Economy, 100*(3), 598–614.

Beck, U. (1992). *Risk society: A new modernity.* Newbury Park, CA: SAGE Publications.

Behn, R. (2004). Performance leadership: 11 better practices that can ratchet up performance, *Managing For Performance and Results Series, IBC Center for the Business of Government.*

Buchanan, A. (1988). Principal/agent theory and decision making in health care. *Bioethics, 2*(4), 317–331.

Feild, T. (1996). *Managed Care and Child Welfare: Are they Compatible?* Westminster, MD: Institute for Human Services Management.

Figgs, J., & Ashlock, S. (2001). Family preservation/foster care/adoption: Kansas public/private partnership initiative. Honorable mention in the Pioneer Institute 2001 Better Givernment Competition. Retrieved February 23, 2006 from the Pioneer Institute for Public Policy Research Institute Web site: http://www.pioneerinstitute.org.pdf/bgc01_kansas.pdf.

Friedman, M. (1995). From outcomes to budgets: An approach to outcome-based budgeting for Family and Children's Services, Center for the Study of Social Policy. Retrieved October 24, 2000 from Center for the Study of Social Policy Web site: http://www.cssp.org/kd13.htm.

Hirsch, G. (1994, May/June). Mastering the transition to capitation. *Healthcare Forum Journal,* 89–97.

Hollingworth, A., & Roth, J. (2006). Implementing performance management and enabling partnership in child welfare. Retrieved June 3, 2006 from the University of Pennsylvania Fels Institute Child Welfare Partnership Web site: http://www.fels.upenn.edu/FGRS/Implementing%20Performance%20Management%20ans%20Enabling%20Partnership%20in%20Child%20Welfare%20-%20March%202006.pdf.

Illinois Department of Children and Family Services. (2001). *Signs of progress in child welfare reform.* Springfield, IL: Author.

Illinois Department of Children and Family Services. (2002). *Signs of progress in child welfare reform.* Springfield, IL: Author.

Illinois Department of Children and Family Services. (2006). *Signs of progress in child welfare reform.* Springfield, IL: Author.

Kiser, E. (1999). Comparing varieties of agency theory in economics, political science, and sociology: An illustration from state policy implementation. *Sociological Theory, 17*(2), 146–170.

Lipsky, M. (1980). *Street-level bureaucracy: The dilemmas of individuals in the public service.* New York: Russell Sage Foundation.

Malloy, M. (1995). *Managed care: A primer for families and consumers.* Arlington, VA: National Alliance for the Mentally Ill.

McBeath, B., & Meezan, W. (2008) Market-based disparities in foster care provision. *Research in Social Work Practice, 18*(1), 27–41.

Meezan, W., & McBeath, B. (2003). Moving to managed care in child welfare: First results from the evaluation of Wayne County foster care pilot initiative. Retrieved November 10, 2008 from the University of Michigan School of Social Work Web site: http://gpy.ssw.umich.edu/projects/foster/Moving_to_Managed_Care_in_Child_Welfare.pdf.

Meezan, W., & McBeath, B. (2008). Market-based disparities in foster care outcomes. *Children and Youth Services Review, 30,* 388–406.

Moynihan, D. (2005). Goal-based learning and the future of performance management. *Public Administration Review, 65*(2), 203–216.

Quality Improvement Center on the Privatization of Child Welfare Services. (2006). Literature review on performance-based contracting and quality assurance. Last accessed November 2, 2008 at http://www.uky.edu/SocialWork/qipcw/documents/QICPCWPBCLiteratureReview.pdf.

Schorr, L. (1994). The case for shifting to results-based accountability. Center for the Study of Social Policy. Downloaded October 24, 2000 from http://www.cssp.org.kd31.htm.

Shott, B. (2007). Who do you think we are? *The New York Times,* Op-Ed Sunday February 25, 15.

Westat & Chapin Hall Center for Children. (2002). State Innovations in child welfare financing. Retrieved August 1, 2005, from the U.S. Department of Health and Human Services Secretary for Planning and Evaluation, http://aspe.hhs.gov/hsp/CW-financing03/report.pdf.

Wulczyn, F. (2005). Linking outcomes and funding: Core challenges and approaches. Retrieved November 28, 2008, from http://www.chapinhall.org/article_abstract.aspx?ar=1394.

11

FOSTERING AND SUSTAINING UNIVERSITY/AGENCY PARTNERSHIPS

Joan Levy Zlotnik

Results-oriented accountability in public child welfare requires an immense array of knowledge and skills. Those working directly with children and families need to be experts in the evidence-supported interventions that effectively address the multitude of problems encountered by families. The cycle of results-oriented accountability put forth in this book envisions that agencies have access to program evaluation and quality improvement staff with the necessary expertise to create and evaluate policies and programs that improve results for children and families. In spite of the increased complexity of the outcome measures required under the Adoption and Safe Families Act (ASFA), the usefulness of data mining, and the growing sophistication of data analysis techniques, public agencies still find it difficult to justify the large number of highly specialized and expensive staff needed to perform these accountability functions. State budget decision makers do not always appreciate the need for such additional staff, particularly if such hires are not engaged in direct service provision. Organizational head count frequently becomes an issue and its reduction provides a mechanism for controlling costs in times of tight state budgets.

The barriers to establishing research, evaluation, and quality improvement departments in public child welfare agencies have prompted public administrators to seek out this expertise and to encourage its development by establishing and supporting partnerships with universities. These research partnerships also emerge from a more general desire to forge tighter linkages between universities and child welfare departments in the training of students and staff for public service careers.

University/agency partnerships are critical components in helping states address their recruitment and retention problems that impact the quality of services and outcomes for children and families (Government Accountability Office, 2003). In two surveys by the American Public Human Services Association (American Public Human Services Association, 2005; Cyphers, 2001) state administrators reported that university/agency partnerships are highly or somewhat effective in addressing staff recruitment and retention. Schools of social work report that their training partnerships lead to research opportunities and vice versa (IASWR, 2008; Zlotnik & Cornelius, 2000).

More recent interest in establishing research partnerships with universities to help meet public accountability demands goes beyond the practice knowledge needed to improve curricula. As discussed in Chapter 3, it involves the creation of technical communities of scholars, researchers, practitioners, and administrators who can deal collaboratively with policy problems, oversee related research, and monitor the quality of the partnership's work on these activities. A critical function of these partnerships is to help bridge the gap between the scientific rigor and significance demanded by scholars and researchers with the value orientations and policy relevance expected by practitioners and administrators.

Misunderstandings over the evidentiary power of randomized experiments, ethical concerns about withholding services from control groups, the importance of publications to ensure knowledge development and knowledge transfer, and the political risks of disclosing negative findings can quickly undermine the trust necessary to sustain such cooperative arrangements. It is therefore useful to explore the benefits of university/agency collaborations and to examine the characteristics, purposes, models, and funding sources for partnerships between child welfare agencies and universities. In addition, many of the obstacles that have impeded university/agency training collaborations in the past can also affect research partnerships. The historical and policy contexts in which they have developed, and the challenges that they face must also be considered.

Developing Partnerships

Child welfare agencies and universities are organizations with different missions, cultures, and systems of incentives. To blend the activities of these organizations requires an understanding of their differences and what constitutes a good partnership. The Council on Social Work Education's (CSWE) Developing Human Services Partnerships Project, funded by the Ford Foundation in the early 1990s articulated the following core principles that address attributes of successful partnerships that can support both their development and maintenance (Zlotnik, 1993, p. 10).

These attributes were reinforced by more recent work focusing on research partnerships (IASWR, 2008):

Attributes of successful partnerships:

- Trusting relationships
- Long-term commitment
- Committed leaders
- Benefits for all collaborators
- Common interests and objectives.

Harris (1996) examined the formation of education and training partnerships and found a typical sequence of events in the development of university-agency partnerships. These also can hold true for research partnerships:

- A precipitating event or circumstance creates the initial interest in partnership development.
- Key leaders from social work education and public agencies become involved in negotiations.
- The purpose and the vision of the partnership are articulated.
- Needed resources are identified.
- Specific tasks and timelines are delineated; issues are resolved and resources are obtained;
- The partnership is implemented.

Precipitating Event

Various factors have precipitated partnership development by child welfare agencies including;

- Class action lawsuits and consent decrees;
- High profile child deaths or agency's inappropriate actions;
- A commitment to improving worker training and competence;
- Legislative mandates to improve accountability, hire new workers, and/or to reduce caseloads

For example, although the University of Maryland School of Social Work and the state's Department of Human Resources (DHR) have a long history of collaborating on research and training, this was further reinforced by legislative action. In 2006, the *Maryland Child Welfare Accountability Act* passed, requiring the Maryland Department of Human Resources (DHR) to develop and implement a system of accountability to measure the efficiency and effectiveness of certain child welfare services. The University of Maryland School of Social Work has a Memorandum of Understanding (MOU) with DHR to measure child welfare services, collect and analyze data, provide guidance on the quality assessment process, and provide reports and analyses to the state (University of Maryland, 2008).

Generally, universities may initiate a partnership to fulfill their mission of public service; engage in research and public education for a particular client population (e.g., children and families), or implement strategies that fulfill the historic child welfare/social work links. Agencies may reach out to universities to fulfill functions that they lack the staff, technical resources, or expertise to carry out, or to have a more independent entity gather information and provide reports (see previous chapter on performance contracting). The agency and university may also come together to take advantage of a source of funding (e.g., Title IV-E training funds) or specific grant opportunities. Beyond creating a pool of new or better trained workers with a commitment to child welfare, partners can also help to guide policy change and service improvement and build, manage, and transfer knowledge through research, data analysis, program evaluation, and development of reports.

Key Leaders

Partnerships are created and strengthened by the involvement and commitment of the chief agency executive and a senior professor, dean/director or department chair. Because so much federal and state funding comes through the state agency, it is important that the agency head be committed to the partnership. University/agency partnerships have experienced changes and sometimes upheavals when the agency administrator changes and the new administrator has a different vision for achieving the tasks that were set out to be accomplished. In some instances, leaders in outside groups, such as the National Association of Social Workers (NASW) chapter or perhaps a legislator or legislative committee or foundation have helped to support the partnership and bring leaders together for a common goal. In Idaho, for example, the child welfare partnership efforts include Casey Family Programs, along with the state's Department of Health and Welfare and several universities; and, in Minnesota, the Bush Foundation played a role in launching partnership activities (IASWR, 2008).

Vision

Developing an agreed upon vision is a critical step in partnership development. It is important to create a win-win situation. Common understandings of goals for child welfare service delivery are often incorporated into this shared vision using terms like family-centered, child-focused, strength-based, and culturally responsive.

Resource Level

Harris (1996) notes that "no discernible national strategy guides the acquisition of funding for reprofessionalizing child and family services" (p. 14).

Neither are there specific federal funds to support research partnerships. Furthermore all partnerships are not funded in the same manner or via the same funding streams (IASWR, 2008; NAPCWA 2005,). The majority of child welfare university/agency education/training partnerships access Title IV-E training funds. In addition, the partnerships may receive other federal funds (e.g., Medicaid, TANF, Title XX, Title IV-B, Title IV-E administrative funds, and/or Child Abuse Prevention and Treatment Act) and/or state and foundation funds to support its activities. As indicated in Table 11.1, these same sources can support research partnerships (IASWR, 2008). When the university and state enter into a contract or an MOU regarding the partnership, the university partner may be unaware of the funding sources used by the state. Such funding might actually entail the pooling of a number of federal funding sources (See Partnership Funding Sources).

Private funds from national, regional or state foundations often are an important part of a partnership's resources. As previously noted, funding from the Bush Foundation helped to launch the Center for Advanced Studies in Child Welfare at the University of Minnesota. Initial funding from the Zellerbach Fund and the Ford Foundation helped to support the launching of the California Social Work Education Center (CalSWEC) at the University of California-Berkeley (CalSWEC, 2008). Foundations can also support valuable adjunctive functions for partnerships. For example, the Stuart Foundation's support of the UC-Berkeley Center for Social Services Research *California Child Welfare Performance Indicators Project* (http://cssr.berkeley.edu/ucb_childwelfare/) helps to fund the Web site and other dissemination efforts including travel for staff to professional meetings.

TABLE 11.1   Potential Federal Sources of Child Welfare Research Funding

- Title IV-B services funding (Parts 1 & 2)
- Title IV-E administration (50% match)
- Title IV-E training (75% match)
- Title IV-E waiver evaluations
- Child Abuse Prevention and Treatment Act (Parts 1 & 2)
- Discretionary grants from the Children's Bureau (e.g., Child welfare training, Adoption Opportunities, CAPTA)
- Discretionary research grants from the Centers for Disease Control and Prevention (CDC)
- Discretionary grants from the Substance Abuse and Mental Health Services Administration (SAMHSA)
- National Institutes of Health research grants, especially from the National Institute of Mental Health (NIMH), National Institute on Drug Abuse (NIDA), and National Institute on Child Health and Human Development (NICHD)
- Medicaid
- Department of Justice grant funding

In the development of partnerships, it is not unusual to seek outside technical assistance and consultation to identify funding sources and to develop strategies to maximize available resources. The complexity of the funding sources and the absence of a specific funding stream can require intricate knowledge of budgeting and the specific parameters of multiple federal programs and use of federal match to finance such efforts.

Task Identification

There is no specific model of task identification that is followed across states in developing its university/agency partnership. Some states have consortia of several universities that work together (e.g., Kentucky, Arkansas) and others have regional collaborations between service delivery regions and universities (Texas, Florida, and Louisiana). In Pennsylvania, the University of Pittsburgh coordinates both the statewide Title IV-E degree education program for agency staff and also delivers the state's child welfare training program. It has recently also expanded its partnership's research agenda (University of Pittsburgh, n.d.).

Some Title IV-E educational partnerships prioritize return to school of current staff to acquire advanced degrees, usually in social work, while others focus their IV-E partnership on attracting new social work students toward child welfare careers. A recent review of retention of Title IV-E educated child welfare workers highlighted the diversity of these IV-E programs (Zlotnik, DePanfilis, Daining, & Lane, 2005). Several partnerships have focused on attracting bi-lingual workers to agencies and others, for example, the University of Wisconsin, Green Bay, includes a focus on tribal child welfare activities.

Information gleaned from child welfare university/agency partnership Web sites found that some partnerships focus specifically on training, some focus on education, and others target a range of education, training, research, consultation, and evaluation tasks to be accomplished through the partnership. For example, the objectives of the Judith Granger Birmingham Center for Child Welfare at the University of Texas, Arlington are:

- To develop, conduct, and disseminate major research to address important policies and practice influencing the lives of children and families.
- To serve as a resource center to child welfare advocates, practitioners, and policy makers.
- To professionalize child welfare practice through the training of professional social workers for a career in child welfare services, and the development of a certification program for practitioners.
- To deliver competency-based training to child welfare practitioners to improve service delivery, and

- To provide assistance to, and promote collaboration among, national, state, and local public and private child welfare institutions. (UTA School of Social Work Judith Granger Birmingham Center for Child Welfare [2008]). (http://www2.uta.edu/ssw/ccw/)

The mission of the Ruth Young Center for Children and Families at the School of Social Work at the University of Maryland incorporates education, research, training and program development priorities, stating that its goal is: "To promote the safety, permanence and stability, and well-being of children, youth, and families in their communities through education and training, research and evaluation and best practice service programs." The work of this center is in the child welfare domain, whereas the School's Family Welfare Research and Training Center partners with the state of Maryland on welfare and child support research, training and policy development.

Barriers to Partnerships

Barriers to successful partnerships primarily arise from the differences in the nature of universities and child welfare organizations. Recognizing these differences from the beginning can help partners understand and manage them. Such barriers to successful collaborations may include:

- Differing organizational values
- Differing philosophies
- Differing reward systems
- Differing priorities
- Lack of institutional commitment for the long term.
- Differing time frames: The needs of agencies are often specific and immediate and the focus of academia is broader and not created to address a specific problem or concern.
- Concerns about the complexity of public child welfare practice: Faculty members may not be interested in developing practice applications or research projects in the complex settings that public agency practice involves.
- Inconsistencies in the recognition of and role for professional social work in public child welfare: Child welfare agencies frequently do not require an MSW or BSW degree for employment or advancement, providing limited incentive for social work graduates to seek jobs in those settings.
- Open contracting processes that require agencies to bid for services, making it difficult to develop a long-range relationship with a partnering university or consortia of universities.
- Absence of a specific federal funding stream for research and evaluation often precludes the development of a long-range strategy

because funding is made according to year to year contracts or through time-limited grants.
- Substantial time and resources are required on the part of both the agency and the university to establish and maintain collaborations, both at the leader level, and among the staff and faculty involved in the partnership activities (IASWR, 2008; Zlotnik, 1993).

Despite these barriers and challenges, however, universities and agencies do make strides to come together to address common concerns and to build partnerships.

Historical Context

The early roots of the social work profession and formation of child welfare agencies are intertwined (Child Welfare League of America, 1982; Zlotnik, 2002). Since at least the 1960s, social work education programs have played a key role in educating prospective child welfare workers, providing advanced degrees to current child welfare workers, providing pre-service and in-service training for agency employees and conducting research and evaluation activities (Zlotnik, 2002). Although the advocacy preceding the passage of the Adoption Assistance and Child Welfare Act of 1980 (AACWA) envisioned partnerships that would occur to implement the law, the change in the federal administration with the inauguration of Ronald Reagan, the withdrawal of draft regulations, the end of large scale Title XX training efforts, and the lack of technical assistance forestalled efforts to promote partnerships to achieve practice enhancements and improve outcomes for children and families (Zlotnik, 1998).

Historical Challenges

Child welfare agencies have reached out to universities, often in times of crisis, for assistance in dealing with growing caseloads, the impact of class action lawsuits, high media visibility resulting from child deaths, the high rates of substance abuse involved in cases of child abuse and neglect, high rates of staff turnover, a workforce sometimes ill equipped to meet the needs of these complex cases and the increasing accountability demands that strained quality improvement and program evaluation staff. However the universities' response to such outreach has not always been consistent and the outreach from the university to agencies has also not always been met with a positive response.

   History has shown that it is difficult for professional schools and state governments to sustain a partnership in the delivery of public child welfare services (Grossman, Laughlin, & Specht, 1992; Illinois Department of

Children and Family Services, 1995). This difficulty is reflective partly of the roots of many human services professions in the voluntary sector, which tended historically to distrust a large public role in the provision of child welfare services. It is also reflective of government's wariness of professional work which it has regarded as encouraging unnecessary and uncontrollable social service spending. This mutual suspicion was further reinforced by a divergence in conceptual orientation at the direct-practice level between professional schools, which typically trained practitioners for "soft-service," therapeutic interventions, and public departments, which frequently leaned toward "hard-service," environmental remedies. Because these tensions (e.g., individual treatment vs. social reform, clinical practice vs. policy analysis) also existed within the profession, the division periodically broke out into acrimonious conflict, especially during periods of social upheaval, e.g., World War I, the Depression, and the civil rights movement (Grossman et al., 1992).

It is now more than forty years since the latest schism between the individualistic approach of clinical work and the environmental approach of social reform frayed relations between professional schools and public social services. This schism was spurred on in large measure by anti-poverty reformers and radicalized students who condemned the therapeutic orientation of direct-practice workers for "blaming the victim." Bolstered by "social labeling" theory, which argued that professionals unintentionally create the very problems they are endeavoring to treat, some agencies initiated programmatic changes that sought to control public costs by "deinstitutionalizing" child placement and "deprofessionalizing" child welfare services (Illinois Department of Children and Family Services, 1995). These policies were reinforced by budgetary constraints that kept institutional placements from expanding, and public unionization that displaced professional credentials as the basis of worker protection and career mobility. With both the loss of therapeutic field placements in child welfare institutions and private agencies and the demise of professionalism in public child welfare services, professional schools and public agencies went their separate ways.

As stated in the proposal by the Illinois Department of Children and Family Services (1995) to establish the Children and Family Research Center at the University of Illinois:

> It wasn't until the mid-1980s that interest in a rapprochement between professional schools and public departments began to gain momentum nationwide. The deans of leading schools of social work reaffirmed their institutions' historic mission of serving vulnerable populations and made outreach efforts to public social service departments. At the same time, public child welfare administrators began arriving at the conclusion that the increasing complexity of child protection, placement, and permanency-planning services and the growing need for sophisticated treatment of child and family dysfunction required a more educated and skilled workforce than what

public unionization and departmental training alone could guarantee. Thus schools and public departments in California, Florida, Illinois, Washington, and elsewhere began hammering out agreements which sought to address the workforce needs of public child welfare services through social work education that was responsive to the mission and responsibilities of public departments. (Illinois Department of Children and Family Services, 1995, p. 3)

Fostering University/Agency Connections

In the late 1980s, a dialogue was renewed among the NASW, public child welfare administrators and deans of schools of social work (University of Southern Maine, 1987). One concern was worker preparation. For example, a national survey indicated that 28% of workers had a social work degree (Lieberman, Hornby, & Russell, 1988). NASW, working with the National Association of Public Child Welfare Administrators (NAPCWA), an affiliate of the American Public Human Services Association (APHSA), the Council on Social Work Education (CSWE) and individual deans and directors, and child welfare administrators, began to identify collaborative models and to track the availability of and access to sources of funding (i e., Title IV-B Section 426 discretionary grants and Title IV-E training entitlement funds) used to support partnerships. The U.S. Children's Bureau fostered technical assistance through a cooperative agreement with Florida International University (Briar, Hansen, & Harris, 1992) and also funded eleven five year child welfare training grants to educate social work students for child welfare practice, to pursue use of Title IV-E training funds, and to foster collaboration and partnerships. The expanded use of Title IV-E entitlement funds and more targeted discretionary training grant announcements under Title IV-B Section 426 funds seem to have achieved some success. Enhancements of partnerships focused on training and education as well as the provision of technical assistance across sites is reflected in more recent staffing data that indicates that close to 40% of child welfare workers have social work degrees (Barth, Lloyd, Christ, Chapman, & Dickinson, 2008).

According to a survey by CSWE, only 6 out of the 68 programs in 29 states that were receiving Title IV-E funds to support degree education in 1996 had begun to receive Title IV-E funding prior to 1991 (Zlotnik & Cornelius, 2000). For over a decade, these partnerships have flourished and about 40 states are involved in such university/agency efforts (CSWE, 2008). However the exact parameters of the partnerships change as leadership changes and as service delivery strategies change, e.g., the privatization of child welfare services in Kansas. These partnerships frequently:

- Prepare undergraduate and graduate students for public child welfare careers.

- Provide opportunities for current agency employees to return to school to acquire a child welfare relevant undergraduate (usually a BSW) or graduate (usually an MSW) degree.
- Develop and implement pre-service and in-service trainings.
- Undertake research, research synthesis, program evaluation, program development, and consultation efforts to test program models and to incorporate research findings into curricula, trainings and enhanced practice techniques.

National Technical Assistance and Information Exchange

The proliferation of partnerships between social work education programs and public child welfare agencies has stimulated ongoing strategies for the exchange of information, dissemination of research and evaluation findings and promotion of innovation diffusion efforts.

In the early to mid-1990s, the Ford Foundation supported the *Social Work Education and Public Human Services: Developing Partnerships* project at the Council on Social Work Education to catalogue and promote research, training and educational partnerships. The project developed several technical assistance documents (Harris, 1996; Zlotnik, 1997, 1993) to provide guidance to the field and also convened sessions at the CSWE Annual Program Meeting and Association of Social Work Baccalaureate Program Directors (BPD) conference and undertook collaborative activities with NASW, CSWE, NAPCWA, the Child Welfare League of America (CWLA) and the Children's Bureau.

National conferences and working seminars later emerged from this collaborative catalyst. The National Association of Deans and Directors of Schools of Social Work (NADD) developed a working committee with NAPCWA and cohosted a symposium focused on "Advancing Professional Education for Child Welfare Practice" (Ferguson, 2002).

More than 100 representatives of Title IV-E partnerships (mostly from schools of social work) convene annually at an all day meeting in advance of the Annual Program Meeting of the CSWE. And for several years there has been robust attendance at the Child Welfare Interest Group initiated at the Society for Social Work and Research (SSWR) Conference. A listserv and Web site (http://louisville.edu/kent/projects/iv-e) facilitate the on-going exchange of information providing listings of partnerships and their characteristics, federal Title IV-E policy guidance and research studies.

Fostering Strengthened Partnerships

After the passage of the Adoption and Safe Families Act of 1997, the Children's Bureau hosted an invitational meeting, *Changing Paradigms of Child Welfare Practice: Responding to Opportunities and Challenges* that brought together teams from several states representing academia and agency administrators to struggle with the impact of child welfare practice on policy and to examine partnership models. The Children's Bureau planned this collaboratively with NASW, NAPCWA, CSWE, and the CWLA. It led to a national meeting in 2000 on child welfare workforce issues and partnerships hosted by the Children's Bureau and a subsequent Children's Bureau-hosted 2005 Child Welfare Workforce Institute. This helped to strengthen the perceived value of partnerships for child welfare outcomes and to provide ideas for partnership development and enhancement.

Policy Imperatives: Accountability Principles and the Children and Family Service Review

The passage of ASFA in 1997 (P.L. 105-89) was a "precipitating event" for the creation and/or strengthening of agency/university partnerships. The focus of AFSA is on accountability for outcomes for children in child welfare and establishing time limits so that children do not languish in foster care. The Children's Bureau encouraged state and local agencies to implement new paradigms for good child welfare practice based on seven key principles:

- Children have the right to a fair chance in life and to the essentials of healthy development, including a sense of belonging, continuity of care, safety, nurturance, and access to opportunities to acquire basic social competence.
- Family-centered practice advances the overall objectives of establishing safe, stable, and permanent families to promote the well-being of children.
- The best care and protection for children can be achieved when service delivery focuses on developing and using the strengths of nuclear and extended families and communities.
- The values and customs of families from different cultures need to be acknowledged and valued, and service delivery, training, policy development and evaluation must be designed to be culturally competent and respectful.
- There is a sense of urgency in all child welfare services to ensure safety and a permanent placement for children.
- Training must provide information and direction regarding strategies and methods that promote high-quality service delivery to children and families.
- A strong network of both informal and formal community-based resources is necessary for prevention and early intervention in child abuse and neglect cases. (US Department of Health and Human Services, Administration for Children and Families, Children's Bureau, 2000).

These accountability demands and the child welfare service delivery principles require states to examine their data reporting and analysis systems, training curricula and competency of their child welfare staff. This stimulated new partnership activities, data analysis and reporting systems, training for workers, changes to practice methods and improvements to social work education child welfare curricula.

To further create a process for child welfare service assessment and improvements, in 2000, the Children's Bureau launched Child and Family Services Reviews (CFSR)—a process to assess states conformity with federal requirements for child protective, foster care, adoption, family preservation and family support, and independent living services. The two-stage process includes a statewide assessment and an onsite review of child and family service outcomes (safety, permanence, and well-being) and program systems. If states are found to be out of conformance on any of the seven outcomes or seven systemic factors that are reviewed they are required to submit a Program Improvement Plan (PIP) for approval and then to address the tasks outlined in the PIP (see Chapter 4, this volume).

Many of the PIPs address the need for increased worker expertise and improvements in agency policy and practice. At an August 2004 symposium hosted by the Institute for the Advancement of Social Work Research (IASWR) and NASW, federal staff, representatives of national organizations and university partnerships came together to examine the implications of the CFSR (see www.iaswresearch.org). Partnerships can be a component of the state's strategy to achieve improved outcomes, noting that:

- States with better training systems were also stronger in meeting standards;
- States find it valuable to include university partners as key stakeholders in both the CFSR and PIP development and implementation process;
- States should consider worker training strategies that bring workers to the job "ready to learn";
- There is a need to build child welfare leadership; and
- States and their university partners need to undertake on-going review of curricula for relevance (IASWR & NASW, 2004).

In several states, e.g., Pennsylvania, the university partner (the University of Pittsburgh) plays a substantial consulting role in the CFSR process, development of the PIP and works with the state toward implementation.

In 2003 and 2004, the University of Illinois Children and Family Research Center convened national organizations and state and university representatives to examine child welfare practice concerns regarding the complexities of consistently defining placement stability and the assessment of safety as a child welfare goal. These symposia, not only facilitated research/practice/education/policy linkages, but they also demonstrated the value of university/agency research partnerships. One outcome of these meetings was the stimulation of research partnerships in Ohio, Iowa, Missouri, and Los Angeles County (IASWR, 2008).

National Research Agenda Development

Recognizing the value of agency/university partnerships, the National Association of Public Child Welfare Administrators and the National Research Center on Child Maltreatment launched a region by region effort to develop a research agenda from the agency's perspective. The report details research needs addressing practice, program evaluation, policy, research synthesis and prognosis (NRCCM/NAPCWA, 2001). Despite the detailed agenda, which can stimulate agency-based research by university partners, there has been no targeted effort to implement the agenda or to review current research to assess new knowledge related to the agenda's questions.

Partnership Implementation

As noted previously, the implementation of university/agency partnerships takes many forms and provides benefits to both the university and the agency. The implementation of partnerships should be an on-going process that continues to evolve as new needs are identified or resources are accessed. In many states, the partnership might be implemented through a specific university-based center or a center that is a consortium of several universities. Partnership implementation can be effected by changes in leaders, funding, and policy. For example, a new agency director may wish to refocus partnership efforts from degree education to staff training, or vice versa, or may want to strengthen the research and consultation component. A governor's initiative to hire more child protective staff might stimulate an interest in developing or expanding a partnership with social work education programs to create a more formal pathway to educate and train the necessary workers.

In Los Angeles County, a research partnership was created among the five MSW programs and the Department of Children and Family Services. With initial county funding to support research studies that addressed the developed research agenda, tighter funding in subsequent years reduced the county's support. However, collaboration was maintained because of the work that had gone into supporting the initial partnership and partnered research efforts continued through funding by Casey Family Programs (IASWR, 2008).

A partnership initially focused on degree education or training, might later incorporate agency staff training and later expand its research collaborations as is the case with the University of Pittsburgh. The University of Maryland School of Social Work recently incorporated its child welfare research efforts together with its child welfare training and degree education programs under the auspices of the Ruth Young Center for Children and Families.

As part of its partnership with the state and county child welfare agencies, the Jordan Institute for Families at the University of North Carolina School of Social Work publishes a quarterly newsletter, *Practice Notes*, which synthesizes research findings to address child welfare practice strategies and to provide practice guidance to workers. Topics covered have included supervision, domestic violence, worker recruitment and retention and chronic neglect (http://ssw.unc.edu/fcrp/cspn/cspn.htm). The newsletter is distributed to all child welfare workers.

Research Partnerships

Although a primary focus of partnerships in social work education programs has been in the education and training realm, implementation of the Adoption and Safe Families Act (ASFA) requirements, increased availability of performance data, focus on measurable outcomes, and the expanded focus on the development of and delivery of evidence-informed interventions has fostered expanded attention to the creation and sustenance of research partnerships. This also results from the recognition that universities have research expertise and research personnel, a mission to develop and disseminate knowledge, access to technology and libraries, and a level of flexibility to implement research and evaluation activities that the agency itself might not possess. In addition, an external and neutral perspective that is respected by the legislature and other stakeholders when reporting findings and outcomes can be invaluable.

Such partnerships take many forms—from informal efforts to develop a shared research agenda as is the case in the state of Iowa, to formal partnerships that are funded through contractual-services arrangements as have occurred in Illinois, Minnesota, Texas, Florida, North Carolina, and California. In these more formal arrangements, most of the contractual work is published under center banners. Ownership of the contractual work is either under the sole proprietorship of the public department or joint-proprietorship of the university and the department. The relationship is typically time-limited and circumscribed by the terms of the contract that purchases specific products and services from the centers. There is little sharing of personnel between centers and departments.

There has been little examination of the characteristics of effective child welfare research partnerships or targeted technical assistance to help implement strategies to strengthen research partnerships. In 2008, IASWR received funding support from Casey Family Programs to identify existing strategies that result in strong child welfare research partnerships and to develop a toolkit that includes practical strategies to strengthen child welfare research partnerships. Casey Family Programs' efforts to catalyze service delivery enhancements, including its 2020 Vision (http://www.casey.org/About Casey/2020 strategy) recognized the value that such partnerships can have to improved foster care outcomes.

The IASWR initiative involved interviews with more than 40 stakeholders including research center directors, agency administrators and research staff, university faculty and deans; focus groups with multiple audiences; and two web-based questionnaires (for social work doctoral program directors and for child welfare researchers). *Strengthening University/Agency Research Partnerships to Enhance Child Welfare Outcomes: A Tool-kit for Building Research Partnerships* is available from www.iaswresearch.org. IASWR identified more than 30 child welfare research centers and research partnerships between public agencies and social work education programs through this process.

Although there is no one way that research is initiated and implemented, the creation of a formal structure to support research partnerships can help facilitate agency-based research efforts. It can highlight the importance of research to service outcomes and create a vetting process to ensure the feasibility, confidentiality, and human subjects protections of the research. A formal partnership can also clarify accountability and roles and responsibilities for each actor in the research process. The greatest barriers to child welfare research partnerships include those previously described. Another sticky issue is the potential and/or perceived mismatch between university scholars' research interests and agencies' research needs. *Of significant concern, however is the absence of a targeted research funding stream.*

Critical to the success of research partnerships is the development of clear guidelines regarding the following:

- Project time frames and timelines
- Data access, data sharing, data retention, and confidentiality
- Review of publications, reports, and presentations from the research, prior to dissemination
- Processes to obtain IRB approval(s) in a timely manner.

Although many research partnerships occur between the university and agency within a particular state, there are some research centers that engage in partnerships at the national level (e.g., Chapin Hall Center for Children—http://www.chapinhall.org/) or with several states (e.g., the University of Kansas Office of Child Welfare and Children's Mental Health—http://www.socwel.ku.edu/occ/).

Research Center and Partnership Examples: University of California-Berkeley

The Child Welfare Research Center at the School of Social Welfare, University of California at Berkeley is one example of a center that is partnering with the state agency. This is part of the Center for Social Services Research, established in 1994, which conducts research, policy analysis and program planning, and evaluation directed toward improving the public social services. The Center collaborates with public social service officials, elected policy-makers, community professionals, and consumers of service, it engages in research activities that are directly and immediately practice and policy-relevant (http://cssr.berkeley.edu/about).

A major Center project is "Performance Indicators for Child Welfare Services in California/California Children's Services Archive (http://cssr.berkeley.edu/ucb_childwelfare/)"(funded by the California Department of Social Services (CDSS) and the Stuart Foundation). The Performance Indicators Project creates and presents timely and useful data about children who are involved in each county's Child Welfare System. This includes ongoing analysis and reporting using statewide and county-specific child welfare administrative data, along with data from other sources. Under an Interagency Agreement with the CDSS, the Center receives quarterly extracts from the Child Welfare Services Case Management System (CWS/CMS). Center staff provide regular training and reports to county agencies and to the states, helping to show how these data can be used to inform and guide practice.

Berkeley also serves as the home for the California Social Work Education Center (CalSWEC), a consortium of the California Schools of Social Work, the California Department of Social Services, and the California Child Welfare Directors Association. CalSWEC supports research grants to faculty on topics that will enhance the child welfare curriculum. It also participates in a partnership effort to implement a practice-focused research agenda and an annual leadership symposium on evidence-based child welfare practices (http://calswec.berkeley.edu/CalSWEC).

University of Illinois Children and Family Research Center (CFRC)

The Illinois Department of Children and Family Services (IDCFS) and the University of Illinois Children and Family Research Center (CFRC) created a partnership, through a cooperative agreement "to provide independent evaluation of outcomes for children who are the responsibility of the department" (Johnson, Wells, Testa, & McDonald, 2003, p. 53). The state used this arrangement to monitor and implement child welfare service enhancements in response to the B.H. vs. Johnson class action lawsuit. The usefulness of this model encouraged the center director and agency director to encourage other states and localities to form such partnerships. The CFRC recently launched quarterly Data Summits to bring together child welfare researchers in Illinois. In addition, there is a staff person who serves as a bridge between the university and the agency, titled the Director of Research Partnerships (see Chapter 1, this volume for the history of this partnership).

The Chapin Hall Center for Children, University of Chicago

The Chapin Hall Center for Children is an applied research center at the University of Chicago dedicated to "conducting and actively disseminating rigorous research that serves children and youth, their families, and the communities in which they live" (http://www.about.chapinhall.org/index.html). Chapin Hall's research agenda is developed in collaboration with public agency directors, elected and appointed officials, philanthropic leaders, and other stakeholders who shape the policies and programs affecting the well-being and healthy development of children and adolescents. A major Center project is Chapin Hall's Multistate Foster Care Data Archive—with the individual case histories of more than 1.5 million foster children. The archive is widely viewed as a national model for the aggregation and analysis of administrative data. It forms one of the core resources of the Center for State Foster Care and Adoption Data, a partnership of Chapin Hall, the American Public Human Services Association, a growing number of states, and other universities.

Los Angeles County

In Los Angeles County, there had been a long standing training and education partnership that implemented research related to workforce issues. The county child welfare agency and the local consortium of schools of social work worked together to build an organized research partnership. Leadership by the director who valued research and a university faculty member with strong standing in the child welfare and policy community helped to build support for this collaborative endeavor (Donnelly, 2008—Personal Communication; McCroskey, 2008—Personal Communication).

Agency Research Needs

From an agency perspective, research findings have become increasingly important. Even those states that may have more sophisticated internal research and data personnel and infrastructures find engaging in university research partnerships valuable. The partnerships can assist with:

- Development and management of the increasing amount of child welfare outcome and performance measurement data that is available as a result of the CFSRs, including, but not limited to, the Adoption and Foster Care Reporting and Analysis System (AFCARS), the National Child Abuse and Neglect Data System (NCANDS), and other performance systems that various states have developed. More information on the child welfare data and statistics sources can be found at http://www.acf.hhs.gov/programs/chb/stats_research/index.htm#cw.

- Development and implementation of a prioritized research agenda.
- Evaluation of existing and new programs. Synthesis of existing research studies to help guide practice.
- Testing of interventions using both quantitative and qualitative methods, including randomized controlled trials, quasi-experimental, and participatory research designs.

Funding Partnerships

Education and Training Partnerships

For training and education child welfare university/agency partnerships, there are two key federal funding sources to help states and localities address child welfare workforce issues. One is the Title IV-E training entitlement created as part of the Adoption Assistance and Child Welfare Act (ACWA) of 1980 (P.L. 96-272). The second source is the Title IV-B, Section 426 discretionary training grant program, begun in 1962 and currently funded at about $7 million. Title IV-E training is an entitlement program with a special 75% enhanced federal match, subject to certain conditions, created as a provision of P.L. 96-272, that states can use for short or long term training of "personnel employed or preparing for employment by the State agency or by the local agency administering the (Title IV-E) plan" (Section 474A, P.L. 96-272). These funds are used to provide support for current workers to return to school, usually to acquire an MSW degree, and provide support to BSW and MSW students who are new to child welfare in order to provide incentives for them to begin their careers in child welfare (Briar et al., 1992).

Section 426 of Title IV-B is a discretionary grant program administered by the Children's Bureau that provides grants to institutions of higher learning, usually social work education programs, to train individuals in the child welfare field. Although the grants are awarded to universities, those universities are required to collaborate with state and local child welfare agencies to carry out their project. Until the recent funding of the National Child Welfare Workforce Institute (www.ncwwi.org) and four Child Welfare Workforce Centers, the Children's Bureau directly provided multi-year grants (2 to 5 years) that support creation of agency-based pre-service and/or in-service training materials, and/or development of enhanced university curriculum materials and traineeships to attract BSW and/or MSW students to child welfare careers.

Advocacy by the social work and child welfare communities has assisted in sustaining the federal appropriation for the Title IV-B 426 program and for directing the funding toward addressing high priority needs and toward schools of social work. In the mid-1990s, funding fell to $2 million annually, but with Congressional support, and targeted advocacy by the Action Network for Social Work Education and Research

(ANSWER), funding was increased to $7 million and has remained at that level. In 2008, the Children's Bureau chose to redirect these programs by funding five year Institutes and Centers to carry out the curriculum development, training and stipend programs through cooperative agreements.

Child Welfare Research Partnerships

For child welfare research, as previously noted, there is no specific funding source. This distinguishes child welfare from fields like substance abuse and mental health. In those fields, there are federal entities (e.g., the National Institute on Drug Abuse and the National Institute of Mental Health) that specifically support research and discovery and the Substance Abuse and Mental Health Services Administration (SAMHSA) that specifically supports service delivery and program innovation. As noted by the National Association of Public Child Welfare Administrators (NAPCWA), "The level of federal and state resources focused on important child welfare research questions ... have long suffered from the relatively low priority legislative bodies have placed upon research (NAPCWA, 2005, p. 5).

In recent years, federal legislation (e.g., the Promoting Safe and Stable Families Program (initiated under P.L. 103-66), the Chafee Foster Care Independence Act of 1999 (P.L. 106-169), and the new Fostering Connections and Increasing Adoptions Act (110-351) include set-aside funds for research, evaluation and technical assistance related to specific child welfare programs. These funds, however, do not necessarily trickle down to states and universities, and have more commonly been used to support national level evaluation and technical assistance efforts.

The Title IV-B 426 provisions of the Social Security Act include a section for research and demonstration programs; however the appropriation for this was zeroed out in 1996 and has not been restored. Title IV-E funds (both training and administration) might be used to support state level research and evaluation efforts through university/agency partnerships. If training funds are used, then they must be tied to enhancement of the Title IV-E training efforts, as noted in the previous discussion of CalSWEC. The provisions of Child Abuse Prevention and Treatment Act (CAPTA) do support some discretionary research, and over the years has supported field-initiated research efforts. Recent requests for proposals have focused on replication of evidence-based programs including Family Connections at the University of Maryland and Nurse Family Partnerships developed initially through research by David Olds of the University of Colorado. As noted earlier, Table 11.1 provides an overview of federal funding sources. Several foundations that support child welfare research include Annie E. Casey Foundation, Casey Family Programs, W.T. Grant foundation, Ballmer Foundation, and the Doris Duke Foundation.

Children's Bureau Re-Focus on Knowledge Development and Knowledge Transfer

The Children's Bureau is the federal entity that administers federally supported child welfare programs. It is the only specific child welfare-focused source of funding for child welfare service delivery, and it has recently re-focused its research, knowledge development, and knowledge transfer efforts implemented through its discretionary grant programs (Adoption Opportunities; Abandoned Infants Assistance; Promoting Safe and Stable Families: CAPTA; Child Welfare Services Training and Infant Adoption Awareness Training) (Brodowski, et al., 2007). This includes "maximizing the use of existing knowledge and evidence gleaned from research and practice to guide policy, funding and ultimately, program practice" (pp. 4–5). Grantees are asked to set aside 10 to 15% of funds for evaluation. This provides an important opportunity for agencies to engage with university partners to carry-out such evaluations. In 2001, the Children's Bureau began to connect research to practice by funding Quality Improvement Centers (QIC). See Box 11.1 for a description of the University of Kentucky's Quality Improvement Center on Child Protective Services, which focused on the importance of enhancing the supervision of workers. The projects of this effort were carried out through numerous university/agency partnerships.

In 2008, in addition to funding several new QICs, the Children's Bureau also added to its training and technical assistance network by funding five regional Implementation Centers (University of Maryland, University of Southern Maine, University of Nebraska, University of Texas, Arlington, and American Institutes for Research). In May 2009, the Children's Bureau hosted a national child welfare evaluation summit, providing an important opportunity to convene key agency and university stakeholders to describe and refine this state of the art.

Title IV-E Waivers

The IV-E child welfare waivers program was another important source of funding for research and evaluation of specialized programs (see Chapter 9, this volume). Authorized by Congress in 1994, the program allowed states greater flexibility to waive certain requirements so that innovative practices could be tried. This allowed spending flexibility while maintaining the basic child protection entitlement. The waiver program required a rigorous evaluation so that federal funds were invested in innovations that were scientifically proven to work. Several states partnered with universities to conduct the required evaluation activities; these states included Illinois, Iowa, Oregon, Maryland, North Carolina, and California (US Department of Health and Human Services, Administration for Children & Families, Children's Bureau, 2008). Over half of the waivers included a research design with random assignment. The effective use of randomized research

---

Box 11.1 Southern Regional Quality Improvement Center (SR QIC)

The SR QIC is a five-year grant to the University of Kentucky funded by the Children's Bureau to improve the Child Protective Services system in these ways:

- Increase the capabilities of agencies in identified geographical areas to improve frontline CPS practices;
- Foster the development of collaborative partnerships on the local and regional level
- Promote collaborative problem solving;
- Develop and implement research and demonstration projects to promote innovation, evidence-based practice improvements, and advancement of knowledge;
- Establish an information-sharing network to disseminate information on promising practices; and
- Improve the quality and availability of CPS delivery systems in a specified geographical area.

The Southern Regional Quality Improvement Center (SR QIC) utilizes working partnerships between child protection agencies, university social work programs, and the community in ten states in a rural, southern region to support and evaluate innovative projects designed to improve the child protective services system within a Learning Lab Model. One of the key objectives of SR QIC is to support practice improvements that build lasting capacity in public and private agencies in the region by expanding university and community partnerships to provide a reinvigorated research and community support base for ongoing work, to train future practitioners in state of the art practices, and to provide training partnerships that allow for expanded use of state and federal funding. (Southern Regional Quality Improvement Center, 2008).

---

designs has stimulated a number of non-waiver, child welfare research studies that use randomization.

Links to the reports and more information about the waiver program and research findings are available at http://www.acf.hhs.gov/programs/cb/programs_fund/cwwaiver/2007/summary_demo2007.htm. The findings from the Illinois Subsidized Guardianship Waiver carried out by the University of Illinois CFRC, and research on independent living carried out by Chapin Hall Center for Children, provided evidence that support provisions enacted in the Fostering Connections to Success and Increasing Adoptions Act of 2008 (P.L. 110- 351). The authority to grant new IV-E waivers expired in March 2006, and there appears to be little interest at the moment in reviving the program.

Evaluating Partnerships

The evaluation of partnerships is important for the multiple stakeholders including the children and families served by child welfare agencies. The ultimate outcome of these efforts is anticipated to be the enhancement of services to children and families so that they will achieve safety, permanence, and well-being. However, there are many factors beyond the enhanced education and training or findings from research that can be incorporated into agency practice that impacts outcomes for children and families. High caseloads and lack of resources are key factors that can interfere with the outcomes of the best intentioned partnership. Inconsistent policies and poor supervision can also impact child and family outcomes. Thus, it is difficult to evaluate partnership outcomes specifically in the context of children and families. Recently, there has also been increased attention to research on organizational climate and culture and the extent to which these factors can impact service improvements. The current attention to the translation of research into practice and implementation of evidence-supported practices is also increasing attention to organizational and structural issues that can enhance or hinder service improvement.

There has been little evidence gathered to support earlier generations of child welfare agency/university partnerships (e.g., Title XX training partnerships). Thus, in the late 1980s and early 1990s, when advocates pushed for building more partnerships, questions were raised about their value and outcomes. Stakeholders were reliant on anecdotal stories and a few research reports.

Title IV-E training regulations require that there be an evaluation process, and there have been multiple calls for evaluation of the current partnership efforts to create a body of research that would document their value and outcomes (Briar-Lawson & Zlotnik, 2002, 2003; Brown, Chavkin, & Peterson, 2002; Smith, 2002). Two special issues of journals (Briar-Lawson & Zlotnik, 2002, 2003) were developed, the *Journal of Public Child Welfare* was launched and CalSWEC convenes an annual meeting of child welfare training evaluators. There have also been dissemination efforts through conference symposia and papers at the Society for Social Work and Research, at the American Evaluation Association and at the Council on Social Work Education as well as at the Children's Bureau conferences described earlier. A systematic review of research on retention in child welfare found, however, that even in evaluating the outcomes of Title IV-E partnerships in regard to worker retention or intention to leave, different partnerships (even within the same state) used differing samples, measures, and timeframes, making it difficult to create a robust research synthesis (Zlotnik et al., 2005).

Despite the existence of research partnerships, there is little evidence that they have been evaluated. Rather their focus and sustenance seems to be driven by committed leaders, utility of products, and the availability of funding. Attributes that would benefit from further study include a number of issues that look at organizational and relational issues. Research is needed on maintenance of effective relationships; sustainability of funding; completion of products and tasks in a timely manner; ability of academic partners to publish findings; and implementation—the ability of the agency partner to use the research findings to guide practice and policy. Better understanding is also needed in regard to how issues of access to and use of data and issues of confidentiality are dealt with as well as strategies for dissemination and implementation of research. The Research Process in the Human Services, edited by Alexander and Solomon (2006) proves useful guidance for agencies and researchers interested in building successful partnerships, with case studies and lessons learned provided by a range of researchers involved in community-based research.

Sustaining Child Welfare Partnerships

It is valuable for agencies to be able to transcend changes in leaders and the ebbs and flows of funding streams to sustain partnerships. However, this is not always what occurs. Changes in leaders bring changes in relationships and desires to go in "new" directions. The lack of evaluation data and clarity of outcomes of the partnership often has an impact on its sustainability. For those who have worked within a successful partnership in one jurisdiction—they may move to a new venue and find it difficult to establish a partnership in the new setting. This might result from the lack of established relationships, difficulty identifying sources of funding, lack of trust, inability to demonstrate the value of such a partnership, competition among different universities, or a previous negative experience by one or both partners. The following, drawn from the IASWR University/Agency Research Partnerships project, provide some guidance for sustainability.

1. Learn from the experience of others:

    a. Develop a cadre of capacity-building experts and peer consultants who can assist states and universities embarking on partnerships or those who encounter impediments along the way.
    b. Create a technical assistance and information exchange strategy through collaboration between deans and directors of schools of social work and child welfare administrators; through creation of listservs and other communication tools; through conferences and newsletters.

2. Identify funding sources:

    a. Use networks to learn how to fund such efforts.
    b. Involve national, local, regional, and state foundations to fund and catalyze a partnership, provide matching funds, create an

endowment that can provide funding for writing grants and planning activities, and that can support certain functions that might not be covered by government funding sources.

c. Develop advocacy efforts that will support child welfare university/agency partnerships and that will create sustainable funding streams for child welfare research.

The Future of Partnerships

As states begin the second round of CFSRs and engage in program improvement, it is an excellent time to strengthen the engagement between universities and agencies. The opportunities that university expertise can bring to agencies in terms of research, evaluation, consultation, and program development can be built on to enhance the well-being of the children and families in need of services. All of the elements of the cycle of results-oriented accountability that are presented in this book can be strengthened in both agencies and universities through partnership agreements. This is a time that is ripe to strengthen the practice/research/practice loop and university/agency partnerships can play important roles in creating and sustaining such efforts.

Fostering university/agency partnerships is an important part of strengthening the evidence-base of child welfare practice and policy. Research and outcome studies that address the value of partnerships and the impact on service delivery continue to be important. In addition to the traditional journals that cover child welfare, the recent creation of a *Journal of Public Child Welfare* is one new outlet for the publication of these studies.

There are other opportunities for promoting collaborations between social work and other disciplines. For example social work and law are both engaged in child welfare reform and improvements. There are opportunities for collaboration with many disciplines, such as psychology, neuroscience, or urban planning, needing to focus on the links between individual development and risk factors, as well as community and neighborhood capacity-building efforts.

The increased attention to the connections between substance abuse and child welfare, as well as the recognition of the high rate of mental health problems of those who are served by the child welfare system creates opportunities to broaden the partnerships and to bring in new stakeholders. New collaborations can strengthen cross-system training, build new research paradigms, and examine service delivery strategies that are more child and family centered, rather than reflecting the diverse funding streams and silos that get created through narrow agency and university departmental structures.

As partnerships move forward, not only is there collaboration between agencies and universities, but increasingly there is involvement of the consumer and community in planning, research, training and program implementation. Initiatives such as the Community Partnership for Protecting Children, coordinated through the Center for the Study of Social Policy (http://www.cssp.org/center/community_partnership2. html) are providing such models in more than 50 communities. This was recently reinforced by the Children's Bureau funding CSSP to be the Quality Improvement Center for Community Partnerships. In addition, to ensure that solutions are attentive to the diversity of cultures and communities, there is an increasing need to undertake participatory action and community-based participatory research efforts. The efforts of the Community-Campus Partnerships for Health (www.ccph.org) can provide guidance to similar initiatives in child welfare and vice versa. The involvement of Casey Family Programs in state foster care enhancement efforts includes an emphasis on using data to guide practice and policy. University partners are key players in helping states use the available data, gather new data, and measure program performance.

As more states seek to privatize child welfare services and/or to more strategically engage private, non-profit, and faith-based agencies in the implementation of service delivery, there need to be organized strategies to ensure that there is a well-trained workforce using evidence-supported interventions. States and universities need to be vigilant to the discussions underway to develop and implement new financing strategies for child welfare services. Title IV-E training entitlement has been an important funding source. In addition, state level service delivery would benefit from an invigorated field initiated research program. As proposals are put forward, it is critical for the partners, and their representatives to be articulate about the potential impact of these changes on the partnership activities and its outcomes.

Summary

Since the late 1980s, there has been both a national and state strategy to strengthen partnerships and to reinvigorate the links between child welfare and the social work profession. We are beginning to see the fruition of those efforts in improved outcomes for children, in improved staff retention, in a growing body of research that examines policy imperatives and child welfare practices and that creates a career trajectory and career ladders for child welfare workers. However, much more needs to be done. Just as the federal investment to develop social work education programs resulted in the building of infrastructure and the expansion of BSW education to attempt to ensure the necessary workforce (Austin, Antonyappan, & Leighninger, 1996; Harris, 1996), so today the use of

Title IV-E training funds can revitalize the social work/child welfare connection and engage universities, especially public universities, and especially social work education programs in child welfare service delivery improvements. The focus on evidence-supported practices, increased attention to data driven performance measures and outcomes, increased accountability at the federal and state level, and the public's concerns about high profile child deaths require a focus on research, research translation, and implementation of evidence supported interventions. University/agency partnerships can and should play critical roles in addressing these priorities. To best meet the needs of our most vulnerable children and families, it is critical that agencies and universities work together to implement the cycle of results-oriented accountability.

Acknowledgment

This chapter draws upon the content of *Strengthening university/agency research partnerships to enhance child welfare outcomes: A toolkit for building research partnerships*, developed by the Institute for the Advancement of Social Work Research with support and technical assistance from Casey Family Programs. The full report is available at www.iaswresearch.org and www.casey.org.

References

Adoption and Safe Families Act of 1997, Pub. L. No. 105-89

Adoption Assistance and Child Welfare Act of 1980, Pub. L. No. 96-272

Alexander, L. B., & Solomon, P. (Eds.). (2006). *The research process in human services: Behind the scenes*. Belmont, CA: Thomson Brooks/Cole.

American Public Human Services Association. (2005). *Report from the 2004 child welfare workforce survey: state agency findings*. Washington, DC: Author

Austin, M., Antonyappan, J., & Leighninger, L. (1996). Federal support for social work education: section 707 of the 1967 social security amendments. *Social Service Review, 70*(1), 83–97.

Barth, R., Lloyd, C., Christ, S., Chapman, M., & Dickinson, N. (2008). Child welfare worker characteristics and job satisfaction: A national study. *Social Work, 53*(3), 199–209.

Briar, K., Hansen, V., & Harris, N. (Eds.) (1992). *New partnerships: Proceedings form the National Public Child Welfare Symposium*. Miami, FL: Florida International University.

Briar-Lawson, K., & Zlotnik, J. L. (2002). *Evaluation research in child welfare: Improving outcomes through university-public agency partnerships*. Binghamton, NY: Haworth Press.

Briar-Lawson, K., & Zlotnik, J. L. (2003). *Charting the impact of University-child welfare collaboration*. Binghamton, NY: Haworth Press.

Brodowski, M., Flanzer, S., Nolan, C., Shafer, J., & Kaye, E. (2007). Children's Bureau discretionary grants: Knowledge development through our research and demonstration projects. *Journal of Evidence-Based Practice, 4*(3/4), 3–20.

Brown, K., Chavkin, N., & Peterson V. (2002). Tracking process and outcome results of BSW students' preparation for public child welfare practice: Lessons learned. *Health and Social Policy, 15*(3/4), 105–116.

CalSWEC. (2008). *About CalSWEC.* Available from http://calswec.berkeley.edu.

Child Welfare League of America (1982). *Child welfare as a field of social work practice (2nd edition).* Washington, D.C.: CWLA Press

Children and Family Research Center (2008). Mission statement. Available from http://www.cfrc.illinois.edu/mission.htm.

Cyphers, G. (2001). *Report from the Child Welfare Workforce Survey: State and County Data and Findings.* Washington, DC: American Public Human Services Association. Available from http://www.aphsa.org/Policy/Doc/cwwsurvey.pdf.

Ferguson, S. (2002). *Proceedings from professional education to advanced child welfare practice: An invitational working conference.* University of Minnesota School of Social Work. Available from http://uky.edu/socialwork/cswe.

Government Accountability Office. (2003). Child Welfare: Enhanced federal oversight of Title IV-B could provide states additional information to improve services. Available from http://gao.gov/new.items/d03956.pdf.

Grossman, B., Laughlin, & Specht, H. (1992). Building the commitment of social work education to publicly supported social services: The California model. In Briar, K, Hansen, V., & Harris, N. (Eds.), *New partnerships: Proceedings from the national public child welfare training symposium 1991* (pp. 55–72). Miami, FL: Florida International University.

Harris, N. (1996). *Social work education and public human services partnerships: A technical assistance document.* Alexandria, FA: Council on Social Work Education.

Illinois Department of Children and Family Services. (1995). *A proposal to the Chicago Community Trust to establish a children and family research center.* Springfield, IL: Author.

Institute for the Advancement of Social Work Research and the National Association of Social Workers (August 3, 2004). *Workforce and Accountability: Child and Family Services Reviews—Implications for Child Welfare Practice.* Available from http://www.charityadvantage.com/iaswr/images/WASReport.pdf.

Institute for the Advancement of Social Work Research. (2008). *Strengthening university/agency research partnerships to enhance child welfare outcomes: A toolkit for building research partnerships.* Available from http://www.iaswresearch.org.

Johnson, M., Wells, S., Testa, M., & McDonald, J. (2003). Illinois's child welfare research agenda: An approach to building consensus for practice-based research. *Child Welfare, 82*(1), 53–75.

Lieberman, A. A., Hornby, H., & Russell, M. (1988, November/December). Analyzing the educational background and work experiences of child welfare personnel: A national study. *Social Work, 33*(6), 485–489.

NAPCWA. (2005). Guide for child welfare administrators on evidence-based practice. Available from http://www.aphsa.org/Home/doc/Guide-for-Evidence-Based-Practice.pdf.

NRCCM/NAPCWA. (2001). *A Research Agenda for Child Welfare.* Retrieved from October 12, 2008 http://www.nrccps.org/documents/2001/pdf/Research-Agenda.pdf.

Smith, B.. (2002). Evaluating federally funded child welfare training partnerships: A worthwhile challenge. *Health & Social Policy, 15*(3/4), 189–201.

Southern Regional Quality Improvement Center. (2008). Accessed on January 26, 2009 from http://www.uky.edu/SocialWork/trc/mainqic.html.

US Department of Health and Human Services, Administration for Children and Families, Children's Bureau. (1999) *Changing paradigms of child welfare practice: Responding to opportunities and challenges*. Report from the 1999 child welfare training symposium. Washington, D.C.: Author

US Department of Health and Human Services, Administration for Children and Families, Children's Bureau. (2000). *Rethinking child welfare practice under the adoption and safe families act of 1997*. Washington, DC: Author

US Department of Health and Human Services, Administration for Children and Families, Children's Bureau. (2008). *Summary of the Title IV-E Child Welfare Waiver Demonstrations*. Washington, D.C.: Author.

University of Maryland. (2008). Child Welfare Accountability: Efficiency and Effectiveness of Child Welfare Services, retrieved December 18, 2008 from the Ruth Young Center for Children and Families, School of Social Work, http://www.family.umaryland.edu/ryc_research_and_evaluation/child_welfare_research_files/cwa08-07.htm

University of Pittsburgh School of Social Work (n.d.). *The child welfare research and education programs*. Pittsburgh: Author.

University of Southern Maine. (1987). *Professional social work practice in public child welfare: An agenda for action*. Portland, ME: University of Southern Maine, Center for Research and Advanced Study.

UTA School of Social Work Judith Granger Birmingham Center for Child Welfare. (2008). Mission. Available from http://www2.uta.edu/ssw/ccw/

Zlotnik, J. L. (1993). *Social work education and public human service agencies: developing partnerships*. Alexandria, VA: Council on Social Work Education

Zlotnik, J. L. (1997). *Preparing the workforce for family-centered practice: Social work education and public human services partnerships*. Alexandra, VA: Council on Social Work Education

Zlotnik, J. L. (1998). *An historical analysis of the implementation of federal policy: A case study of accessing title IV-E funds to support social work education*, University of Maryland School of Social Work.

Zlotnik, J. L. (2002). Preparing social workers for child welfare practice: Lessons from an historical review of the literature. *Journal of Health & Social Policy*, 15(3–4), 5–22.

Zlotnik, J. L., & Cornelius, L. (2000). Preparing social work students for child welfare careers: The Use of title IV-E training funds in social work education. *Journal of Baccalaureate Social Work, 2*(5), 1–14.

Zlotnik, J. L., DePanfilis, D., Daining, C., & Lane, M. M. (2005, July). Professional education for child welfare practice: Improving retention in public child welfare agencies. *IASWR Research Brief 2: Child Welfare Workforce Series*. Available from http://www.charityadvantage.com/iaswr/images/IASWRBrief2.pdf

12

CONCLUSION

Mark F. Testa and John Poertner

Fostering accountability in pubic child welfare involves holding agents answerable for the validity and integrity of the actions they take on behalf of their principals. It is demonstrated by presenting valid evidence of the efficacy and effectiveness of child welfare interventions, and by showing that agency relationships reliably and efficiently achieve the results valued by children, families, and the public at large. Assembling the best available evidence and minimizing agency risks are not simple tasks. They are made difficult by the variable scope of public interest in the safety, permanence, and well-being of children and by conflicting perspectives on the best types of agency relationships for accomplishing these public purposes. Although public policy remains in flux along these dual dimensions of interest and organization, the dynamic situation also presents opportunities to make better use of empirical evidence to guide and improve child welfare practice and policy.

The nature of the challenges and opportunities are apparent in the latest U.S. child welfare legislation enacted into law: The Fostering Connections to Success and Increasing Adoptions Act of 2008 (P.L. 110-351). The new law expands federal support for grandparents and other relatives who assume permanent legal guardianship of children formerly under their foster care. The same legislation authorizes direct federal payments to Indian tribal organizations for the operation of foster care, adoption, and guardianship assistance programs, renews the bonus program for improved adoption performance, and gives states the option of extending federal foster care assistance to youth adults beyond their 18th birthday.

One is hard pressed to find a unitary ideological thread that weaves together these different provisions of the law. Although there is a discernable tilt toward primordial agency (tribal sovereignty and kinship care), the new federal law also reinforces bureaucratic agency with adoption incentives (contractual agency) and enlarges state responsibility for the health, educational stability, and transitioning to independence for children in foster care (fiduciary agency). The disparateness of these provisions reflects to some extent the cross-cutting influences of alternative ideological visions (Sowell, 2002), which have been competing to fill the void left by the collapse of the once dominant progressive narrative that equated human betterment with the unidirectional displacement of primordial solidarities by the centralized bureaucratic institutions of an all encompassing welfare state. But, the appeal of these competing ideological visions is also tempered by the insistence that policy proposals be supported by empirical evidence of actual results and not just by their consistency with underlying value premises and ideological beliefs.

Empirical evidence played an important role in the development and passage of the Fostering Connections legislation. Even though every child's right to permanent guardianship of the person had been enunciated by U.S. government officials and child welfare advocates as far back as the 1950s (Smith, 1955), serious consideration wasn't given to federally subsidized legal guardianship until state IV-E waiver demonstrations in the late 1990s showed guardianship to be a cost-effective and safe alternative to maintaining children in long-term foster care (The Pew Commission on Children in Foster Care, 2004; Testa, 2002). Similarly, even though the lengthening dependence of youth into their twenties had been a middle-class trend since the 1960s (U.S. President's Science Advisory Committee Panel on Youth, 1974), it was only after longitudinal surveys of foster youth documented a plausible connection between termination of foster care at the age of 18 years and adverse educational and well-being outcomes that Congress elected to give states the option of using federal dollars to extend foster care assistance to 21 years of age (Courtney et al., 2007).

This is not to say that every provision of the Fostering Connections Act was based on credible empirical evidence of effectiveness. Tribal access to title IV-E entitlement funding belatedly made good on the federal government's original acknowledgement of tribal governments' legal authority and jurisdiction to provide child welfare services under the Indian Child Welfare Act of 1978. But, it is also the case that the generally positive research findings on kinship care (Winokur, Holtan, & Valentine, 2009) also helped to reinforce the affine principle that tribal organizations "are in the best position to understand and effectively respond to the needs of their American Indian and Alaskan Native (AI/AN) children and families" (Kids Are Waiting and National Indian Child Welfare Association, 2007, p. 2).

Similarly, adoption incentives were initially included in the Adoption and Safe Families Act of 1997, because of the ready acceptance by the Reagan-Bush and Clinton administrations of the applicability of market principles to the delivery of child welfare and other government services. But beliefs in the value of such bonuses have also been reinforced by studies that point to an association between increases in the numbers and likelihood of adoption and the introduction of adoption bonuses (McDonald, Salyers, & Testa, 2003; Wulczyn, Chen, & Hislop, 2006).

What the future may hold for results-oriented accountability and the use of empirical evidence to guide and improve child welfare policy is hard to say. Is it a temporary infatuation that will fade as soon as another ideological vision cycles into dominance? Or, is it likely to exert a lasting impact on future practice and policy developments in child welfare? In this concluding chapter, we address these questions by considering the five facets of results-oriented accountability outlined in the introduction to this volume—scope of interest, transparency, evidence-supported, causality, and reflexivity—and assess where current child welfare policy stands on each of these dimensions. We comment on those stages of results-oriented accountability that appear to be gaining the greatest ground—outcomes monitoring and data analysis—and contemplate the implications of the stage that appears to be losing the most in child welfare—experimental evaluations. We consider the alternative directions that results-oriented accountability might take with respect to what we call the accountability mismatch between the enlarged scope of public interest and the limited technical capacity of states to meet public expectations. We offer our thoughts about the future of waivers and the flexible funding of child welfare interventions, the continued viability of market-oriented solutions to the principal-agent problem, and the future role of university-agency partnerships in fostering accountability in child welfare.

Scope of Public Interest in Child Welfare Outcomes

In Chapter 2, we advanced the proposition that many historical develop-ments in public child welfare can be conceived as stemming from different perspectives on the diversity of organizational forms that parent–child agency relationships can take (primordial or bureaucratic) and conflicts over the proper scope of public interest in the results of those relationships (narrow or diffuse). We suggested that the main historical trend has been a widening of public interest from a narrow *safety* focus on the protection of children from parental cruelty and exploitation in the workforce in the late 19th century to a broader *permanency* concern with family continuity, placement stability, and legal permanence in the 20th century, to finally a more diffuse interest in child and adolescent *well-being* in the early 21st century. This main trend, however, has not been unidirectional and at different times has been moderated by changing public acceptance of and confidence in different forms of agency relationships for achieving the desired results of child safety, family permanence, and child and adoles-cent well-being.

The interaction between scope of public interest and agency relation-ship currently takes a curvilinear shape in the United States. The scope of interest tends to be most narrow at the mid-range of the primordial-bureaucratic continuum, where institutions of family privacy limit state intrusion into the affairs of the nuclear, conjugal family and gradually broadens as child-caring agents shift towards single (birth) parent, adoption, legal guardianship, foster family care, supervised independent living, group homes, institutions, and more restrictive (less family-like) forms of bureaucratized care. Correspondingly, on the primordial side of the continuum, the scope of interest also widens as the child-caring agent departs from the nuclear family norm towards extended families (kinship care), faith-based communities, and tribal organizations.

The curvilinear pattern in which public interest in child welfare outcomes and direct public investment in agency capacity is least for birth families and greatest for groups and organizations at the farthest ends of the primordial-bureaucratic continuum is problematic for many who see the solution to child maltreatment and foster care as necessitating greater public funding of preventative services and support of birth families. Although this imbalance could quickly change in the future, the current structure reflects both public deference to the value of nuclear family autonomy and a lingering reluctance to engage in redistributive policies that seriously encroach on the value of competitive economic achievement in order to equalize the developmental opportunities of children from less affluent households.

The presumption that the well-being of children who reside with one or both of their birth parents (96% of U.S. children) ought to depend primarily on their parent's own economic success and cultural preferences for raising children as they deem fit becomes less constraining after children have been removed from parental custody. After the norm of family autonomy is breached, the scope of public interest is expected to widen so that children's developmental opportunities and future well-being aren't unduly compromised by child protective intervention.

Public acknowledgement of a diffuse rather than narrow standard of state accountability for the well-being of children who have been removed from parental custody has grown in recent years. This is reflected in the numerous consent decrees and settlement agreements that more than 30 states have entered into since 1995, as a result of class-action litigation to remedy specific faults and systematic defects in the delivery of state child welfare services (Kosanovich & Joseph, 2005).

Approximately two-thirds of these decrees and settlements require that foster children shall have access to a comprehensive array of services that address their physical, emotional, educational, and other well-being needs. The enlarged scope of public interest is also reflected in the recently enacted Foster Connections Act. The new law builds on the Adoption and Safe Families Act's (ASFA) recognition of child well-being as an outcome and holds public agencies accountable for foster children's educational stability and enrollment as full-time elementary or secondary school students; for oversight and coordination of their mental health treatment, dental care, medical prescriptions, and other health care services; and for the development of personalized transition plans for children aging out of foster care, which include specific options on housing, health insurance, education, mentor opportunities, work force supports, and employment services.

The wide array of results for which public child welfare agencies are to be held accountable poses special challenges to carrying out the first stage of results-oriented accountability: outcomes monitoring. Measured against appropriate baselines, the reporting of results shows where efforts appear to be successful, but also where the outcomes appear less than desirable. This variable quality of results poses challenges to the integrity of child welfare management. If results are less than desirable, what will be the effect of reporting them to the community? To what extent will risk-averse agencies allow the accurate reporting of results? It takes courage to accept unvarnished results, explain them to a skeptical public, and use them for program improvement.

For monitoring to be effective, you not only need courageous administrators and judges, but also consensually agreed upon child and family outcomes that are measured validly and reliably. Given the history of child welfare this is a substantial challenge. AFSA and the Foster Care Independence Act (FCIA) are two of the most recent federal child welfare policies that explicitly focus on outcomes. In each case, the United States Department of Health and Human Services (USDHHS) was charged with implementing these outcome provisions. They have determined how these outcomes are to be measured and the source of the data.

Chapter 4 provided a good critique of the implementation of these provisions. A major revision of the federal data collection systems is necessary to guide improvement in the measures just as outcome monitoring guides improvement in outcomes. It is by examining the strengths and weaknesses of current and future measures that administrators can best develop a set of statistical indicators that can validly and reliably guide program improvement. In this regard, it is important that the set of indicators be counterbalanced and sensitive to the interrelated nature of child welfare outcomes. This will necessitate greater investments in the systematic collection of a larger set of data elements than is now routinely monitored as part of the current Child and Family Services Review (CFSR) process. A wide array of child well-being elements are currently being collected on a probability sample of children investigated for child maltreatment as part of the National Survey of Child and Adolescent Well-Being (NASCW). A smaller array are contemplated as part of the proposed modifications to the Adoption and Foster Care Analysis and Reporting System (AFCARS) requirements for states to collect and report data on children in out-of-home care and in subsidized adoption and guardianship arrangements (Federal Register/Vol. 73, No. 8/Friday, January 11, 2008/Proposed Rules). They include items on current immunizations, special education, grade repetition, and physical, behavioral, and mental health conditions.

Adding these and other indicators of child well-being to the existing mix of safety and permanency indicators that are now routinely monitored as part of the CFSR process will require some major modifications in the way that the federal government currently assesses state performance in operating child protection and child welfare programs. Numerous scholars have pointed out the limitations and weaknesses of the existing federal safety and permanency standards, which fail to take into account the interrelated nature of child welfare outcomes (Courtney, Needell, & Wulczyn, 2004; Testa & Rolock, 2006; Webster, Usher, Needell, & Wildfire, 2008). States that are better at preventing child removal and ensuring social continuity score lower on most federal standards because they often end up with a more troubled foster care population and fare worse on family permanency and child well-being measures than high-removal states.

Transparency in Accounting for Results

Developing a reliable and counter-balanced set of outcome indicators is a prerequisite for the second stage of results-oriented accountability. When less than adequate performance is noted, sub-group analysis of which populations of children and families are most at risk of undesirable outcomes can help refine the search for promising solutions. The example of permanency trends that is woven throughout this volume is illustrative of this process. By examining time to outcome data it is possible to estimate the likelihood that an individual will experience the outcome of interest in a given interval of time. Applying this data analysis method to Illinois led, in part, to the finding that one group of children not experiencing timely permanency outcomes were those children placed into homes of relatives. Illinois child welfare policy makers responded to this situation with their Home of Relative (HMR) reform. This is clearly a complex task requiring that agencies have considerable expertise in the use of a variety of statistical procedures or develop a partnership with a university research center to gain access to this expertise.

The impact of HMR reform on the cohorts of children entering and exiting the Illinois foster care system also illustrates the sensitivity of federal outcome standards to changes in the demographic composition of the foster child population and the distribution of their living arrangements along the primordial-bureaucratic continuum. Unless sample selectivity is taken into account at both the front-end and back-end of the system and appropriate risk-adjustments are made, serious misreading of performance trends can occur. In the past, reliable readings of performance trends were hampered by the cross-sectional design of federal data collection, which inhibited longitudinal tracking of children into and out of different living arrangements and legal statuses. Fortunately, the newly proposed AFCARS regulations address the most serious limitations of the current system that were outlined in Chapter 4. The most important change is the restructuring of AFCARS to support longitudinal data analysis. Instead of states' reporting the living arrangement, provider information, and exit type for only the last placement of a child's most recent removal episode, states will be required to report information on every removal episode, including details on each placement type and the timing and circumstances of each of the child's exits from out-of-home care. This set-up helps to alleviate some of the selectivity problems associated with federal permanency measures that look only at exits and allows the sorts of time-to-outcome analysis of agency performance which was presented in Chapter 5. For the first time, AFCARS will also track children who enter adoption and legal guardianship arrangements. This will allow for more accurate assessment of post-permanency stability and offer better insight into the average well-being of the residual group of foster children who are unable to exit to permanence before transitioning to adulthood.

Other new AFCARS elements, such as prenatal alcohol and drug exposure, juvenile justice involvement, and children who are out of their own homes to obtain mental health services, will enhance data analysis of performance trends by allowing for statistical adjustments for these and other risk factors that affect children's safety, permanence, and well-being. As accountability for results becomes more transparent, a more realistic assessment can be made of what needs to be done to improve agency performance. Instead of concealing pertinent facts from stakeholders or misrepresenting spurious change as actual improvement, administrators can turn their attention to providing a candid account of the possible reasons for performance shortfalls, the resources required, and the interventions that will be pursued to attain the desired results.

The Need for Evidence-Supported Interventions

An honest acknowledgement of performance gaps coupled with a rigorous analysis of the conditions that may need to change will place a higher premium on the search for evidence-supported interventions (ESI). To be reasonably confident that a program or policy will have the intended effect, it will be important to base the selection on the best available evidence of its efficacy and effectiveness. Identification of the contributing factors and the populations most at risk helps in formulating hypotheses that link risk factors to the promising interventions and desired outcomes. For example, if declining reunifications is a cause for concern and data analysis points to a rise in the number of substance exposed infants (SEI) as a possible explanation, attention can focus on interventions with substance-dependent parents rather than on the myriad of other factors that are correlated with reunification rates, such as parental visitation, kinship placement, and inadequate training of workers.

There are a number of web-based resources that can facilitate the search for relevant literature. Many of them were cited in Chapter 6 and include the Casey Decision-Making Guidelines (americanhumane.org/protecting-children/resources/casey-decision-making-guidelines), which are hosted by the American Humane Association, Results-Oriented Management in Child Welfare (www.rom.ku.edu) at the University of Kansas, and The California Evidence-Based Clearinghouse for Child Welfare (cachildwelfar-eclearinghouse.org). Although the opportunities are expanding for finding research pertinent to the hypothesis of interest, the likelihood of finding an exact match that meets a high standard of evidence is still low. The contents of Web sites devoted to cataloging promising programs and ESI have evolved from best-practice guidelines compiled by experts (Casey) to narrative reviews of the empirical literature (Kansas) to standardized assessments of program efficacy (California). The latest development is systematic research review (SRR), which employs quantitative techniques to cumulate the sizes of intervention effects over a number of published and unpublished studies (Shadish, Cook, & Campbell, 2002). The most sophisti-cated model of this approach can be found in the work of the Cochrane (cochrane.org) and Campbell Collaborations (campbellcollaboration.org).

SRR represents an important advance over expert consensus, narrative reviews, and standardized assessments of ESI for drawing causal infer-ences about the effectiveness of a proposed course of action. Although narrative reviews of the empirical literature are superior to expert con-sensus, it becomes very difficult to reach a summary judgment about effectiveness when the number of studies grows large. Systematic assess-ments that count up studies with statistically significant and non-signifi-cant results can more efficiently handle larger numbers, but its major weakness is that it ignores the magnitudes of intervention effects. SRR, or more exactly, the component that cumulates effect sizes (also called meta-analysis), yields a pooled estimate of effect sizes, which can account for variations in sample sizes and within-in sample variances of different studies (Littell, 2008). SRR is alert to the potential influences of publication bias that tends to favor studies with positive findings over those with null or negative results. It can also assess the external validity of an interven-tion with demonstrated efficacy by exploring potential moderators of effect sizes across populations, places, and contexts.

The aims of SSR are to find a representative sample of published and unpublished randomized controlled experiments that test an intervention related to the hypothesis of interest and to compile these in a way that allows examination of critical features of the research. The number of SRR titles registered with the Campbell Collaboration (C2) on topics that are pertinent to child welfare is steadily increasing. As tabulated in Chapter 6, approximately one-half (N = 26) of the registered social welfare titles deal with interventions that are generally aimed at improving the safety, family permanence, or well-being of children and adolescents. Nonetheless, the output of published reviews remains meager. Only half of the registered titles have resulted in published reviews (N = 13) as of 2008. Furthermore a quarter of these were "empty" reviews, which found no studies that met the reviewers preset criteria for inclusion.

Where randomized controlled experiments are lacking, research review must turn to quasi-experimental and observational research with the next strongest level of evidence. Sifting through the best available evidence will typically yield potentially promising policy options. However, before implementing any policy it is important to examine them to gain insight into how they might fit the specific agency context. This includes gaining intelligence from clients and community through advisory committees or focus groups. Implementation of a new policy may also fail if the organization does not have the proper support. This requires managers who back the use of evidence to improve outcomes, proper training of staff in methods of causal inference, and a quality assurance system that helps monitor the fidelity with which the policy is implemented.

Restoring Rigor to Child Welfare Evaluations

Satisfying the demand for high-quality research reviews and program implementation is facilitated by the training of child welfare staff in advanced research methods in graduate social work and other social science programs. But, more importantly, it requires renewed dedication of the field to boosting the output of rigorous evaluations that are most valid for assessing the efficacy and effectiveness of child welfare interventions. Chapter 9 detailed the loss of the most ambitious federal effort to date for increasing the output of randomized controlled experiments in child welfare. At its height, the IV-E waiver demonstrations functioned much like a federal program of research that approved replications by other states of an efficacious intervention in a lead state to learn whether the intervention worked across populations under different conditions of real-world implementation. This was the model followed for the federal subsidized guardianship demonstrations. The replication of the positive results from Illinois by the states of Wisconsin and Tennessee was a key reason behind Congress' passage of the guardianship provisions of the Fostering Connections Act in 2008 (Zlotnik, 2008).

With the demise of the IV-E waiver program in 2006, there is not much counter-weight to the reticence that many child welfare administrators and practitioners feel when it comes to evaluating the delivery of child welfare services under controlled experimental conditions. Although such reluctance is sometimes justified by concerns over the ethics of denying services to children and families, more often the objection merely assumes what the experiment is trying to ascertain. Specific reforms are advocated as though they were certain to be successful without adequate evidence of this fact in the first place (Campbell, 1969). This results in widespread indiscriminate "experimentation" on vulnerable children and families by well-meaning administrators and workers who have no real knowledge of whether their interventions are beneficial, harmful, or just plain useless. For example, when Donkoh, Underhill and Montgomery of the Centre of Evidence-Based Interventions at Oxford University set out in 2005 to evaluate the effectiveness of independent living programs (ILPs) in improving outcomes for foster care youths leaving the care system, they were unable to find a single randomized or quasirandomized controlled trial that compared ILPs to standard care among the 54 studies they were able to cull from the 2,196 citations they screened (Donkoh, Underhill, & Montgomery, 2006).

To compensate for the paucity of rigorous evaluations in child welfare, systematic reviewers are often obliged to turn to related fields, such as mental health, substance abuse, and juvenile justice, which are more adequately funded and less adverse to randomized controlled trials. Many of the C2 titles that pertain to child welfare involve mental health therapies of one type or another. But, as Julia Littell, a SRR pioneer in child welfare, notes, it is unclear how such evidence compiled in related fields generalize to children and families in child welfare (Littell, 2008). She concludes that there have been far too few controlled trials in child welfare and too many haphazard reviews of these trials to produce enough valid evidence for guiding practice and policy: "More scientifically sound syntheses of credible empirical studies are needed to provide a valid evidence base for practice" (Littell, 2008, p. 89).

Public child welfare is currently heading toward what may be called an accountability mismatch: On the one hand, accountability for results is increasing as the scope of public interest in child well-being outcomes widens and becomes more diffuse. On the other hand, the ability to provide a valid evidence base for guiding practice and policy is falling farther behind as federal support for rigorous child welfare evaluations evaporates and systematic research reviewers must turn to related fields for ESI.

The arena in which the accountability mismatch between expectations and capacity is perhaps most acute is the federal Children and Family Services Review. After the first round of reviews was completed in 2004, all 50 U.S. states, the District of Columbia and Puerto Rico had to complete Program Improvement Plans (PIP) and comply with ongoing monitoring that carried the risk of financial penalties. As of 2008, all 52 jurisdictions completed the initial 2-year PIP implementation period. Although the federal government does not publish penalties, several large states have disclosed that their penalty assessments run into the millions of dollars for failing to achieve the measurable benchmarks established in their approved PIP.

The National Association of Public Child Welfare Administrators (NAPCWA) raised concerns about the utility of assessing financial penalties on states for failing to achieve child welfare benchmarks (Friedman & Deibert, 2008). Financial penalties are appropriate for regulating agency relationships when contractual agents defect from an agreed upon course of action that parties to the bargain are reasonably confident will have the intended effect. Because the evidence base for child welfare interventions is so underdeveloped, there is little guarantee that planned action steps will produce the desired improvements. Thus, NAPCWA argues that it is counterproductive to levy penalties on states that make good faith efforts to implement a PIP but fail to achieve the desired results, because the interventions turn out to be ineffectual. Instead of exacting penalties from states, the federal government would do better to require under-performing states to invest penalty funds into technical assistance for identifying relevant ESI or rigorously evaluating an untested but promising service innovation. Financial penalties would be imposed only if the state failed to implement the agreed upon interventions or to conduct credible evaluations of its service innovations.

Reflexivity of the Child Welfare Policy Process

U.S. congressional action may ultimately be required to lessen the mismatch between federal performance expectations and state technical capacity. How this will be accomplished should ideally be influenced by parents, foster youth, and caregivers as well as by caseworkers, attorneys, judges, researchers, editorial boards, and citizen groups. These and other stakeholder groups are increasingly being engaged or inserting themselves in the reflexive process of using information about results as a means of understanding how we may lay claim to know something worth acting upon (Holland, 1999).

In Illinois, for example, the plaintiffs' attorneys under the *B.H.* consent decree sought to ease the accountability mismatch by backing the creation of the Children and Family Research Center and looking to it for credible evidence of which service innovations were accomplishing the desired results and which ones were falling short of expectations. The CFRC and the Office of the DCFS Research Director (later absorbed into the Center) subsequently assisted the state in securing three IV-E waivers to mount innovative service demonstrations and to conduct rigorous experimental evaluations of service efficacy. Similarly, the Illinois Adoption Advisory Council to DCFS culled the findings from the Illinois study of children's needs in adoptive and guardianship homes (Fuller et al., 2006) to build a case for additional investments in post-permanency services. As a final example, the Research Office and Center engaged members from the DCFS Youth Advisory Programs in two projects: The Young Researchers Program and Foster Youth Seen and Heard (Children and Family Research Center, 2004). Their advocacy was instrumental in putting the issues of sibling placement in foster care and sibling association after termination of parental rights on the CFRC research agenda (Testa, Curtis, Kang, & Kidd, 2003).

Reflexivity in public policy means cultivating an awareness of the construct validity of one's own assumptions and beliefs about how others act and what motivates them to change. In Chapter 3, the concept of logic models was introduced as a way of making explicit both the causal model of change and the underlying interpretive framework of assumptions and desired end-values. A distinction was drawn been single-loop learning, which leaves the underlying interpretative framework unchanged and double-loop learning, which results in a change in the theory of action and its assumptions and values (Argyris & Schön, 1996). Many of the recent advances in child welfare policy at the state and federal levels have been outgrowths of double-loop learning. The mismatch between the once prevailing assumption that relatives don't adopt and the results from focus groups (Testa, Shook, Cohen, & Woods, 1996), which suggested otherwise, led to the experimental reforms that Illinois pursued in the 1990s, the results of which changed the nature of the association between kinship and family permanence (Testa, 2002). Similarly the lack of fit between actual data on child maltreatment and people's intuitions captured by the proverb, "the apple doesn't fall far from the tree," caused policymakers to rethink their hesitancy about placing children with relative foster parents (Garnier & Poertner, 2000; Testa, Bruhn, & Helton, 2010).

Encouraging reflexivity in the policy process means bringing decision-makers into direct contact with the subjects of those policies who can hold them answerable for their decisions and help to surface the underlying assumptions and end-values on which public policies are built. Admittedly this is an uncomfortable situation for some administrators and policymakers, but the process can be made less onerous by regularly convening learning forums in which the latest results are shared and the public is enlisted to help define future courses of action. This was the model that Illinois followed in rolling out performance contracting and subsidized guardianship (see Chapter 10, this volume). Although the exchanges were initially heated, by the second or third meeting the discussions cooled down as participants focused on the practical tasks of improving performance and getting results.

Future Scope of Public Interest

Encouraging transparency, technical proficiency, and reflexivity in the use of evidence for guiding and improving child welfare practice and policy suggests one potential solution to the accountability mismatch problem. An alternative is simply to scale back public accountability by narrowing the scope of public interest. As mentioned in earlier chapters, leading national judicial and legal organizations declined to adopt measures of child well-being in assessing the performance of juvenile courts on the grounds that courts do not have direct responsibility for these outcomes (The American Bar Association, The National Center for State Courts, & The National Council of Juvenile and Family Court Judges, 2004). Even for measures of safety and permanence, there is some reticence on the part of state agencies and court offices to make performance measures publicly available. Some of the most respected researchers in the field have also raised concerns about making child protective agents accountable for child well-being outcomes, which could lead to heightened public surveillance of parenting practices and massive governmental intrusion into formerly autonomous family life (Wulczyn, Barth, Yuan, Harden, & Landsverk, 2005).

After decades of reducing government's role in assisting families, there appears to be renewed interest in policies that can equalize children's developmental opportunities for healthful growth, emotional security, and educational success by supporting and upgrading the capacity of parents to act as responsible agents of their own children's well-being. An enlarged scope of public interest in child well-being could conceivably translate into an enlarged primary prevention system of comprehensive family support, early education, children's allowances, parental leave, and health care, which is universally accessible to all families (Donnelly, 1997; Garrison, 2005; Kamerman & Kahn, 1990). An undertaking of this magnitude would, of course, entail a massive overhaul of government involvement, which, in Fishkin's terms, is currently narrowest for birth families (upholding achievement and family autonomy at the expense of equality), broadest for children in bureaucratized substitute care (sacrificing family autonomy for achievement and equality), and gradually enlarging for children under primordial substitute care (encroaching on achievement in favor of group autonomy and equality).

Currently, for the 96% of child living with their birth families, parents are free to raise them or delegate this responsibility to other parental surrogates (e.g., relatives, neighbors, day care centers, or boarding schools) as they deem appropriate. The only limitation on parental autonomy arises from the surveillance systems that are necessary to assure that children's safety and health can be verified, for example, mandatory reporting laws, universal home visitation, school registration, and from the public interventions that could result if the children's safety and health are deemed inadequate. If the children are doing poorly in school or changing residences often, these are matters typically referred to educational, public aid, or public housing authorities. More could be done by way of public investment in comprehensive primary prevention programs, such as new parent training, crisis nurseries, and family resource centers to preserve the continuity of children's care when heightened risks to their safety, health, and well-being bring them to the attention of child protective authorities.

The central message of this volume is that any future expansion of child and family services that emerges from a broadened scope of public interest should be based on the most credible evidence of program efficacy and effectiveness. As discussed in Chapter 7, randomized controlled experiments are generally considered the strongest evaluation design and the "gold standard" for estimating intervention effects. The Obama Administration has committed to spending billions on nurse home visiting programs that have been empirically supported by randomized controlled trials (Haskins, Paxson, & Brooks-Gunn, 2009). Future funding should also take heed of rigorous studies conducted by child psychologists to evaluate parent training programs, which show reductions in conduct disorders and physical aggression among children randomly assigned to the treatment group compared to the control group (Brotman et al., 2009). After initially eschewing experimental methods, educational researchers are increasingly using randomized experiments to produce unbiased estimates of the impact of early literacy, school choice, after-school programs, and drug and violence prevention. Criminologists have launched the *Journal of Experimental Criminology* to advance the science of systematic research reviews and experimental methods in criminology and criminal justice.

Child welfare once appeared poised to join its sister disciplines in producing high quality experimental and quasi-experimental research for the development of evidence-supported policy. As detailed in Chapter 9, sixteen states initiated 21 randomized controlled experiments under title IV-E waiver authority to evaluate the demonstration of new approaches to the delivery of child welfare services. With the expiration of waiver authority in 2006, however, and especially the loss of federal matching funds at the 50% rate for independent waiver evaluations, state willingness to conduct randomized controlled experiments in child welfare has seriously eroded. To reinvigorate federal and state interest, IV-E waiver authority should be reinstated immediately along the lines recommended by the Pew Commission on Children in Foster Care and the American Public Human Services Association. These recommendations include among others:

- Granting USDHHS the authority to grant new waivers indefinitely and lifting the cap on the numbers of waivers that it can approve.
- Allowing county and municipal child welfare systems to apply through their state to obtain their own waiver authority to test innovations.
- Offering challenge grants to states that undertake waiver demonstrations as part of their Program Improvement Plan (PIP) to address performance deficiencies as identified in federal Child and Family Services Reviews.
- Establishing a multi-tiered evaluation system that consists of a Phase I for previously untested innovations that require randomization and is reimbursed at a higher rate than Phase II evaluations

for already tested innovations that can be replicated with less rigorous quasi-experimental and observational designs.

- Offering states the option of graduated IV-E match rates to stimulate innovation at the front-end of the child protection system.
- Establishing a national Waiver Demonstration Resource Center to assist states in developing the expertise to plan, implement, evaluate, and manage waivers.
- Acting on the results from waiver demonstrations by allowing states to add approved programs to their IV-E state plans, without further evaluation and cost-neutrality requirements.

The reinstatement of IV-E waiver authority with the recommended improvements would grant states greater flexibility in the use of IV-E dollars without sacrificing the funding guarantees of entitlements or the cost neutrality afforded by block grants. The phased evaluation requirements would help to ensure that dollars are invested in only those innovations that have been empirically demonstrated to work. Cost-neutrality calculations would reward states for successful innovations while limiting the federal risk for failed experiments. To fully realize the promise of child welfare waivers, however, Congress would need to act periodically on the results from successful demonstrations by making them statutorily allowable IV-E expenses for all states.

The Agency Problem in Child Welfare

Strengthening the validity of child welfare knowledge is a necessary, but not entirely sufficient condition for fostering accountability in public child welfare. Unless agency relationships are embedded in an institutional framework that discourages opportunistic gaming and self-interested defections from responsible stewardship, the aims of even the most rigorously tested programs can easily be subverted. Chapter 1 outlined the various risks that can arise from different types of agency relationships in child welfare. These include the risks of excessive control and physical violence by superiors in hierarchical agency relationships, such as parents, foster caregivers, guardians, teachers, and judges. They also include the risks of neglect or overinvestment that can result from dysfunctional affine relationships, such as between children and parents, relatives, neighbors, church members, and family friends who customarily are trusted to have the best interests of their children at heart. On the bureaucratic side, there are the risks of exploitation and shirking by contractual agents whose interests in the children are mostly instrumental. Finally there are the risks of malfeasance by public agents who fail to live up to their ethical responsibilities or alternatively overinvest in their fiduciary role and become excessively paternalistic in their agency relationships with children and families.

As previously noted, many lawmakers, administrators, and advocates came to view the fiduciary model of public child welfare that dominated most of the 20th century as wasteful and inadequate for serving the interests of children and families. They argued that far more children than necessary were being removed from their homes, too many were allowed to languish in interminable foster care, and too few were reunified with their families or placed into permanent homes in a timely fashion. At the front-end, reformers called for family-centered policies that could retain children in affine relationships of care, commitment, and trust with parents, relatives, neighbors, and other primordial agents. At the back-end, policymakers advocated market-oriented solutions, which would raise output levels and guard against agency risks through performance contracting and public surveillance of private provider activities.

Child welfare researchers have turned their attention in recent years to evaluating the gains from these alternative types of agency relationships and estimating the costs of containing different kinds of agency risk. A good deal of the recent focus has been on the comparative benefits and harms of primordially-based foster care by relatives compared to bureaucratically credentialed (traditional) foster care by non-relatives. A systematic research review of experimental and quasi-experimental studies concluded that children in kinship foster care may do better than children in non-related foster care in terms of their behavioral development, mental health, and placement stability (Winokur et al., 2009). But, the authors cautioned that this conclusion is tempered by the pronounced methodological and design weaknesses of the reviewed studies.

Evaluations of the benefits and harms of market-oriented approaches to service delivery compared to more traditional fiduciary arrangements are also beginning to appear. Chapter 10 presented observational data on permanency trends in Illinois before and after the introduction of performance-based contracting (PBC) among contractual agencies serving children in kinship and non-kinship foster homes. The staggered nature of the PBC implementation first in Chicago and a year later in downstate Illinois helped to strengthen the authors' conclusion that PBC rather than a general time trend boosted permanency rates in Illinois. Although these results were later replicated in Philadelphia, more rigorous evaluations of performance contracting have failed to reproduce consistently those beneficial impacts across variations in intervention models and market environments. Only one of four completed evaluations of randomized PBC and managed care experiments conducted under IV-E waiver authority reported increased permanency rates associated with the intervention. The remainder showed no differences (James Bell Associates, 2008).

An important series of studies of PBC conducted in Wayne County (Detroit), Michigan relied on the county's rotational assignment system to allocate comparable groups of children to a performance-based, managed care regime, which coupled fixed per-diem reimbursement with substantial financial bonuses for permanency outcomes (intervention group) and to a traditional fee-for-service regime, which reimbursed agencies for their service-related expenses on a higher per-diem, per-child basis (comparison group). The findings were that children allocated to the PBC group were significantly more likely to be placed in the custody of kin and slightly more likely to adopted (n.s.), but significantly less likely to be reunified compared to children allocated to the fee-for-service group (Meezan & McBeath, 2008). There were no statistically significant differences in the proportions of children who experienced TPR or remained in state custody at the end of the study (between 8% and 9% were still in custody in both groups). Of greater concern to the authors, children and their families allocated to the PBC intervention received significantly fewer service contacts and referrals for out-of-agency service than children and families allocated to the comparison group (McBeath & Meezan, 2007).

The results of the Chicago, Philadelphia, and Detroit PBC studies suggest that permanency outcomes can be substantially impacted by the structure of financial incentives. But, whereas the time-series in Chicago and Philadelphia implied that the impact was largely salutary for children and families, the Detroit study raised concerns about the agency risks that PBC may pose to family reunification. Referring to the large disparities in reunification rates, the authors of the Detroit study argued for specific financial incentives for reunification but concluded that state child welfare systems should ensure that foster care placement decisions are influenced more by child and family conditions than by financial considerations. The reasons for the reunification disparities in the Detroit study remain unclear. The initial bonus amounts for reunification were the same as for relative placement, guardianship, and adoption. Unmentioned in the Detroit study was how the bonuses for stability after discharge might have affected permanency choices. In Illinois, rates of foster care re-entry from reunified families are substantially higher than re-entry rates from adoptive and guardianship homes (Rolock & Testa, 2008). The Detroit study did not report post-discharge stability rates, but the authors called for future research to examine whether certain market-based models alter service providers' efforts with biological parents and whether caseworkers perceive kinship placement to be easier to achieve than reunification (Meezan & McBeath, 2008).

Child welfare research is beginning to evolve beyond the simple conditions-to-outcomes "black-box" model of intervention research and to adopt the more complex conditions-agency-outcomes perspective on how different types of agency relationships structure the ways in which purposive actions of individuals combine to produce social outcomes (see Chapter 1, this volume). Future research should continue to refine our understanding of the comparative benefits and harms of contractual versus fiduciary models of agency relationships in using instrumental and expressive incentives to encourage practitioners and administrators to adopt child welfare interventions with demonstrated empirical efficacy and effectiveness. This should include not only the degree of compliance with intended interventions but also the risks that such incentives may unwittingly create for agents to maximize their own self-interests at the expense of their principals.

Greater attention should also be paid to the comparative benefits and harms of hierarchical agency relationships in which the incentives are of a more threatening and coercive nature. For example, arresting domestic batterers has been shown experimentally to be more effective in reducing subsequent domestic violence than ordering the offender off the premises for 8 hours or some form of advice that might include mediation (Berk & Sherman, 1988). There have been randomized controlled experiments of the impact of drug courts on recidivism and drug use, but more work needs to be done to understand how treatment compliance under threat of sentencing sanctions impacts drug recovery, family reunification, and other child welfare outcomes (Gottfredson, Kearly, Najaka, & Rocha, 2005). There also needs to be a better understanding of the limitations of potentially threatening interventions, such as allegation-driven, child maltreatment investigations as compared to alternative or differential response in which family stresses and strengths are assessed and, if needed, the family is referred for voluntary services (Loman & Siegal, 2005).

Sustaining Research and Training Partnerships

The technical expertise and organizational culture required for fostering results-oriented accountability in public child welfare are difficult to sustain in highly bureaucratized settings and swiftly politicized environments. The usual top-down style of public management and its chronic vulnerability to leadership shake-ups in response to high-profile tragedies make it extraordinarily challenging to sustain the high levels of scientific validity and agency integrity that are advocated in this volume. Although public child welfare systems have invested significant resources in building a rich storehouse of data on children and families for monitoring performance and holding agents accountable, there is still a sizeable mismatch between public expectations and the capacity of these systems to develop valid measures, assess performance accurately, scan for promising practices, evaluate the effectiveness of hypothesized solutions, and make the appropriate adjustments based on information feedback on child and family outcomes.

One of the ways that some of the more successful child welfare systems have adapted to these contingencies is by entering into research and training partnerships with universities to bring the methods and culture of systematic research into their day-to-day operations. Chapter 11 by Joan Zlotnik gave examples of some of the leading university partnerships and identified many of the ingredients that are necessary to sustain these relationships. As noted in the chapter and by previous writers (Grossman et al., 1992), many of the barriers to successful collaborations arise from institutional differences in decision-making authority, organizational tempo, and reward structures.

In public departments, for example, decision making tends to be hierarchical and vested in the hands of a director who is ultimately accountable for the organization's activities; whereas in universities, decision making tends to be more collegial and shared. Frustrations arise when heads of public departments learn they cannot depend on school deans or center directors to exercise the same degree of control over faculty members that they exercise over departmental staff. These differences sometimes result in the creation of separate research structures within universities which are staffed by non-tenure track, research professors and associates who are attuned to the variation in decision-making styles and accept the indirect lines of communication through academic administrators. At the same time, the status of these research positions and their role in the governance of the host institution remains a chronic source of tension in the university.

Another potential source of friction is the differences in tempo at which work is expected to be done. A frequent complaint lodged against university-based research is that it takes too long and fails to meet a department's need for short-term problem solving. This is especially true for experimental and longitudinal studies where by the time the results become available, the stakeholders who were originally interested in the idea are no longer in office and the new policymakers and administrators are concerned with a different set of policy issues (Shadish & Cook, 2009). In many respects, this discontinuity argues for locating long-term projects in university settings where the interest in cumulative knowledge building can withstand cost-cutting measures by policymakers and administrators who must rely on immediate and often incomplete information to deal with short-term problems. Thus, a partnership structure that meets the agency's need for "quick-response" information can often earn the goodwill, time and funding required for long-term projects that contribute to cumulative knowledge building in the academy.

Reconciling the short-term information needs of administrators with the long-term knowledge interests of academics will ultimately require dealing with the differences in how rewards are earned in public departments as compared to university settings. In public departments, rewards tend to be given for innovative solutions to the practical problems of the organization. In universities, rewards tend to be based on the quantity and quality of scholarly information that is communicated to academic peers. This difference creates another source of potential strain between university researchers and service providers who engage in collaborative studies. To some extent, this tension can be mitigated by engaging practitioners and administrators as co-authors of published works and by giving greater weight to public engagement in academic promotion, retention, and tenure decisions. At a more fundamental level, it requires cultivating, in Terry Moore's terms, a "results-oriented culture" that prizes scientific validity and agency integrity by public leadership (see Chapter 8, this volume). Service providers sometimes feel betrayed by academics whose scientific norms of disinterestedness (Merton, 1996) make them appear indifferent to their concerns and willing to ignore political considerations for the sake of scientific rigor and publishable results. Likewise, academics sometimes feel misunderstood by service providers who seem unsympathetic to the norms of skepticism, disinterestedness, transparency, and intellectual integrity upon which the scientific enterprise is built. Of course, the public's willingness to accept the validity of science rests, to a great extent, on its practical accomplishments in achieving valued outcomes through technical applications and service demonstrations. In this regard, administrators and academics can find common ground in fostering institutional arrangements that orient researchers to solving the practical problems of child welfare and confer academic rewards on applied research that contributes to the solution of these problems.

To carve out this common ground, it will be necessary to invest greater resources in results-oriented accountability in child welfare. The easiest place to start is to restore what has been lost, namely reinstating IV-E waiver authority. Beyond this, it will be necessary to establish a dedicated source of federal research funding, which, although available in medicine, mental health, education, substance abuse, and juvenile justice, has inexplicably been denied to child welfare. As Joan Zlotnick forcefully stated in her chapter, the absence of a targeted research funding stream for child welfare research is one of the greatest barriers to creating the necessary partnerships to improve the validity and integrity of child welfare social work. It is not sufficient just to enumerate the many ways that we as public guardians of the over half-million children in foster care should hold ourselves accountable for their safety, permanence, and well-being. It is essential that we give the agents to whom we have delegated this responsibility the resources to develop the knowledge-base and accountability systems for making good on these promises.

References

The American Bar Association, The National Center for State Courts, & The National Council of Juvenile and Family Court Judges. (2004). *Building a better court: Measuring and improving court performance and judicial workload in child abuse and neglect cases.* Washington, D.C.: Author.

Argyris, C., & Schön, D. A. (1996). *Organization learning II: Theory, method, and practice.* Reading MA: Addison-Wesley Publishing Co.

Berk, R. A., & Sherman, L. W. (1988). Police responses to family violence incidents: An analysis of an experimental design with incomplete randomization. *Journal of the American Statistical Association, 83*(401), 70–76.

Brotman, L. M., O'Neal, C. R., Huang, K., Gouley, K. K., Rosenfelt, A., & Shrout, P. E. (2009). An experimental test of parenting practices as a mediator of early childhood physical aggression. *Journal of Child Psychology and Psychiatry, 50* (3), 235–245

Campbell, D. (1969). Reforms as experiments. *American Psychologist, 24*(4), 409–429.

Children and Family Research Center. (2004). *Youth programs.* Urbana, IL: Children and Family Research Center.

Courtney, M. E., Dworsky, A., Cusick, G. R., Keller, T., Havlicek, J., Perez, A., . . . Bost, N. (2007). *Midwest evaluation of the adult functioning of former foster youth.* Chicago: Chapin Hall Center for Children.

Courtney, M. E., Needell, B., & Wulczyn, F. (2004). Unintended consequences of the push for accountability: The case of national child welfare performance standards. *Children and Youth Services Review, 26*(12), 1141–1154.

Donkoh, C., Underhill, K., & Montgomery, P. (2006). Independent living programmes for improving outcomes for young people leaving the care system. *Cochrane Database of Systematic Reviews,* 3, CD005558. DOI: 10.1002/14651858. CD005558.pub2.

Donnelly, A. C. (1997). An overview of prevention of physical abuse and neglect. In M. E. Haelfer, R. S. Kempe, & R. D. Krugman(Eds.), *The battered child, fifth edition, revised and expanded* (pp. 579–593). Chicago: The University of Chicago Press.

Friedman, J., & Deibert, K. (2008). American Public Human Services Association and National Association of Public Child Welfare Administrator, to Christine Calpin, U.S. Department of Health and Human Services (May 13, 2008).

Fuller, T., Bruhn, C., Cohen, L., Lis, M., Rolock, N., & Sheridan, K. (2006). *Supporting adoptions and guardianships in Illinois: An analysis of subsidies, services, and spending.* Urbana, IL: Children and Family Research Center.

Garnier, P. & Poertner, J. (2000). Using administrative data to assess child safety in out-of-home care. *Child Welfare, 79*(5), 597–613.

Garrison, M. (2005). Reforming child protection: A public health perspective. *Virginia Journal of Social Policy and Law, 12*(3), 499–534.

Gottfredson, D. C., Kearley, B. W., Najaka, S. S., & Rocha, C. M. (2005). The Baltimore city drug treatment court: 3-year self-report outcome study. *Evaluation Review, 29*(1), 42–64.

Grossman, B., Laughlin, S., & Specht, H. (1992). Building the commitment of social work education to the publicly supported social services. In K. H. Briar, V. H. Hansen, & N. Harris (Eds.), *New partnerships: Proceedings from the national public child welfare training symposium 1991* (pp. 55–72). North Miami, FL: Florida International University.

Haskins, R., Paxson, C., & Brooks-Gunn, J. (2009). Social science rising: A tale of evidence shaping public policy. *The future of children: Policy brief, fall,* Princeton, NJ: The Future of Children.

Holland, R. (1999). Reflexivity. *Human Relations, 52*(4), 463–484.

James Bell Associates. (2008). Profiles of the child welfare demonstration projects. Arlington, VA. Last accessed March 1, 2009 at http://www.jbassoc.com/ reports/documents/final%20waiver%20profiles%20060308.pdf.

Kamerman, S., & Kahn, A. (1990). Social services for children, youth, and families in the United States. *Children and Youth Services Review, 12*(1–2), 1–184.

Kids Are Waiting and National Indian Child Welfare Association. (2007). *Time for reform: A matter of justice for American Indian and Alaskan native children.* Philadelphia: The Pew Charitable Trusts.

Kosanovich, A., & Joseph, R.M. (2005). *Child welfare consent decrees: Analysis of thirty-five court actions from 1995 to 2005*. Washington, D.C.: Child Welfare League of American and ABA Center on Children and the Law.

Littell, J. (2008). How do we know what works? The quality of published reviews of evidence-based practices. In D. Lindsey & A. Shlonsky (Eds.), *Child welfare research: Advances for practice and policy* (pp. 66–93). Oxford: Oxford University Press.

Loman, A., & Siegal, G. (2005). Alternative response in Minnesota: Findings of the program evaluation. *Protecting Children, 20*(2&3), 78–92.

McBeath, B., & Meezan, W. (2007). Market-based disparities in foster care provision. *Research on Social Work Practice, 18*(1), 27–41.

McDonald, J. M., Salyers, N. S., & Testa, M. (2003). Nation's child welfare system doubles number of adoptions from foster Care. *Fostering Results Report*. University of Illinois at Urbana-Champaign, Children and Family Research Center, Urbana. Last accessed October 1, 2008 at http://www.fosteringresults.org/results/reports/pewreports_10-01-03_doubledadoptions.pdf.

Meezan, W., & McBeath, B. (2008). Market-based disparities in foster care outcomes. *Children and Youth Services Review, 30*(4), 388–406.

Merton, R. K. (1996). *Robert K. Merton: On social structure and science*. In P. Sztompka, (Ed.). Chicago: The University of Chicago Press.

The Pew Commission on Children in Foster Care. (2004). *Fostering the future: Safety, Permanence, and well-being for children in foster care*. Washington, D.C.: The Pew Commission on Children in Foster Care.

Rolock, N., & Testa, M. (2008). *Conditions of children in and at risk of foster care in Illinois*. Urbana, IL: Children and Family Research Center.

Shadish, W.R., & Cook, T. D. (2009). The renaissance of field experimentation in evaluating interventions. *Annual Review of Psychology, 60*, 607–629.

Shadish, W. R, Cook, T. D., & Campbell, D. T. (2002). *Experimental and quasi-experimental designs for generalized causal inference*. Boston: Houghton Mifflin Company.

Smith, A. D. (1955). *The right to life*. Chapel Hill: University of North Carolina Press.

Sowell, T. (2002). *A conflict of visions: Ideological origins of political struggles*. New York: Basic Books.

Testa, M. (2002). (Subsidized guardianship: Testing an idea whose time has finally come. *Social Work Research, 26*(3), 145–158.

Testa, M., Bruhn, C., & Helton, J. (2010). Comparative safety, stability, and continuity of children's placements in informal and formal substitute care arrangements. In Webb, M. B., Dowd, K., Harden, B. J., Landsverk, J., & Testa, M. F. (Eds.), *Child welfare and child well-being: New perspectives from the National Survey of Child and Adolescent Well-Being* (pp. 159–191). New York: Oxford University Press.

Testa, M., Curtis, A. Kang, H., & Kidd, Z. (2003). *Conservation of sibling bonds*. Urbana, IL: Children and Family Research Center.

Testa, M., & Rolock, N. (2006). *Conditions of children in and at risk of foster care in Illinois*. Urbana, IL: Children and Family Research Center.

Testa, M., Shook, K., Cohen, L., & Woods, M. (1996). Permanency planning options for children in formal kinship care. In D. Wilson & S. Chipungu (Eds.), *Child Welfare. Special Issue: Kinship Care, 75*(5), 451–470.

U.S. President's Science Advisory Committee Panel on Youth (1974). *Youth: Transition to adulthood. Report of the panel on youth of the president's science advisory committee*. Chicago: University of Chicago Press.

Webster, D., Usher, C. L., Needell, B., & Wildfire, J. (2008). Self-evaluation: Using data to guide policy and practice in public child welfare agencies. In D. Lindsey & A. Shlonsky (Eds). *Child welfare research: Advances for practice and policy* (pp. 261–270). Oxford: Oxford University Press.

Winokur, M., Holtan, A., & Valentine, D. (2009) Kinship care for the safety, permanency, and well-being of children removed from the home for maltreatment. *Cochrane Database of Systematic Reviews*, Issue 1. Art. No.: CD006546. DOI: 10.1002/14651858.CD006546.pub2.

Wulczyn, F., Barth, R. P., Yuan, Y. T., Harden, B. J., & Landsverk, J. (2005). *Beyond common sense: Child welfare, child well-being, and the evidence for policy reform.* New Brunswick, NJ: Aldine Transaction.

Wulczyn, F. H., Chen, L., & Hislop, K. B. (2006). Adoption dynamics and the adoption and safe families act. *Social Service Review, 80*(4), 584–608.

Zlotnik, J. (2008). *Strengthening university/agency research partnerships to enhance child welfare outcomes: A toolkit for building research partnerships.* Washington, D.C.: Institute for the Advancement of Social Work Research.

INDEX

Note: Page numbers followed by t and f refer to pages containing tables and figures respectively.